INTEGRAL RELATIONSHIPS

A Manual for Men

By
Martin Ucik

First Edition 2010

Integral Relationships: A Manual for Men
Copyright © 2010 by Martin Ucik

Published and distributed worldwide by singles2couples.org Publishing
Santa Rosa, CA
www.singles2couples.org

All Rights Reserved. No part of this book may be reproduced or distributed in any form or by any means, or stored in a database or retrieval system, without the prior written permission of the publisher.

ISBN-13: 978-0-9845703-0-0
ISBN-10: 0-9845703-0-6
Library of Congress Control Number: 2010906440

Cover design and inside illustrations by Annette Berlin

Text layout and additional illustrations by Renate Elhardt

Most excellent help with flow/structure/grammar and content editing
by Harriett Hardman of Wizard Publications LLC

Manufactured in the United States of America

DEDICATION

To all women, especially my mother Renate and my daughters Laura, Lisa, and Anna Lea. I love you very much.

TABLE OF CONTENTS

Preface	xvii
Introduction	1
Chapter 1: Understanding the Dimensions of Love	9
PART I – THE BIOLOGICAL AND PSYCHOLOGICAL MAKEUP OF MEN AND WOMEN	**15**
Chapter 2: Understanding the Differences Between the Sexes	17
Chapter 3: Lines of Development for Human Intelligences	29
Chapter 4: Levels of Growth	41
Chapter 5: States of Falling in Love	67
Chapter 6: Evaluating Personality Types	73
Conclusion Part I	79
PART II – MEN AND WOMEN COMING TOGETHER	**81**
Chapter 7: Primary Fantasy and Personality	83
Chapter 8: Our Drive To Connect	93
Chapter 9: Passion/Intimacy/Dependence	107
Chapter 10: Differences in Male and Female Consciousness Development	119
Conclusion Part II	131
PART III – APPLYING THE INTEGRAL RELATIONSHIP MODEL IN THE REAL WORLD	**133**
Chapter 11: Where Am I Coming From? Where Is She Coming From?	135
Chapter 12: Locating Your Partner and Yourself on the Compatibility Matrix	153
Chapter 13: Dating Using the Integral Relationship Model	163
Conclusion Part III	173
EPILOGUE	175
APPENDIX I: Relationship Books for All Levels/Colors	179
APPENDIX II: Links and References	199
BIBLIOGRAPHY	201

Endnotes 213

Index 267

Detailed Table of Contents

Preface	xvii
Introduction	1
A Few Facts and Figures	1
The Integral Approach	2
The Integral Relationship Model	3
Some Notes About This Manual	7
A Final Suggestion	8
Chapter 1: Understanding the Dimensions of Love	9
The Spiritual Dimension of Love	9
The Evolving Physical and Psychological Dimensions of Love	10
In Summary	14
Part I – The Biological and Psychological Makeup of Men and Women	15
Chapter 2: Understanding the Differences Between the Sexes	17
Sex: Physical/Biological Differences Between Males and Females (Body)	18
Gender: Cultural/Learned Differences Between Men and Women (Mind)	22
Polarities: Masculine/Feminine Potentials for Both Sexes (Soul)	23
In Summary	28
Chapter 3: Lines of Development for Human Intelligences	29
The Many Facets of Humanness	30
Building Relationships through Shared or Compatible Passions and Interests	30
Identifying and Discussing Capacities, Values and Ideals	33
Talking About Needs and Neediness	34
Opening Up to Feelings	35
In Summary	40
Chapter 4: Levels of Growth	41
Consciousness Development (Colors)	42

Spiritual Development	51
Development of Sexuality	56
Anima and Animus Complex Development	58
In Summary	66

Chapter 5: States of Falling in Love — 67

Phase 1 – Lust	68
Phase 2 – Romance	68
Phase 3 – Commitment	69
Your Gift That Keeps On Giving	70
Addicted to Love	70
Integrating Chemistry With Reason	70
In Summary	71

Chapter 6: Evaluating Personality Types — 73

NLP Types	73
Five Love Languages	74
The Enneagram	75
Myers-Briggs Type Indicator	77
Astrology	78
Other Types and Beliefs	78
In Summary	78

Conclusion Part I — 79

Part II – Men and Women Coming Together — 81

Chapter 7: Primary Fantasy and Personality — 83

Attractiveness at Different Levels of Consciousness	83
Personality Matrix	87
In Summary	91

Chapter 8: Our Drive To Connect — 93

Holons, Always Partial, Already Whole	93
Characteristics of Individual Holons	94
Social Holons	101
In Summary	105

Chapter 9: Passion/Intimacy/Dependence	107
The Three Sides of the Triangle	107
The Eight Forms of Love	111
Aligning His and Her Triangle	116
In Summary	118

Chapter 10: Differences in Male and Female Consciousness Development	119
The Male-Female Co-Creation of Consciousness	119
From Archaic to Transpersonal	121
Transcend and Include/Exclude	122
Feminine Flow and Masculine Structure Create The River	124
Errors Along the Way	125
Ladder, Climber, View	126
Psychological Healing	127
In Summary	129

Conclusion Part II	132

Part III – Applying the Integral Relationship Model in the Real World — 133

Chapter 11: Where Am I Coming From? Where Is She Coming From?	135
What is a Kosmic Address?	135
Identifying Her Perspective and Level of Consciousness	136
Identifying Her Spiritual State-Stage	145
Identifying Her Sexual Stage	147
Identifying Her Animus Complex	149
Identifying Her Type	150
In Summary	151

Chapter 12: Locating Your Partner and Yourself on the Compatibility Matrix	153
Conflict Resolution and Forgiveness	159
To Be Or Not To Be – That is the Question	160
In Summary	162

Chapter 13: Dating Using the Integral Relationship Model	163
The Integral Approach	163
Dating Strategies	164
Internet Dating	165
In Summary	172

CONCLUSION PART III	173
EPILOGUE	175
APPENDIX I: RELATIONSHIP BOOKS FOR ALL LEVELS/COLORS	179
Books for Red Singles	180
Books for Amber Couples	182
Books for Single Amber Women	185
Books for Orange Couples	185
Books for Orange Single Women	189
Books for Orange Single Women And Men	190
A Book for Orange Single Men	191
Books for Green Singles and Couples	192
Books for Green Singles	195
A Book for Green Men	197
Conclusion to Appendix I	198
APPENDIX II: LINKS AND REFERENCES	199
BIBLIOGRAPHY	201
ENDNOTES	213
INDEX	267

List of Figures

Figure 1: The model with man and woman in spiritual context	3
Figure 2: The model with body and mind	4
Figure 3: The model with feminine and masculine polarities	4
Figure 4: The model with lines and levels of development	5
Figure 5: The model with Primary Fantasy, Personality Matrix, and Triangles of Love	5
Figure 6: The complete model with Kosmic Address and Compatibility Matrix	6
Figure 7: Man and woman in spiritual context	9
Figure 8: The core elements of men and women	15
Figure 9: Body/mind of men and women	17
Figure 10: The four polarities of both sexes	23
Figure 11: The four polarities	23
Figure 12: Understanding ascending, descending, agency, and communion	25
Figure 13: The elevator metaphor for mutual exclusivity	26
Figure 14: The mutual exclusivity of the four polarities	27
Figure 15: Graph showing an individual's development on various lines	41
Figure 16: A summary of spiritual levels in world religions	55
Figure 17: The Enneagram	75
Figure 18: Integrating the Primary Fantasy and Personality Matrix through Triangles of Love	82
Figure 19: Divergence in male/female Primary Fantasy	86
Figure 20: The Personality Matrix—allowing you to map your and her development	88
Figure 21: Example showing nested holons	94
Figure 22: The four quadrants of individual holons.	95
Figure 23: Characteristics of each quadrant	97
Figure 24: The four quadrants applied to individual holons	97
Figure 25: Every human possesses four quadrants	98
Figure 26: Example of dancing couple and the four polarities	102
Figure 27: The passion/intimacy/dependence triangle	107
Figure 28: Examples of differently shaped triangles of love	108

Figure 29: The eight forms of love — 112

Figure 30: Each lover experiences passion, intimacy, and dependence to various degrees. — 116

Figure 31: Examples showing two triangles overlaid to evaluate the form and quality of love that is experienced — 116

Figure 32: Joke about divergent psychological complexity of men and women — 122

Figure 33: Male-female dynamic in consciousness growth — 123

Figure 34: Compatibility Matrix for men and women at different levels of consciousness development — 154

Figure 35: Global challenges facing humanity — 176

LIST OF TABLES

Table 1: List of passions and interests	31
Table 2: List of capacities, values, and ideals	33
Table 3: List of needs	35
Table 4: List of interpretations versus feelings	38
Table 5: Developmental stages, their colors, and proportions of U.S. population	44
Table 6: Fear and desire to be in partnership or alone	104

Acknowledgments

My gratitude goes to the women who gave me firsthand experiences of how wonderful, challenging, rewarding, and painful relationships can be, and so inspired me to grow in consciousness to become a better man. You know who you are if you happen to get a copy of this manual. Liza Braude-Glidden for her loving friendship, for introducing me to Ken Wilber's work, and for the early encouragement; Christel Rene and Kim Hansen for spending countless hours on hikes while discussing ideas as the manual took shape; John McCoy, Bill Henderson, and Frederick Ernst for proofreading the first drafts; my friends at the Santa Rosa Integral Salon for their wisdom, support, feedback, and encouragement; the countless men and women who shared their relationship experiences with me in groups and individual sessions; Ken Wilber for the Integral Model that this manual is based on; the many authors whose writings provided the wisdom that allowed me to fill in the blanks (see Appendix I and the Bibliography); Mark Johnson, Bruce Kunkel, Professor Allan Combs, Steve Blackmer, and Gore Yaswen for peer reviews; Rebecca Davenport for proofreading the final manuscript; Annette Berlin for the cover design and inside illustrations, Renate Elhardt for text layout and additional illustrations, and last but not least Harriett Hardman for her guidance and excellent editing.

Preface

*The proof of the depth and embodiment of your realization will be seen in your love relationship. That's where the proof is in the pudding.
If it all collapses in your relationship, you have some work to do.
And people do have a lot of difficulties in their relationships.*
~ Adyashanti ~

On July 15, 2006, a woman that I loved and felt truly happy with left me. Until she walked out, I believed that we were in a good place. We seemed to be compatible in almost spooky ways, she loved me (or so she said), we lived together, held good day jobs, and, ironically enough, shared in running singles2couples.org, an Association for Healthy Relationships. A week before her departure we had returned from a romantic trip to Paris and a vacation with our children in Germany, where I introduced her to my family who also fell in love with her.

Through books, groups, workshops, therapy, a spiritual path, and previous relationships (among them a 14-year marriage with three children) I had already practiced how to overcome my commitment phobia, as well as how to love unconditionally, communicate compassionately, be emotionally available, engage in tantric lovemaking, resolve conflicts, do my share of the housework, and put down the toilet seat.

Still she left. What the $$%& ?!?!?!

I felt by turns bewildered, ashamed, angry, frustrated, and sad. Six weeks after the breakup, I sat on my bedroom floor, contemplating what had happened to us.

Earlier that year, I had become an avid student of Ken Wilber's Integral Model of human growth and potentials. All of a sudden I had an epiphany that his insights not only held the answer to my burning question why there are so many singles and unhappy couples in this country (I had grown up in a happy family in Germany and came to the US with my (then) wife and children in 1995), but also why my girlfriend had moved out. I realized that **her leaving me was neither her nor my fault, but an inevitable consequence of our different perspectives and levels of development.**

I thought, surely others must have applied Wilber's model to love relationships, but to my surprise there were no books or writings that did. None of my friends, some of them relationship book authors, Integral pioneers, therapists, spiritual teachers, and workshop leaders, had heard of any such application either, but were all very interested and encouraged me to write down my thoughts.

In the process of developing this manual I attempted to describe Wilber's fascinating insights in a more accessible way for newcomers and made several extensions to his model that may be of interest to readers who are already familiar with his work.

However when I shared my ideas with women that I dated, I realized that most of

[handwritten margin notes: "my picture / my different" "boring / drinking / m. story" "demeaning / disparaging" "i rewrite."]

them were more interested in chemistry with a successful man than in considering and integrating the multiple dimensions that are vital to a healthy love relationship. I quickly learned that walking my talk by being genuinely curious and meeting women with understanding and compassion as an opposite and equal was more conducive to creating the intimate connection that I was yearning for than sharing my Integral knowledge. As I explored how the Integral Model applied to relationships, my love life improved significantly and many of the women that I dated became my friends instead of breaking my heart. This led me to the decision to write this manual for men.

I call it a manual because it is all about how to, ~~rather than me too.~~ After this preface, I won't bore you with any more "I" statements, details of my life, or stories about others. Instead, this manual will provide you with a practical map that you can use; a comprehensive analysis of male-female relationships in the context of Ken Wilber's Integral Model.

The manual's purpose is simple and clear: to make you familiar with the Integral Relationship Model and how its application will support you in improving all your relationships, especially romantic relationships with women, no matter whether you are currently single or with a partner.

[handwritten: → I found the intro a compelling "hook" & boring]

Introduction

It is not a measure of health to be well adjusted to a profoundly sick society.
~ Jiddu Krishnamurti ~

Men generally benefit more from being in a committed love relationship/marriage than women do, but are frequently less informed about what makes love work.[1]

As a consequence, many emotionally and financially independent modern and postmodern women have gotten tired of taking the lion's share of the responsibility for making their partnerships with men work. **Such women no longer want to feel miserable, they blame men for their relationship problems, leave them in frustration, and prefer to remain single** rather than live with relationship morons.[2] In this process, women often turn to self-help books for advice.

Hence, thousands of politically correct and oversimplified[3] relationship books that are targeted at women and women's interests flood the market. **These books usually have a narrowly defined focus and discuss men and love relationships from a feminine perspective.** If the advice in these books actually worked, then we would see an increasing number of people in healthy partnerships, not a decline.

At the same time, women tend to get overwhelmed, uncomfortable, defensive, and sometimes even outright hostile when offered views on relationships that take a masculine perspective and integrate evolutionary differences between the sexes with feminine and masculine polarities along levels of developmental lines. Pushing this unconscious button would only alienate them further from men, which is NOT the intention of this manual.

Thus this manual is **for men only**—providing a sensible solution for men who want to co-create a healthy, sustainable love relationship with a woman.

A Few Facts and Figures

A multitude of studies have evaluated the status of adult relationships today, generating lots of statistics. Some of the most relevant results are:

84 million Americans (44% of the adult population) live alone.[4]

Over 30 million adults are trying to find a partner online or through singles organizations.[5]

The number of singles is constantly increasing, with negative effects for their physical and emotional health, their socioeconomic status, and the size of their ecological footprint.[6]

Between 40% and 50% of marriages in America will end in divorce,[7] with only 7% of first-time marriages and 15% of all couples experiencing marital satisfaction over an extended period of time.[8]

Over two-thirds of divorces are initiated by women.[9]

The emotional and financial suffering of men tends to be larger after a divorce or breakup than that of women.[10]

The suicide rate of divorced fathers is ten times higher than that of divorced mothers[11] and four times higher for men in general.[12]

The prospects for physical and emotional health, income, job security, promotions at work, sexual satisfaction, and life expectancy generally increase for men who are in a partnership or marriage. The same holds true for women only if they are with a supportive partner, otherwise they decrease.

Men find most women to be sexually attractive, while modern and postmodern single women consider less than 5% of available men to be suitable partners.[13] Since men naturally compete for attractive women, they get repeatedly ignored, rejected, or dumped,[14] while many single women complain that there are no good available men out there.

Some women even believe in the urban myth that there are two women for every man in our adult population, while in actuality the overall US population is fairly balanced between the sexes.[15]

Relationship books top the self-help category and approximately 90% of those books are purchased and read by women.[16] Women are also the main consumers of partnership-oriented media content such as newspaper articles, magazine articles, and radio and TV programs. Women also typically outnumber men at churches, support groups, singles events, dating websites, and relationship seminars/workshops (unless the event has "sex" in the title).[17]

These resources appear to make women even more critical, unsatisfied, and demanding in their relationships with men, while they are often suspicious and feel manipulated if men try to improve their relationship skills by the same means.[18]

The bottom line is that an ever-increasing number of men who try to find a new partner or to improve their current love relationship find themselves in a confusing, painful, frustrating, and damaging mess in their partnerships with women, and none of the currently available approaches seems to solve their problems.

THE INTEGRAL APPROACH

Albert Einstein said, "The significant problems that we face cannot be solved at the same level of thinking we were at when we created them." This new level of thinking about love needs to come from men who are integrally informed and motivated to take responsibility for their part in the co-creation of male-female partnerships.

Integral means whole, complete, or comprehensive. The term was adopted by the renowned American philosopher, psychologist, and writer Ken Wilber (1949-), who spent over four decades of his life creating a coherent map of human growth and potentials.[19]

Introduction | 3

He considered all recurring patterns of human wisdom and knowledge from the East and West and integrated the largest amount of research from the greatest number of disciplines—including the natural sciences (physics, chemistry, biology, neurology, and ecology), art, ethics, religion, psychology, politics, business, sociology, and spirituality—that had stood the test of time. The result was his **Integral Model** which has already been used in such fields as politics,[20] ecology,[21] economics, medicine, law, art,[22] management, education, and spirituality.

This manual describes an **Integral Relationship Model**—the first application of Ken Wilber's Integral Model to dating and the co-creation of healthy love relationships.[23]

THE INTEGRAL RELATIONSHIP MODEL

In this manual we will integrate the multiple dimensions and potentials of our humanness to explain how men and women co-create different forms of love relationships. Below is an outline of how the manual is organized and how the Integral Relationship Model is constructed.

In Chapter 1 we will explore how our evolutionary past shapes the spiritual, physical, and psychological dimensions of our love relationships today. Note the larger spiritual context which is indicated by the outer circle in the diagram below.

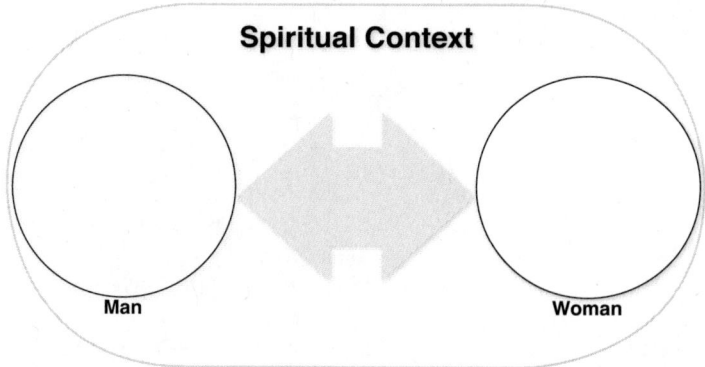

Figure 1: The model with man and woman in spiritual context

Part I of the manual focuses on individuals—what we're looking for, how we develop, and how we're different. We will begin by differentiating between the body and mind of males and females, as indicated by the divided squares inside the male and female circles in the diagram below.

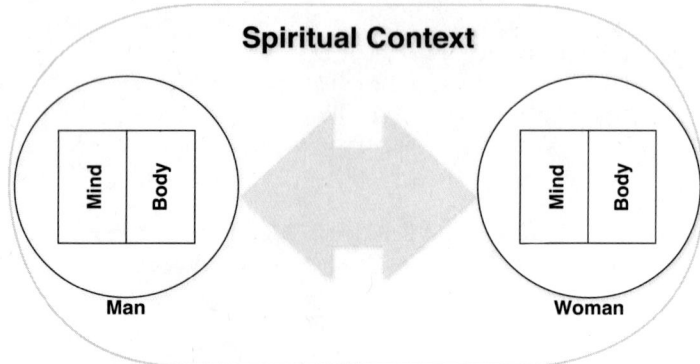

Figure 2: The model with body and mind

This will be followed by a description of the two opposing feminine and masculine polarities that both sexes can equally embody. These polarities are indicated by four arrows pointing away from the square inside the male and female circles.

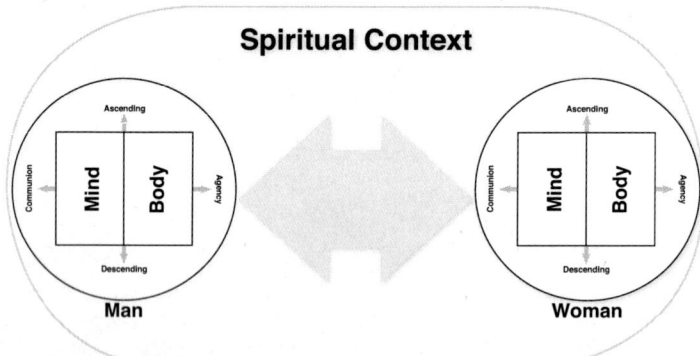

Figure 3: The model with feminine and masculine polarities

The final chapters in **Part I** explore multiple intelligences (lines) and growth potentials (levels), indicated by the four arrows inside each of the squares below, as well as states of consciousness and personality types.

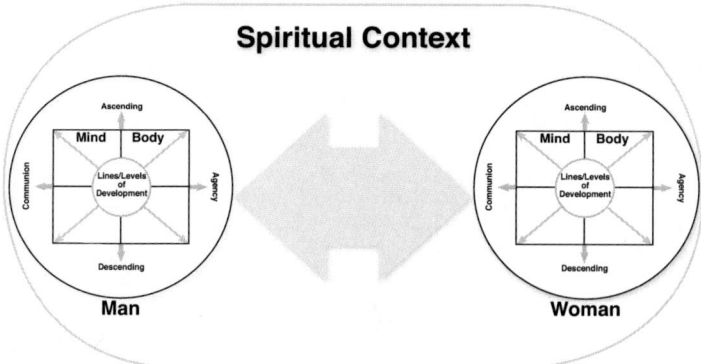

Figure 4: The model with lines and levels of development

Part II of the manual looks at relationship dynamics between men and women, including various forms of love. These forms of love are indicated in the diagram below by triangles that integrate the Primary Fantasy and personality traits that are outlined in Part I of the manual.

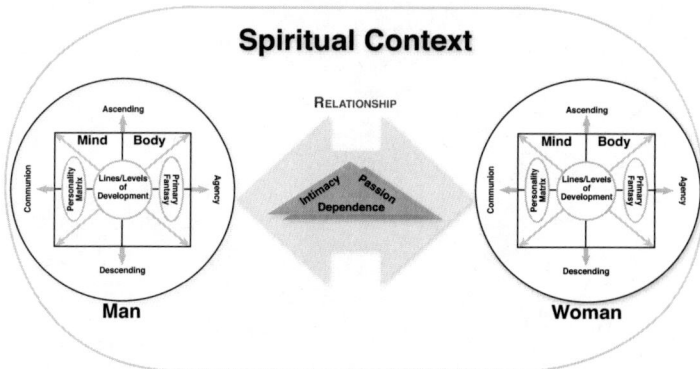

Figure 5: The model with Primary Fantasy, Personality Matrix, and Triangles of Love

In **Part III** of the manual, we will explore how to apply the model in real life by identifying her Kosmic Address through questions and observations. This will allow you to place both of your Kosmic Addresses into a Compatibility-Matrix which will provide you with insights about the quality and sustainability of your love relationship.

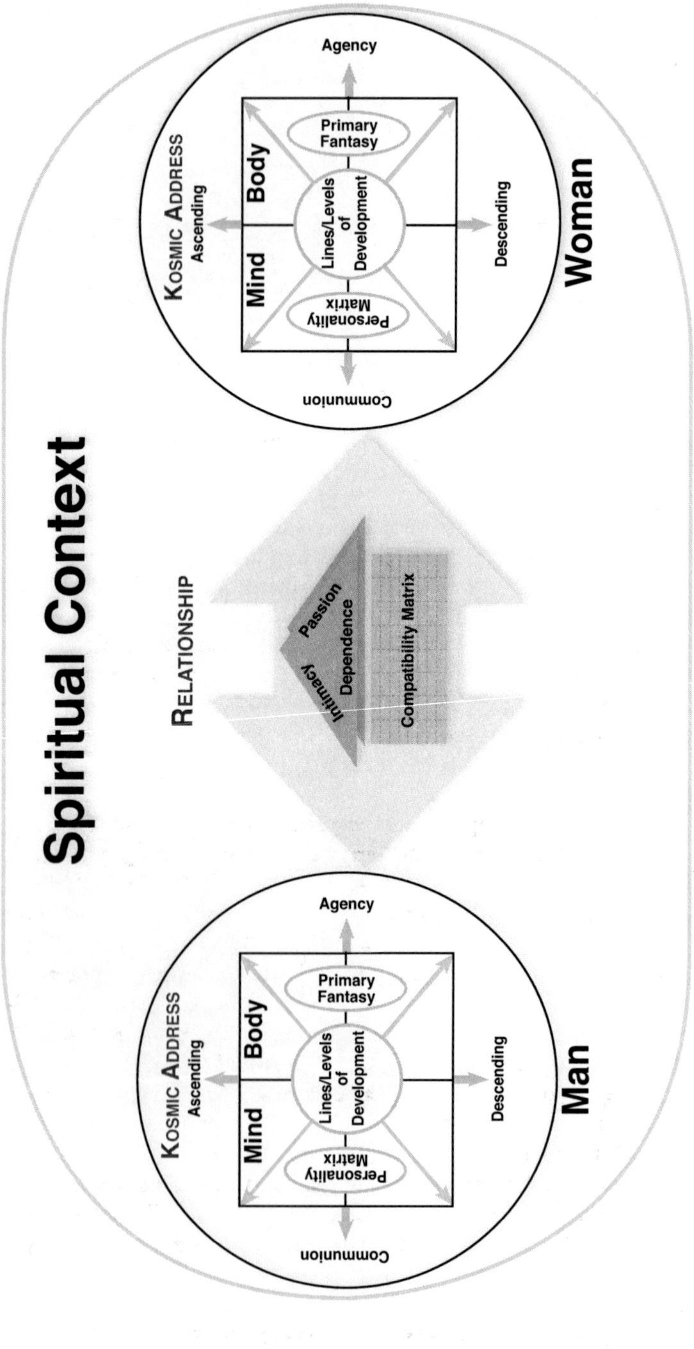

Figure 6: The complete model with Kosmic Address and Compatibility Matrix

Some Notes About This Manual

Throughout the manual you will learn that everyone (including you) is right from their own point of view, what these views are, how they evolved over time, and how men and women with various views relate to each other. As you embrace an increasing number of views, and balance and harmonize whatever is present in your own being, you can approach others with ever-increasing integrity,[24] compassion, love, and understanding. This will not only reduce your own suffering, but also that of others, and will drastically improve all your relationships, especially your love relationships with women. You may then open up to further growth potentials and work towards achieving them if you so choose.

This book is based on four general premises:
  (1) We are only self-aware through our relationships
  (2) We are here to procreate
  (3) The meaning of life is to grow in consciousness towards awakening to our authentic life purpose and full capacity to love unconditionally[25]
  (4) Love may be unconditional but relationships are not[26]

If these premises hold true, then male-female partnerships define our past (we would not be here without our ancestors), present (we would not be aware of our male existence and have no purpose without female reflection), and future (males and females can only fully awaken and sustain the human race together).* If we are at all concerned with our own health and happiness, the future of our children, the well-being of others, the sustainability of our ecosystem, and the further evolution of humanity, then we need a new, complete, accurate, multidimensional, and comprehensive Integral map of the entire territory of male-female relationships, which this manual provides.

However, keep in mind that **the map is not the territory**, no more than a cookbook is the meal. Maps and words are only pointers to reality. The gap between the map (your vision of a healthy, happy love relationship) and the territory (your reality of being single or in an unfulfilling partnership) is called the reality gap. This is where you come in, to bridge this gap. Only if you apply the Integral Relationship Model to your real-life dating strategy and love relationships, can you make the model work for you.

Also be aware that there are limitations to the empirical findings that this manual is based on, especially those that result from social and gender studies. The studies may tell us a lot about randomly selected groups of men and women, such as "on average men are taller than women," or "women are more emotional than men," but little about individuals. While based on the latest scientific research from the West and enduring wisdom traditions from the East, the content of this manual can only serve as a generalizing orientation that needs your careful verification on an individual level, such as, "am I really taller than she is?" In no way should you use what you learn in the following pages to label, discriminate against, or take advantage of women.

To keep the text succinct and flowing, you will find additional thoughts, details, references, and resources for further reading in an abundance of endnotes. You may also skip to the summaries at the end of each chapter if you are already familiar with the chapter's topic.

---

* These statements are in no way intended to discriminate against gays and lesbians. Their world is just not familiar to the author. Most principles that are outlined in this manual may apply to their relationships as well.

Throughout the manual we will refer to women whom you romantically relate to as partners and love relationships as partnerships, to distinguish them from the people with whom you have non-romantic relationships.

A Final Suggestion

Don't share the content of this manual with your date or partner, no matter how excited you might feel. Rather, surprise her with your presence, kindness, understanding, warmth, confidence, curiosity, empathy, and integrity. When it comes to dating and love relationships, women want to know who you are by experiencing your genuine and authentic self, so that they can learn to trust you. If you share your theoretical book knowledge with them, you will *always* get the same reaction: "You have all these ideas and concepts in your head, but I don't feel them coming from your heart. I want to get to know the real you who I can trust and connect with." In other words, "I don't feel any intimacy, connection, attraction, or chemistry when you talk about stuff from books."

In effect, she is saying, "Don't explain the map to me, just drive me to the ocean."

[Handwritten annotations: "NO!" in margin; "you" inserted above "your date"; "TYPICALLY" above "always"; bracket around paragraph]

[Handwritten note at bottom:] a huge red-flag. If I hadn't met you, this paragraph (after the preface) the implied misogyny of the discounting of non-... relationship" would cause me to so question your understanding of and appreciation of women as to abandon the book without proceeding. etc. This statement is "oversimplified" sg. Better to stick w/ map is not the territory. "Don't wave your map..." better to demonstrate your understanding.

Chapter 1

Understanding the Dimensions of Love

You have to know the past to understand the present.
~ Carl Sagan ~

Throughout this manual we will discuss two conditional dimensions of love relationships between men and women: First, the physical dimension, which is motivated by our persistent drive to procreate and to raise healthy offspring. Without this drive we would not be here today and would have no future as a species. We may call this dimension selfless love or Agape, which requires compassion and self-sacrifice. Second is the psychological dimension of love, which is driven by our yearning to become complete and to transcend our illusionary sense of separation and aloneness in the universe. This dimension we may call the art of love or Eros, as it requires creativity and skill to co-create a healthy love relationship. Both of these dimensions are set in the larger context of the ever-present unconditional spiritual dimension of Love, which is the ground of all being.

THE SPIRITUAL DIMENSION OF LOVE

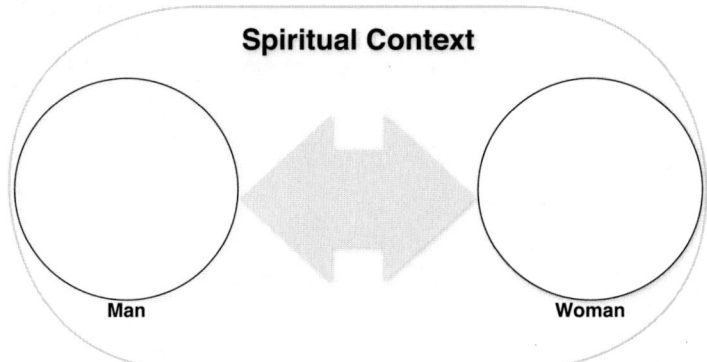

Figure 7: Man and woman in the spiritual context

Modern physics, philosophy, and mysticism all point us to an infinite and eternal/timeless oneness or connectedness. Everything, including you, is part of this oneness that has been given many names such as God, Spirit, the Absolute, the Infinite/Eternal, Pure Awareness, Ever-Present Origin, Unified Field, or Ground of All Being. This oneness can only experience itself by splitting into the "two-ness" that we perceive as the duality of past and future, emptiness and form, light and dark, male and female, feminine and masculine, etc. By forgetting that these opposites are ultimately the eternal and infinite One, the illusionary play of time, emptiness, and form can begin. The deep yearning of our soul to love and to be loved unconditionally is the call to return to this oneness through ego transcendence.

The mind cannot grasp this oneness. Unless you are permanently enlightened (whatever that means), you can only get glimpses of oneness at moments of absolute stillness and presence, during a peak or near-death experience, in certain drug-induced states, or in transcendental tantric sexual union.[27] This oneness cannot be thought of or spoken about either, since that would split one into two and make it separate from you. Words and concepts can only point to it, and many sacred texts and poems attempt to do so.[28] Why this oneness "went through all the bother to bring the universe into existence"[29] remains a mystery to scientists, philosophers, and mystics to this day. True unconditional Love (with a capital L) can be seen as the experience of a return to this oneness.[30] So now that we are done speaking about the unspeakable (that was easy, wasn't it?), we can move on to talk about the physical world and evolution as we understand it today.

THE EVOLVING PHYSICAL AND PSYCHOLOGICAL DIMENSIONS OF LOVE

Throughout history, human males and females have co-created mutually compatible biological and psychological characteristics that drive us to sustain the human race. What may look like male oppression of females from today's perspective was actually (with the regrettable exceptions that we see to this day in some parts of the world) a mutually beneficial arrangement for the survival of both sexes, which has resulted in significant increases in human population, longer life expectancy, and more comfort. Today we experience this evolutionary drive to procreate and to complement each other's psyche through various forms of love.

Let's now take a brief look at history from the point of view of the evolution of the sexes.

For a long time after the Big Bang about **13.7 billion** years ago, there was only space and dead matter (quantum particles, atoms, clouds of gas, rocks, stars, planets, and galaxies).

About **4 billion** years ago the first biological life forms appeared on earth as simple sexless organisms.[31]

About **1 billion** years ago, the opposite sex emerged when certain life forms evolved to reproduce by combining their genetic material through sexual reproduction and so passed it on to future generations. Today it is widely believed that mutations in genes generated an increasing variety of species[32] of which, through sexual and natural selection, only the fittest and/or most adaptable/cooperative survived to further procreate.[33]

About **225 million** years ago, the first warm blooded mammals came into existence.

About **7 million** years ago, the predecessors to our human ancestors, the great apes, began to inhabit the African jungles.[34]

Understanding the Dimensions of Love | 11

About **5 million** years ago, receding forests and declining supplies of plant foods forced our predecessors, the great apes, to descend from their trees. Males learned to hunt small, sick, and injured animals, while females specialized in the gathering of edible fruits, roots, shoots, and leaves. The addition of animal protein to their diet allowed the brains of our ancestors to grow and created a literal meat hunger inside of them.[35] Males began to band together to hunt ever larger animals to satisfy their own and the carnivorous appetites of their female mates and offspring. This required males to design and implement clever plans, display good judgment, operate inside hierarchical structures, sit silently for hours, be single-focused on their prey, kill without remorse, and to develop simple verbal and non-verbal communication skills. The most productive hunters, who were naturally tall, well-built, intelligent, clever, industrious, and competitive, became capable of providing up to three times more meat than their weaker peers. This gave them access to females with the best reproductive qualities—who were naturally young and healthy-looking—while less productive males partnered with physically less attractive and older females. At the same time, females sharpened their sensory awareness to scan the land for edible vegetables and fruit, identify them through their colors and smells, share information about their location with other females, and monitor the ripening cycles of nature. To ensure that their own genetic material would be passed down to future generations, males became protective of the females they had mated with. At the same time, it became advantageous for females to be sexual with only one male to ensure his ongoing commitment as her protector and provider once she became pregnant and bore their children.[36] This led to the earliest forms of monogamous partnerships and the establishment of nuclear families[37] that bonded together in small bands and clans.

Through sexual and natural selection, the offspring of the most successful male hunters and healthiest (by today's standards sexiest/prettiest) females survived long enough to procreate. The resulting mating behavior became deeply embedded in the physical and psychological makeup of modern humans.[38] This can be seen today in the universal male desire for young, vital, and healthy-looking females (most men are turned on by a hot Playboy model or porn star), and the female fantasy of a committed, successful protector/provider who is benevolent towards her and her children, while competing aggressively with other males (most women like chick flicks and romance novels with a striking James Bond-style hero in them).[39]

About **750,000 years** ago, the ability to harness fire for protection from wild animals, for cooking food (which makes it much easier for the body to absorb nutrients), and for seeing in the dark allowed for communal gatherings at night and further advanced the physiological growth and social bonding of these early family clans.

About **400,000 years** ago, swinging the biggest club and killing the largest animals became no longer good enough to woo the most desirable females, who started to look for additional fitness indicators in their suitors; they wanted to be romanced and entertained. In response, early Stone Age males forayed into the creation of art (cave paintings, body ornaments, drumming, and dances) and developed language.[40]

About **200,000 years** ago, the first modern humans (Homo sapiens) entered the scene. Like their ancestors, they were nomadic hunters and gatherers.

About **12,000 years** ago, the lifestyle of some families became more settled when horticultural communities found ways to cultivate a variety of crops and to herd small animals around their dwellings. These activities could be largely performed by pregnant and child-rearing women, while men expanded their hunting territories ever further from home to find enough game to feed their growing families, bands, clans, and tribes. By that time, about **1,000,000** humans had spread to all livable areas of the planet.

About **8,000 years ago**, the invention of the plow (most likely by a man) pulled by domesticated large animals such as oxen, heralded the era of agriculture[41] when hunting, gathering, and horticulture alone could no longer feed the human population, which had by then grown to 5,000,000. Plowing was handled exclusively by men, because pregnant and child-rearing women could not perform the strenuous work. Consequently, patriarchal[42] social structures developed as men—in addition to being hunters and protectors—took on the major responsibility for providing foodstuffs. As a result, men started to dominate the emerging public sphere of government, education, religion, and politics, while women dominated the private sphere of family, hearth, and home. This division of labor is often referred to as male production and female reproduction,[43] which allowed women to focus on the lighter and less dangerous chores around the house and of tending to their offspring, while males risked their lives through hard labor, dangerous hunts, and defending the territory of their families and clans.

Further advancements in farming techniques helped to produce a surplus of food, especially in fertile regions of the world with milder climates, such as the Mediterranean, along the Nile River, and in China. This freed up a certain number of creative men to pursue endeavors like specialized warfare, new inventions such as the wheel and axle, beer, sailboats (around 5000 BCE), competitive sports (in China by 4000 BCE), architecture, and the creation of more elaborate art objects, while women continued to focus on homemaking and raising their children.

About **6,000 years ago**, small cities and states were founded by men to house some of the **10,000,000** humans that lived on earth by then. With more people on the planet, new conflicts arose between them, and larger wars started to be fought by men to protect their families and farming/hunting territories, gain status, and win the hearts of women.

About **4,000 years ago**, the first monotheistic religions that worshipped a male God, and generally saw women as inferior, were conceived by men, and recorded history began with the earliest written documents that we know of today.

About **3,000 years ago**, **50,000,000** people populated the earth and the first large city-states were established in Greece. Athens became the home of such influential philosophers[44] as Socrates, Plato and Aristotle. The latter wrote in his book *Politics*: "the male is by nature superior, and the female inferior; and the one rules, and the other is ruled." These philosophers laid the foundation for modern civilization and the Western thought systems that remain highly influential to this day.[45]

About **2,000 years ago**, **200,000,000** humans were alive, and the Romans had built their empire, which was later broken up into the European states as we know them today.

About **500 years ago**, the world's population had doubled again to **400,000,000** when Columbus and other modern male explorers made their land discoveries, which led to worldwide trading and exploration, while Copernicus, Galileo, Kepler, and Newton made the first modern scientific discoveries. In an ongoing effort to gain the love of women and to improve their quality of life, men made tremendous technical, philosophical, social, and political advancements during the Enlightenment Period in the eighteenth century.[46]

About **200 years** ago, (around the year 1800), the human population hit the billion mark, and the physical strength of males and animals started to be replaced with the power of steam engines and modern weapons during the Industrial Revolution.[47] These new technologies allowed women to gradually enter into domains that had been previously developed and occupied exclusively by men, and gave rise to the female liberation movement,[48] which later led to the various forms and waves of feminism.[49]

Around **1900**, men granted [PATRONIZING] women the right to vote,[50] to receive an equal education,[51] and to work in any profession they were qualified for, gradually earning equal or even higher pay for equal work.[52] By that time **1.6 billion** humans walked the earth, only to rise to **6 billion** by the year 2000, which is, from an evolutionary standpoint, an incredible success story.

In **1960**, the sexual revolution was spurred by the invention of the Pill (by a man),[53] which gave women control over their reproductive capacity.

In **1970**, no-fault divorce laws started to be established throughout the US,[54] which caused divorce rates to double when wives started to initiate divorce twice as often as husbands did to end their marriages.[55]

In **1990**, third-wave feminism empowered modern and postmodern women to forge their independent way into all areas of Western society as we see it today.[56]

While modern and postmodern women have been liberated from their traditional gender roles and economic dependence on men by gaining unlimited (if they choose) access to traditionally male-dominated domains and full control over their reproductive capacity, men remain largely stuck in their traditional roles as protector and provider[57] and continue to depend on females for sex, love, purpose, and emotional support.[58]

To win the hearts of desirable women, men still have to be success-oriented in their educational and career choices, take higher risks of losing their lives through stressful, hard, and dangerous work,[59] or be the disposable sex in wars.[60] Modern and postmodern women, on the other hand, can afford to be fulfillment-oriented by generating income from professions that are personally satisfying and financially rewarding, while benefitting from husbands (and ex-husbands),[61] benevolent men (who are often naïve/needy), sex partners, and/or boyfriends who support and pay them in exchange for love, company, and sex (think dinner, movies, vacations, diamond ring, car, house, etc.). In other words, males throughout history have had to become ever more successful, sophisticated, creative, inventive, and competitive to amass increasing amounts of power, status, and wealth to win the hearts of desirable females. This dynamic, as we slowly realize, cannot be endlessly sustained without destroying our ecosystem and forcing others into poverty and starvation. On the other hand, it continues to suffice for females to be healthy in body and mind, as well as sexually available, supportive, and understanding towards males to attract them.

Gender Mainstreaming is the latest emergence in the evolutionary development between the sexes. It was formulated at the United Nations by women who realized that advocating for the rights, viewpoints, and benefits of one sex only (women) is against both sexes.[62]

In the October 26, 2009 issue of *Time* magazine, the article "The State of the American Woman"[63] concluded that,

> " … we will soon be having parallel conversations: What needs to be done to free American men to realize their [emphasis added] full potential? You can imagine the whole conversation flipping in a single generation. It's no longer a

man's world. Nor is it a woman's nation. It's a cooperative, with bylaws under constant negotiation and expectations that profits be equally shared."

These latest insights about gender issues, if seen and accepted by both sexes, open up new possibilities for the co-creation of partnerships between integrally informed men and post-feminist/post-postmodern women, who do not only demand equal rights but also assume equal responsibilities, for example to protect our ecosystem and to reward non-violence. These new couples will treat each other as equals while honoring their sexual differences and so point the way into a sustainable and peaceful future for all humanity.[64]

In Summary

Seen from an absolute spiritual perspective, Love is the everpresent ground of all that is. On the relative physical and psychological plane, love is our means to sustain the human race and to overcome our sense of separation.

For thousands of years, males have advanced their fitness to win the hearts of desirable females and to augment the life quality and safety of their families through protecting and providing. In return, women cared for men and rewarded them with their admiration, love, support, company, sex, and children.

With the rise of modernity—which gave birth to female liberation and the feminist movement--this long-time equilibrium started to shift. It now provides modern and postmodern women with equal rights and opportunities without equal responsibilities. They have become legally, financially, and emotionally independent, and only consider being in a partnership with a man if he can significantly augment their quality of life. This leaves many average and disadvantaged men struggling to prevent their wives from divorcing them or to find a partner in the first place. The latest development in the evolution of the sexes is called Gender Mainstreaming. It holds the possibility of partnerships between men and women as opposites and equals and promises a peaceful and sustainable future for all humanity by promoting true gender equality (rights and responsibilities) while honoring sexual differences.

Part I – The Biological and Psychological Makeup of Men and Women

> *Romantic love is either all I want to talk about, or the last thing I want to talk about, depending on the hour. When I'm in the mood to discuss it, it seems huge and important. When I'm not in the mood, it seems almost neurotic. One thing remains constant, however, regardless of how I view it: romantic love is a mystery.*
> ~ Marianne Williamson ~

In Part I of the manual we will define the core elements of the Integral Relationship Model:
1. Body (sex-based differences, including the Primary Fantasy), mind (learned gender roles), and soul (feminine/masculine polarities)
2. Lines of human development (intelligences and other potentials)
3. Levels of consciousness, anima/animus complex, sexual, and spiritual development
4. States of falling in love
5. Personality types

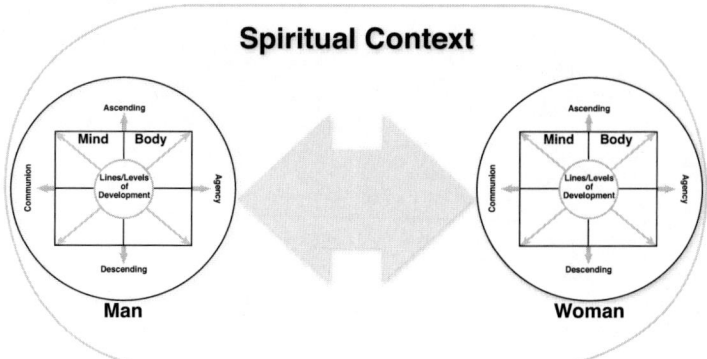

Figure 8: The core elements of men and women

Elements two to five are based on Wilber's original Integral Model, so if you're familiar with his work, the labels match. Note that we'll discuss Wilber's first element, the four quadrants, in Part II.

Chapter 2

Understanding the Differences Between the Sexes

In this country, you gotta make the money first. Then when you get the money, you get the power. Then when you get the power, then you get the women.
~ Al Pacino in "Scarface" ~

While the 20th century brought legal and socioeconomic equality with men for modern and postmodern women, the unique biological and genetic makeup that distinguishes the sexes has remained the same. To gain a deeper understanding of the male-female dynamic, we will now further distinguish between (1) essential sex differences between males and females (body), (2) learned gender roles of men and women (mind), and (3) the feminine and masculine polarities that can be uniquely embodied by both sexes (soul).

Throughout this manual we'll use the following terminology:

When referring to biological differences (sex), we'll speak of **male/female**.
When referring to learned social patterns (gender), we'll speak of **men/women**.
When referring to polarity (soul), we'll speak of **masculine/feminine**.

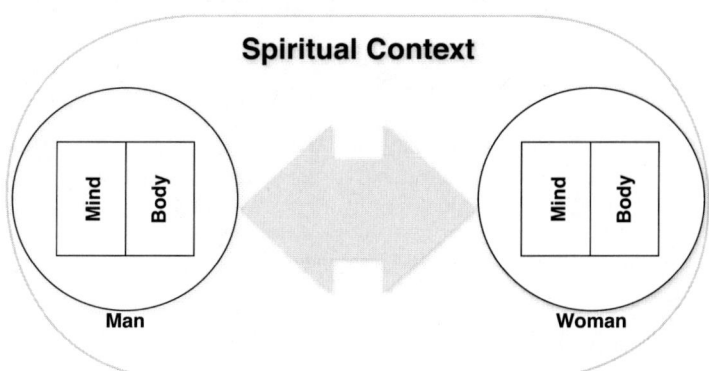

Figure 9: Body/mind of men and women

In this chapter, we will explore each dimension as the first element of our Integral Relationship Model.2

---
2. We will cover the four quadrants, which are the first element in Wilber's original AQAL model, in Part II, Chapter 7 of the manual.

Sex: Physical/Biological Differences Between Males and Females (Body)

Sex (as a noun) refers to the physiological, biological, and genetic makeup of males and females. It has evolved over billions of years and is unaffected by social change. Typical human males have a penis and XY chromosomes, grow more body hair, turn bald, and produce ten times more testosterone than females, who have a vagina, XX chromosomes, breasts, higher-pitched voices, more estrogen, and think less often about sex. These differences have been hardwired into our bodies by evolution, and require a sex change procedure to be altered. As a consequence, there are distinct mating behaviors for heterosexual men and women that have become equally hardwired:

Men are conditioned to be physically attracted to young (or at least, younger), vital, and healthy-looking females with smooth skin, shiny hair, well-aligned complete white teeth, symmetric facial and body features, wide hips, small waists (ideally with an 0.7 hip-to-waist ratio),[65] sparkling eyes, and full breasts, which are all indicators for fertility and the ability to bear healthy children.[66]

Women are intuitively drawn to benevolent, strong, tall,[67] successful, intelligent, healthy-looking, and entertaining males with money, future earning potential, power, and social status, who commit to and love them exclusively. These attributes are all indicators for good genes and a male's capacity to be a strong protector and provider.[68]

The sexual fantasies of males are objectified in the offerings of the porn industry[69] (which are condemned by society), while romance novels[70] and "chick flicks" (which are sanctioned by society) represent the equivalents that cater to the sexual fantasies of females.

Sex-Based Differences in Male/Female Primary Fantasy

Researchers have identified how biological sex differences result in sex-based fantasies that are consistent throughout all cultures.

These fantasies run deep in our unconscious, are almost impossible to transcend,[71] and their fulfillment is the prerequisite for any romantic interest in a member of the opposite sex. We're going to refer to them collectively as the Primary Fantasy. All other qualities that lovers typically seek in a partner are secondary to the Primary Fantasy and usually gender-neutral. They include shared values, interests, lifestyle choices, temperaments, plans and dreams for the future, and compatible needs around time spent together, money, and sex.[72]

Once the Primary Fantasy is fulfilled, a male's loving feelings for a sexy female and hers for a successful male are experienced as absolutely real and authentic. Their bodies signal the potential to produce and raise healthy offspring to their owners by increasing the production of thrilling hormones that foster lust, desire, and intimacy, while temporarily impairing the rational faculties of the love-struck couple's brains so that they ignore red flags and have sex with each other.

Lovers with this experience often speak of the chemistry between them and they are right.[73] Lust is triggered in males and females by an increased production of testosterone, feelings of intimacy are promoted by dopamine, norepinephrine, and serotonin, and attachment forms through elevated levels of oxytocin in females and vasopressin in males.[74] Some of these hormones are as potent as illegal drugs. They can send their recipients on unknown highs, get them addicted, and lead to painful withdrawal symptoms when they drop.[75]

Males get attracted and fall in love much more quickly than females, since their Primary Fantasy is solely based on her physical appearance and sexual radiance.[76] Seeing an attractive woman, looking at sexy pictures, watching an erotic movie, or a stripper in a bar can be enough to elevate the testosterone levels that turn him on. And often, to the utter frustration and puzzlement of females, he can be turned off as quickly once he has conquered the object of his desire and goes on the hunt for another sex object to get his fix.

Attractive females, in alliance with the cosmetic, beauty, and fashion industry,[77] as well as clever advertisers for goods and services have, of course, been long aware of the effect that images of sexy females have on males. They constantly bombard men with seductive messages that suggest how making and spending large sums of money for status symbols (e.g., diamond ring, car, watch), consuming the right products (e.g., beer, aftershave), or risking their health and lives (fighting in the army, embarking on dangerous adventures, and engaging in violent/competitive sports), will get them the woman of their dreams.[78]

Females usually experience the same initial spark when they see a physically attractive male, but get turned off quickly if his socioeconomic status and personality do not meet their Primary Fantasy (unless they are looking for a one-night-stand or "boy-toy").[79] Unlike males, females are much more likely to warm up romantically to an older and physically less attractive partner over time if his financial assets, social status, and character traits meet their expectations. While the attention of males is almost exclusively directed towards her body, jumping her bones, and how she will look on his arm, to her, his income, character, intelligence, wit, loyalty, stature, security, use of language, manners, education, job, accomplishments, health, lifestyle, car, home, other material possessions, retirement plan, circle of friends, and integrity are of high significance in addition to (and sometimes instead of) good looks.[80]

If the sexual attraction is mutual, she will still often need more time to build the confidence that he is able, willing, and available to make an exclusive commitment as her benevolent, generous, trustworthy, and consistent protector and provider. The evolutionary reason for her scrutiny and selectivity before choosing him as a lover and partner lies in the possibility of her getting pregnant. To conceive a child is a much larger emotional and life-changing investment for her than for him.[81] Even if couples use methods of contraception or can no longer conceive children, her hormonal system responds in very much the same way as if she could get pregnant, in which case she would have to endure nine months of physical discomfort, could not conceive another man's child, would risk her life during childbirth, and would be obligated to take care of the child for years to come, while the father could easily abandon her and give his semen, love, and support to another woman.[82]

THE SEX-BASED FEMALE FEAR—MALE SHAME DYNAMIC

The biological differences between the sexes also lead to the primary emotional reactions of *fear* in females and *shame* in males. Fear (typically fear of abandonment) arises in her when she experiences an emotional disconnect, usually after the initial chemistry is gone, or if she worries that he falls short as her committed protector and provider. Her fear is triggered when their communication breaks down, if he shows an interest in other women, if he reveals weaknesses, appears incompetent, complains or worries about his job, becomes unemployed, engages in addictive behaviors, or gets defeated. In her efforts to get him to reconnect with her emotionally, to receive reassurance of his support, or to improve his performance, she often starts to withhold sex, and to nag, criticize, challenge, humiliate, compare, or passive-aggressively ignore him, without having a clue how she is undermining their partnership by doing so.[83] If he does not respond in a favorable way, she is quick to lose her faith and to accuse him of not listening to or understanding her, and of being insensitive, emotionally unavailable, passive aggressive, or in denial, which may or may not be the case.

Her efforts to re-connect and to support him to perform better only push him further away so that he can avoid her ongoing emasculations[84] and hide his primary emotion of shame for not being good enough to make her happy. Instead of providing her with the connection, emotional safety, strength, and reassurance that she is longing for, he may get angry at her, start to work longer hours, try to make more money, spend more time with his buddies, engage in his hobbies, embark on a spiritual path, or become whiny and depressed.[85] She, on the other hand, does not know how to inspire and reward him by showing empathy and to appreciate him for the things he does (even if they are little) by recognizing/praising and having sex with him, which would often open him up to provide her with more of the support, love, and reassurance that she craves.[86] Both partners are then prone to discuss their unhappiness and frustration with members of the opposite sex outside their relationship who show more empathy. Such behavior is called emotional infidelity and is obviously a slippery slope, as sexual infidelity lurks right around the corner.

Because of their different evolutionary conditioning, he is usually better equipped to handle her emotional infidelity as long as she does not cheat sexually on him, while she can be forgiving about his sexual infidelity as long as she is assured of his love, financial support, and commitment to her.[87]

If you experience the fear-shame dynamic in your love relationship, you may be able to turn things around by listening to your partner's fears and concerns without guilt and without getting defensive or withdrawn, and by reassuring her of your love, loyalty, and support.[88]

THE SOCIAL TABOO AROUND THE SEXUAL SELECTION PROCESS

The Primary Fantasy and the resulting sexual selection process that underlies most of our partnerships is a highly vulnerable and emotionally charged issue for singles and couples alike, and is therefore rarely addressed scientifically or publicly for several reasons:[89]

(1) Hardly anybody wants to publicly state or admit that the primary criteria for the attractiveness of females are their age, physique, looks, and sexual radiance—in short, their "fuckability factor," and those of males are their socioeconomic status, competitiveness, and generosity.[90]

(2) It is hard for singles to face the fact that they may have unresolved psychological

issues that prevent them from having a healthy partnership, or that they date way outside their league. Women often have unrealistic expectations of attracting a "prince in shining armor" or "sugar daddy" who they are too old and ugly for, while men may fantasize about younger, sexually attractive Playboy model types whom they can't afford.

(3) Social, radical, and eco-feminists[91] are in denial about the role that sexually attractive and partnership-oriented females (oops ... they are women too) play in the creation of social injustice, wars, and the destruction of our ecosystem, by rewarding those males who are most ruthless in competing for power, status, and wealth (at the expense of the environment as well as other women and men) with their love, company, and sex, in exchange for a safe and carefree lifestyle.[92]

(4) Couples don't want to be confronted with the possibility that they have confused the fulfillment of each other's Primary Fantasy with real love, especially if their partnership is in trouble after the initial chemistry faded away.

(5) Singles who lack the necessary physical or material assets to attract a partner don't want to be reminded of the painful feelings that they have endured after previous rejections from members of the opposite sex whose hearts they could not win.

While the Integral Relationship Model doesn't ignore the important role that the Primary Fantasy and the resulting hormonal reactions play in the co-creation of partnerships, it also does not reduce partner choices or the quality of love relationships to these criteria. In Part II of the manual we will therefore further differentiate how the Primary Fantasy is experienced at different levels of consciousness development, and integrate it with the other elements of the Integral Relationship Model.

Understanding Sex-Based Differences Reduces Suffering

As many psychologists, anthropologists, and sociologists have confirmed,[93] and as you know from your own experiences and observations, "men look for sex objects, and women look for success objects," "men want the one thing from every woman, while women want everything from one man," and "for men the physical attraction (and sex) causes the relationship, while for most women, the relationship causes the physical attraction (and sex)."

Your investment in this manual may have already paid off if you were unaware of the extent that the often unconscious Primary Fantasy plays in the sexual selection process. This insight can **save you a lot of money, grief, and frustration** if you can avoid an expensive and devastating breakup/divorce by becoming more understanding of your spouse or by separating amicably if mutual chemistry was the primary motivator for your partnership in the first place and is now gone. If you are single, you can stop going on costly dates with attractive, high-maintenance females whom you can't afford and can't make happy in the long run.[94]

Gender: Cultural/Learned Differences Between Men and Women (Mind)

Gender refers to the roles that society and culture have assigned to each sex. Gender roles are learned during childhood and beyond, as we observe and are told how to think and behave appropriately as men or women in our society.[95] These roles vary among cultures, as they are not hardwired, unlike the sex-based Primary Fantasies that are consistent throughout the world and human history.[96] Nevertheless, gender roles are deeply ingrained into our mind and often unconscious. Social scientists and feminists still debate which characteristics of males and females are created by nature (sex) or nurture (cultural background and social conditioning). The boundaries between them are arguably fluid and certainly blurred.[97] For example, we speak of *transgender* if a man or woman feels themselves to be in the body of the wrong sex and acts accordingly, such as a cross-dresser.

Gender is usually expressed through the type of clothes we wear, customary length of hair, the professions we choose, hours we spend at work, what and whom we play with, who proposes and buys the diamond ring, assignment of chores around the house,[98] and all other gender-related social roles and cultural norms. It is hard to break out of one's assigned gender roles, as society puts much pressure on men and women to act according to their sex (for example that men marry younger women, can't be fulfillment-oriented, or have to be the main breadwinner), but it is certainly possible if we make them conscious and intelligently question the status quo that limits us in our freedom of expression (e.g., the recent trend of older women, so called *cougars*, dating younger men).

Social researchers have found that across 25 nations, the most common and widely accepted gender stereotypes for men are: adventurous, dominant, forceful, independent, strong, aggressive, autocratic, daring, enterprising, robust, stern, active, courageous, progressive, rude, severe, unemotional, and wise.

Women are stereotyped as sentimental, submissive, superstitious, affectionate, dreamy, sensitive, attractive, dependent, emotional, fearful, soft-hearted, weak, sexy, curious, gentle, mild, charming, and talkative.[99]

It can be quite illuminating and entertaining to learn about sex- and gender-based differences between men and women through pop psychology books and workshops[100] that go into more depth about stereotypes, such as:

Men are from Mars, single-focused,[101] compartmentalize, go the shortest route between points A and B, don't ask for directions, think before they feel, retreat into their cave or watch TV to deal with problems, think hierarchically, build structures, are rational, have a hunter's "fuck it or kill it" instinct, pursue women for sex, want to problem-solve, and work harder to become better providers when their partner seems unhappy.

Women are from Venus, multi-task, network, like to meander, ask for directions, feel before they think, need to talk to deal with problems, think laterally, go with the flow, are passive and peaceful, have healing energy, give sex, receive, follow, radiate, and are more visual.

As we will explore in Part II, gender roles are not as closely tied to the sexes as is suggested by stereotyping, and the dynamics shift and can be transcended as men and women evolve.

POLARITIES: MASCULINE/FEMININE POTENTIALS FOR BOTH SEXES (SOUL)

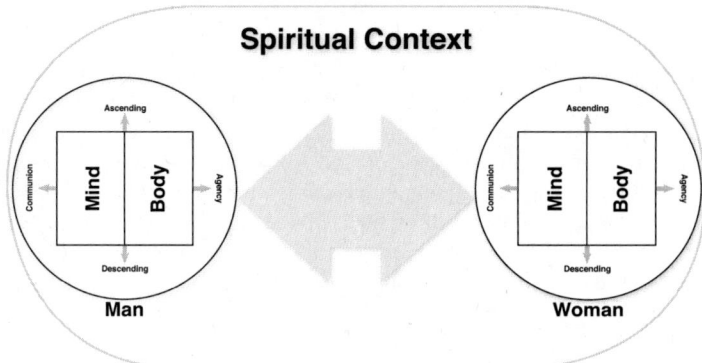

Figure 10: The four polarities of both sexes

While sex-based differences are biological (body) and gender roles are learned (mind), the potentials to embody womanly (or feminine) and manly (or masculine) qualities are equal for both sexes (soul).[102] The Integral Relationship Model equates the feminine with **descending** and **communion**, which are opposed by the masculine qualities of **ascending** and **agency**. The two pairs of polarities can be visualized as a graph (shown below) with ascending and descending on the vertical axis, and communion and agency on the horizontal axis. You may envision these polarities as the positive and negative poles of a battery or magnet that are necessary for sexual energy to flow and to keep the human psyche in a healthy balance.

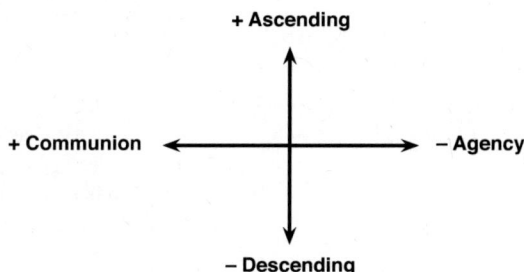

Figure 11: The four polarities

Consider which qualities resonate most with you and which sound familiar from observations in others while you read the descriptions of the four polarities below.

Ascending

Ascending[103] (or self-transcendence) is the upward drive towards heaven, the absolute, union, spirit, or Godhead, away from the fragmented details of the manifest world and its many forms. Einstein's famous quote aptly describes ascending: "I want to know how God created this world. I am not interested in this or that phenomenon, in the spectrum of this or that element. I want to know His thoughts, the rest are details."

Ascending is also characterized as "the love that reaches up" (Eros) that brings forth new creations by arranging fragments into larger wholes, such as notes into symphonies, ingredients into meals, colors into paintings, words into sentences, knowledge into wisdom, individuals into couples, or communities into societies. Ascenders look at reality from a distance and see fractions as part of the larger whole or a greater totality. They perceive the world from an extended bird's eye view and try to rise ever higher in consciousness to encompass everything. Ascending energy expresses itself through wisdom, creativity, novelty, visionary concepts, emptiness, and stillness.

Healthy ascending is characterized by a desire to improve, to go beyond, to grow, to transcend, to create, and to think big. This is accomplished by gaining wider perspectives of the self and the nature of things. It requires a willingness to change by letting go of old paradigms and not sweating the small stuff.

Unhealthy ascending ignores, represses, controls, and dominates the lower, instead of embracing and caring for it. It denies feelings, the body, sexuality, and nature.

The fear of ascenders is to get dragged down, engulfed, absorbed, and lost (Phobos).[104]

Descending

Descending[105] (or self-immanence) is the downward drive towards earth, into the world of many manifestations and the body. Descenders celebrate life and its many forms, the body, and their sexuality. They go with the flow, are in touch with the richness of the manifest world, and experience things from the fullness of existence by diving in deep. Descending is also characterized as "the love that reaches down" (Agape), embracing everything—including earth and all its inhabitants—with selfless compassion and devotion.

Descending energy expresses itself through feelings, empathy, emotions, warmth, movement, surrender, fullness, and flow. A descender perceives the world from the inside.

Healthy descending means to be connected with and sensitive to the richness and fullness of the world, to be down-to-earth and in touch with one's body, feelings, emotions, and sexuality.

Unhealthy descending means to be overwhelmed, fused with, and run by the many details of life and its manifestations, feelings, earthly desires, and needs.

The fear of descenders is to lose touch, to get lost, or to be dissociated from the fullness of life and its forces (Thanatos).[106]

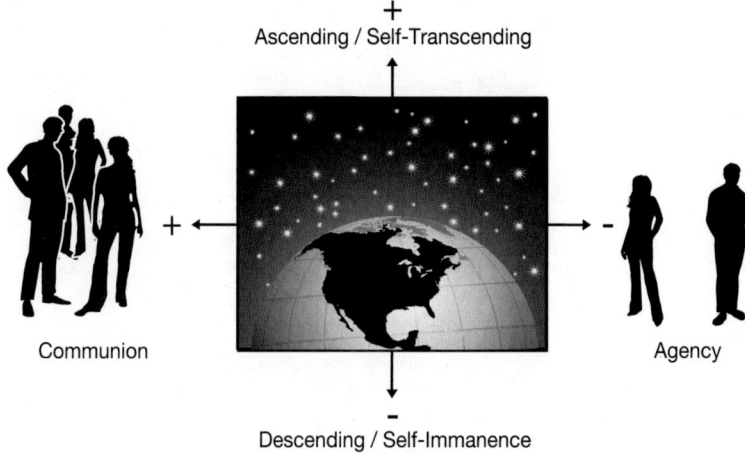

Figure 12: Understanding ascending, descending, agency, and communion

AGENCY

Agency[107] (or self-preservation) is the drive towards wholeness, taking action through one's own will, making independent choices, and exerting power. People with a tendency towards agency have a desire to maintain their own identity, personality, individuality, independence, and autonomy. They focus on rights, rules, laws, and justice that protect and serve the interests of the individual, and are defined by their own decisions, success, and free will, rather than their environment and the opinion of others (it is better to fail at living your own life, than to succeed at living someone else's).

Healthy agency supports the autonomous functioning of the individual.

Unhealthy agency leads to alienation and dissociation from others.

The fear of agentic people is to lose the freedom to make independent choices, and to become dependent on others for their well-being.

COMMUNION

Communion (or self-adaptation) is the drive to connect (commune) with others, to be part of and act in the interest of the unit or group, and to cooperate. Communion is expressed through qualities of care, responsibility, relationship, lateral bonding, connection, communication, empathy, intimacy, joining, and participation. Communal people feel that their well-being depends on their ability to contribute, trust, depend on others, fit into their environment, and maintain a mutual support system of give and take.

Healthy communion is expressed through the peaceful, responsible (response-able), considerate, and caring connection between people.

Unhealthy communion leads to fusion, dependency, neediness, and clinging—with the loss of one's own will, individuality, and autonomy—which eventually leads to resentment.

The fear of communion-oriented (communal) people is to be abandoned, unsupported, and alone.

Mutual Exclusivity

A person can either be agentic or communal, or ascending or descending, but not communal and agentic or ascending and descending at the same time—just as it is impossible to simultaneously breathe in (descend) and out (ascend), or to be together (communion) and apart (agentic).

It can be challenging to clearly differentiate between the four polarities of ascending/agency and descending/communion, because they may initially sound and feel the same. One way to do so is to realize that you can ascend or descend in either an agentic or communal way (think of going up or down in an elevator alone or in a group).

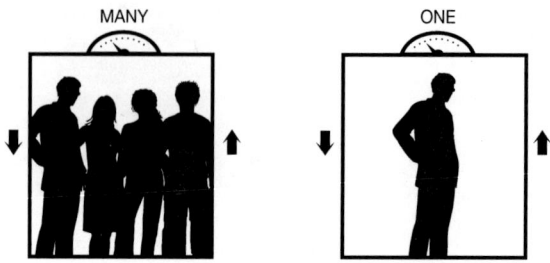

Figure 13: The elevator metaphor for mutual exclusivity

You may—for example—want to experience Godhead (ascend) and go off alone into the desert (agency) to meditate, empty your mind, and chastise your body, or chant mantras in a group with others (communal). Or you may want to comfort and nurture your body (descend), either by taking a hot herbal bath and eating chocolate-covered strawberries in solitude (agency), or by joining a group of friends for a healthy meal and intimate sharing of feelings, followed by ecstatic group dancing (communal).

In other words, ascending or descending either appears in a communal or an agentic way. The resulting intersection between the two lines provides you with the feminine or masculine address.

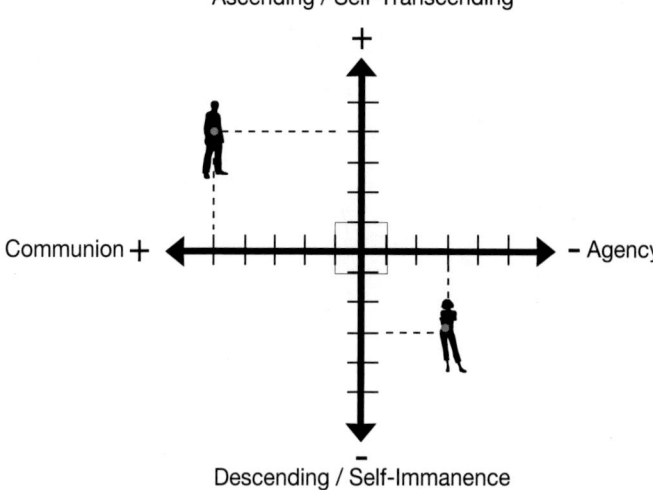

Figure 14: The mutual exclusivity of the four polarities

Our natural impulse is to equate the two feminine polarities (descending and communion) with females and the masculine polarities (ascending and agency) with males, which is the original meaning of the terms.[108] This congruency may have been the norm (or at least expected behavior) in the past, but it often shifts in modern and postmodern individuals, as we will explore in more detail later. It is therefore important **not to** automatically link the two, as both sexes have the potential to embody any of the four polarities in a healthy or unhealthy way. Some people are pathologically stuck in either one of the positive or negative directions, while others have learned to move more freely between the healthy expressions of all of them as their needs or the situation at hand require.

Balancing Polarities for Better Relationships

The goal is to balance and harmonize the healthy qualities of the feminine and masculine polarities at all levels of our being (body, mind, heart, and soul), which can be only effectively achieved in an intimate love relationship. It takes two people with opposite polarities to create the feminine-masculine dynamic that is then experienced as the sexual attraction and synergy of the couple. In this respect, opposites certainly attract and similarities repel, just as the positive and negative poles of two magnets do.

The level of appreciation for the different qualities of each polarity defines the couple's ability to complement each other, and to co-create a whole that is larger than the sum of its parts. If partners are energetically too close, little or no sexual magnetism and synergy will be experienced; if they are further apart than they can tolerate, especially in an unhealthy way, they will experience a disconnect, aversion, and ongoing conflict.[109]

By becoming aware of the four polarities, you can gain a sense of where you and your partner's energies are at any given moment in time, and complement and balance each other by developing a wide range of fluidity in its healthy form in each direction.

Tantra,[110] which means "to weave and expand continuously," or the union of wisdom (ascending) and compassion (descending), is an accumulation of Eastern spiritual practices that attempts to harmonize the four polarities, especially ascending and descending, heaven and earth, or Shiva and Shakti—expressing the assumption that God manifests through both.

In the West, Tantra has become largely associated with the art of using ritual and techniques to reach transcendental states of consciousness (or to experience God) through sexual union. No wonder lovers often exclaim "Oh my God" during ecstatic lovemaking and orgasm. In the Eastern traditions, tantric sex was reserved for highly realized spiritual practitioners after they had passed through many years of rigorous non-sexual tantric training.[111]

A Metaphor for the Polarities: The River

A wonderful metaphor to envision the feminine and masculine polarities is to see them as a river. The depth and span of the water represent the feminine qualities of descending and communion. The height and distance of the banks indicate the masculine capacities for ascending and agency. Together they co-create the river, with the feminine fullness/flow and the masculine emptiness/structure. It is a true co-creation, as neither the banks nor the flow can be said to have come first, nor can they exist without each other. Without the structure and direction of the banks, the feminine is without orientation and uncontained; without the fullness and flow of the water, the masculine is without purpose and fulfillment.

Even though males and females may equally embody the feminine fullness/flow or the masculine structure/direction, they can't do so at the same time, just as you can't simultaneously inhale and exhale, be still and moving, alone and in company, empty and full, on top and at the bottom, etc. Yes, you can try to alternate back and forth—and many singles do so—but something will always be lacking and so contributes to the stress and depression in modern and postmodern people. Only through the feminine-masculine co-creation between opposites and equals can there be a return to oneness (awakening) on all levels of our being and a balanced life.

In Summary

Males and females are characterized by their sex, gender, and feminine/masculine polarities. Sex refers to the hardwired biological makeup which leads to the different Primary Fantasies, gender refers to learned social and cultural roles as men and women, and the feminine/masculine polarities represent universal "mannish" and "womanish" qualities that may be embodied equally by both sexes. Denying, confusing, or leaving out any of these three dimensions will lead to a partial or distorted view of male-female partnerships.

Chapter 3

Lines of Development for Human Intelligences

Everything that irritates us about others can lead us to an understanding of ourselves.
~ Carl Gustav Jung ~

In the Integral Model, Lines of Development[*] (or simply lines) refer to the various kinds of skills, traits, or intelligences[112] that humans possess, such as maths, sports, music, or connecting with the feelings of others. To which degree these lines develop and the sequential levels through which they develop will be covered in the next chapter "Levels of Growth." Without getting into the nature versus nurture debate,[113] we can safely say that the potential for the development of each line is either hardwired from birth or formed in early childhood. You are either musical or have mathematical talents etc., or you don't. **Out of these lines arise a multitude of passions, needs, interests, hobbies, and lifestyle choices that are important factors in your compatibility with your partner.** Below is a list of the lines (the ten most significant in bold) that Wilber mentions in various places in his writings:[114]

aesthetics *(what is beautiful)*
affect/emotion *(feelings about things)*
altruism
care
cognition *(awareness of what is)*
communicative competence
concern
creativity
death seizure
defense mechanisms
empathy
gender identity
idea of the good
interpersonal capacity *(interacting with others)*
kinesthetic
mathematical
meditative stages
morals/ethics *(what to do)*
modes of space and time
musical
needs *(immediate needs for well-being)*
psychosexual *(expression of Eros)*
role-taking
self-esteem
self-identity *(who are you)*
socio-emotional capacity
spiritual *(what is of ultimate concern)*
values/worldviews *(what is important)*

One person may have developed their musical, mathematical, and cognitive lines, but have little emotional intelligence and low morals. Another person might be highly kinesthetic, empathetic, and show deep concern for others, while having a limited sense of space and time, and weak defense mechanisms.

---

[*] Lines are the second of five elements in Wilber's original AQAL model. We will cover his first element, quadrants, in Part II of the manual.

The Many Facets of Humanness

While the Primary Fantasy and opposing feminine and masculine polarities create sexual attraction and synergy, **couples with similar values, interests, passions, personalities, lifestyle choices, relationship skills, needs, and cultural/ethnic backgrounds—which we may call gender-neutral secondary fantasies—have a higher chance of staying together.**[115] **Both sexual attraction and compatible secondary fantasies are essential for a healthy partnership:** the opposite attractors that present the opportunity for psychological healing and spiritual growth through heavenly feelings of passion, intimacy, and unconditional love,[116] AND the similarities that unite by providing the practical earthly structure and conditional foundation for a sustainable love relationship.[117]

Below you will find lists of characteristics. As you read through them, you may find it useful to mark the words that express the qualities that you:
1. Bring to a partnership
2. Must have, would like, can tolerate, and can't stand in a partner
3. Would like to develop further with or without a partner
4. Would like to be mutual
5. Would like to have a conversation about with your partner

Building Relationships through Shared or Compatible Passions and Interests[118]

The Latin root for the word passion is passio, which means suffering. We suffer if we can't follow our passions, and sometimes we exercise them to a degree of suffering. A passion is intrinsic to our being and emerges passively without conscious doing,[119] while an interest or hobby is more of an active choice, externally motivated, passing, or inspired by the egoic mind. **Identifying your own and your partner's passions is essential for any healthy relationship, as you either have to be able to share them, support each other in expressing them, or at the very least be able to tolerate them.**

If she is passionate about dancing, gardening, and horseback riding, and insists on sharing these activities with you, while you loathe them, your relationship will obviously become strained. The words below provide good topics for questions and conversations about your own and your partner's passions and interests.[120]

PASSION/INTEREST	MUST HAVE	CAN'T TOLERATE	WOULD LIKE	CAN TOLERATE	WANT TO DEVELOP	NEEDS DISCUSSION
activism						
animals						
antiques						
appearance						
art						
bathroom/hygiene						
camping						
children						
concerts						
cooking/food						
dancing						
dining out						
environmental concerns						
entertainment						
family						
fishing/hunting						
friends						
future						
gaming						
gardening/plants/landscaping						
golfing						
groups						
hiking						
hobbies						
holidays						
home-improvement & decoration						
household						
massage						

Table 1: List of passions and interests

PASSION/INTEREST	MUST HAVE	CAN'T TOLERATE	WOULD LIKE	CAN TOLERATE	WANT TO DEVELOP	NEEDS DISCUSSION
material lifestyle						
money/investing						
movies/videos/DVD						
museums						
music (playing and listening)						
nightclubs						
painting						
past						
performing arts						
personal growth						
pets						
philosophy						
physical health						
politics						
reading						
religion						
romance						
sensuality						
sexuality						
shopping						
spirituality						
sports (watching and active)						
travel and sightseeing						
TV						
vacations						
vehicles/transportation						
video games						
volunteering						
wedding						
wine tasting						
work						
writing						

Table 1: List of passions and interests (continued)

Identifying and Discussing Capacities, Values, and Ideals

In addition to passions and interests, we have our uniquely developed capacities, values, and ideals. These also deserve consideration and make good topics for conversations.

CAPACITY/VALUE/IDEAL	MUST HAVE	CAN'T TOLERATE	WOULD LIKE	CAN TOLERATE	WANT TO DEVELOP	NEEDS DISCUSSION
ATTENTIVENESS						
AVAILABILITY						
BEAUTY						
CHARITY						
COMMITMENT						
COMPASSION						
CREATIVITY						
EFFORTLESSNESS						
EVEN TEMPER						
FAITHFULNESS						
GENEROSITY						
GENTLENESS						
GOOD HUMOR						
CONSISTENCY						
HOPE						
HOSPITALITY						
INTEGRITY						
JOY						
JUSTICE						
KINDNESS						
LOVE						
MERCY						
MONOGAMY						
PATIENCE						
PERFECTION						
PLAYFULNESS						
RICHNESS						
SELF-CONTROL						
SELF-SUFFICIENCY						
SERVICE						
SIMPLICITY						
TRUST						
TRUTH						
UNDERSTANDING						
UNIQUENESS						

Table 2: List of capacities, values, and ideals

Talking About Needs and Neediness

The words that are listed below describe needs.[121] All human needs are legitimate and deserve consideration on an individual level. Some needs have been identified to be universal.[122] **There is, however, a very important difference between needs and neediness that is often confused:**

Needs are things that we must have for our well-being.

Neediness is the projection of emotional needs onto others, and expecting, nagging, manipulating, or forcing people to meet our needs, while punishing them through accusations, rejection, threats, or violence if they don't. We all know how babies and small children react if they don't get what they need. Of course, a baby dies if its parents or caregivers do not meet its needs for survival (food, warmth, safety, physical contact), and a child that wants something has little to no concern for the reality of others.

In the healthy process of maturing/awakening, humans learn how to satisfy their own needs rather than depending on others, by transforming (1) needs into wants, (2) wants into desires, (3) desires into preferences, and (4) preferences into "no preference."[123] If you and your partner follow this continuum, then destructive emotional, sexual, and material neediness can be transformed into a voluntary and loving exchange of give and take that leads to the gratitude and mutual appreciation that is one of the characteristics of a healthy partnership.[124]

As you read through the list below, mark the words that express the needs, wants, desires, and preferences that you and your partner have and expect to meet for each other—both in kind and degree. When you listen to your partner, note the words **need** and **want** in her language and which of those you are willing and able to meet for her.

If she makes many demands, such as "you need to make me …" or "you need to be…" or "I have a need for…," then you should make sure that you can accommodate her by asking upfront what she exactly means and expects of you.[125] Otherwise, the two of you won't have much fun together. **Partnerships that are largely based on satisfying each other's needs become quickly problematic as needs tend to change in kind and degree over time, and the willingness or ability of partners to meet them diminishes.** The words below may help you to have a conversation with your partner about your and her needs, wants, desires, preferences, and no preferences.

acceptance	contribution	integrity
affection	cooperation	intimacy
aliveness	creativity	joy
appreciation	discovery	learning
authenticity	ease	leisure
awareness	efficacy	moderation
beauty	effectiveness	mutuality
belonging	empathy	nurturing
celebration of life	equality	order
challenge	freedom	participation
choice	fun	peace
clarity	growth	play
closeness	harmony	presence
communion	honesty	protection
community	humor	purpose
companionship	inclusion	quality time
consciousness	independence	
consideration	inspiration	

Table 3: List of needs

OPENING UP TO FEELINGS

Emotional intelligence[126] is the capacity to be in touch with our own feelings and the feelings of others, and to use this information to guide our thinking and actions.[127] The variety and intensity of feelings and emotions that humans experience, witness, and tolerate in themselves and others are directly correlated with their level of consciousness and psychological health.

The English language names over 3,000 feelings,[128] but we usually only distinguish ten to twenty common ones. Feelings range from shame, guilt, apathy, grief, fear, desire, anger, sadness, disgust, pride, envy, and surprise on the negative side, to courage, neutrality, willingness, acceptance, reason, love, joy, peace, and enlightenment on the positive side.[129] Scientists recently confirmed that the brains of females are better equipped to be in touch with their own and the feelings of others, and to communicate them in more subtle ways than males.[130]

Not surprisingly, almost every modern and postmodern woman says that she wants a man who is "emotionally available."[131]

What she **means** by that is his ability to stay mentally present (or at least physically in the room) when she shares her feelings or gets emotional, that he intuitively interprets her emotional state and feelings correctly at all times (yes, even if she is ambiguous or does not verbalize them at all), and that he responds to her with kindness, empathy, compassion, and love in a reassuring way, without being condescending or trying to fix, change, or belittle her.[132]

What she **doesn't mean** is for him to share his own vulnerable feelings, especially if they are negative. Even worse for most women are angry emotional outbursts that mask his underlying (often unconscious) fear, hurt, shame, guilt, jealousy, neediness, or insecurity in an aggressive or passive-aggressive way (see "submerged unconscious" in Chapter 9 for more). Such feelings and emotions lie outside the comfort zone of almost every woman and bring up primal fears of abandonment (that he will no longer be a provider) and insecurity (that he will no longer be a protector) from her unconscious female shadow, that will prompt an unpleasant fight or flight reaction from her.

It is of course desirable for men to be in touch with, and to be guided by their own feelings. But even if she invites you to share your thoughts and feelings openly, you should be cautious with expressing critical ones in reference to her, such as disapproval, frustration, sadness, loneliness, ambivalence, coldness, or distance.[133] She will lose her attraction to your masculinity and feel that she is with a woman in a male body if you emote[134] too much or show vulnerabilities.[135] She may still (or may not) appreciate you as a sensitive friend, but certainly not as a man that she can trust, whom she is sexually attracted to, and whom she wants to be in a partnership with.[136]

Communicating positive feelings of your love and commitment that provide her with the sense of intimacy, connection, and safety that she longs for is of course welcome, and you will get brownie points and sex for that. The best way to deal with your negative emotions is to heal the underlying wounds with a therapist and to start a meditation practice that allows you to stay present with your and her emotional pain when it emerges.[137]

To be compatible with your partner in your emotional development is obviously an important factor for a healthy love relationship.

The list of feelings and emotions below may help you to expand your vocabulary and bring you in touch with your own and the feelings of your partner. The first word (in capital letters) provides a primary emotion or feeling, while the following words give you a more subtle differentiation.

FEELINGS WHEN NEEDS ARE SATISFIED[138]

AFFECTIONATE: *Compassionate, friendly, loving, open-hearted, sympathetic, tender, warm*
CONFIDENT: *Empowered, open, proud, safe, secure.*
ENGAGED: *Absorbed, alert, curious, engrossed, enchanted, entranced, fascinated, interested, intrigued, involved, spellbound, stimulated*
INSPIRED: *Amazed, awed, wonder*
EXCITED: *Animated, ardent, aroused, astonished, dazzled, eager, energetic, enthusiastic, giddy, invigorated, lively, passionate, surprised, vibrant*

EXHILARATED: Blissful, ecstatic, elated, enthralled, exuberant, radiant, rapturous, thrilled
GRATEFUL: Appreciative, moved, thankful, touched
HOPEFUL: Expectant, encouraged, optimistic
JOYFUL: Amused, delighted, glad, happy, jubilant, pleased, tickled
PEACEFUL: Calm, clear-headed, comfortable, centered, content, equanimous, fulfilled, mellow, quiet, relaxed, relieved, satisfied, serene, still, tranquil, trusting
REFRESHED: Enlivened, rejuvenated, renewed, rested, restored, revived

FEELINGS WHEN NEEDS ARE NOT SATISFIED:

AFRAID: Apprehensive, dread, foreboding, frightened, mistrustful, panicked, petrified, scared, suspicious, terrified, wary, worried
ANNOYED: Aggravated, dismayed, disgruntled, displeased, exasperated, frustrated, impatient, irritated, jerked
ANGRY: Enraged, furious, incensed, indignant, irate, livid, outraged, resentful
AVERSION: Animosity, appalled, contempt, disgusted, dislike, hate, horrified, hostile, repulsed
CONFUSED: Ambivalent, baffled, bewildered, dazed, hesitant, lost, mystified, perplexed, puzzled, torn
DISCONNECTED: Alienated, aloof, apathetic, bored, cold, detached, distant, distracted, indifferent, numb, removed, uninterested, withdrawn
DISQUIET: Agitated, alarmed, discombobulated, disconcerted, disturbed, perturbed, rattled, tasteless, shocked, startled, surprised, troubled, turbulent, turmoil, uncomfortable, uneasy, unnerved, unsettled, upset
EMBARRASSED: Ashamed, chagrined, flustered, guilty, mortified, self-conscious
FATIGUE: Beat, burnt out, depleted, exhausted, lethargic, listless, sleepy, tired, weary, worn-out
PAIN: Agony, anguished, bereaved, devastated, grief, heartbroken, hurt, lonely, miserable, regretful, remorseful
SAD: Depressed, dejected, despair, despondent, disappointed, discouraged, disheartened, forlorn, gloomy, heavy hearted, hopeless, melancholy, unhappy, wretched
TENSE: Anxious, cranky, distressed, distraught, edgy, fidgety, frazzled, irritable, jittery, nervous, overwhelmed, restless, stressed out
VULNERABLE: Fragile, guarded, helpless, insecure, leery, reserved, sensitive, shaky
YEARNING: Envious, jealous, longing, nostalgic, pining, wistful

INTERPRETATIONS VERSUS FEELINGS

Words like ignored express how we interpret the behavior or reality of others, rather than how we feel. Below is a sampling of words that are not feelings but interpretations:

abandoned	*threatened*	*provoked*
co-opted	*betrayed*	*unsupported*
misunderstood	*distrusted*	*cheated*
taken for granted	*patronized*	*let-down*
abused	*unheard*	*put-down*
cornered	*boxed-in*	*unwanted*
neglected	*interrupted*	*coerced*
unappreciated	*pressured*	*manipulated*
attacked	*unseen*	*rejected*
diminished	*bullied*	*used*
overworked	*intimidated*	

Table 4: List of interpretations versus feelings

COMMUNICATING FEELINGS AND NEEDS MORE EFFECTIVELY

A good strategy to express feelings and needs in a considerate way (but not beyond her comfort level) is to put them into a sentence that expresses (1) an objective observation, (2) the feeling that is created, (3) an underlying need that is not met, and (4) that makes a doable request which is specific in time and place (in short, an OFNR … Observation, Feeling, Need, Request).

It goes like this:

(1) State an observation that is factual (when you … e.g., showed up late, did not keep your promise, etc.);

(2) Describe the feeling that was created for you— which is called owning your feelings or making an "I statement"—such as (I felt … e.g., irritated);

(3) Explain the need that was not met (because I have a need for … e.g., respect for my time); and

(4) Make a doable request (would you be willing to … e.g., call me when you are late next time?). If the answer is no, you can either make another request (would you be willing to … e.g., accept that I won't wait for you and meet you later at …) or state in the same structure how you feel about her saying no.

Some examples of OFNR's:

When you showed up late, I felt annoyed because I have a need for the effective use of my time. If that happens again, would you be willing to call me in advance?

When you didn't reply to my email, I felt anxious because I have a need for clear communication. Would you be willing to send me a brief reply so that I know that you received my email and that you are just too busy to reply in more detail at that time?

When you stopped talking to me after I hugged my former girlfriend, I felt puzzled because I have a need for understanding. Would you be willing to write me a note about what is going on for you if you can't talk to me?

A good strategy to connect with her feelings is to guess them without interpretation or judgment in the following form:

(1) Guess her feeling (are you feeling ... e.g., frustrated?)

(2) State or guess a fact why she may feel that way (because I did/did not .... e.g., "listen to you")

(3) Guess a need (and you have a need for/to ... e.g., be heard and understood?) and

(4) Make a doable/realistic offer that is specific in time and place (would you like me to ... e.g., listen to you tonight at home in the living room from seven to eight?)

Some examples of this kind of communication, which is sometimes called an "empathy guess":

Does it frighten you when I tell you about my problems at work because you have a need for safety? Would you rather have me share my fears of being fired in my men's group and reassure you that I am strong enough to handle the situation without getting you involved?

Do you feel furious because I left my dirty clothes on the bathroom floor and you have a need for tidiness? Would you like me to put my dirty clothes into the laundry basket right after I take them off?

Do you feel frustrated because I forgot to buy you flowers for Valentine's Day and you have a need to be recognized on a day like this? Since I hate to buy flowers, would you feel honored if I take you out to a nice dinner tonight at 7:00?

This way of communication is called *Non-Violent Communication*[139] (NVC) or Compassionate Communication. The goals of NVC are (1) to make everybody feel better after a conversation, (2) to get emotional needs, typically for understanding and connection, met, and (3) to not be attached to certain outcomes or solutions.

NVC does not judge or evaluate feelings, does not demand that people make each other feel/not feel a certain way, does not criticize others for the way they feel, and does not make people responsible for the feelings of others.[140] **This is a very feminine way of communicating that often feels inefficient and inauthentic to males, because it does not get to the point, does not focus on the dialectic of good/bad, right/wrong, or win/lose, and often does not get things accomplished in an expedient manner.**[141] **But the long-term benefits for partnerships are undeniable, because "winning the argument" or "being right" often means losing the relationship.** NVC has not only proven to be more effective in one-on-one intimate relationships but also in areas of modern management and politics.[142]

Please refer to the list of books in Appendix I if you want to gain a deeper understanding of this vital relationship topic.

In Summary

While we may love another human being unconditionally, being in a healthy partnership/marriage is always based on practical conditions. It requires certain compatibilities in intelligences, passions, interests, lifestyle choices, and life-purpose/dreams. Many people say that they want to love and be loved unconditionally, which is possible and desirable, but romanticize this notion at the expense of practical considerations, only to realize later that their partner is too different. On the other hand, some people are so overly focused on having all the needs from their endless laundry lists exactly met, that they completely miss the opportunity to learn and grow in a partnership by staying open to new possibilities and expanding their horizon. The Integral Relationship Model considers both the spiritual and practical dimensions of love relationships equally: the desire for intimacy and to love and to be loved (unconditionally), and the compatibility requirements to co-create a (conditional) life together.

Chapter 4

Levels of Growth

He who desires to see the living God face-to-face should not seek him in the empty firmament of his mind, but in human love.
~ Fyodor Dostoevsky ~

Humans have different potentials to develop their capacities in each of the lines of development discussed in the previous chapter. This development occurs in levels or stages (Wilber also uses the terms waves or spirals) from lowest towards highest, and may do so over a lifetime. **Understanding what level of development you and your partner have reached in each of these lines and what your future growth potentials are will help you to evaluate your long-term compatibility.** In which particular line and for how long people develop depends on many complex factors, including their predisposition, socio-economic environment, cultural background, available nutrition, and personal circumstances.[143]

The number of levels given for each of the lines can vary. The granularity of simple models may be three levels, such as low, medium, and high, or pre-conventional, conventional, and post-conventional, while more complex models may specify twenty levels or more.[144] The grades in our public school system provide an analogy. We could talk about three levels (elementary, middle, and high-school) or we could talk about twelve levels (dividing the same span into first through twelfth grade).

Some lines depend on each other for their development, while others develop independently. For example, highly intelligent people (cognitive line) may be low in their moral development, such as the Unabomber, while people with highly developed moral values like Mahatma Gandhi, Nelson Mandela, or Martin Luther King, Jr., are always intelligent.

You obtain a simple psychograph if you rate an individual's level of growth for some or all of the developmental lines listed in Chapter 3 as low, medium, or high.[145]

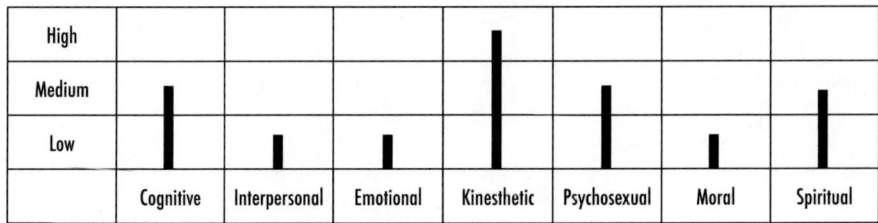

Figure 15: Graph showing an individual's development on various lines

The Integral Model **does not** suggest that every human being needs to be at the highest level known to man in every line in order to be fully realized—which would be impossible anyway, as intelligences and capacities are all open-ended and continually evolve. It rather suggests that it is desirable to (1) be integrally informed about the existence of these lines, (2) understand their individual significance, (3) accept that lines are differently developed in people, (4) recognize the potential for future growth in yourself and others, (5) have a desire to foster the development of each line in yourself and others to the highest individual potential (called self-actualization), and (6) balance and harmonize your development in relationship with an equal and opposite partner.

An *Integral Life Practice* (ILP) that includes multiple modules for the health of body, mind, spirit/soul, shadow, ethics, sexuality, work, emotions, and relationships is a proven method to support growth in the major developmental lines.[146] Being in an integrally informed partnership is not only beneficial but mandatory to effectively engage in these practices.

In this chapter we will focus on the levels of consciousness, spiritual, sexual, and anima/animus complex development, which are pivotal for love relationships.

Consciousness Development (Colors)

A key factor in creating a good relationship is to have a partner with a matching level of consciousness development. In this section we will discuss what consciousness is and how it develops in humans through stages. Each stage will be identified with a different color.

To be conscious means "to know, be aware of, sense, feel, or experience things."[147] For humans these things include physical objects that can be looked at or measured (such as the physical body, the manifest world, or invisible forces such as electromagnetic waves), AND non-physical *objects in consciousness* (such as thoughts, beliefs, feelings, intentions, dreams, concepts, theories, etc.). In other words, what's out there (objectivity), and what's in here (subjectivity). To the level that we are conscious, we know of and/or experience these things; if we are unconscious, we don't.[148]

So, simply put, we can say:

"The world consists of things plus consciousness that experiences things."[149]

This implies that consciousness is neither a thing (object) in itself, nor necessarily local; it just IS.[150]

Feel inside yourself for a moment and ask "who is conscious of things?" You may say "me, I, myself, the witness, my ego (a.k.a. self-organizing principal or separate/false sense of self),[151] my conscious self," or something like that. How we can experience an "I" or a "self" that is conscious of "itself" in a physical body is quite a miracle if you think about it for a moment, and still a mystery to philosophers and scientists alike. They call it "the hard problem," because it is hard (and perhaps impossible) to explain.[152] This conscious self that experiences—and in a sense creates[153]—its own story about the world in a unique way as it selectively receives, evaluates, sorts, names, compares, prioritizes, stores, and remembers information also develops.

People sometimes call this development growing up, self-development, personal development, or personal growth. We will call it *consciousness development*.

Women often intuitively say, "I want to be with a man who knows who he is," or "I want a man who has done some growth work," or "I want a man who is aware, loving, intuitive, creative, spiritual, compassionate, wise, mature, emotionally available, understanding…" Note that all these terms point to consciousness and not to things. She is basically saying "I want a man who sees me, himself, the world, and God/Spirit from the same level of consciousness as I do," usually without knowing that there are multiple levels of consciousness or what they entail.

Today, hardly any social scientist questions that humans became increasingly conscious throughout evolution and that children develop cognitively from gestation to the end of adolescence.[154] However, it is not widely known, and sometimes vehemently rejected—especially by women and postmodernists—that adults are at different levels of their consciousness development, with an open-ended potential for future growth. The critics tend to ignore the fact that there is a lot of carefully conducted research that supports the idea of growth hierarchies in adult development.[155]

The refusal to rank people on a hierarchical scale as more or less evolved, conscious, or developed results from the well-founded concern that individuals and groups who are presumed to be at lower levels (such as indigenous people, the poor, the less educated, people of color, women, children, etc.) may be dominated, abused, marginalized, exploited, or oppressed by those who are or who put themselves at higher levels.

The fallacy of people who are critical of developmental hierarchies is to confuse natural growth hierarchies[156] of increasing integration and complexity (which allow for more perspectives, cooperation, care, love, responsibility, creativity, and compassion) with dominator hierarchies in which power and superiority are abused. It is therefore important to understand the difference between the two forms of hierarchies when we discuss the stages of growth and development in any of the developmental lines so that we don't offend those who are sensitive to this issue (e.g., women) or abuse our knowledge.[157]

Adult growth in consciousness appears in three different ways: (1) almost unnoticed over long periods of time; (2) through a structured meditation or contemplative prayer practice (typically two levels in four years); or (3) when particular beliefs, capacities, and views of a certain stage no longer provide adequate answers to life's questions, challenges, and demands. The latter is often the case for men who want to win the heart of a woman, are in a troubled partnership, or have gone through a painful breakup/divorce. Each consecutive level provides better solutions to life's challenges, deeper insights, wider perspectives, and more capacity for love and compassion than the previous one.

THE EIGHT STAGES OF CONSCIOUSNESS DEVELOPMENT AND THEIR COLORS

We will use eight levels of consciousness development for our Integral Relationship Model. The initial six stages are grouped together in **first-tier consciousness**, while the two highest stages are grouped in **second-tier consciousness**. A different color of the rainbow is assigned to each level to deflect from ranking or labeling individuals, and to avoid confusion between the various numbers and names of the multitude of developmental systems.[158] It is important to understand that the various levels of consciousness do not describe different types **of** people (such as primitive or intelligent, good or bad, right or wrong, sensitive or insensitive, functional or dysfunctional, etc.), but look at the underlying motives and worldviews **within** people that guide their thinking and behavior. The question to ask is therefore **NOT** "how are people behaving," but "what are the underlying values and worldviews that motivate and drive their behavior."

Keep in mind that (1) each level carries its own assets and liabilities, (2) everybody (including you) started at square one, (3) higher levels are **always** achievable, (4) altered states of consciousness can cause temporary shifts to lower or higher levels at any time, and (5) people who express personal judgments always do so from their own limited level of consciousness.

The table below summarizes the different stages and colors and the proportion of the American population that falls into those levels.

Group	Level/Stage	Color(s)	Approx. Proportion of U.S. Population
Second-tier	Post-post-conventional	Turquoise Teal	1/30
First-tier	Post-conventional	Green	1/10
First-tier	Conventional	Orange Amber	2/3
First-tier	Pre-conventional	Red Magenta Infrared	1/4

Table 5: Developmental stages, their colors, and proportions of U.S. population

You may visualize the sequential stages as a vertical string of light bulbs with different colors that become illuminated as higher stages of consciousness emerge, musical notes on a piano that get arranged in ever more complex ascending chords, or the seven chakras.

As you read through the descriptions below, you can get a sense for the levels of consciousness that are alive in you.

The Six Levels of First-tier Consciousness

Pre-conventional stages

The first three stages are called *pre-conventional*, as only a first person "I, me, mine" perspective can be taken. The ability to conform to the conventions of other individuals, a society, a single supreme power (God), or scientific evidence, which requires the ability to take a second- and third-person perspective, has not emerged yet.

1. Infrared—archaic—dead or alive

The infrared level is called *archaic* and covers all the levels of human consciousness that had emerged up to about 50,000 years ago. It concerns our basic needs for survival: food, water, shelter, warmth, and sex. These needs are closely related to our animal nature and are embedded in our reptilian brain stem. At this level, behavior is guided by instincts and impulses for physical comfort. There is little awareness of the past or future, and the world is perceived through the senses, which can be highly developed in functional adults at this stage e.g., in indigenous tribes. Some spiritual seekers confuse this stage of total fusion with the environment (called a-duality) with higher stages of non-duality.[159]

Only few adults in the developed world are exclusively at the infrared level, such as the mentally ill, delusional street people, individuals in deep shock, or Alzheimer's patients. They represent less than 1% of the U.S. adult population.

2. Magenta—magic—safe or unsafe

The magenta level is called *magic* or *superstitious* and started to emerge about 50,000 years ago, when humans became self-conscious, realized the threats and dangers of their immediate environment to their survival, and sought solutions for their safety. As a result, all kinds of superstitious explanations and beliefs were created to explain natural phenomena such as lightning, thunder, natural cycles, birth, illness, and death. This lead to the formation of close bonds—often based on kinship—with others for protection.

For today's people at this level, being part of a family, tribe, clan, or cult supersedes individuality and rationality. "One for all, and all for one" is their motto. False beliefs in the power of magic, group rituals, sacred places and objects, voodoo-like curses, spells, ghosts, good-luck charms, astrology, or magical healing powers are indicators of magenta. To this day, primal "fight or flight" reactions are triggered from this level when individuals feel threatened by situations and experiences that they can't rationally explain or control. On the positive side, sharpened sense perceptions, sensitivity to nature, and supernatural capacities such as remote viewing or telepathy, as seen in members of indigenous tribes and shamans, are qualities of magenta that often get diminished or completely lost in later, higher stages of development.

Green (see below) often confuses the pre-rational superstitious fantasies and behavior of magenta with verifiable trans-rational phenomena and capacities that can only be differentiated at higher levels of consciousness.[160]

Magenta awareness is seen in members of clan-like families, street gangs, athletic teams, corporate "tribes," cults, and pagan/earth-oriented Goddess-worshipping religions. It represents about 10% of the U.S. adult population.

3. Red—egocentric—good or bad

The red stage is called egocentric and emerged about 10,000 years ago, when young males started to break free from the dictates of their elders and confinements of their family clans to claim their own autonomy. Self-serving choices, power, independence, high risk-taking, stubbornness, and unrestrained creativity are used by red to control their environment and destiny, instead of being controlled by it.[161] In an attempt to feel good, red energy is focused on behaviors that provide instant gratification, often through sex, food, gambling, alcohol, illegal drugs, shopping, or mindless entertainment, without concern for others or negative consequences for its own future. "I want it all and I want it now" is the motto. To red, the world appears like a jungle in which only the fittest survive. The resulting value system is polarized between good and bad. People in this stage tend to identify with powerful gods or idols (rock stars, movie or video-game heroes, etc.) who are on their side, demand respect from others, and fight everyone who tries to control, dominate, or shame them. In its healthy form, red energy can be refreshingly spontaneous, creative, innovative, original, uninhibited, emotional, carefree, and alive.

Red consciousness is seen in leaders of street gangs, narcissistic New Age communities (with claims that egoic thoughts manifest objects, physical well-being, and material abundance, or that being "In The Now" is sufficient for the development of a functional self), pimp and prostitute relations, wild rock stars, pre-conventional artists, Rambo- and Terminator-type fighters, ruthless dictators, characters in violent video games, and James Bond villains. Red represents about 20% of the U.S. adult population.

Conventional Stages

The amber and orange stages are called *conventional*, as amber can take a second-person (you, thou) and orange a third-person (he, she, it, its, them) perspective. This allows individuals in these stages to conform to the conventions (norms) of others, a religion, society, or scientific evidence.

4. Amber—mythic—right or wrong

The amber stage is called *mythic* and emerged about 5,000 years ago through males who sought to transcend their red egocentric short-term thinking. They realized their eventual mortality, searched for deeper meanings of life (which they found in mythic religious beliefs), and developed ethical codes of conduct (laws) for the growing number of peoples in their communities. This stage satisfies the human need for stability, order, purpose, rules, hope, recognition, and future rewards for right behavior.

Amber values are derived from literal interpretations of mythic scriptures, such as Jesus was born to a virgin, Lao Tzu was eighty years old when he was born, Moses parted the Red Sea, or that obeying the Ten Commandments and confessing one's sins will open the gates to heaven after death. Hence, amber thoughts allow for only one right way of belief and doing things. The resulting value system labels things as either right or wrong.

The **right way** is based in conformist political, religious, or social belief systems (e.g., Marxism, Islam, patriarchy) and governed by a single authority such as a father, the church, the government, the ruler of a nation, a superior commander, or a teacher/guru. Amber is therefore found in members of fundamentalist religious and spiritual communities (my God/Guru is right, no matter what), patriarchal families (the father is right, no matter what), law and order societies (my people are right, no matter what), extreme patriotism (my country is right, no matter what), organizations (our mission is right, no matter what), the military (superior orders are right, no matter what), and hierarchical corporations (the boss and making profits is right, no matter what).

Right conduct and following the proper rules, laws, orders, religion, or a spiritual path promise future rewards, such as ongoing support from a family, being promoted, receiving a medal of honor, going to heaven after death, or enlightenment. Wrongdoing will cause chaos and leads to punishment, such as losing family support, being dishonorably discharged, being fired or asked to leave, ending up in prison, burning in hell after death, or being subject to an endless cycle of suffering and rebirth. In its healthy form, amber provides stability, security, and order for families, groups, organizations, and societies to flourish. In its unhealthy form, amber is dogmatic, intolerant, repressive, and irrational.

Amber values are seen in patriarchal family structures, government and military organizations, hierarchical corporate structures, fundamentalist churches, spiritual communities, and the Republican Party. It represents about 40% of the U.S. adult population.

5. Orange—rational—win or lose

The orange stage is called rational and emerged about 300 years ago during the *Enlightenment Period*—which brought the rise of modernity—when a number of men questioned the feudalistic systems and supreme power of monarchies, and challenged the church dogma. Today, orange represents the human desire for the good life of material abundance and personal liberty through objective reasoning, use of scientific methods, democratic capitalism, individual choice, excellence, and acceleration through taking controlled risks. The resulting value system is "win or lose." Winners are those who effectively use their higher education, superior talents, and the best information available to succeed financially, politically, or academically. Orange individuals think and act globally, show confidence, believe in their own abilities, have a "can-do" attitude (Yes We Can), play hard, and take risks to try to win big.

From this level, the world looks like an ever-changing and evolving place, with limitless possibilities and opportunities for those who are flexible, clever, and fast. Intelligent and witty people with knowledge, financial assets, or social/political status (think Albert Einstein, Bill Gates, Ted Turner, Donald Trump, or Barack Obama) are the icons of orange who replace the mythic superiors of amber as authority figures and role models. Efficiency, effectiveness, positive thinking, visioning, strategic planning, goal setting, innovation, and the evaluation of progress (where are we, where do we want to go, how do we get there) are the highest priorities. Orange wants the facts and nothing but the facts, and conflicts are resolved in a rational way (getting to yes without giving in),[162] through expensive lawyers, or acceptance of collateral damage.

Even though orange energy can be ruthless in the pursuit of its goals and lack conscience when harm that is done to others is justified as "necessary and eventually good for them,"[163] it also considers the long-term effects of its actions (otherwise it is red egocentric). Repeat customers are valued, bridges don't get burned easily, the past is forgiven if it is beneficial for the future, and networking with others is seen as an important tool for success. Orange may also appear like Teflon when it doesn't allow emotions that could alienate others or reveal weaknesses to get in the way or distract it from being efficient. Problems that would devastate others slide right off. When things fail, depression does not last very long. "Pick yourself up, dust yourself off, and start all over again" is the motto.[164] Instead of asking others for support or advice, which would imply weakness and is therefore to be avoided, orange asks for input, data, and information to be evaluated by itself for arriving at its own conclusions and decisions.

The U.S. constitution and many of the laws that are written to protect individual freedoms and rights originate from the rational level. Through advancements in many areas, such as medicine, transportation, information-technology, architecture, agriculture, and the industrial production of goods, orange has also contributed (and continues to contribute) to the abolition of poverty in most parts of the Western—and now increasingly in the developing—world, our modern comfortable lifestyle, and the increasing longevity that many people enjoy today. It is also responsible for much of the environmental damage and global social injustice that has emerged from this stage.

Orange consciousness is seen on Wall Street, in the cosmetic and fashion industry, scientific community, upper management, emerging middle-class, success churches, self-improvement and wealth seminars, and among left-wing Republicans, Democrats, and the liberal feminist movement. Orange represents about 25% of the U.S. adult population.

Post-conventional stage

The green postmodern pluralistic stage is also called post-conventional, as it can take a 4th person "all of us" perspective that transcends the conventional norms of the previous stages.

6. Green—pluralistic—sensitive or indifferent

The green stage is called *pluralistic*. It emerged about 100 years ago and came into full bloom in the 1960s, when postmodern male artists and intellectuals challenged the theories, assumptions, and ideologies of modernity. Green is characterized by multiple interpretations of history, language, science, religion, spirituality, politics, culture, and social systems—with the belief that absolute truth doesn't exist in any objective sense, but is created individually rather than discovered. The ability to take a fourth-person (cultural) perspective allows for greater compassion, idealism, and involvement. A sense that all human beings—regardless of race, gender, or class—are born equal and should be equally heard and respected becomes prevalent. Green feels strongly that the human spirit must be freed from masculine orange greed and amber dogma. It is against hierarchy/patriarchy and establishes lateral social structures with an emphasis on friendships, empathy, non-violent or compassionate communication, and consensus, often with the downside of endless processing and inability to reach decisions.

Green has the capacity for subjective, nonlinear thinking, and shows a great degree of affective warmth and sensitivity towards others. The concept that all souls are connected in a big web of life with a deep caring for mother earth and all its inhabitants emerges. Along comes the desire to find peace and happiness within, which triggers an exploration of the inner feelings and experiences of the self and others, with an increasing attention to the unconscious. This often brings green men in touch with their anima (deconstructing their ego, which makes them more feminine), and women with their animus (strengthening their ego, which makes them more masculine).

While it seems that green would love and embrace everything and everyone, it opposes orange rationality and patriarchal amber conformity, with the idea that men should let go of their egos, and women should stand up for themselves. Green also denies the existence of higher stages of consciousness development and considers such notions as arrogant, judgmental, and ranking. "What stages?" says green, "we are all equal! Everything is relative!" By denying any kind of hierarchy and calling it ranking, oppressive, and outdated, green quickly gets caught up in "performative contradictions,"[165] such as "lateral systems are better than hierarchy," (and therefore unwittingly creating its own hierarchy which says no hierarchy is better than hierarchy) "people should not be judgmental," "I hate people who are unloving," or "let's fight for peace," and prohibits itself from further growth.

At the same time, green often identifies red (egocentric) as a victim of orange's rational greed and amber's conformist repression, and romanticizes magenta's superstitious tribal living and their assumed sensitivity towards mother earth and its inhabitants. This sometimes makes the pre-conventional red and post-conventional green stage look alike, since they are both un-conventional. The energies of these two stages often resonate with each other in a very confused and destructive way, e.g., when instant gratification is mistaken for being present in the now, red violence erupts during a Greenpeace or anti-globalization demonstration, or when green people consider it to be healthy to let red emotions erupt in an uncontrolled way.

Green consciousness is seen in the civil and animal rights, environmental protection, ecology, human liberation, radical and eco-feminist, and humanistic sciences movements, which gave birth to organizations such as Greenpeace, Amnesty International, Doctors Without Borders, the Sierra Club, and the National Organization of Women (NOW).[166] Green represents about 10% of the total U.S. adult population, with higher concentrations in pockets such as Boston, Northern California, Boulder Colorado, New Mexico, and Oregon.

The Two Stages of Second-tier Consciousness

Post-post conventional

With less than 3% of the U.S. adult population at teal (below), and less than 1% at the highest, turquoise level, second-tier consciousness is still extremely rare, and represents the leading-edge of human consciousness evolution.[167]

7. Teal—Integral—integrated or partial

The teal stage is called Integral. It first emerged in the early 20th century in India and Europe,[168] and was widely recognized by pioneering U.S. psychologists and social researchers in the 1970s.[169] Teal is not just another stage, but marks the shift into what is called second-tier consciousness. Previous levels insist that their particular views are the only way to see the world. Whenever threatened or challenged, individuals in first-tier consciousness react negatively and lash out, using their own tools (magenta voodoo-like spells, red anger and crude violence, amber moral wars and shaming, orange cold logic and collateral damage, and green emoting, victimizing, demonstrations, activism, and endless processing).

Teal and above intuitively recognizes the importance of all preceding levels—including the process of development itself—and integrates them with the healthy qualities of masculine agency and feminine communion. It is the first stage that doesn't force its own values onto others by "should"ing them to be more like me/us. In teal, knowledge and competency supersede rank, power, gender, or status. Flexibility, spontaneity, and functionality become the highest priority. Unlike green, which does away with developmental hierarchies and maintains that all humans are equal, teal sees the liabilities, contributions, benefits, values, and limitations of each previous stage. It supports the cultivation of healthy feminine and masculine qualities (a.k.a. self-actualization[170] and horizontal translation)[171] at each level, communicates with others in their voice, facilitates their healthy growth through the stages, and acknowledges that higher levels of development are always possible. Teal can see beyond a fourth-person perspective and recognizes the prevailing world-order as a result of the existence of developmental stages, as well as the movement of individuals and groups through them.

Seen from the perspective of first-tier consciousness, people in the teal stage may seem cold, calculating, opportunistic, manipulative, analytical, distant, cynical, or arrogant—and sometimes they are. Teal can feel quickly discouraged, bored, and frustrated, as it thinks it has seen and had it all. And while it can easily connect with others in earlier stages of development when making the effort, teal often feels isolated and alone, as it gets tired of the limited worldviews, self-created drama, narrow-minded labeling, and naive stereotyping of people in first-tier consciousness.

8. Turquoise—transpersonal—wisdom and compassion

The turquoise stage is called transpersonal (or post-Integral)[172] and represents all the stages above Integral.[173] While teal tends to observe, analyze, and evaluate the inner and outer world in an analytical, left-brained, righteous, distant, and ascending way, people in these higher stages display an actual embodiment, full embrace, or interweaving of all the healthy qualities of the previous stages and the four feminine/masculine polarities. They have reached the top of the developmental pole and gone one step further, plunging into the fullness of their own being and the world, but without getting lost in it. They have a sense of "being in the world but not of it"[174] and transcend good/bad, right/wrong, win/lose, sensitive/indifferent, and integrated/partial thinking, representing the leading edge of human consciousness development—with higher stages possible in the future.[175] Desires, attachments, and fears, with the resulting striving for ever more exterior comfort, luxury, safety, power, order, status, wealth, peace, and knowledge, are replaced with inner qualities of increasing wisdom, compassion, presence, and surrender. This transformation is caused by a conscious, stepwise deconstruction of unconscious habits of the mind and the healing of negative emotions. An awareness of the intersubjective and interobjective co-creation of experiences and a sense of a universal unified order that is the result of all manifestation comes into focus. For turquoise and above, a grand unification is possible in theory and in actuality, and ever more perspectives can be taken. This often involves the emergence of a new spirituality as a meshwork of all existence.

Turquoise consciousness may be seen as aloof and indifferent about the condition of others (e.g., a partner), as well as the earth and all its inhabitants, but nothing could be further from the truth. People in turquoise are simply no longer attached to certain outcomes that are governed by their ego, and have no preference to have things one way or another. Turquoise and above has the wisdom to accept what is, proactively respond where action is needed, and to leave a situation at its own devices if opposing it would do more harm than good.

THE PRE/POST OR PRE/TRANS FALLACY

Both, the **pre**-conventional infrared to red stages, which are also referred to as pre-modern or pre-rational, and the **post**-conventional green and higher stages, which are also called postmodern or trans-rational, are **non**-conventional/non-rational and are therefore often confused with each other by people who are not integrally informed. They are prone to mistake the pre-rational infantile stage of a-duality with trans-rational stages of non-dual awareness, or pre-conventional unrestrained but ultimately narcissistic/egocentric behavior in children or adults with responsible authentic expressions of post-conventional personal freedom.[176] Thus, the pre/post or pre/trans fallacy leads to many misunderstandings in spiritual circles, confusion in postmodern groups and organizations, and irresolvable conflicts in love relationships between pre- and post-conventional partners.

SPIRITUAL DEVELOPMENT

The word spiritual generally means "that which is not bound to time, the physical world, or mental concepts,"[177] which is all the domain of the mind and our senses. Spiritual may also refer to obtaining a sense of self, happiness, joy, and peace from an inner or higher source, instead of external objects and pleasures.

To be spiritual implies different things for different people. It is therefore crucial to verify what concept, teaching, experience, insight, wisdom, belief-system, or practice a woman refers to when she mentions the word. Her answer will most likely fall into one of four general categories: (1) random spiritual and paranormal phenomena, (2) a particular attitude or quality, (3) superhuman achievements in one or several of the developmental lines, or (4) a permanent level or stage of spiritual realization that is attained through a practice such as yoga, meditation, Tantra, or contemplative prayer.

The first definition describes random, blissful, transitory, altered states that arise spontaneously during a peak experience, use of illegal drugs, transcendental sex, after a dark night of the soul, birth of a child, death of a loved one, energetic healing session, or a psychic episode.

The second refers to a particular attitude of openness, loving kindness, humility, devotion, compassion, joy, or wisdom. Your grandparents may have lived by the Golden Rule all their life and never heard about spirituality, and yet appeared to be totally spiritual by this definition.

The third form is experienced through exposure to superhuman achievements in any of the developmental lines, such as sports (Michael Jordan), music (Mozart), poetry (Rumi), visual art (Michelangelo), knowledge (Einstein), or wisdom (Gandhi). It creates a sense of divine awe, as their gift seems to originate from a realm beyond human possibility, from a "spiritual place."

The fourth description points to a formal spiritual practice, often conducted under the guidance of a teacher (or guru), lineage, or religion, that aims to transform temporary spiritual states into permanent stages which then become accessible by choice rather than by chance. **States that become accessible through formal study/practice are often called *state-stages* and their unfolding will be the focus throughout the following paragraphs.**

STATE-STAGES

Spiritual state-stages tend to unfold in a certain order that are likened to the three broad states of *waking* (in which we are aware of physical objects), *dreaming* (in which we are identified with nonphysical objects in our mind), and *dreamless sleep* (in which we fall into a state of timeless emptiness) that every human being, regardless of age, education, or cultural background, experiences during the course of a normal day.

Two advanced state-stages that are called the *witness* (in which a conscious awareness of timeless emptiness arises) and *non-duality* (in which awareness and that which we are aware of unite) become available through grace or advanced practices.

Another helpful way to look at spiritual state-stage development (or any growth for that matter) is to make a clear distinction between (1) the self and (2) the things that the self can observe, such as physical objects in our surroundings, our own physical body, or the thoughts that create objects in consciousness. This "I" or "subject" that is doing the seeing, witnessing, or observing is by nature unaware of itself. Once it can be seen, it becomes an object, so who/what is doing the looking?

This may sound quite strange, and it is. Think about it this way: You can look at the words on this page, observe your surroundings, and think about things (symbols, objects, concepts, ideas, etc.), but you can't see the actual observer. The objects that you observe are those aspects of your experience that are apparent to you, and can so be thought of, related to, reflected upon, engaged with, manipulated, or connected to something else. You can be "objective" about them because you don't experience them as the self or witness. The objects can so be differentiated from the aspects of your experience that you are identified with, embedded in, or fused with.[178]

In a nutshell, we can say that spiritual growth appears when the subject that we identify with becomes the object of the subject of the next stage. As mentioned above, this growth unfolds in five general state-stages:[179]

1. Gross/Waking

The initial level of spiritual awakening is called the gross/waking (or psychic) state-stage, and marks the major transition from a complete identification with the material world and the physical body into the spiritual realm. It emerges with the realization that you are defined by neither your body with its needs, impulses, and emotions,[180] nor your material possessions or social status. Instead of having knee-jerk reactions to inner habits and other people's behavior, you increasingly learn how to stay present, and how to respond in mindful ways.[181] You become the witness of your environment and the master of your body, instead of its slave. This may sound easier than it is, and may require the support of practices such as yoga, conscious breathing,[182] relaxation techniques, physical exercise, contemplation (such as reading this manual), or—in severe cases of pathological attachments—psychotherapy. Just think how often you may consume unconsciously, have a negative emotional reaction to somebody else's reality, avoid physical exercise, fail to properly nourish your body, identify with the car you drive and other material possessions, derive your self-worth from the amount of money you have (or don't have), or the physical appearance of the woman on your arm.

The awareness of "I have a body—but I am not my body," with the ability to observe and use it, instead of being used by it (often through addictive behavior),[183] is very liberating. People who enter this state-stage of spiritual realization may start to have psychic,[184] synchronistic,[185] or mystical experiences in nature,[186] and have a clear sense of awakening to a different reality. They realize that the physical and emotional pains of the body may be inevitable, but that suffering is optional. As the body becomes the object of the subject, more compassion for the self and others emerges.

The feminine in this state-stage tends to move consciously into the body (descend) and the manifest world. This downward movement gave rise to earth-bound and Goddess-worshipping religions such as paganism. The masculine tends to move away from the body (ascend) and deny its pleasures, as seen in male God-worshipping religions such as Christianity, Buddhism, Hinduism, and Islam in their fundamentalist forms.

2. Subtle/Dreaming

The subtle dream stage is entered by grace or through a regular spiritual practice such as meditation or contemplative prayer. It emerges with the realization that you are not your thoughts and beliefs. Similar to awakening from a dream after sleeping, you realize that random and unobserved thoughts (assumptions, projections, etc.), which are frequently fed by pain from the past and fears of the future, are just as unreal as your dreams at night. These thoughts can play in your head like a radio station that repeats the good old "coulda, shoulda, woulda" blues over and over. If this is the case, you are essentially just one step away from an insane person who talks out loud while walking down the street. This self-talk may then trigger negative emotions, which in turn feed more paranoid thoughts that can become a cause for depression[187] and other pathologies. People who enter the subtle state-stage awaken from this nightmare (or cognitive prison), and learn to recognize their random thoughts as unreal objects in consciousness. They can then either turn down the volume (quiet the mind), push the Off button, change the radio station from KFUCK to KLOVE (positive thinking), or simply observe their thoughts and allow them to move freely like the wind through the branches of a tree, without being affected by them.

Advanced forms of insight meditation, such as Vipassana, that focus on the breath or the reciting of mantras, are practices that can support individuals in their ability to observe, quiet, and focus the mind. They can then use their mind as a tool for visualizations, introspection, contemplation, creativity, and critical thinking, instead of being used by it. With the realization that "I have thoughts, but I am not my thoughts,"[188] individuals may start to dream lucidly,[189] have experiences of subtle illuminations, or experience unconditional love for all creation.

In an effort to enter this state-stage through observing and quieting the mind, the masculine tends towards repressing and dissociating from emotions and the ego, while the feminine tends to strengthen the self and connects more deeply with feelings and the heart.

3. Causal/Deep Sleep

The causal formless state is likened to deep dreamless sleep. It is experienced as a timeless openness or emptiness with the realization that you are not your feelings (happy, sad, afraid, content, etc.), intuitions, or intentions. It becomes a state stage with the arising of a permanent sense of "I AM-ness" that observes—and therefore transcends—time[190] and separation. In this state-stage, any identification with the physical world and objects in consciousness disappears. You intuitively sense that there is a Ground of all Being that transcends the physical world and the egoic mind, which both create the illusion of a separate self. This state-stage is often likened to emptiness, except that it is not a mere blank, but an utter fullness of Being or Godhead that enters the space as light. It feels so full that no other manifestation can contain it. Lucid dreaming becomes more regular and there is a clear sense of "I have experiences but I am not my experiences."

The masculine tends to experience this state as radical stillness and emptiness; the feminine experiences it as radical fullness and flow.

4. Witnessing

The witnessing state is entered when the observer that experiences the timeless emptiness of state-stage three drops away. In Zen this experience is called "Satori," "Radical Emptiness," "the Cloud of Unknowing," "Beginner's Mind," or "the Vertical Drop." In this state there is no more separate you or witness that would experience time, form, emptiness, or even enlightenment (who would be there to be enlightened?).[191] It is a state-stage to which many mystics and sages point. But instead of looking at their pointing finger, you become the finger AND that which it points to.

Lao Tzu, the first Taoist philosopher, wrote in the opening verse of the Tao Te Ching (or Dao De Jing), "the Tao that can be spoken of is not the true Tao" (and then goes on to write eighty more verses that point TO the truth that can't be spoken of).

If you fall into this radical egoless state you may lose any sense of the manifest world and need to have caretakers in place, otherwise you may starve or freeze to death. A sense of "I witness Being but I am not Being" emerges. The witnessing state becomes a state-stage when you can access complete non-attachment or non-desire by choice, similar to accessing language, and retain a subtle awareness during dreamless sleep.[192]

In this state-stage, the feminine-masculine duality is fully transcended.

5. Non-dual

Non-dual awareness is not as much a state-stage as it is a merging of the ever-present infinite ground of all the previous levels. In the preceding witnessing state-stage, one can become completely absorbed in blissful emptiness and oblivious to all form. In non-duality, both are integrated: Emptiness manifests as form, and form as emptiness. Both are simultaneously real and unreal. Non-dual awareness cannot be really experienced, since all experiences (including the witnessing state) come and go and require a witness who has the experience. It also cannot be contained in words.

As soon as you talk or think about "it," it would become separate from "you" and therefore dual. Non-duality has been described as reaching the top of a pole and then climbing one step further. What follows is a complete emptying of the subject (climber) into the object (world), so that there is, in a sense, no more subject (observer/witness)/object duality at all. It is devoid of any looking out on the world from any vantage point that is apart from it. You are then the world's perspective or one with Godhead (sorry, you are still not God—or a Goddess if you happen to be a woman reading this—this notion would be a psychotic[193] delusion that many New Age narcissists have fallen into).

In this latest state-stage of development that we are aware of, the self has become entirely identified (but not fused in an a-dual psychosis) with the world. There is recognition of the oneness of the uni-verse, a realization that wisdom literature from the East and West has pointed to repeatedly. Only few humans (if any) have attained this state-stage as a permanent realization, which could be called full enlightenment, Buddha or Christ nature. It may well be that duality can only be temporarily overcome during transcendental sexual union between lovers who have both reached witness consciousness (which can be a permanently accessible stage or a temporary drug-induced state or peak experience), since it entails male-female union on all levels from the physical/gross to the witness level.

Individual humans are obviously never complete on the physical level (one is either male or female),[194] and can't be feminine or masculine at the same time (you can't breathe in and out simultaneously), but they can find wholeness through sexual union in an enlightened relationship.

Spiritual but Not Religious

Many modern and postmodern women identify themselves as "spiritual but not religious." They may say this without any deeper understanding, or have a certain spiritual teacher, practice, belief system, or realization, but are not members of an organized church, sangha, temple, mosque, or cult with a common creed. However, women who are religious may still be spiritual, as all religions, and even some New Age movements, have developed branches that represent the initial four state-stages of consciousness, which lead to different religious denominations and branches; from atheist to polytheist, monotheist, and mystical.[195]

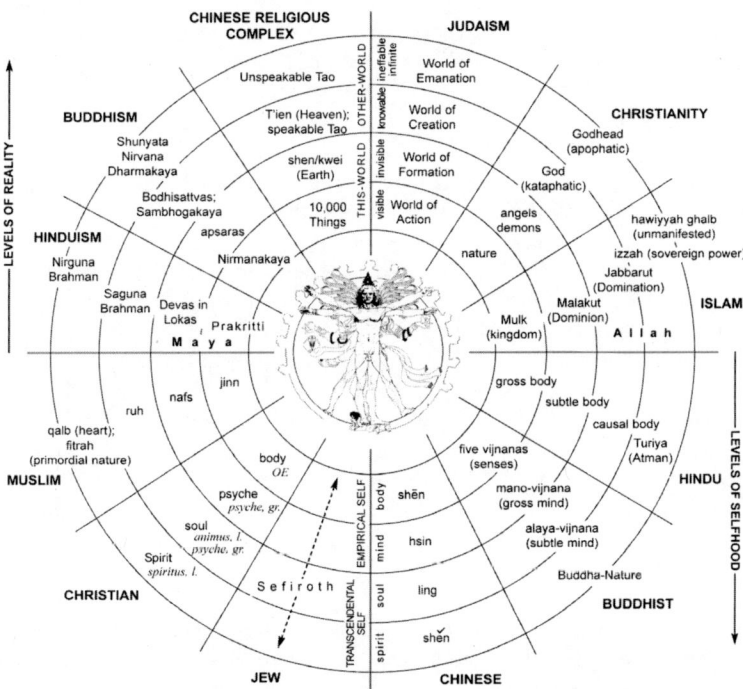

Figure 16: A summary of spiritual levels in world religions

Design by Brad Reynolds, used by permission.

To assume that some religions are more spiritually advanced than others is a fallacy, as all enduring religious or spiritual practices lead through the same state-stages of realization, insight, and illumination that we outlined above. To be in a partnership with a woman who is at the same or next higher state-stage of spiritual development is obviously conducive for the spiritual alignment and growth of both partners, and mandatory for an Integral Life Practice that includes spirituality. Compatible partners can support each other in transforming temporary spiritual states into more permanent state-stages. This often requires the woman to challenge her partner's ego,[196] while the man may support her in building her self-esteem. It can, however, be difficult for a partner who has not experienced certain states, is arrested in a lower state-stage of spiritual development, or only pursues a feminine or masculine form of spirituality to stay in a partnership with a more evolved practitioner.

Development of Sexuality

There are five general levels of sexual exchange between partners that are a direct reflection of their physical, psychological, and spiritual health.[197] Similar to the unfolding of the spiritual realizations outlined above, these levels can be experienced as a temporary state or become permanently accessible state-stages through practice with a partner.

1. Repressed Sexuality

In this lowest stage, the body and sex are viewed with suspicion as something negative and dirty. Usually driven by shame, guilt, and fear that originate from childhood trauma and abuse, adults at this level either avoid sexual activities altogether, perform out of duty in a dissociated way (with closed eyes, under the sheets, in the dark), or develop forms of obsessive-compulsive disorders around their sexuality that can lead to sexual addiction and other abusive behaviors. Oral sex or similarly playful sensual activities are usually out of the question for people at this stage, where modesty is confused with shame.

2. Fucking

In the *fucking* stage, sexuality is instinctual, self-serving, and limited to the physical, hedonistic pleasures of the body. Sex partners tend to objectify each other without seeking a deeper personal connection. They want to have fun, "get off," and don't care much about their partner's emotional needs, feelings, or sexual desires. There is no shame or guilt, and "everything goes," which can be confused with the higher, unrestrained forms of transcendent sexuality (see below), which is another form of the pre/trans fallacy (see above). In this stage, males often dominate and manipulate females into having intercourse and to engage in hurtful practices such as anal sex or deep-throating/gagging.

In the *fucking stage,* everything is seen as OK, as long as the partner cooperates or at least does not call the police. Rarely is there a prior conversation about consent, sexual preferences, sexual history, sexually transmitted diseases (STDs), no-no's, expectations for a monogamous commitment, or possible consequences such as emotional/sexual dependence or pregnancy. Women at this stage often have an unspoken expectation of their partner to make an exclusive commitment after intercourse and feel used and abused if he moves on. They may also become intentionally pregnant without their partner's consent to "hook him" and/or to collect child support and social security payments.

Once the excitement of the newness vanishes, couples in this stage often lose interest in sex with each other and stop having sex or seek a new fuck buddy.[198]

3. HAVING SEX

In this stage, mindfulness comes into play. Sex becomes a conscious choice between a couple that has a mutual understanding and agreement about the implications and consequences of being sexual. Having sex is seen as a beautiful and important activity which brings two people together and provides many physical and emotional health benefits.[199] There is usually an agreement for monogamy or openness about multiple lovers, and partners try to find the time and energy to be sexual with each other. Sex partners in this stage go beyond the pure physical aspects (fucking), and see each other as conscious subjects. They focus on pleasing the other within the context of individual boundaries, rather than trying to openly express and meet their own sexual needs, desires, and fantasies. This leads to sexuality at the lowest common denominator that often leaves both partners unfulfilled over time.

Relationship difficulties such as power struggles or emotional withdrawal tend to be carried into the bedroom, but don't get resolved there. Instead of working on deeper issues to improve their sexual relationship, couples in this stage sometimes try new positions or locations, engage in role playing, apply sex-toys, watch porn movies, or join swinger clubs to keep their sex life interesting. Unless they evolve to the next higher stage of sexual development, merely *having sex* will eventually turn stale, die completely, or become so difficult that their partnership ends when one of them falls in love/lust with a new sex partner.[200]

4. LOVEMAKING

In the *lovemaking* stage, a couple's sexuality becomes the expression of their genuine love, mutual acceptance, deep emotional intimacy, and the joy of being together. Body, mind, and heart are integrated in their lovemaking which is no longer just "a thing that couples do," but an expression of who they are as sexual human beings. No special effort to find the time or energy to be sexual needs to be made by them. Their love making is a life-giving and rejuvenating affirmation of their bond and the depth of their connection. They are open to talking about their desires and exploring all forms of healthy sexual play that bring pleasure and deepen their union. They naturally stay in verbal and non-verbal communication (eye contact) with each other during their love making. Sex at this level is not used to cover up conflicts, to keep score, or to manipulate each other. Instead, sexual and emotional blocks that may arise are worked out between them, and therapeutic help is sought if they can't resolve the problems that they face.[201]

5. Transcendent Sex

This stage represents all advanced sacred or tantric practices that lead to spiritual state experiences through sexual union (such as Kundalini),[202] that transcend the lovers' sense of separation from each other and the universe. This kind of sexuality emerges as a stage between partners that share a deep soul connection, enjoy a high level of physical, emotional, and relationship health, and have reached an advanced stage of spiritual development (see above) with the ability for intense presence and full surrender. Spiritual practices such as meditation, partner-yoga, and ecstatic dance are often interwoven in this form of lovemaking.

Partners who consciously engage in transcendent sexuality allocate ample quality time for their lovemaking (instead of waiting until they are in the mood); create sacred space in their home or away (think of a tastefully decorated warm room, soft sheets, various sized/shaped pillows, dimmed lights, scented candles, burning incense, veils around the bed, oils and lotions, and soft sacred music); and co-create a wide range of experiences through rituals such as sharing sensual food (think strawberries, chocolate, ice-cream, etc.), eye gazing, erotic dance, synchronized conscious breathing into the seven chakras, reciting of mantras, reading poems,[203] alternate giving and receiving of arousing touch and massage, playfulness with objects (think feathers, boas, silk, flower petals, ice cubes), gentle intercourse, or unrestrained ravaging (that may be falsely interpreted as a form of rape).[204]

A common position for deep tantric connection is for the man to sit cross-legged (or on a chair) and the woman on top of him, allowing them to meet each other face-to-face as opposites and equals.[205] The goal of transcendental sexuality is not solely to pleasure and to reach orgasms, but to move (Kundalini) energy up the spine or through the seven chakras, and to deepen the soul connection between the lovers that leads them to consciously experience the divine, instead of unconsciously exclaiming "oh my God" during a short orgasmic release.[206] This requires the ability for men to delay or avoid orgasm, and/or to have orgasms without ejaculating by squeezing their PC muscle.[207] Often, deeply rooted emotional blocks that are embedded in the body and inhibit a further spiritual awakening get revealed and can be released through transcendental sex.

Anima and Animus Complex Development

In Jungian psychology, the anima and animus are seen as the bridge to the soul. One way to experience the soul is to get in touch with the unique sense of self that remains after we strip away all learned conceptions and false beliefs (ego) about who we are.[208] What remains is the deepest possible authentic expression or essence of our unique being that is still personal, the subject that cannot be made into an object, or the soul. This unique core of our existence knows nothing about the duality of the opposite sex, gender, or the feminine-masculine polarities.[209]

As our self-identification as boys or girls develops during childhood, we invariably cover up, split-off, disown, repress, or dismiss qualities of the opposite sex to various degrees.[210] Since we are all born to a mother, this intricate process is different for males and females.

Little boys soon learn that they are not like mother, painfully dissociate from her, and identify with father figures, while little girls learn that they are like her, but not like father, who becomes somewhat of a mystery to them.[211] **Carl Jung[212] discovered this split-off and called the disowned feminine in males the anima, and the disowned masculine in females the animus.**[213] The parts of these disowned (and therefore unconscious) realities that are not recognized and reclaimed in later life appear as inward shadows that cover parts of the soul and consequently become outward projections onto the opposite sex, which is called a complex.[214]

You experience the projection of your anima when you feel a strong emotional (versus sexual or otherwise) attraction to, or threat from, a woman's aura. If the attraction is mutual and you decide to become a couple, it will feel as if you have found and come home to your long lost other, your soul mate, or "twin-flame." The blissful feelings of completeness when you are harmoniously together, the longings that you feel when you are apart, and the fears of loss and abandonment that you experience when she withdraws or challenges you are expressed in the lyrics of many love songs, such as "when I found you, there was no more emptiness inside," or "if you leave me now, you take away the biggest part of me," and movie dialogs such as "I love you, you complete me," and her "you had me at hello."[215]

Lovers with these experiences have fallen in love with a partner who has a compatible anima/animus complex. After a while, the pain of separation and missed love/care during childhood which created the complex in the first place will resurface. This especially happens once the honeymoon is over and the lovers fail to live up to their unrealistic expectations of meeting each other's every need for comfort, acceptance, assurance, understanding, closeness, kindness, appreciation, approval, empathy, support, autonomy, etc. (see list in Chapter 3 under "Needs" and the difference between needs and neediness). In other words, they will start to push each other's emotional buttons which they did not install in the first place.[216]

If you cling and never want to let her go, miss her badly when she is away, get easily jealous if she turns her attention to somebody or something else,[217] withdraw in shame if you can't make her happy,[218] run if she seems to threaten, manipulate, control, or suffocate you, or if you feel that you can't live without her—but need to change her so that you can live with her—then you know where the edge of your complex lies and where the healing work of your wounded anima begins.[219] Your soul calls you to transcend your complex (shine light into your shadow) by realizing the wholeness of your essence and your oneness with all creation (Love), while your ego tries to protect you from being hurt again by defending its separate sense of self or clinging to what seems to be its salvation.[220]

If she shares your emotional attraction and you decide to stay together as a couple despite the inevitable conflicts that will arise, then you can serve each other as catalysts to uncover your soul's essential nature by starting your healing, growth, and awakening process together. You then become soul mates in the true sense; two people who lovingly but relentlessly challenge each other to transcend their egos. This will bring forth your soul's full potential to love unconditionally, not only for your own sake, but also for that of your partner and all sentient beings.[221] This dynamic answers the question of how a soul mate is different from family members or friends whom we may love dearly, but not in the unique way that we experience with a romantic partner.[222]

The five stages of anima/animus complex development that are outlined below provide you with a generalizing orientation to how a woman's animus and a man's anima may evolve. The actual stage and severity of the complex that an adult displays depends largely on his or her childhood and past relationship experiences. As you read through the descriptions below, one or more stages of the anima may resonate with your own level of development, just as you will recognize the animus of women that you are—or have been—in a relationship with. Note how stage five is almost identical for both sexes.

STAGES OF ANIMA DEVELOPMENT IN MEN

1. Women as mother

He needs a mommy to take care of him.

In this first stage, a man's anima is completely tied up with the mother. She is not necessarily his personal mother but the image of a woman that is a faithful provider of nourishment, security, and love. She represents all that is natural, instinctual, and biological.[223] A man with an anima complex of this type cannot function well without a vital connection to a woman, and is easy prey of being controlled and exploited by her. He frequently suffers from impotence or has no sexual desire at all, and is therefore called a mama's boy. This type of anima possession also manifests through fear of accidents or disease, or in a sort of dullness of personality. The Greek Sirens and the German Lorelei personify these dangerous aspects of the anima, which may even lead a man to his death over a lost love relationship through suicide.

2. Women as sex object

He wants her to make him feel good.

In the second stage, the anima is a collective sexual image. She is a Marilyn Monroe, Madonna, or Playboy model. Men in stage two are often Don Juans who see all women as sex objects, and engage in repeated sexual adventures, sometimes developing into sexual addictions. These relationships are invariably short-lived, because he is not faithful, is always looking for his next conquest, and no woman can ever live up to his unrealistic image of the ideal female partner.

3. Women as wife

He wants her loyalty and support.

In the third stage of his anima complex development, a man becomes ready to care for a wife and be devoted to his family. He is the loving protector and provider that women in the equivalent stage three of their animus development seek. Men with this anima accept their partner as she is, as long as she fulfills her role as supportive, undemanding, caring, and faithful wife, available sex partner, and loving mother to his children. His sexuality is usually integrated into their relationship and not an autonomous function that drives him. He can differentiate between love and lust, which allows him to create a lasting partnership (if she stays), because he can tell the difference between the objects of his sexual desire and the benefits of being a faithful partner/husband.

4. Women as guide to creativity and awakening

He struggles with her need for independence.

In the fourth stage, a man's anima functions as a guide to his inner life. As women in this stage become emotionally and financially independent from men, they often turn away and abandon their partners against their will. This challenges him to seek other sources of fulfillment, happiness, aliveness, passion, joy, purpose, peace, and love. Through his quest arises a desire to answer life's deeper questions of "who am I," "where do I come from," "why am I here," "what is the meaning of my life," "what should I do," "what is my purpose," and "where do I go"?

Contemplating these questions, reading books like the one that you are holding right now, meditating, or seeking a bond with others on a similar path in men's groups, New Age churches, and personal growth workshops allow him to bring deeper levels of his unconscious anima into his awareness. This leads to a liberating process of awakening to his authentic nature, true purpose, genuine passions, and capacity to love unconditionally that are independent from a partnership with a woman.[224]

On the flipside, he may show behaviors that are usually described as a midlife crisis,[225] become commitment phobic, avoid deeper intimacy with women altogether, or engage in serial monogamy or polyamory,[226] since he does not want to sacrifice his newfound freedom or to be limited by one partnership. This partial awakening (the idea of living alone is not Integral, fully realized, or the ultimate realization of human development) is transcended when a man enters stage five of his anima development.

5. Women as equal partner

He meets her as an opposite and equal partner.

Similar to a woman in this stage (see below), a man in stage five of his anima complex development has accepted the fact that conflicts and ambivalence are intrinsic to human relationships, and sees how their resolution contributes to his ongoing healing, personal growth, and spiritual realization. He feels confident, secure, and comfortable to authentically express his sexual essence (which tends to be masculine in heterosexual men), while he embraces his feminine (anima).[227] This allows him to invite differing views, experiences, and feelings of his female partner without feeling threatened, offended, or puzzled by them.

Her authentic stage-five feminine qualities naturally complement his masculinity and vice versa. Since he has found his own purposeful identity that does not depend on her inspiration, support, or approval, he appreciates his partner's independent authority,[228] and doesn't feel responsibility, shame, or insecurity if she is unhappy—even though he shows empathy, care, and devotion—and enjoys when she is happy.

He neither clings, nor pushes her away, but fully opens to embrace her at all levels of his being when they are together, and stays content and fulfilled when they are apart. This allows him to enter into a mature monogamous relationship of opposites and equals from which radically new life experiences, emotional healing processes, and deeper spiritual realizations that often become the foundation for altruistic acts of kindness and service towards others emerge.[229]

Stages of Animus Development in Women

1. Men as alien outsiders

She fears, hates, and loves him.

Because of abuse or abandonment from men that she indentified with during childhood, such as a father, father figure, older brother, uncle, or family friend, a woman in this stage completely denies and suppresses her animus as alien inside and outside of herself. She trusts her mother and other females, while she distrusts, hates, or fears men. This is often countered by a strange curiosity about men, which she cannot differentiate.

This ambivalence can make her extremely seductive, needy, and clingy, and cause severe symptoms of the "seduce and withhold"[230] syndrome. As soon as a man gets close to her she withdraws, only to come back to ask for more after he becomes distant. She can break the heart of a weak man who tries to prove that he is different, attempts to rescue her from her fears, and so becomes codependent[231] as she lures him into her pathological cat and mouse game.

Within the limits of her domain in household, family, and female-oriented work environment (e.g., school teacher, nurse, artist, gardener, therapist, healer, working with animals, etc.), such a woman may seem grounded and self-confident. Outside those limits, she leaves the work and responsibility to men and more mature women.[232]

2. Men as father, God, or king

She wants his approval.

The self-esteem of a woman in this stage is directly connected to the response and approval that she receives from men. She is often driven by a need to be seen as the most attractive female, and constantly monitors her value by her internalized masculine judgment and through externalized male reflection. This may lead to a split in her personality when she imitates male behavior to be liked by them, and at other times presents herself as a sexually seductive *femme fatale* (such as in the movie *Basic Instinct*) to be desired.

She either hides behind a feminine mask of beautiful appearance, graceful charming manner, and entertaining wit, or develops a tomboyish attitude through teasing, competing, and challenging, or some other facade that suggests success. Women in this stage gravitate towards men that they perceive to be more attractive, intelligent, and exciting than they could ever be themselves. They often try to live up to men by dietary restrictions, vigorous physical exercising, adapting to their intellectual interests, developing new talents, and being sexually available to become the perfect mate.

If a woman remains in this stage, she is at great risk of entering a profound depression when her beauty and sexual attractiveness wane, and the number of heads that she is turning, and men who admire her diminishes. She may then isolate herself from all intimate relationships, because her perfectionism overrides her ability to be compassionate and to forgive her own and others' mistakes. This may lead her to withdraw into a cold and bitter self-denial in which her anxieties create all kinds of psychosomatic illnesses, such as panic attacks, vomiting, heart problems, fatigue, and body aches.

A strong, conscious, and patient man (or a good psychotherapist) can support a woman in this stage to find her own worth, passions, and identity, independent of male approval, which then allows her to enter into stage three.[233]

3. Men as hero

She wants him to take care of her.

Women in stage three seek a man as protector and provider with strength, courage, and ability, who can meet her needs, cherish her, and whom she wants to marry. He represents her ideal (and often unrealistic) image of the knight in shining armor who fulfills her expectations for good looks, intelligence, solid reputation, stable finances, generosity, loyalty, humor, kindness, care, integrity, and faithfulness.

To be in a good bargaining position, this woman will focus on her appearance, health/fitness, and adapting to the world of men by seeking a higher education, pursuing a career, fighting for social justice, or saving a failing business. She will appear as self-affirming and expects something in return. She functions well in the competitive world of men, sees herself as equal, is willing to share responsibilities, and will contribute and perform as long as her partner is able to provide more in return, since women want to marry up.

As long as he meets her expectations for financial security, social status, and devotion, she will support him to achieve his full potential while often denying such achievements to herself. This can lead to feelings of resentment and anger when she sees that she has been "denied" the right to experience her own competence, and when her partner/husband fails to live up to her ever-growing expectations. Some women in this stage will enter an inward journey once they become aware of the transitory nature of their physical attractiveness, ability to succeed with men, and limitations of finding acceptance in the male world. This may lead them to the restoration of their female authority[234] as they take responsibility for their own identity once they have moved into stage four of their animus complex development.[235]

4. Men as independent beings

She wants her independence.

A woman in stage four makes an active choice in favor of her self-interest and self-fulfillment—independent of a partner or husband. This transition takes place with the realization that she has constructed her own experiences throughout her lifetime in relationship to men, and now wants to find her own identity. She will stop trying to be perfect in all things in order to please her partner (who was a heroic father figure in the previous stage), as she becomes emotionally free from his approval and support. Having discovered her own source of worthiness and foundation, she is working to restore her female authority. Financial independence through her own labor or through other sources of money that are often only available to women, such as "divorcing well," alimony and child-support payments, generous lovers, support from parents, or Social Security benefits, are the prerequisite for this transition.

You will notice if your partner enters into stage four of her animus development when she starts to challenge you, cares less about your needs, seeks her financial independence, and refuses to take responsibility for holding your relationship together. If you are in partnership with a woman in this stage, it is important to know that it is **not your fault** that her pain of staying will eventually be greater than her fear of leaving, and that there is **nothing you can do** but to take care of yourself emotionally[236] and sexually, protect the financial assets that are legitimately yours (if you have to, with the help of a CPA or lawyer), and, if you can, support her with love and compassion in her transition. Once separated and/or divorced, she will feel free from the evaluation and needs of men for the first time in her life.

These newly single women are then much occupied with challenging work, their animals and children, social activities, educational advancements, maintaining their household, hobbies, world-travel, and their friendships.[237] At the same time, they look down at women who show more feminine or balanced qualities and who desire to be (or are) in a committed partnership with a man. To women in stage four, partnered women still seem to be in the pitiful stage two or three of dependence on a male partner (which they have just escaped). However, married women may have actually advanced into stage five, which women in stage four cannot fathom yet. They discredit partnered women as unevolved and often compete with them in merciless ways. Women in stage four frequently break with the conventional role of caring mother, show tough love, and feel fulfilled outside a partnership with a man.

Still, there remains an underlying fear of abandonment, especially in older women, when concerns about the disappearance of their skills and autonomy in the midst of a crisis arise. This often leads to feelings of ambivalence. On one side there is a secret longing for the stability and support that a partnership with a man could provide during times of stress, fatigue, loneliness, or desire for sex. On the other side there is the fear of becoming emotionally dependent, used, and dominated again.

Frequent complaints about the lack of good men who are physically fit and attractive, highly intelligent, successful, accomplished, mature, kind, loving, generous, evolved, supportive, spiritual, and available when they need/want them, but who remain flexible, undemanding, and unattached otherwise, are a hallmark of women in stage four.[238] Becoming men-hating diehard singles, settling for "friends with benefits" whom they string along, or serial monogamy are often the only solutions that seem to solve their dilemma.

It is **not your fault** if you get mixed messages, are rejected, or are ignored altogether by women in stage four that you try to date or get a commitment from, as these women are highly independent, endlessly demanding, impossible to please, and commitment-phobic.[239] This is, of course, no problem for men who have entered stage four of their own anima development, which many single males and females falsely see as the highest stage of their personal and spiritual development (as in, I am so whole and complete, I don't need a partner to complete me).

If you have matured into stage five and meet a woman who is at the end of her animus stage four development, then you may be able to patiently support her to transition into stage five and find a wonderful partner in her.

5. Men as equal partners

She wants him as an equal and opposite partner.

Just as a man, a woman in stage five of her animus development has accepted that conflict and ambivalence are intrinsic to human relationships, and realized the significance of a partnership to balance her further psychological growth and spiritual awakening.[240] Having fully claimed her own authority after transcending her animus complex, she no longer sees men as alien, superior, inferior, or independent. The realization that the idea of living and going it alone was a distorted conception of human existence emerges in her, because we never live alone.

She sees that in being human we have a variety of economic, physical, sexual, psychological, and spiritual needs that cannot be met by living alone. At last she has the insight that a balanced personality always develops in a self-other conception, and never through the discovery of an independent self.[241] This woman then desires the material, intellectual, emotional, sexual, and spiritual synergy that is co-created with a man who meets her as an opposite and equal (which means opposite feminine and masculine polarities with equal levels of consciousness, rights, and responsibilities). Since she may have never experienced a stage five partnership, she needs guidance from a man (like you?) at the same stage of his anima development, who is able to meet her in an integrally informed way. These couples can then form interdependent[242] partnerships in which they heal, learn, grow, and enjoy family and social activities together, while contributing to the well-being of others.[243]

Growth

The stage of anima/animus development in which individuals find themselves at the end of adolescence depends largely on the relationship that they have had with their parents during childhood, especially their opposite-sex parent.[244] People may then remain stuck at that post-adolescent level for the rest of their lives, or they may advance to higher stages once the possibilities of one stage have been exhausted and pain stimulates a move to the next. This move rarely appears without struggle or crisis, such as fights with a partner, addictions, job loss, relocation, breakup, or divorce.

If a man's anima in any of the first four stages feels lonely and desperate for attention, he will experience an emotional attraction to a woman at a similar stage of her animus development, and vice versa. For example, a man in a mother-bound stage one will choose a woman who clings and takes care of him in exchange for getting her codependent needs met by him. A man in stage two who is not living up to his true potentials will be attracted to a woman who spurs him on and makes more of him than he would otherwise be, in exchange for getting his approval. A man in stage three may project his complex onto a woman who wants to get married, cared for, and provided for, and is thus led away from his responsibility to himself. He has the opportunity to enter stage four when his wife/partner leaves him, when he no longer wants to put up with her constant unhappiness and ignorance, or when he embarks on a spiritual journey to discover his own identity and passion—independent of a committed partnership (the latter is usually triggered by a midlife crisis). This may eventually lead him into stage five, in which his complex becomes increasingly conscious and transcended, which feels like a big awakening. He then no longer depends on women to complete him AND he can open up fully to a committed partnership without emotional neediness or fear of abandonment. This allows him to attract a woman in stage five of her animus development who wants to co-create a partnership with a man who is an opposite and equal.

In other words, the feminine and masculine qualities that men and women have denied within themselves will confront them in their relationships with the opposite sex.[245] What is often painfully experienced as a difficult or failed marriage can actually support men and women in moving forward in their anima and animus complex development and spiritual awakening. This move forward is always worthwhile, for it leads us ever closer towards the discovery of our true essence (soul). Individuals who ignore or repress the calling of their anima or animus and avoid growth through intimate relationships (although there are, of course, times in life where it is prudent to be alone) risk becoming depressed, cynical pseudo-intellectuals. They may then lose all joy, capacity to love, meaning, purpose, and spontaneity in their lives. Active avoidance of a partnership out of fear of becoming engulfed or abandoned, or out of arrogance (the feeling that no one is good enough for me) is therefore an indication that more growth-work is needed, and by no means a sign of maturity, transcendence, wholeness, or enlightenment.[246]

As men and women transcend their anima/animus projections in the course of their partnerships and increasingly develop internally what they seek or avoid externally, they will be rewarded with becoming deeper, more vibrantly alive and creative human beings as well as more balanced partners in their love relationship.[247]

In Summary

Not only children, but also adults have the potential to advance in all the developmental lines. This growth appears in progressive levels from lowest to highest, one step at a time. Each higher level provides better answers to life's questions and challenges than the preceding one. In this chapter we defined the levels of four developmental lines that are particularly relevant to partnerships: (1) eight levels of consciousness development (from archaic to magic, egocentric, conformist, rational, pluralistic, integral, and transpersonal); (2) five state-stages of spiritual development (from gross to subtle, causal, witness, and non-dual); (3) five levels of sexual expression and experience (from repressed sexuality, to fucking, having sex, lovemaking, and transcendental/tantric sexuality); and (4) five levels of the feminine and masculine shadow that cover up the soul/essence of males and females, called the anima and animus complex.

In Chapter 7 we will introduce a Personality Matrix that ties these four lines together with personality types (see below) and the feminine/masculine polarities.

Chapter 5

States of Falling in Love

Sometimes with the Heart
Seldom with the Soul
Scarce once with the Might
Few—love at all
~ Emily Dickinson ~

All temporary experiences that come and go in a fluid way and are recognized as such by the subject (e.g., I was angry, happy, sleeping, awake, stoned, drunk, in love, etc.) are called states of consciousness (not to be confused with the vertical/hierarchical structure stages of consciousness from which states are observed and interpreted). **In the context of this manual, this chapter will focus on the states of falling in love.**[248]

Feelings such as sexual lust, infatuation, bliss of romance, emotional bonding, or pain/depression after a breakup or divorce are all temporary states (versus permanent stages) that are caused by elevated or lowered levels (imbalances) of specific chemicals in our body, called hormones and neurotransmitters.[249] These hormonal responses originally evolved through our ancestors, who chose the fittest and most compatible sex partners, excluded others once they found a mate for procreation, moved on if pregnancy wasn't the result of their efforts in due time,[250] stayed together while raising their young, and, if they were to become depressed during times of hardship, abandonment, or loss, solicited compassionate responses from others.[251] These powerful chemicals still play an important role in our mating behavior to this day, as they can send us on incredible highs when we fall in love, and cause deep pain when we get cut off from the object of our desire.

The intensity of the chemistry that lovers experience is directly related to the degree that they meet each other's Primary Fantasy. Other factors include, compatible genes,[252] the matching of their mutually compatible unconscious anima/animus complex and other shadow elements, and the level of their preceding loneliness.[253]

Even though many people fantasize about, and even anticipate falling in love at first sight, only 11% of married couples report having had this experience when they first met.[254] For the remaining 89%, the love hormones kicked in over time once they had a neutral or positive first impression of each other, but experienced no particular initial sexual or romantic attraction. Proximity, their general state of vulnerability and unsettlement,[255] as well as frequency, duration, and intensity of the ensuing contacts were crucial factors for romantic feelings to emerge, especially in women.[256]

Once infatuated, lovers see the object of their desire through rose-colored glasses, and often falsely interpret their chemistry as a sign of true love and compatibility that will last forever—the "happily ever after" fantasy that is the theme of many romantic movies, love songs, romance novels, and fairy tales.

Fortunately, all hormone-driven states of falling in and out of love are **temporary states** and not **permanent stages**. The three major states/phases of attraction that are outlined below provide you with a very general overview of the intricate and mysterious role that chemicals play in the human experiences of lust, romance, commitment, and painful breakups.[257]

Phase 1 – Lust

Sexual urges and lust are driven by the sex hormone testosterone. It is not only present in males—even though levels in their bodies are usually ten times higher than in women's bodies, which leads men to think about and crave sex more often[258]—but also plays a role in the sexual desires and emotional well-being of women. However, estrogen is the dominant cuddle hormone in females and stimulates seductiveness, openness, and receptiveness, as well as longing for physical closeness, skin-to-skin contact, and sex.[259] Estrogen is also important for vaginal health (thick viscosity of lubrication, firm muscle tone, elasticity, and thickness of the vaginal walls) and often diminishes during and after menopause, when frequency of intercourse diminishes.[260]

Sometimes a role reversal in sexual appetites appears around midlife when testosterone levels and the resulting libido naturally decrease in men, while the libido of women increases as the testosterone-masking effects of estrogen decline.[261]

At any rate, increased levels of testosterone create sexual desire and get men and women out there looking for somebody, and healthy levels of estrogen make women seductive and receptive.[262]

Phase 2 – Romance

This is the truly love-struck phase. After people get infatuated and enter the romance state, they can hardly think of anything else, lose their appetite, need less sleep, spend hours at a time daydreaming about their new love, engage in endless phone conversations, email exchanges, and text messaging, and try to spend as much time together as possible. In the infatuated romance state, a group of neurotransmitters called monoamines play an important role. These are:

Dopamine—also activated by cocaine, nicotine, heroin, and other addictive substances. It creates the drive to seek the rewarding stimulus and is therefore associated with any kind of major addiction, in our case to a member of the opposite sex.[263]

Norepinephrine—similar to its better known cousin adrenaline, increases energy, memory function for new stimuli (men really listen and remember after they have fallen in love), perspiration, heart rate, and blood pressure, with the downside of lowered appetite, sleeplessness, and exhilaration. It also stimulates more "fight or flight" responses, which often leads new lovers to be over-reactive or edgy.[264]

Serotonin—suspected to be one of love's most important chemicals. Lowered levels of serotonin allow for an increase of the love hormones testosterone, dopamine, and norepinephrine.[265] Similar to patients with obsessive compulsive disorder (OCD), the serotonin-starved brains of lovers obsessively think about the object of their desire, which renders them temporarily insane, especially if their love is unrequited. Serotonin-enhancing antidepressants (a.k.a. selective serotonin seuptake inhibitors or SSRI's) such as Prozac, Celexa, Lexapro, Luvox, Paxil, or Zoloft can help in such situations, but are also known to lower a person's sex drive and romantic feelings towards others. So it is advisable to stay away from these medications if you can.[266]

The drug-induced romance phase lasts between 3 and 24 months, which, again, has evolutionary reasons. This was the period of time that it took for our ancestors to try to get pregnant. Otherwise they would move on to find a new partner. Even modern couples who don't want children couldn't stay infatuated forever, otherwise they wouldn't get any work done, which does not mean that you should no longer be romantic after the romance phase—quite the contrary.

If lovers manage to resolve the inevitable conflicts that arise at the end of the romance phase in a constructive way and stay together,[267] they may reap the long-term benefits of increased social status, financial stability, physical health, and sexual satisfaction, as well as personal and spiritual growth in the commitment state that follows.

PHASE 3 – COMMITMENT

Two attachment hormones support couples in sustaining their commitment to each other beyond the romance phase, especially if pregnancy occurs. These chemicals evolved through the descendants of devoted parents who were more successful in raising their young to maturity by staying together and supporting each other, than those who separated.

Oxytocin—released during childbirth and causes the female breasts to produce milk. It helps cement the strong bond between mother and child. Oxytocin is also released in both sexes during orgasm and is thought to promote the bonding between adults who become sexually intimate. It also reduces stress, especially in women, and is believed to have many other health benefits for both sexes.[268]

Vasopressin—the monogamy hormone that plays an important role in the long-term commitment between partners. Levels increase before and during orgasm. The bonding effect of vasopressin was discovered when scientists injected different amounts into the bodies of prairie voles.[269]

Long-term partnerships can stay satisfying and exciting beyond the romance phase if the couple is compatible along crucial developmental lines, is dedicated to ongoing personal and spiritual growth in the context of their union, and shares rewarding activities such as travel, hobbies, joint projects, realization of common dreams, participating in growth workshops, and a vibrant tantric sex life with each other.[270]

Your Gift That Keeps On Giving

The seminal fluid (ejaculate/cum) that surrounds sperms contains dopamine, norepinephrine, testosterone, various estrogens, oxytocin, and vasopressin, which all contribute to the physical and emotional health of women.[271] The theory goes that the more sex a couple has, the deeper their bond becomes—so go for it if you want her to stick around, and be responsible if you are not serious and don't want to hurt her feelings.[272]

Addicted to Love

Some people, especially those who are highly desirable to the opposite sex and have no problem attracting partners, can get addicted to the hormonal thrill during the infatuation and romance state, and often move from one lover to the next, which can become destructive to their own and other people's lives (think movie stars and rock stars). There is even a 12-step group for sex and love addicts, called Sex and Love Addicts Anonymous, or for short SLAA.[273] Such behavior is called "digging many shallow holes," as it never leads to the rewards that staying and doing the work in a committed, healthy, long-term partnership provides. Some people try to prolong the romance phase by engaging in the excitement and drama of codependent, polyamorous, or open relationships,[274] which are rarely sustainable. Yet others are afraid of the distracting, challenging, and sometimes emotionally devastating effects that the rise and fall of the love hormones can have on their life, and avoid partnerships altogether.

Therapists have suggested to their female clients to run in the opposite direction when they feel a strong attraction to a man. From their experience with pathologically feminine clients who only follow their chemically-induced feelings without verifying them with their rational mind (ignoring red flags), such relationships usually end in a disaster. This leaves many females confused between their chemistry-driven instincts and their reasoning mind, instead of learning how to integrate them both in a functional way and to see a partnership as an opportunity for their healing and growth.[275]

Integrating Chemistry with Reason

On one hand, chemistry is the prerequisite for any romantic interest to emerge and for good reasons—it is the ancient wisdom of our body and unconscious mind that signals to us that we have found a physically/socially (see Primary Fantasy), genetically, emotionally, and spiritually compatible mate to procreate, heal, grow, and awaken with.

On the other hand, chemistry effectively impairs our rational faculties, which leads us to conveniently ignore incompatible values, worldviews, intellects, relationship skills, passions, interests, lifestyle choices, and dreams for the future.

The ability of a man to differentiate between chemistry and rationality, and to integrate them both is therefore essential for the co-creation of a sustainable, healthy love relationship—if that is what you and your partner desire. If you don't take this responsibility, your mate is likely to deny any fault and say that she overlooked red flags, lost faith in you, grew apart, no longer loves you, or that you seduced and manipulated her for sex, when she dumps you after the romance phase is over.

In Parts II and III of the manual we will dive deeper into the factors that allow you to determine if a temporary love-struck phase (or a marriage that went sour) can be transformed into a healthy partnership or not. This will put you in command of your emotional, time, and financial investment in a woman. It will also allow you to make responsible choices with integrity about engaging her further and working inside the partnership to resolve problems (if she happens to be willing to do so), or to let her go gracefully with love and compassion when it is time for her to move on.

In Summary

The various feelings of lust, infatuation, romance, and commitment are temporary hormone-driven states and not permanent stages. Even though chemistry plays a vital role in the sexual selection process, the love hormones can blind lovers to the red flags, indicating that a long-term healthy partnership may fail to flourish. By differentiating and integrating both aspects of love—the hormone-driven thrills of chemistry AND practical compatibility factors—integrally informed men can make responsible mate choices and minimize the risk of bad emotional, financial, and time investments in infatuated women who will eventually move on and break their hearts. It also allows men to show compassion and patience if their partner suffers because of hormonal imbalances.

Chapter 6

Evaluating Personality Types

He who knows others is learned. He who knows himself is wise.
~ Lao Tzu ~

All humans possess certain personality characteristics that stay consistent throughout their lifetime. The Integral Model refers to these fixed character traits as *personality types* or simply *types*. Most commonly known are introverts and extroverts, Type-A (impatient, hostile) and Type-B (calm, laid-back) personalities, the nine types of the Enneagram, and the infamous astrological signs of the Zodiac. Less recognized but equally relevant are the three NLP types, the Five Love Languages, and the Myers-Briggs type indicator.

Knowledge about viable personality types and their integration with the other elements of the Integral Model provide you with crucial information that can make or break a relationship. Unfortunately, women often reduce questions of compatibility to types (he is just not my type, I don't get along with Capricorns, I don't like introverts, etc.), so knowing about the validity of typologies can be useful. Exploring and analyzing types is relatively simple, can be fun, usually resonates with women, and can provide a lot of insights, so here we go.

NLP Types

Neuro-Linguistic Programming, or NLP, is a method that originated in the 1970s to improve therapeutic and personal successes by replicating effective patterns of behavior and communication. The model soon became popular in sales, education, and change management to create better rapport with customers, students, and employees[276] and can also be applied to improve success with a woman.[277] NLP identifies three basic learning and communication modalities in people—auditory, visual, and kinesthetic.

Auditory types connect through verbal exchange and might say "I **hear** what you say," or "let me **tell** you something." They learn and communicate through words.

Visual types like to **see/show** things and might say "I **see** what you mean" or "let me **show** you how I see things." They learn and communicate through images.

Kinesthetic types like to feel and touch and might say "this really **touches** me" or "don't you **feel** what is going on." They learn and communicate through shared feeling and hands-on experiences.

NLP Techniques

To effectively communicate and build rapport with women (or others in general), it is helpful to understand their NLP type and to communicate in the language that resonates most with them.

The Eye Accessing Cue technique (described in more detail in the endnotes) helps to identify if people are thinking in images (visual), in sounds and self-talk (auditory), or through their feelings (kinesthetic), and if they are focused on the past or constructing ideas for the future.[278] Reading these cues correctly can support you in understanding and responding to your partner with more empathy.

Another NLP technique called mirroring can be used to build instant rapport. During mirroring/pacing you synchronize your body language, facial expressions, tone of voice, and breathing pattern with your partner. This will give her a sense of comfort, ease, and safety through familiarity.[279]

Five Love Languages

Based on the three NLP types that we discussed above there are five different ways through which people give and receive love.[280] These are:

1) **Words of affirmation** (NLP auditory) such as "I love you," "you are wonderful," "I miss you," and by calling frequently or, sending emails, text messages, cards, and handwritten love letters.

2) **Quality time** spent together while doing enjoyable things such as going to the movies, playing board/card games, sharing time with friends and family, shopping sprees, sports, cooking, or travel.

3) **Gifts** (NLP visual) such as chocolate, flowers, candles, books, CDs, clothes, jewelry, a car, boat, house, island, or country.

4) **Acts of service** such as cooking dinner, cleaning the house, bringing breakfast to bed, driving the car, fixing things, or running errands.

5) **Physical touch** (NLP kinesthetic) such as holding hands, cuddling, kissing, giving and receiving massages, taking baths together, or sensuality/sex.

All people have a primary and secondary Love Language that resonates most with them. Often, partners are not aware of their different love languages and therefore miscommunicate their affection and appreciation for each other; for example, if he washes her car and buys her gifts, while she would rather receive a love letter and cuddle.

You can identify your partner's love language through skillful questions and answers (ask for a list of 10 or more things that make her feel loved, and do a few every day), observations, by asking her to take an online test,[281] or by having her answer the questionnaire in the back of the book, *The 5 Love Languages* by Gary Chapman.

The Enneagram

The Enneagram is a synthesis of several ancient wisdom traditions that has become one of the most popular typologies in recent years. Today it is widely applied in business (team building/change management), psychotherapy, personal growth, and spirituality.[282] The Enneagram symbol is composed of three interlaced "triangles" that form a geometric figure with nine points around a circle, with each of them representing a specific personality type. It is common to find a little of yourself in all of the types, although one of them will stand out prominently as being closest to yourself. *Each of the nine types has unhealthy, average, and healthy expressions (or assets and liabilities).* The number above or below a person's main type represents the secondary quality or "wing," while the two inner lines point to the corresponding types that individuals gravitate towards under stress/disintegration and during healthy integration/growth.[283]

Courtesy of The Enneagram Institute
Copyright 2005, The Enneagram Institute. All Rights Reserved. Used with Permission.

Figure 17: The Enneagram

The Nine Enneagram Types[284]

1. The reformer, judge, perfectionist

Is focused on personal integrity and seeks truth. Can be a teacher, crusader, or advocate for change. Is often ignorant of his/her own flaws and overly critical of others. Fears being corrupt, evil, or defective—wants to be good, balanced, perfect, and have integrity.

2. The helper, giver, caretaker

Is compassionate, attentive, generous, and caring. Can be clingy, needy, flattering, people-pleasing, and manipulative. Often well-meaning and driven to be close to others, but can slip into doing things for others in order to be needed. Fears being unwanted and unlovable—wants to be loved and needed.

3. The achiever, performer, status seeker

Is adaptable and changeable. Walks the world with confidence and acts in ways that will bring approval and accomplishments, sometimes at the expense of his/her true self. Fears failure and being worthless—wants to feel valuable and worthwhile.

4. The individualist, romantic, aesthete

Is driven by the desire to understand and to find his/her place in the world. Embraces individualism, is creative, intuitive, and humane. Fears having no identity or personal significance—wants to be significant.

5. The investigator, expert, thinker

Is driven to understand the world and derives self-worth through contribution, can be withdrawn, observant, and quiet, until he/she can impress with a witty remark. Fears incompetency or uselessness—wants to be capable and knowledgeable above all else.

6. The loyalist, hero, rebel, defender

Longs for secure stability and exhibits unwavering loyalty and responsibility. Is slow to trust again if betrayed and prone to fearful thinking. Displays emotional anxiety as well as reactionary and paranoid behavior. Fears being without support and guidance—wants to have security and support.

7. The enthusiast, adventurer, sensationalist

Is adventurous and constantly busy, embraces life with all its various joys and wonders, and moves frantically from one new experience to another. Fears being unable to provide for him/herself, and is afraid of missing out on life with all of its richness—wants to be satisfied, content, and to have his/her needs fulfilled.

8. The challenger, boss, maverick

Is strong, with a desire to be a powerful and controlling leader. Can be friendly and charitable, or dictatorial, manipulative, ruthless, and willing to destroy anything that stands in the way. Fears being harmed or controlled by others—seeks self-protection and wants to be in control of life and destiny.

9. The peacemaker, mediator, preservationist

Is empathetic, receptive, gentle, calm, and at peace with the world. Avoids conflict, withdraws, shuts down, and goes along with other people's wishes. Is prone to dissociation and passive-aggressive behavior. Fears loss and separation—wants to have inner stability and peace of mind.

THE ENNEAGRAM COMPATIBILITY COMBINATIONS

No pairing of types is particularly blessed or doomed. You can have a healthy relationship between any two types. Free or affordable assessment tests on the Internet allow you to determine your and your partner's type and the assets and liabilities between the two of you.[285]

Myers-Briggs Type Indicator

According to the Myers-Briggs type indicator, all people can be classified using four opposing criteria:

>Extroversion - Introversion
>Sensing - Intuitive
>Thinking - Feeling
>Judging - Perceiving

Introvert and Extrovert[286]

These are the attitudes that show how a person orients and receives their energy. The extrovert's energy flow is outward, and the preferred focus is on other people and things. The introvert's energy flow is inward and the preferred focus is on his or her own thoughts, ideas, and impressions.

Sensing and Intuition

These are the perceiving and non-rational functions. People don't have much control over their perceptions, only how to process them once they have them. Sensing people tend to focus on the present and on concrete information gained from their five senses. Intuitive people tend to focus on the future, with a view towards patterns and possibilities, and prefer to receive guidance from their unconscious or the spiritual realm.

Thinking and Feeling

These are the judging functions. Both types strive to make rational judgments and decisions based on the information from their perceiving functions, above. Thinkers tend to base their decisions on logic such as "true-false, if-then" connections and on objective analysis of cause and effect. Feeling people tend to base their decisions primarily on values and subjective evaluations based on concerns for other people. They use "more-less, better-worse" evaluations. It could be said that thinkers decide with their heads, while feelers decide with their hearts. When thinking or feeling is extroverted, decisions tend to rely on external sources and the generally accepted rules and procedures. When introverted, thinking and feeling judgments tend to be subjective, relying on internally generated ideas for logical organization and evaluation.

Judging and Perceiving[287]

People who favor judging like a planned and organized approach to life and prefer to have things settled. People who prefer perceiving tend to like a flexible and spontaneous approach to life and prefer to keep their options open.

Combinations

Different combinations of the four either/or criteria determine a type. For example:
ISTJ - Introvert Sensing Thinking Judging
The sixteen possible combinations are ISTJ, ISFJ, INFJ, INTJ, ISTP, ISFP, INFP, INTP, ESTP, ESFP, ENFP, ENTP, ESTJ, ESFJ, ENFJ, and ENTJ.
You can identify your own and your partner's types with their associated strengths and weaknesses by taking an online Myers-Briggs typology test.[288]

Astrology

According to a Harris poll, 31% of Americans believe in astrology (25% of men, 36% of women).[289] Astrological charts and computer programs claim to provide solid information about personality types, compatibilities, and one's destiny. At the very least, they make for interesting and revealing conversations; so no matter if you are one of the 25% of male believers or not, you may want to stay open-minded. Some women will not even consider you as a partner if you are not a good astrological fit, while others may determine that you are their soul mate after doing your chart without ever having met you.[290]

Other Types and Beliefs

You may come across some other typing (and stereotyping), such as numerology, human design,[291] birth order,[292] genetic types,[293] the inner animal, cultural background (e.g., European versus Asian), or race. Unfortunately, most of these ways of typecasting people are not very scientific, but rather stem from magical thinking or judgmental projections.

Showing an open and discerning interest in unscientific approaches to typologies and acceptance of superstitious, magical, or mythic beliefs (see pre/trans fallacy in Chapter 4), such as tarot card readings, divination cards, psychic readings, horoscopes, past-life experiences, shamanic voyages, Reiki healing, out-of-body experiences, etc. that your partner might subscribe to can provide new insights for you and her that create more intimacy and expand your horizons.

In Summary

Personality types describe character traits that stay consistent throughout human growth and stage development. Most classifications, such as how people give and receive love, or their Enneagram type, are based on viable psychological tests or self-assessments and describe habitual responses to reality that lie under the surface of our normal awareness. Other typologies originate from superstitious beliefs or cultural stereotyping and can, at best, provide interesting topics for authentic self-revealing conversations. To explore and discuss your own and your partner's types in different areas can be a lot of fun and reward you with new personal insights that will improve your self-understanding and partnership.

Conclusion Part I

We started out with a brief evolutionary history of the sexes that culminated in our modern-world reality, in which liberated modern and postmodern women have gained equal rights and access to virtually every male domain (often without assuming equal responsibilities), while males have remained largely stuck in their traditional gender roles as disposable protectors and providers. We discussed the UN strategy of Gender Mainstreaming as a concept for the co-creation of a desirable future for humanity, between post-feminist/post-postmodern women and integrally informed men. This led us to the five core elements of the Integral Relationship Model: (1) sex/gender/polarities, (2) lines of development, (3) levels of development, (4) states of falling in love, and (5) personality types—which have been identified in the East and West as the essential facets of our human experience and growth potentials.

Part II – Men and Women Coming Together

In every age men have tried to assemble all the knowledge and experience of their day into a single whole which would explain their relation to the universe and their possibilities in it. In the ordinary way they could never succeed. For the unity of things is not realisable by the ordinary mind, in an ordinary state of consciousness. The ordinary mind, refracted by the countless and contradictory promptings of different sides of human nature, must reflect the world as manifold and confused as is man himself. A unity, a pattern, an all-embracing meaning—if it exists—could only be discerned or experienced by a different kind of mind, in a different state of consciousness. It would only be realisable by a mind which had itself become unified.
~ Rodney Collin ~

It is one thing to take a holistic approach and to consider all the essential elements of our human nature, but a totally different task to integrate those factors into a coherent model. This is what Ken Wilber elegantly accomplished with his Integral AQAL model of human growth and potentials.

In this part of the manual we will take Wilber's original ideas one step further to explore interpersonal dynamics between men and women on a physical, psychological, cultural, and social level (or body, mind, heart, and soul). We will:

(1) Look at the *Primary Fantasy* at different levels of consciousness
(2) Construct a *Personality Matrix* that integrates the developmental lines (consciousness, spiritual, sexual and anima/animus) personality types and the feminine/masculine polarities that we outlined in Part I
(3) Introduce the concept of *holons*, which clarifies how humans can be simultaneously whole in themselves and part of a relationship
(4) Add the missing "Q" element (the four quadrants) of Ken Wilber's original AQAL model that we omitted in Part I
(5) Construct several *Triangles of Love*
(6) Investigate differences in male and female growth in consciousness

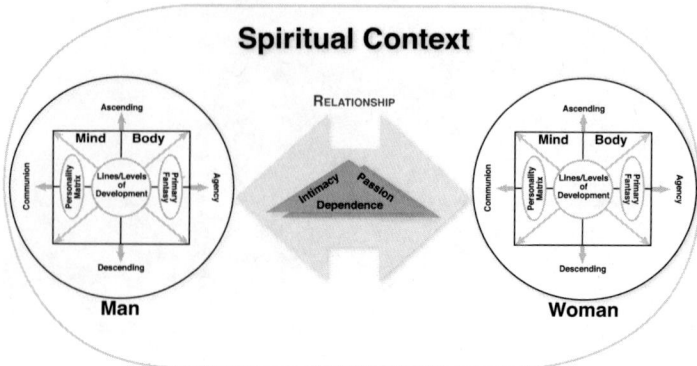

Figure 18: Integrating the Primary Fantasy and Personality Matrix through Triangles of Love

Chapter 7

Primary Fantasy and Personality

Women marry men, hoping that they will change. Men marry women, hoping they will not. So each is inevitably disappointed.
~ Albert Einstein ~

Men and women tend to fall in love with members of the opposite sex who meet their Primary Fantasy and have a charming personality. In this chapter we will explore how the attractiveness of men and women changes at different levels of consciousness development and what makes partners compatible in their psychological makeup.

Attractiveness at Different Levels of Consciousness

From your personal experiences in partnerships and observations of other couples, you have most likely seen that the most successful males have access to the sexually most attractive females and vice versa. Less desirable singles either settle for a partner with comparable social assets (looks/age, status/money), try to augment their socioeconomic status (males) or sexiness (females),[294] keep holding out for the off-chance to attract a partner who is "out of their league" (these relationships usually don't last very long), settle for uncommitted "friends with benefits" or "fuck-buddies" (where meeting each other's Primary Fantasy is not so important), or give up on finding a partner for a love relationship altogether.

The parameters that define male success in the eyes of females significantly increase in complexity with each level of her consciousness development, while the definition of sexiness that makes females attractive to males (a healthy body, sexual availability/radiance, and support of his vision) is consistent throughout human evolution, across cultures, and within vertical stage development of men.[295]

In the archaic infrared stage of consciousness development (1% of U.S. adult population), male success is defined by day-to-day survival skills. In females, a healthy sexy body that indicates fertility and sexual availability are seen as attractive.

In the superstitious magenta stage (10%), male success is defined by the ability to adapt to their immediate natural environment, cleverly exploit its resources, appease threatening ghosts or spirits through perceived magical powers, and loyalty to their family clan, band, or gang. In females, a healthy sexy body that indicates fertility, sexual availability, and healthy instincts are seen as attractive.

In the egocentric red stage (20%), male success is measured by their level of independence, confidence, aggressiveness, potency, creativity, and ability to cleverly exploit others for their own immediate gain. In females, a flashy sexy body, a high "fuckability" factor, and respect for his needs/attitude are seen as attractive.

In the conformist amber stage (40%), male success is measured by their level of reliability, job security, and devotion to family, religion, and country (the conservative, consistent, law-abiding husband). In females, a healthy sexy body, sexual willingness, elegance, and devotion to him are seen as attractive.

In the rational orange stage (25%), male success is defined by their levels of income,[296] future earning potentials,[297] overall net worth, displays of status symbols (e.g., Rolex watch, luxury car, designer clothes, penthouse apartment, or mansion—and lately some pseudo-environmental consciousness, for example driving a hybrid or electric car, or installing solar panels), social status, advanced degrees and titles, professional achievements, international travel experience, ambition, cleverness, wit, generosity, and physical fitness (the winner). In females, a healthy sexy body, being "sex-positive," physical fitness, classiness, and support of his mission are seen as attractive.

In the pluralistic green stage (10%), male success is evaluated by the amount of available time, level of passive income, accumulated wealth, altruism,[298] emotional availability, environmental awareness, natural health consciousness, worldliness, and sensitivity (the affluent, kind, semi-retired activist, philanthropist, healer, teacher, artist, etc.). In females, a naturally beautiful, healthy, sexually radiant body, and support for his vision are seen as attractive.

In the Integral teal and transpersonal turquoise stages (4%), male success is defined by increasing wisdom, ability to integrate all the healthy qualities from the previous stages (survival skills, natural instincts, power/creativity, devotion, financial success/status, and sensitivity), and embodiment of higher state-stages of spiritual realizations and ego transcendence. In females, a healthy sexy body, sexual shine, skills as a tantric lover, and ability to meet him as an opposite and equal at the level of all seven chakras in kind and degree are seen as attractive.

WOMEN MARRY UP

As we have seen above, the demands of females to have their Primary Fantasy fulfilled increases in complexity and financial cost with each higher stage of their consciousness development (from survival to protection, heroism, stability, material abundance, independent wealth, and integration of all the former qualities), while the desire of males for a healthy-looking, sexy, and sexually available female who supports him in his particular mission and purpose stays consistent as he evolves, and is rather narrowly defined (see Chapter 2).

As a consequence, we find most adults in the pre-conventional red and conventional amber stage in a partnership, while many modern orange and postmodern green women stay single, because it is harder for them to find suitable partners who meet their high standards. Red women tend to depend on the approval, protection, and support of men, and only leave their partner if they find a more successful protector. Women in amber usually stay with their husbands "for richer or poorer, in sickness and in health, for better or worse, till death does them part" … until they enter into the rational orange and/or animus complex stage four of their development and often leave. Because the different gender roles and feminine/masculine polarities in the pre-conventional and conventional stages are clearly assigned and divided between the sexes (males are masculine producers/protectors, females are feminine reproducers/caretakers), it is easy for women to fall in love and to choose a partner that they can "marry up to."

This changes dramatically for women who have entered the rational and pluralistic stages with an animus complex at level four. By definition, they have climbed the social ladder and become emotionally and financially independent from a partner through their own education and professional careers, "divorcing well" (70% of divorces are filed by women), and/or trust funds (the modern trust-fund baby). Having reached full gender equality with men in terms of rights (without the same responsibilities), and often exceeding their socioeconomic status, it becomes ever harder for these women to find the elusive Mr. Right ("where are all the good men?????") to "marry up to."[299] This is especially true for those who are older, overweight, out of shape, or otherwise physically unattractive.[300]

It is of course understandable and legitimate that healthy, intelligent, successful, and highly independent women don't want to become "a nurse and a purse" for older "loser men" who are typically interested in them. It simply leaves many former trophy wives and self-fulfilled career women without a steady partner after they successfully divorced their husbands, or were abandoned by them for a younger woman. Those who like to have sex (called "sex-positive") and who are still physically attractive may become "cougars"[301] who engage significantly younger men (who often can't attract/afford women at their own age or younger) as uncommitted lovers, fuck-buddies, and boy-toys.

This dynamic leads to an ever-increasing number of attractive single women who get "piled up" at the top of the social ladder, and less attractive "loser men" (such as divorced and child-support-paying fathers, failed business men, men in their midlife crisis, starving artists, lower- and middle-class workers/managers, socially/environmentally conscious dropouts, as well as the unemployed, disabled, ill, addicted, insecure, depressed, etc.) at the bottom.[302]

On the other hand, the assets of financially successful males (less than 5% of the population) tend to appreciate as they get older, while the primary assets of women (age/looks) inevitably depreciate.[303] Consequently, these highly desirable and sought-after men have no real incentive to become a "one-woman man" or to get married, especially if they have been burned financially and emotionally in previous relationships or have not dealt with unresolved psychological issues.[304]

These changes in the socioeconomic fabric have led to a sad reality for many modern and postmodern men and women who have a "flatland"[305] perspective, and objectify the opposite sex for their looks, wealth, and social status.

The following diagram illustrates this dynamic: On the horizontal X axis you find the increasing attractiveness of men based on their income/wealth and that of women based on their sexual desirability. On the vertical Y axis you find the number of males and females. While the U.S. median income in 2006 for people age 25 and older was $32,140 (with only 5.2% making more than $75K),[306] most attractive women (of which there is a high number) desire men who make $75K-150K or more. This leads to the dynamic that many man with average incomes (see the bump in the center of the graphic) look at sexually attractive women (see the bump in the right side of the graphic) whom they can't afford, while these women look for men with high incomes, who are few and far between. As a consequence we see an increasing number of frustrated single men and women.

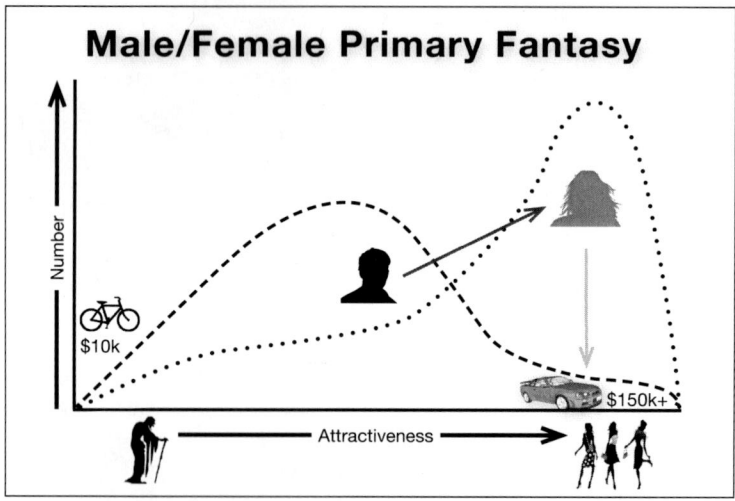

Figure 19: Divergence in male/female Primary Fantasy

There is one more (widely unacknowledged) twist to this new social dynamic: the professional medical community and public health organizations urge people to maintain a healthy body mass index (BMI)[307] and to stay physically fit through regular exercise (at least thirty minutes daily).[308] Women who follow these guidelines become—as a side effect—sexually more attractive to men. On the other hand, we slowly come to realize that, as Rabbi Michael Lerner has observed, "the unrestrained pursuit of money and power lead to huge ethical distortions for human life, and the destruction for our ecosystem and society."[309] Ergo, the Primary Fantasy of males (unless taken to rare extremes, such as men longing for significantly underweight women with enlarged breasts) has positive effects for the health and well-being of females, while the Primary Fantasy of most women (if taken to the unsustainable levels that have become the norm in modern societies of the twentieth and twenty-first centuries, especially in the U.S.) has become a liability for all humanity and our ecosystem.[310] This is quite a dilemma, as men have little choice but to be attracted to healthy sexy women, who are naturally highly demanding, and women have little choice but to desire financially successful, competitive, and powerful males whose actions are often socially and environmentally irresponsible.

One possible solution to this dilemma would be that more men start to live responsible single lives than to compete with other males for the admiration, love, sex, and company of physically and mentally healthy women. The less likely alternative would be that women start to reward men who pursue an environmentally sustainable and non-violent existence through downsizing their lifestyle and through cooperation instead of competition. "What a wonderful world this would be"…at least for us men and our environment.

Personality Matrix

The relationship dynamic that develops between partners beyond the fulfillment of the individuals' Primary Fantasy is determined by their personalities. Of special relevance are the eight levels of consciousness (from archaic to transpersonal), the feminine/masculine polarities, the five state-stages of spiritual, sexual,* and anima/animus complex development, as well as the various personality types, all of which we covered in Part I of the manual.

To better grasp how these multiple dimensions interconnect and affect the quality and sustainability of a partnership beyond the love-struck phase, we will weave them together in a Personality Matrix[311]. We'll place the eight stages of consciousness development on a vertical axis. Next to it are two vertical lines, showing the most common tendencies of the feminine and masculine polarities for men and women as they grow in consciousness. Then we'll map the spiritual, sexual,† and anima/animus complex lines onto a horizontal axis, since these aspects can develop independently from each other at each level of consciousness. This gives you 1,000 different correlates (8 x 5 x 5 x 5) for the fluid feminine/masculine polarities and personality types of every person (deep breath now). Using this matrix allows you to identify compatibilities and differences between you and your partner, and provides you with directions towards future growth potentials.

You may, for example, be a pluralistic (green), feminine, kinesthetic, Enneagram type seven man at stage three of your spiritual, stage two of your sexual, and stage four of your anima complex development, who is in a partnership with a rational (orange), masculine, visual, Enneagram type three woman at stage four of her sexual, stage one of her spiritual, and stage five of her animus complex development. In the future, you may both remain at your vertical level of consciousness or grow further, become more masculine or feminine, or evolve along some or all of the three horizontal lines (or not).

---

* In this context, sexual development refers to the interior awareness and emotional health which determine a person's sexuality, and not the physiological development of the sex organs and release of sex hormones (e.g., testosterone).

† The spiritual and sexual levels can be experienced as temporary states or permanent stages.

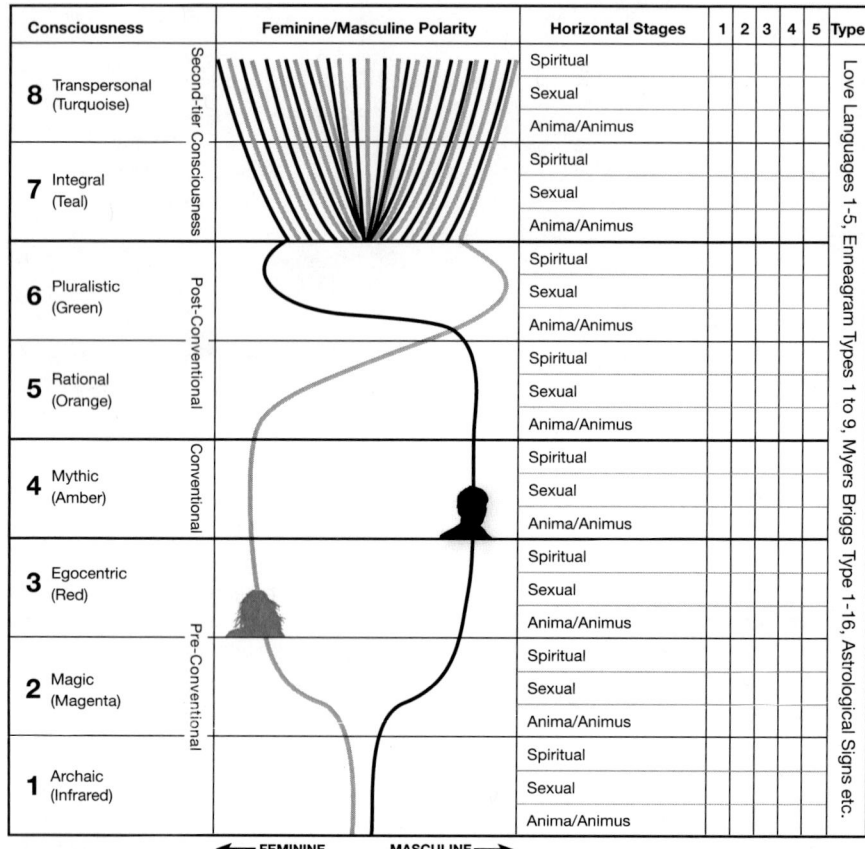

Figure 20: The Personality Matrix—allowing you to map your and her development

Couples with similar lifestyle choices, interests, intelligences, and passions, who are at the same level of their consciousness, spiritual, sexual, and anima/animus complex development, with opposite feminine/masculine polarities and complementary personality types experience the most fulfilling long-term partnerships. These compatibilities allow them to enjoy their sexual attraction and synergy, and to resolve conflicts by the same means (see Chapter 12 under Conflict Resolution and Forgiveness) until they grow apart in their developmental lines or lose their opposite sexual polarities.

Partners with minor differences in their horizontal stage development may be able to get along and support each other in their growth, while couples with larger discrepancies will experience conflicts that are irresolvable[312] once the initial hormonal rush that impaired their rational perception and made them look at each other through rose-colored glasses wears off, and the day-to-day reality of life sinks in.

THE POLARITIES (FEMININE/MASCULINE DYNAMIC) ALONG THE WAY

As males and females grow in consciousness, their feminine/masculine polarity attributes tend to shift.[313] The two curved lines in the Personality Matrix that are next to the eight vertical stages of consciousness development show this dynamic. Both males and females start out relatively undifferentiated in their polarity in the two earliest stages of development. In the egocentric red and conformist amber stages, males display predominantly masculine, and females predominantly feminine qualities, hence the origin of the terms.

The opposite polarities are neutralized in the rational orange stage when females swing towards the masculine side and become androgynous[314]—often being communal and ascending, or agentic and descending—while most males further strengthen their masculine capacities. As a result, the energetic flow that created sexual attraction and synergy between males and females in earlier stages vanishes[315] and many relationships start to struggle and fall apart in the orange stage where the clearly divided gender roles that are found in red and amber get blurred and females become economically (through their own career and/or "divorcing well" from a financially successful husband) and emotionally (through personal growth work, therapy, a spiritual practice, or a shift in their hormonal balance) independent from men.[316]

In the green pluralistic stage, males and females start to connect more deeply with the interior qualities that they had denied in themselves in earlier stages of development. For males this often means fully embracing their anima—with a swing over to their feminine side—while females tend to transcend their animus complex and fully embrace their masculinity.[317] Green men are perceived to be in their midlife crisis or Sensitive New Age Guys (SNAGs) when they get in touch with their feelings, pursue a spiritual or altruistic path,[318] and lose their drive to be aggressive providers and protectors (often accompanied or caused by lowered levels of testosterone).[319] At the same time, financially and emotionally independent green women strengthen their masculine qualities and embrace radical (or eco-) feminist ideals,[320] which claim female superiority over men, and blame hierarchical patriarchal structures for all the problems in the world, such as wars, pollution, poverty, oppression of minorities, abuse of women and children, etc.

Other women in this stage muse how they can establish an authentic female spirituality and shape a better future for humanity and the world by asserting their feminine power (a contradiction in terms if seen from an Integral perspective) independent of men.[321] This forces many abandoned and confused green males to lick their wounds in men's groups of the male liberation movement or in New Age and Eastern-oriented spiritual communities. This role reversal is very confusing and makes healthy and nurturing love relationships between the sexes in green almost impossible as the socially accepted gender roles are reversed, while the underlying biological makeup and Primary Fantasy that create the sexual polarity/attraction remain intact. Green men are still sexually attracted to healthy feminine women, while green women can't help but be drawn to successful males with a strong masculine streak (which often leads both of them back to "bad boy/girl" red partners ... see Chapter 4 under pre/post fallacy).

In the second-tier Integral teal stage, both sexes become aware of the benefits that healthy ascending, descending, agency, and communion play in their lives and balance and harmonize them along the first-tier stages that they have transcended. They can now consciously embody their feminine or masculine polarities as the life-situations at hand require, and are able to co-create synergy with an equal and opposite partner.

The transpersonal turquoise stage heralds the return to the authentic embodiment of one's sexual essence, but this time with a conscious recognition, honoring, valuing, appreciation, and enjoyment of opposite polarities in other human beings. At last, men and women can comfortably relax into and embrace all the healthy facets of their authentic masculine and feminine expression from moment to moment. This allows them to effortlessly engage with each other without elevating their own way of being over that of their mate, forcing their way onto the other, or being offended by their differences.

Integrating the Spiritual, Sexual, and Anima/Animus Complex

Located to the right of the two vertical lines of the feminine and masculine polarities on the Personality Matrix are three rows with the five stages of spiritual, sexual, and anima/animus complex development that we explored in Part I of the manual. They are arranged separately on a horizontal axis for each of the vertical stages for three reasons: (1) they can develop independently at each level of consciousness and are then interpreted from that altitude,[322] (2) they can be experienced as temporary states that may or may not be developed into a state-stage, and (3) their development can be interrelated.[323] This indicates that (1) every human being has the potential to reach higher levels of their spiritual, sexual, or anima/animus complex development at every vertical stage of consciousness, (2) the experiences at each level can be a temporary state or—through tantra, meditation, and/or psychotherapy—be transformed into permanently accessible state-stages, and (3) the three lines are interrelated, since a peak experience or stage development in any one of them can positively affect the others.[324]

For example:

A modern magenta male shaman may be fully present in his body (spiritual stage 1), while being in sexual tantric union with a woman (sexual state-stage 5), and fully accept her as an equal and opposite human being (anima complex stage 5). He may then interpret his experience as a magical spirit flowing through him to the woman and being reflected back from her.

An amber male priest who conforms to the mythic laws of the Bible may have had a mystical experience (spiritual state-stage 4) of Christ consciousness, see women as sex objects (anima stage 2), and, while on a vacation in Thailand, fuck several prostitutes (sexual state-stage 2). He may see his spiritual experience as grace from God, treat women as inferior to men whom they should obey, and curse his sexual addiction, which he can't control, as a Satanic affliction.

An orange female biology teacher who has never had any spiritual experiences (spiritual stage 0) may enjoy various "boy-toys" as sex partners (sexual state-stage 3), and see men as being as equally independent as she is (anima complex stage 4). She may reject any spiritual notion as irrational, enjoy sex as a pleasurable and healthy physical activity, and value men as competent colleagues but not as romantic life partners.

INTEGRATING STATES AND TYPES

The final two elements of the Integral Relationship Model, temporary states such as falling in love, and the consistent personality types, are located at the very right side of the Personality Matrix. States represent the fleeting experiences that are observed by the subject and interpreted from his or her level of consciousness. In the context of this manual we focused especially on the states of falling in and out of love, while other common examples include the waking, dreaming, and dreamless states, drug-induced euphoria, meditative states, and peak experiences.

Personality types such as the Five Love Languages and Enneagram remain consistent throughout stage development and vary only in the way they are expressed and how an individual identifies with them.

IN SUMMARY

In this chapter we established that increasing levels of social status for men provide them access to sexier (younger/healthier) women (and vice versa), and that most women (especially in first-tier consciousness) want to marry up. The quality of a partnership between two individuals who fulfill each other's Primary Fantasy and fall in love is determined by their individual stage of vertical consciousness, and the five levels of their horizontal spiritual, sexual, and anima/animus complex development. By integrating these elements (8 x 5 x 5 x 5) we arrived at a Personality Matrix with 1000 possible combinations for the feminine and masculine polarities, and the various states and types for each partner.

Chapter 8

Our Drive to Connect

A hundred times every day I remind myself that my inner and outer life are based on the labors of other men, living and dead.
~ Albert Einstein ~

At one point or another, lovers may ask themselves how they can be simultaneously part of a partnership and maintain individual wholeness. Lovers may also wonder how they can balance and harmonize physical and emotional/spiritual attraction to a partner in a healthy way. The answer can be found in the concept of holons and the four quadrants that are part of Ken Wilber's original AQAL model.[325]

Holons, Always Partial, Already Whole

In Ken Wilber's Integral Model, a holon[326] is a whole that is simultaneously a part of a larger whole, while being made up of parts that are whole in themselves.

An example is right in front of you: take a closer look; whole **words** that contain whole **l e t t e r s** make up whole sentences, which are parts of whole paragraphs, etc. Or whole atoms are parts of whole molecules, which are parts of whole cells, which are parts of whole organs, which are parts of whole humans, which are parts of whole couples, which are parts of whole families, communities, societies, nations. Letters > words > sentences > paragraphs >; ... atoms > molecules > cells > organs > humans > couples > families > communities … all are holons.

These groups of related holons, or *holonic structures*, lead to natural growth *hierarchies*[327] (often called *holarchies*) in which the higher levels are always more inclusive and therefore have more depth. At the same time, the higher level requires the presence of the lower; otherwise it will cease to exist. Therefore, the lower level is always larger in numbers and has "more span." For example, there are more letters than words in this manual, and more individual humans than couples in the world.

The higher level depends on two factors for its existence: to maintain its wholeness (such as a marriage) AND the presence of the lower (such as the individual spouses). Otherwise it will eventually disintegrate into its parts and disappear. A cell can exist without organisms, but not without molecules; sentences can exist without a paragraph but not without words; partnerships can exist without communities but not without individuals.

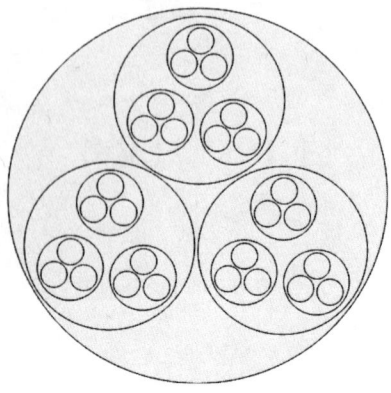

Each circle represents a holon
Figure 21: Example showing nested holons

By definition, holons always have their unique characteristics and can't be reduced to the sum of their parts.[328] For example, an organism is more than just the sum of its cells, it has its own unique structure and function; a word is more than the sum of its letters, it has its own meaning; a partnership is more than the sum of two individuals, it creates its own dynamics, values, and experiences (think of your two hands working together, or two people having sex.)

Ken Wilber's Integral Model specifies four different types of holons:

(1) Individual holons (everything that is conscious and has its own volition (choice/will) or experience, such as cells, dogs, or humans).

(2) Social holons (groups of individual holons, such as flocks of geese, male-female partnerships, families, or communities).

(3) Artifacts (objects created by individual holons, such as paintings, books, cars, or houses).

(4) Heaps (structures created by nature, such as sand dunes or a pile of leaves).[329]

For our Integral Relationship Model we will now focus on individual and social holons.

Characteristics of Individual Holons

In the following paragraphs we will discuss three unique characteristics that are exclusive to individual holons and of relevance for the formation of social holons as love relationships:

1. Individual holons have a single governing force (dominant monad).
2. Individual holons have an interior/exterior and individual/collective dimension (which we will diagram as four quadrants).
3. Individual holons have four drives (related to the masculine/feminine polarities that we discussed in Chapter 2).

Who's in Charge?

The first unique quality of individual holons is their independent will or consciousness that acts as a single governing force which all its constituent parts (holons) have to follow. In Wilber's language, this single governing force is called a dominant monad. If you, as the dominant monad of an individual holon that is a single organism, decide to walk across the room to talk to a woman, all of your constituent parts, such as organs, tissues, cells, molecules, and atoms, have to follow—no exceptions. The three other forms of holons (social, artifacts, and heaps) do not have a *dominant monad* (see below under "social holon").

The Four Quadrants

Individual holons have four distinct dimensions that are intrinsic to the holon's existence:[330]

(1) An individual **interior** subjective/experiential "I" or mind.
(2) An individual **exterior** objective/material "it" or form/body.
(3) A collective **interior** intersubjective "we" or shared values/culture.
(4) A collective **exterior** inter-objective "its" social environment.[331]

For easy reference, the AQAL model diagrams these four dimensions as four quadrants that are labeled:

(1) Upper Left (UL) "**I**"
(2) Upper Right (UR) "**It**"
(3) Lower Left (LL) "**We**"
(4) Lower Right (LR) "**Its**"

UL "I"	UR "it"
Subjective	Objective
Individual	Individual
Interior	Exterior
LL "we"	LR "its"
Cultural	Social Collective
Collective	Exterior
Interior	

Figure 22: The four quadrants of individual holons

In other words, the four quadrants represent your individual consciousness in the upper left, and physical body in the upper right-hand quadrant, and how these two dimensions are extended and connected to the world around you in the lower quadrants.

You—being an individual holon—can experience these four dimensions right now:[332]

(1) The Upper Left (UL) quadrant represents your subjective individual interior "I" dimension. You experience this dimension when you focus your attention inward and ask yourself, "what is alive in me right now?" It includes the full spectrum of your awareness,

from sensations, to feelings, thoughts, dreams, intentions, intuitions, perceptions, and sense of beauty. The levels of consciousness development, spiritual state-stages, and personality types that we explored in Part I are located in this quadrant. Introspection, psychotherapy, cognitive development, and meditation are UL practices.

(2) The Upper Right (UR) quadrant represents your objective individual exterior, physical "it" dimension that can be observed by you or anyone else. It includes your sex, skin, muscles, cells, hormones, enzymes, brain structures, smell, voice, height, size, etc. Differences in male and female bodies, such as their gender characteristics (breasts, penis, vagina, body hair, etc.), hormonal levels (testosterone, estrogen, etc.), and genetic makeup (X and Y chromosomes, etc.), are located in the Upper Right. Behaviors such as physical exercise, body language, and emotional outbursts fall into the UR quadrant.

(3) The Lower Left (LL) quadrant represents your collective interior (cultural) "we" dimension. You experience this dimension when you focus your attention outward and ask yourself, "how do I relate to others and how do they affect my awareness?" This includes everything that you have learned through your culture, such as language, religious beliefs, worldviews, moral values, commitments, humility, empathy, compassion, devotion, and faith. Your way of creating mutual understanding with others, intimacy (which we can rewrite as "into-me-you-see," emphasizing the interpersonal nature of intimacy),[333] and vulnerability, as well as the lines of moral, communicative, worldview, value, and anima/animus complex development, are located in this quadrant. Communication and management training, couples therapy, conflict resolution, mediation, petitionary prayer, and religious beliefs fall into the LL quadrant.[334]

(4) The Lower Right (LR) quadrant represents your collective exterior (social) "its" dimension. You experience this dimension when you focus your attention on the physical world around you and ask yourself, "what is the social, economic, and ecological environment that sustains my body?" This includes the air that you breathe, the food that you eat, shelter, possessions, occupation, financial assets/liabilities, social status, physical relationships, family, friends, and community. How a woman evaluates you as a protector/provider, and how you are seen by others with her on your arm are located in this quadrant. Family relations, social activities, educational systems, community building, team sports, money management, relationship laws (such as legal marriage and divorce), and acceptable conduct between men and women (such as sexual harassment, who buys the diamond ring, who pursues and takes the risk of rejection, etc.) fall into the LR.

	Interior	Exterior	
	UL "I": Individual interior. Intentions, consciousness, awareness, states, types, cognition, feelings, volition, feminine/ masculine.	(UR) "it": Individual exterior. Behavior, physical appearance, sex, biological and genetic makeup, brain-chemistry, hormones, body-language.	Individual
	LL "we": Collective interior/ culture. Language, worldviews, values, religion, morals, communication, devotion, trust, humility, anima/animus complex.	(LR) "its": Collective exterior/ social. Work, economic and legal systems, clothing, material assets, ecology, gender roles.	Collective

Figure 23: Characteristics of each quadrant

You may already see how these four dimensions are essential for partnerships in which two individual (UL) "I's," with two (UR) "it" bodies, experience a (LL) "we" mutual understanding/resonance (or misunderstanding/dissonance), that is embedded in their (LR) "its" social structure.

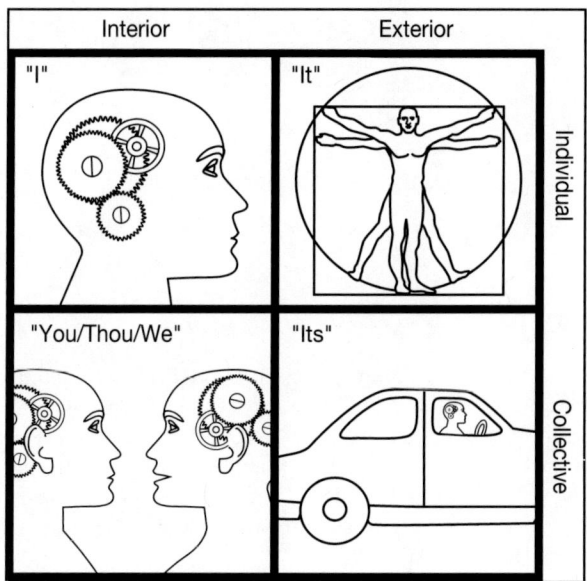

Figure 24: The four quadrants applied to individual holons

If you ignore or marginalize any of these four dimensions, you get a distorted perspective of your inner and outer world, your relationships, and your social environment.

Development Inside the Quadrants

Each of the developmental lines that we outlined in Chapter 3 can be placed into one of the four quadrants—for humans, the stages of consciousness development in the UL, increasing complexity of their physical body and brain in the UR, emergence of cultures and worldviews in the LL, and advancements of social structures in the LR. These lines co-emerge (which Wilber calls *tetra arise*) in all four quadrants simultaneously. For example, consciousness at the rational level (UL) requires a neocortex (UR) to produce a scientific worldview (LL), which leads to an industrial society (LR).[335]

Figure 25: Every human possess four quadrants

THE FOUR DRIVES OF INDIVIDUAL HOLONS

The third unique characteristic of an individual holon that is paramount for partnerships is the four drives that moderate its ability to be simultaneously a whole and a part.[336] In humans, these four drives are closely related to the feminine and masculine polarities that we outlined in Part I, Chapter 2. We named them ascending and descending (displayed on a vertical axis), and agency and communion (displayed on a horizontal axis). We will simply stick with this terminology. Again, you as an individual holon can feel these four drives right now.

Ascending (self-transcendence) is your drive towards the higher, the creation of larger holons, bigger and more complex ideas/concepts, the greater good, and to reach beyond the limited self.[337] This drive is the creative love that reaches up (Eros). Examples include the forming of a partnership/marriage, creation of a family, and founding of organizations, teams, groups, businesses, communities, nations, etc. This drive represents the capacity for creativity, integration, presence, vision, and to see the larger picture. If you resist this drive, your life will be without purpose. In its unhealthy form, the ascending drive will neglect the needs of the individual holons that make up the larger whole.

Descending (self-immanence) is your drive towards the lower, to embrace and to care for the parts/members that make up the larger whole. This drive is the selfless, altruistic, and caring love that reaches down (Agape). Examples include concerns for the health and well-being of your body, spouse, and individual members of your family, team, group, or community. This drive represents the capacity to show compassion, to feel, accept, allow, and to surrender. Resisting this drive will lead to burnout, illness, depletion, emptiness, and loss of support from the base. In its unhealthy form, the descending drive will lead to the dissolution, decomposition, or deconstruction of the larger whole by losing sight of the greater good.

Agency (self-preservation) is your drive to stay whole, complete, independent, and separate—the autonomous functioning of the holon. Examples are maintaining and protecting the integrity and functionality of yourself and your family, group, team, or organization. This drive represents the capacity for autonomy, self-reliance, and free will, and to act and exert power. If you resist this drive, you will become invaded, taken over, fused, attached, or dependent. In its unhealthy form, agency leads to conflict, isolation, alienation, and loneliness.

Communion (self-adaptation) is your drive to act in partnership with others—to connect, join, communicate, participate, fit in, consider, take responsibility, compromise, and cooperate. This drive represents the capacity for understanding, empathy, linking, and openness. If you resist this drive, you will become alienated, isolated, and cut off from others. In its unhealthy form, communion will lead to dependence, fusion, and loss of independent functioning, and free will.

Differentiating the Four Drives

It can be challenging to clearly differentiate ascending/agency and descending/communion, as they may sound and feel similar. One way to do so is to realize that every individual or social holon, once created through ascending, needs to balance healthy agency and communion, and embrace its members through descending in order to exist and survive over time.

We need to take care of our cells and organs to maintain our body (descending), otherwise we will get ill and may even die/decompose into molecules, atoms, quarks, strings…all the way down. We also need the emotional and material support of others (communion) to survive, while maintaining our autonomy as individual beings (agency), and creating partnerships and communities (ascending) to sustain the human race.

An extreme example of unhealthy development of the four drives is Hitler's Nazi Germany which initially succeeded at ascending (creating a large, unified "us") and agency (isolating itself and fighting the rest of the world), but failed miserably at descending (caring for its individual members – including six million German Jews and other fringe groups who were brutally murdered in concentration camps), and communion (cooperating with its neighbors). This endeavor, as history has shown, not only caused unimaginable harm to millions, but collapsed as a whole within a short period of time.[338]

But we don't need to go back that far to see dysfunction in social holons. A look at most relationships, the high divorce rates, the increasing number of singles who are unable to form healthy partnerships and families, the pollution of our environment, and many other social, economic, ecological, and humanitarian problems that our species is facing, provides enough evidence for the imbalance of the four drives. Clearly, we need to learn to balance and harmonize all four capacities in their healthy expression from the lowest (our bodies and ecosystem), to the highest (the whole of humanity and all creation)—and everything in between (our partnerships, families, communities, nations, etc.)—to lead our planet and all its inhabitants into a better future.

Interior/Exterior Conflicts

Sometimes, conflicts between the four drives in our interior and exterior world arise. For example, you may be physically attracted to a woman and would like to have sex with her (exterior communion), but you sense an inner fear of rejection or are afraid to lose your autonomy and instead withdraw into your shell and meditate (interior agency). Integrity is when you align your intentions (values/beliefs) with your behavior in the face of opposition.

To address potential conflicts between your interior and exterior, and to make sense of love relationships, we will consider the four drives separately in the left-hand "I/we" and right-hand "it/its" quadrants.*

This gives us eight combinations that you can experience right now:

Interior

Your interior is ascending if it is directed towards creative thinking/mindfulness, seeing the bigger picture, experiencing God above, stillness, emptiness, and presence.

Your interior is descending if it is directed towards feelings, wandering thoughts, sensing, self-love, embracing the lower, compassion, fullness, and surrender.

Your interior is agentic if it is directed towards keeping your thoughts and feelings to yourself, and to deal with problems alone (introverted). As many relationship books indicate, most men prefer to go into their cave when they experience stress (watching TV, working alone on a project, meditating, going on a solo hike, etc.).

Your interior is communal if it is directed towards sharing your thoughts and feelings with others (extroverted) and showing empathy. As we know from experience, most women prefer to deal with their problems by sharing them with others, without expecting any constructive feedback or needing to be fixed.

Exterior

Your exterior is ascending when it is directed away from the body with its lower impulses, fears, needs, and desires through repression/dissociation or self-discipline and control.

Your exterior is descending if it is directed towards embracing your body, to surrender to its impulses (indulge/allow), to have compassion (suffer with), to be passive and to adapt.

Your exterior is agentic if it is directed towards being alone, physically distancing yourself from others, not touching or wanting to be touched.

Your exterior is communal if it is directed towards being in the company of others, physical closeness, touching others, and being touched.[339]

---

* This is a variation onto the standard AQAL model which applies the four drives equally to all four quadrants.

Examples

You may, for example, want to have sex with your partner (exterior-communion), do her (exterior-ascending), or be done by her (exterior-descending), feel an inner space and emptiness (interior-ascending), or emotional charge (interior-descending), and want to be silent/have no eye contact (interior-agency) while fucking her from behind (exterior-agency), or want to talk/make eye contact while facing her during your lovemaking (interior-communion).

Alternatively, you may want to be alone (exterior-agency), fast (exterior-ascending), or eat a delicious five-course meal (exterior-descending), daydream about a lost love (interior-descending), or think about a creative dating profile (interior-ascending), write your thoughts into a personal journal (interior-agency), or post them on a public Internet blog (interior-communion).

SOCIAL HOLONS

Individual holons (such as humans) that group together are called social holons. Typical examples include couples, families, communities, groups, work-teams, organizations, and nations.[340] **Unlike the constituent parts of individual holons that are governed by a single dominant monad, social holons have members who share a mutual resonance at the level of their body, mind, heart, and soul, on a conscious and unconscious level.** They are usually free to join or leave the group at will, getting married or divorced, taking a job or quitting, becoming a member of or resigning from a team or association, or moving from one community/country to another.[341] Since social holons have no singular mind/consciousness or physical body, they also–by definition–**don't have four quadrants.**[342]

However, most social holons have hierarchies with a dominant power structure (or "pecking order") that direct and hold them together. We find these structures in corporations, politics, military, sports, churches, families, and partnerships. They are formed through a dominant mode of resonance (versus a dominant monad) and shared mode of discourse that is usually necessary and beneficial to create a functional unit, such as a partnership, family, group, business, organization, or society. These hierarchies serve very real needs for expedience/effectiveness/efficiency (corporate world), survival/protection (military), awakening/realization (religious/spiritual community), learning/maturing (school/family), maintenance of social order/justice (politics/law enforcement), or recreational/fitness activities (groups/games/sports). Individuals who are not willing or able to fit into such hierarchical group structures may be marginalized, denied access, or be asked to leave.

Hierarchical structures become problematic if individuals at higher or more powerful levels wield unjustified control over people at the lower levels, instead of caring for them. Unfortunately we see this all around us, including in love relationships. An integrally informed man is aware of the difference between abusive dominator and natural growth hierarchies, and sensitive to where his (or her, for that matter) vision, direction, leadership, and power are desired and necessary to maintain the wholeness of a social holon (partnership, organization, nation, etc.), and when his or her actions start to oppress, manipulate, coerce, dominate, or take unjustified advantage of others. Simply put, we need to make our relationships the highest priority in order to maintain their wholeness while caring for and maintaining the health of the individuals (parts) that comprise them–and this is best practiced in an intimate committed love relationship with a woman.[343]

BALANCE AND HARMONIZE

To maintain their individual wholeness and partialness in a co-created healthy love relationship, both partners need to balance and harmonize the healthy forms of the four drives in their interior and exterior quadrants in an opposite and equal fashion. This creates attraction and synergy through an energy flow (think of a magnet, battery, or sex), and harmonizes the couple's giving and receiving through a shared resonance and mode of discourse between them. Otherwise the couple will experience an inner and outer stagnation or conflict.

Partner dancing with a leader (ascending) and follower (descending) that allows a couple to move in (communion) and out (agency) of embrace in a fluid way may serve as a simple example for the dynamic in the exterior.

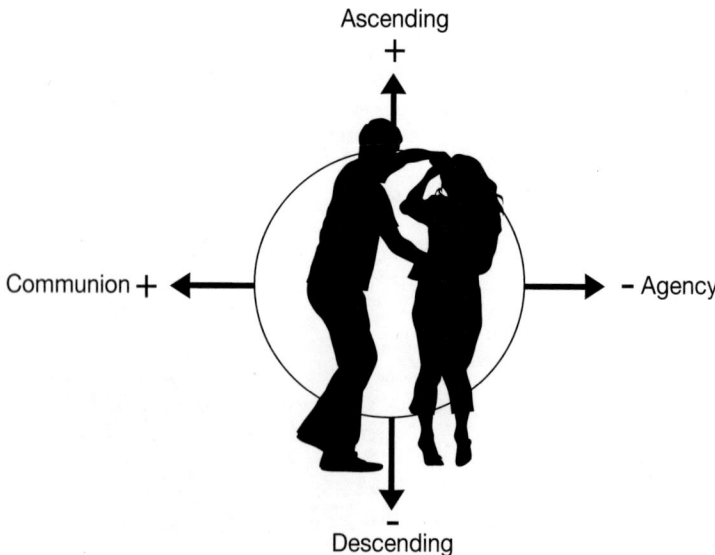

Figure 26: Example of dancing couple and the four polarities

Dance partners may share (interior) thoughts and feelings in a conversation (communion) with one of them speaking (ascending) and the other listening (descending), or remain both silent (agency).

If neither partner leads nor follows, they will be static or stumble over each other. If they don't flow in and out of embrace, they will either suffocate each other or drift apart. If neither of them talks, they might as well be mechanical puppets or zombies. If they both incessantly talk all the time with no one listening, they are like two radios playing without a listener or an Off button.

An integrally informed man will work towards harmonizing his interior and exterior vision (ascending) for his partnership/marriage by considering his own needs and the needs of his spouse (descending).[344] He will also balance his interior and exterior needs for autonomy (agency) with his and her desire for deep harmonious intimacy, closeness, and connection (communion).

Without this balance, two extremely agentic people will have a hard time coming together; extremely communal partners will become fused and codependent; two ascenders will rarely connect on a deeper emotional/sexual level and their separate visions may constantly collide (unless they have a shared vision, which is desirable); and two descenders may get lost in the morass of their emotions and details of their life.

Opposites Versus Equals

In pre-conventional magenta or red, and conventional amber relationships, we often see couples that are opposites but not equals.[345] They share opposite polarities/drives which attract and make them compatible, but are not equals, as the ascending/agentic partner (often, but not always the male) holds the economic, physical, intellectual, and emotional power (often through anger or repression of feelings), while the descending/communal partner tends to be financially and emotionally dependent and cares for the members of the family (partner/children/aging parents).

These relationships begin to fall apart in the modern orange stage of development when women start to gravitate towards the masculine polarities (ascending/agency), claim their authority, and pursue their financial and emotional independence from men. Since men retain their masculinity in orange, the sexes become *equals* but are no longer *opposites* that synergize and attract.[346]

Things get even more confusing in the postmodern green stage of development, when men embark on an inner journey of self-discovery and get in touch with their feminine side (anima), while women fully embrace their masculinity (animus). The sexes are then *equals* and *opposites* but with a complete role reversal in which emancipated women neither want to care emotionally or financially for "sensitive New Age loser men," nor engage with insensitive orange workaholics, or conservative amber patriarchs, while green men find women at this level to be insensitive to their needs (neediness) and emasculating.

In post-postmodern integrally informed relationships, both partners become fully aware of, and integrate the feminine-masculine dynamic. They become opposites AND equals by relaxing into their sexual essence while embracing the opposite feminine and masculine polarities in a conscious, balanced, and harmonized way, as the situation or mood warrants. This way, they co-create synergy between them, keep their sexual passion/attraction alive, and allow each other to express their male or femaleness in a natural and healthy way, without feeling limited, manipulated, oppressed, victimized, or used by the opposite sex.

READY OR NOT?

You may find some deeper answers about your ability to balance and harmonize the four quadrants and drives in a healthy partnership by answering the four questions below:[347]

What are your desires/needs to be in a partnership? **(ascending)**	What are your desires/needs to be alone? **(agency)**
What are your concerns/fears of being in a partnership? **(descending)**	What are your concerns/fears of being alone? **(communion)**

Table 6: Fear and desire to be in partnership or alone

If little or no specific needs and fears come up for you in any of these four areas, and if your answers seem to express reasonable concerns and healthy desires, then you possess the best prerequisites to co-create a healthy partnership. If your answers indicate imbalances, neediness, or fears, then you may want to address those issues first before seeking and engaging with a partner.[348]

In Summary

Congratulations! You made it through the most abstract and technical (but hopefully not boring!) chapter of the manual in which we established that humans are individual holons who are simultaneously whole and partial in their relationships. They possess individual and collective interior and exterior dimensions which we placed into four quadrants for ease of reference. We looked at the four drives that mediate the individual holon's capacity to be whole in itself and part of a social holon, and explored opposite versus equal relationship dynamics in pre-conventional, conventional, post-conventional, and integrally informed partnerships.

Chapter 9

Passion/Intimacy/Dependence

In the arithmetic of love, one plus one equals everything, and two minus one equals nothing.
~ Mignon McLaughlin ~

Even though love is experienced by the individual in the upper left "I" and upper right "it" quadrants, the actual love relationship is created through the lower "we" and "its" quadrants, plus an unconscious dimension.

In this chapter, we will look at the resulting three core elements of love relationships: *LL intimacy, LR passion* **and** *unconscious dependence*. By drawing the levels for each of these core elements as lines, we can combine them into differently shaped metaphorical triangles. These triangles are indicative of eight forms of love that we will discuss in detail below. Understanding the shape and congruency of the triangles will allow you to understand the type and quality of love that you and your partner experience.

The Three Sides of the Triangle

The length of the triangle's left side represents the level of intimacy that individuals experience with another person through their lower left-hand **"we"** quadrant (language, values, worldviews, interests, etc.). They may say "we understand each other," "we click," "we resonate with each other," "we share the same values," "we see the world in the same way," or "we are best friends."

The length of the triangle's right side represents the level of passion that individuals experience through their lower right-hand **"its"** quadrant towards members of the opposite sex who meet their primary sexual fantasy (looks, status, etc.). If the attraction is mutual between two lovers, they may say "we have a lot of chemistry," "we are physically attracted to each other," "we can't keep our hands off each other," "we have great sex," "we have fun together," "we like to do things together," or "we are a great team."

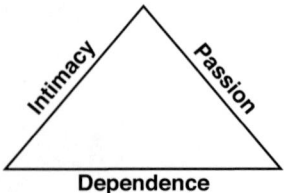

Figure 27: The passion/intimacy/dependence Triangle

The length of the triangle's bottom represents the various levels of dependence that individuals may experience in a partnership through their unconscious (in second-tier couples, which are extremely rare, dependence increasingly becomes an act of choice and will, instead of an unconscious attachment). They may say "we complete/complement each other," "we can't live without each other," "we push each other's buttons," "we fight a lot," or "we are soul mates/twin flames/worthy opponents." The unconscious dimension of love relationships is always experienced as mysterious, miraculous, or magical, as the "love-struck" couple has no rational explanation for their magnetic push/pull.

Figure 28: Examples of differently shaped triangles of love

To better understand the mysterious dimensions of love that affect all three sides of the triangle, and especially the lower part of dependence, we will first take a look at the unconscious and the role that it plays in our attraction to certain members of the opposite sex. After this journey into the underworld of our psyche, we will combine the three core elements of love into eight forms of love.

The Unconscious

We all carry a psychological blueprint that holds the details and lingering imprints of our heritage and life experiences. The unacknowledged/unconscious parts of that blueprint contain the information that drives our irrational fears, anxieties, coping mechanisms, and defenses, as well as our creativity, dreams, and passions. And just as the conscious aspects of our interior and exterior dimensions have opposing feminine and masculine polarities that complement and attract each other, so do the unconscious parts.

There are five major components of the unconscious[349] that are of relevance for the mysterious magnetism or aversion that lovers experience on the level of their bodies, minds, and hearts:

(1) The **ground unconscious** represents our unrealized embedded potentials. All humans carry the potential to grow in awareness (from body to mind, soul, and spirit) after birth. The unrealized stages of these future growth potentials are not actively suppressed or involuntarily repressed; they just have not entered into conscious awareness yet. Examples are certain aspects of a child's sexual impulses and preferences that have

not emerged due to their young age, or an acorn that will grow into an oak tree, and not into a tomato plant. The child or the acorn is not suppressing anything; they just have not started to grow. Even though each human or tree will develop its own unique qualities, the individual's deep structures are embedded in the as-yet unconscious of their kind. In case of the child, we know it will become a man or a woman, in the case of the acorn it is already determined that it will not become a dandelion or a birch tree. The *ground unconscious* explains why people are unconsciously attracted to an opposite partner that they can grow with in kind and degree.

(2) The **archaic unconscious** is linked to the unique predispositions and instincts that individuals have inherited from their ancestral past. These are embedded in their reptilian brain stem and DNA, and existed before language was learned or personal events were remembered. This facet of the unconscious causes people to experience and respond to the world similarly to the ways that their forefathers interacted with the world. This explains why most people feel more comfortable with a partner who shares their own heritage.

(3) The **submerged unconscious** is what people call the *shadow*, or the subconscious.[350] It represents all experiences and memories that were once conscious and are now screened out of awareness, either through simple forgetting, or a more forceful repression, negation, or dissociation. These are the elements of our existence that are considered to be incompatible with the ego—which is also called our *false self*. If we are faced with these elements, we react defensively or aggressively, out of fear of re-experiencing the hurt that made us repress the memory of the event in the first place. As psychologists know, "anger masks fear, and fear masks hurt."[351]

The anima and animus complex is a sub-component of the submerged unconscious that gets projected onto the opposite sex. A man who tends to repress his feelings may be attracted to a woman who is overly emotional. A woman who is unsure of herself and constantly seeks approval from others may be attracted to a self-centered and arrogant man. A man who thinks of himself as unworthy may be attracted to a successful woman with a higher education. A woman who finds life to be meaningless may be attracted to a spirited man who is full of passion and purpose. Sooner or later, though, these lovers will become irritated by their partner's qualities that they had repressed in themselves in the first place, and conflicts in the form of fighting (trying to change the other) and withdrawing emerge...unless the unconscious projections are made conscious through "owning"[352] and used for healing and growth (see below in Chapter 9). This explains why people are attracted to an opposite partner who challenges them to heal their psychological wounds.

(4) The **embedded unconscious** was called the "super ego" by Freud, referring to aspects of the self (ego) that can critically observe other parts of its existence, such as the body, behavior, thoughts, feelings, emotions, or even its essence—but never itself. It is the inner voice (judge, protector, skeptic, controller, seeker, etc.),[353] that consciously represses, but is unconscious of its own existence. Others—especially a soul mate—may recognize this embedded unconscious "self" and mirror it back, until the subject of the previous level of awareness becomes the object of the subject of the next level, as we examined in the section about spiritual growth in Chapter 4. This explains why we are attracted to an opposite and equal partner who sees beyond our false self, as it is our deepest soul desire to be seen for who we truly are and awaken to our deepest essence.[354]

(5) The **emergent unconscious** is similar to the **ground** and **archaic** unconscious above, as its potentials have not emerged yet. The difference is that the ground and archaic unconscious are based in the past (in our examples above, the evolution of oak trees throughout history, and the resulting givens for its growth as an oak tree—both unconsciously embedded in the acorn) and the emergent unconscious is based in the future (the novel unfolding of this particular oak tree). For example, people who reject ideas of higher levels of consciousness development, such as amber rejecting orange, don't do this by actively repressing views from a higher altitude. They have simply not evolved to higher levels of consciousness yet, and hence are unconscious of them. This explains why people–and especially women–who struggle at a particular level are attracted to a partner at the next higher level.

The Unconscious Fit

Humans appear to have an intuitive capacity to scan another person's unconscious makeup.[355] The women that we are most drawn to emotionally (rather than sexually) mirror our unconscious most prominently in two ways: (1) they had experiences similar to ours during their upbringing, and—more significantly—(2) they developed coping mechanisms that are different from our own. This unconscious fit of "mutually compatible pathologies" causes us to gravitate towards, and fall in love with, a partner who complements our psychological makeup most aptly (which holds an evolutionary advantage) and so provides us with an opportunity to heal, learn, grow, and awaken. This "other half" is then experienced as a soul mate—which she exactly is—as she provides us with the best opportunity to transcend our false self/ego, become psychologically whole, and develop the capacity to love unconditionally.[356]

Although no two relationships are ever the same, psychologists have noticed common patterns of the unconscious fit in couples:[357]

- **Parent and child**—often have shared issues with dependency and trust.
- **Master and slave**—have problems with authority and control.
- **Distancer and pursuer**—(also known as "seduce and withhold/withdraw") are in desperate need—and at the same time deeply afraid—of intimacy, and have found their perfect match.[358] One is pursuing—but never quickly enough to get really close; the other is running—but never fast enough to really get away. As one moves closer, the other withdraws, only to reverse the roles for the next episode.
- **Idol and worshipper** – insist on putting the other on a pedestal. This often indicates issues with competition and inadequacy.
- **Babes in the wood** – look alike, share the same interests, and—more importantly—dislike the same things.
- **Cat and dog** – look on the surface as they should have never even met. They argue incessantly over anything and avoid intimacy by living in a war zone.

You may recognize elements of these opposite pairs in your own love relationship or that of others.

Romancing the Unconscious

Dr. Ayala Malach Pines[359] aptly summarizes the attraction of the unconscious and the potentials for healing and growth in her excellent book *Falling In Love,* on pages 194-5 [quoted by permission]:

- Unconscious forces more than logical considerations dictate with whom we fall in love.
- An intimate relationship provides one of the best opportunities for mastering unresolved childhood issues.
- The unconscious choice is of a person with whom we can reenact childhood experiences; thus, the person combines the most significant traits of both parents.
- Negative traits of both parents have more of an impact on romantic choices—especially in obsessive loves—than do positive traits, because the injury or deprivation caused by them needs healing.
- The more traumatic the childhood injury, and the greater the similarity between the lovers and the injuring parent, the more intense the experience of falling in love is.
- In falling in love, there is a return to the primal symbiosis with the mother, a perfect union with no ego boundaries. This is why we only fall in love with one person at a time. The return to the lost paradise creates the expectation that the lover will fill all our infantile needs.
- Because falling in love is dictated by an internal romantic image, lovers feel as if they have known each other forever. And because it involves a re-enactment of specific and powerful childhood experiences, lovers feel that the beloved is "the one and only," and that the loss of the beloved will be unbearable.
- When a couple falls in love, their unconscious choice is mutual and complementary, enabling both partners to express their own core issues. Together, they create their core issue as a couple, the issue around which most of their later conflicts center.
- Understanding the connection between unresolved childhood issues and later problems reduces the feelings of guilt and blame, and helps both partners take responsibility for their parts in the relationship problem.
- Couples who listen to each other's feelings, express empathy, and give each other the things they ask for, can keep the romantic spark alive indefinitely.
- Expressing empathy and granting the partner's wishes is the best way to grow. As partners grow, their relationship grows. And growth is the antithesis of [relationship] burnout.

Many sources provide overwhelming evidence that healthy love relationships between opposite and equal partners hold the best opportunity to heal our unconscious psychological wounds and other emotional scars at every level of our development. They lead us ever closer to awakening to our inborn capacity to love unconditionally, to live our true purpose, and to realize the full potential which was resting in our souls all along.[360]

Terminating an abusive, damaging, or unfulfilling partnership can be justified and necessary in the healthy process of development. However, leaving an emotionally and/or spiritually challenging, but otherwise supportive, loving, and compatible partner—or avoidance of love relationships altogether as "more enlightened" or "to enjoy life more fully"—is not the answer to our existential questions, problems, and challenges. Instead, living together in a healthy relationship and sharing resources is the responsible choice, as it leads us to long-term happiness, emotional health, sexual satisfaction, spiritual growth, and environmentally sustainable living.[361]

THE EIGHT FORMS OF LOVE

Varying levels of the three core elements of love relationships that we outlined above (intimacy, passion, and dependence) produce eight basic forms of love that people may experience.[362] Some of the relationships are platonic in nature, or may feel like love, but are not—at least not in the healthy definition. Others denote actual love relationships by aligning two, and ultimately integrating, balancing, and harmonizing all three sides of the triangle in a healthy way. Below is the description of the eight forms of love:

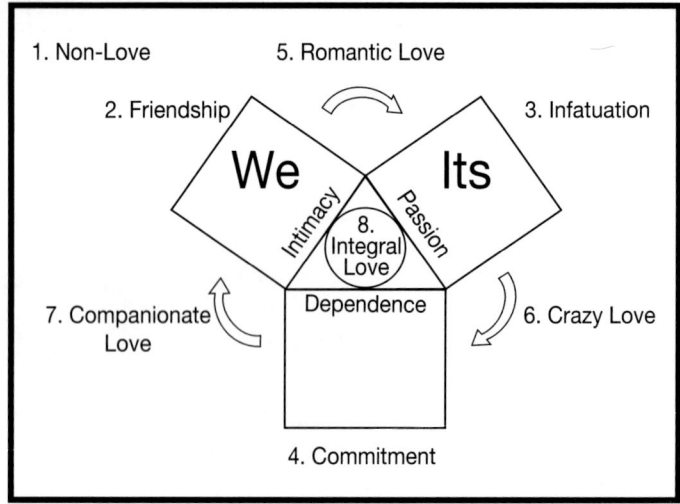

Figure 29: The eight forms of love

1. Non-love is present if there is no mutual experience of intimacy, passion, or dependence between two individuals. However, sometimes people keep meeting at school, work, social groups, or in other environments for some time without feeling any particular attraction before noticing each other as potential mates, and one or more sides of the love triangle may start to evolve and align between them. Hence "nonlove" may grow into other forms of love over time if two people engage in fun or meaningful activities together on a regular basis, and if their first impression of each other is neutral or at least not negative.[363]

2. Friendship develops when two people share *intimacy* through an intellectual, interest-based, or spiritual resonance in kind and degree through their lower left quadrants. The quality and depth of their friendship are determined by the alignment of their respective interior lines (cognitive, communicative, worldviews, values, moral, spiritual, etc.), as well as shared interests and hobbies. Friendship is often the pre-requisite for a woman to enter into a sexual relationship, while men tend to be more driven by their physical/sexual attraction in the right-hand quadrants that may (or may not) lead to friendship after sex. Vulnerability, truthfulness,[364] and honesty are vital factors for the development of mature friendships through intimacy, since integrity is the main ingredient for building trust.[365]

3. Infatuation[366] is experienced when a *passionate* physical attraction—triggered through the fulfillment of a man's or woman's Primary Fantasy in the right-hand quadrants—is the sole factor that draws an individual to a member of the opposite sex, and his or her body secretes the "falling in love" hormones that we discussed in Chapter 5. For males, a seductive sexual female image (a suitable sex object) is usually enough to experience passion and to get infatuated. For most females, a combination of power, social status, wealth, wit, humor, and intelligence (since women want success objects), combined with physical attractiveness and kindness towards her and dominant aggressive behavior towards others (protection) are the prerequisites to get infatuated.

Unlike the left intimacy side of the triangle, which requires a mutual resonance between two people to develop into a friendship, infatuation can be a one-way street. It can be quite painful if the passionate sexual longings of one person are not met by an equal amount of fervor from the object of their desire. In any case, met or unmet infatuation may lead to sexual addiction, destructive behavior, emotional havoc, social isolation, depression, and financial ruin.

Increasing sexiness of individuals leads to deeper feelings of infatuation for the people who fall for them; for example, men losing their heads over much younger, curvaceous, or otherwise attractive women (e.g., poor Goethe at age 73 agonizing over Ulrike von Levetzow, age 18), or women over powerful males, (e.g., Monica Lewinsky and Bill Clinton). Similar to the propensity of certain people to become alcohol or drug addicts while others don't, some people get infatuated more frequently while others never experience this form of love.

4. Commitment between partners arises through various forms of *dependence* that result from a mutually compatible unconscious fit between the partners. The energetic push/pull always appears to be mysterious to the lovers that are negatively afflicted or positively graced by it,[367] but nevertheless, it can be understood with effort.

There are two underlying dynamics for the appearance of dependence that are often confused. One originates from pathological (unhealthy) split-offs, negations, repressions, or dissociations that create a sense of lack, neediness, and deficiency (see submerged unconscious shadows and anima/animus complex above) that the lovers project onto each other. The second results from a sense of fullness, abundance, or wholeness—along with the desire to share one's blessings, to complement, balance, harmonize, synergize, expand, grow, and to be understood in a partnership (see ground, embedded, and emergent unconscious). Elizabeth Gilbert's grandfather said, "sometimes life is too hard to be single, and sometimes life is too good not to be shared," which nicely illustrates the two motives that lead to commitment between two people. Since both dynamics tend to be unconscious and vary in kind and degree for different domains and phases of life (money, sexuality, time, work, family, spirituality, worldviews, feminine, masculine, etc.), neither partner can know for certain which parts of their hidden self cause the unconscious attraction, and which of the five general facets of dependence that are outlined below may be the result:

A) **Codependent** relationships develop between individuals with severe pathologies (usually from childhood trauma) and other forms of psychosis[368] that typically require treatment from a professional therapist to be healed.[369] These lovers are often fused (along with the accompanying separation anxiety and jealousy attacks), or engage in endless "seduce and withhold" games.

B) Milder forms of shadow and neurosis[370] may create a sense of closeness or bond between **dependent** couples. Conflicts in these love relationships are often ignored, attributed to the differences between men (are from Mars) and women (are from Venus), accepted as the inevitable reality of any partnership, or—at best—dealt with and accepted through empathetic dialog and compromise that may be supported by self-help books, workshops, or a marriage and family therapist.

C) Women who reach a certain level of emotional and financial freedom enter the stage of **independence** and often leave their partners unilaterally (or cause them to leave) to live alone and to claim their full authority (animus stage four). This forces an everincreasing number of men to find new meaning and purpose in their life, independent of a female partner. Some people—especially women in the New Age and feminist movements, but also pathologically agentic men—see the pursuit of independence as the highest level of any personal and spiritual development, as they strive to be autonomous, whole, complete, and self-fulfilled without a partner. Any desire to be in a healthy love relationship that may arise in them or others is seen as a weakness and regression towards "un-evolved" dependent or codependent partnerships that they have just escaped. This motivates individuals who are stuck at this level to move ever further towards pathological agentic ascending, or descending, instead of recognizing independence as a healthy and necessary (but ultimately transitory) pre-requisite to enter the next stage of human relating: interdependence.

D) Individuals in the **interdependent** stage realize that nobody exists independent of others,[371] and that a balanced and harmonized personality development at all levels of our being (body, mind, heart, and soul) always occurs by integrating the healthy aspects of the feminine/masculine polarities in their interior and exterior quadrants in self-other relationships.[372] For them, sharing material resources by living together, cherishing differing views that stem from a shared level of consciousness, practicing sacred sexuality, doing shadow work,[373] being of service to others, and the desire to awaken to their true purpose, take center stage. Unlike individuals in the independent stage who pretend to be whole and complete—and hence avoid partnerships that would challenge their ego (false separate sense of self)—interdependent couples cherish their differences as the by-product of their "pretension to completeness"[374] and welcome opposing views as a vehicle for their deepest healing, learning, personal growth, spiritual realization, and service to others.[375]

E) Singles and couples who have advanced into transpersonal stages of consciousness and deeper levels of spiritual realizations may still experience a devotional yearning towards their "divine other," but feel no more emotional or sexual neediness. They are at peace and grounded in their essential "Being" and are neither desperate for, nor avoid a partnership. If in a love relationship with an opposite and equal, they experience what we may call **"Inter-Being"** in which each partner just is, without any need to change the other, to accommodate, or to be accommodated. Neither of them lusts for anybody else, nor do they fear to be consumed or abandoned, which opens up the possibility for mature monogamy[376] and unconditional Love that is by definition devoid of any need or fear.[377]

5. **Romantic love** develops between partners who share *intimacy* and sexual *passion*, but don't experience a deeper commitment through a mutually compatible unconscious fit. This is the kind of love that most women desire and is romanticized in countless movies, novels, and love songs. These women dream of a supportive, wealthy, powerful, and generous partner with similar interests, values, and lifestyle choices as their own,

who shares their passionate sexual attraction (chemistry), but does not challenge them to heal, grow, and awaken to a deeper realization.[378] In other words, they want someone with "no baggage" who loves, cherishes, and accepts them for who they are, with all their emotional wounds, dysfunctions, and ignorance of their ego. This kind of love is called romantic as it seeks to avoid all unpleasant aspects, work, and challenges that inevitably arise in any long-term partnership, instead of welcoming conflict as an opportunity for healing, growth, and awakening.

Once the hormones that created the passion for one or both partners wear off—which usually takes between 3 and 24 months—romantic love relationships either deteriorate into friendships if there was a sufficient level of shared interests and intimacy, or break up altogether when unconscious facets of the self creep up from the bottom of the triangle and neither partner wants to—or knows how to—deal with them in an effective way (typically through appropriate therapy and/or a spiritual practice).

6. Crazy love (also called mania) develops when two people share *passion* through a strong sexual attraction and *dependence* through a pathological mutually compatible unconscious fit, but have no friendship that is rooted in shared values, lifestyle choices, interests, and worldviews. This kind of love is largely driven by elevated levels of testosterone, dopamine, and norepinephrine, and lowered levels of serotonin,[379] and can afflict people from all walks of life. These love relationships are characterized by an addictive emotional and sexual (co)dependence that is not mediated by much (or any) rational consideration. It is called "crazy love" because the afflicted lovers are initially "crazy about each other" and any uninvolved bystander finds the soon-to-follow drama that often involves emotional and physical abuse to be crazy.[380] Crazy love relationships are still positive, as they force the individuals who repeatedly engage in them to eventually grow to higher levels of consciousness through their painful fights and devastating breakups. This may lead them to engage in healthier romantic and eventually integral love relationships.

7. Companionate love develops if a couple shares *intimacy* and *commitment*, but experiences no (more) sexual passion. This kind of love is often seen between conventional (amber/orange) and older couples. They may have gotten together because of religious or cultural conventions and pressures (such as arranged marriages), or to conceive and raise children in a family environment (conformist stage), or they saw the benefits of marriage for their social status, careers, and material success (rational stage). Companionate love may arise out of an initial friendship, but rarely out of romantic or crazy love. Couples who experience companionate love may advance towards an integrally informed love relationship if they address the issues that prevent them from having a passionate sex life, by overcoming physical problems through exercise, partner yoga, healthy eating, or medication, and through the removal of emotional blocks with the help of self-help books,[381] a sex therapist, intimacy workshops, and tantric practices.[382]

8. Integral love develops when a couple experiences healthy *intimacy*, *passion*, AND *dependence*, and integrates them in a balanced and harmonized way. Partners who share this kind of love either feel incredibly blessed and lucky that they found each other—often without actually knowing why their relationship is so satisfying—or have reached later/higher stages of development (second-tier consciousness, anima/animus complex stage five, transcendental sexuality, and spirituality beyond the psychic level) that allow them to consciously co-create an integrally informed love relationship between opposites and equals.[383]

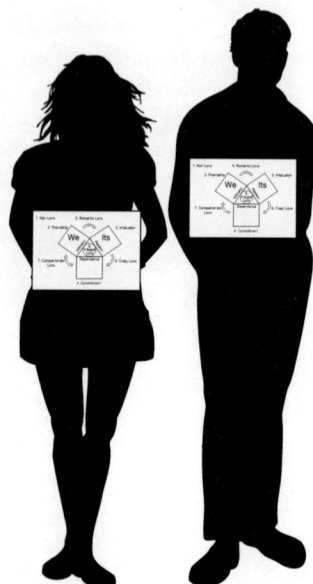

Figure 30: Each lover experiences passion, intimacy,
and dependence to various degrees.

Aligning His and Her Triangles

If you draw two triangles, one for each partner, showing the levels of intimacy, passion, and dependence (indicated by the length of the triangle's three sides) that each partner experiences in a relationship, the triangles will be shaped differently. You can then superimpose the triangles to see how they line up.

To the extent that the three sides overlap, the relationship is experienced as balanced, harmonized, and rewarding; where they don't, the couple will feel challenged, conflicted, unsatisfied, and unmet in their needs.

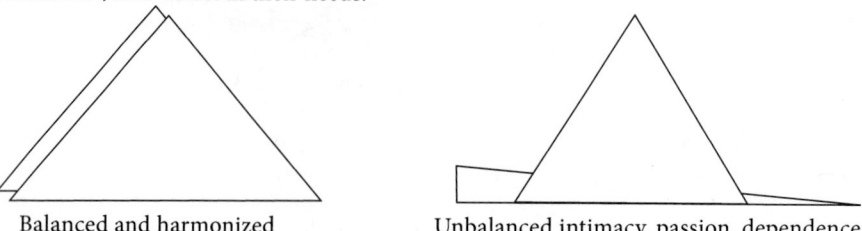

Balanced and harmonized · Unbalanced intimacy, passion, dependence

Figure 31: Examples showing two triangles overlaid to evaluate the form
and quality of love that is experienced

THREE PAIRS OF TRIANGLES

In addition to the pair of triangles that represents the actual reality of the two people in a partnership, there is a second pair for the projected ideals, and a third pair for the intentions (versus the actual behavior) of each lover.

The projected ideals originate from experiences in previous love relationships such as great sex, a deep emotional bond, sharing of rewarding activities, intellectually stimulating conversations, or a divine spiritual resonance, or are inspired by friends, romantic movies, or novels. Nobody can be completely free from these projections, which increase with the amount that the actual relationship deviates from positive memories of previous partnerships and the attachment to unrealistic romantic fairy tales and sexual fantasies. Both partners will then sooner or later try to get their mate to align with their individual projected ideals. As the saying goes—"I love you—you're perfect—now change." Hence the suggested Zen practices of "Beginner's Mind" to let go of these memories.[384]

Men may expect their partner to stop nagging them and to be more supportive of their vision, to be less moody, to lose weight, have their breasts enlarged, or to be more accommodating in the bedroom. Women may expect him to become more emotionally available and to complain less about his job, to make more money, exercise more, be more supportive around the house, take care of the kids, spend more quality time with her, romance her more often, not lust after other women, and to be more considerate as her lover.

The third pair of triangles represents the intentions of each partner. The difference between these intentions and the actual reality (first pair of triangles) represents the integrity of the relationship. For example, a woman may intend to stay with a man forever—only to end the partnership when he doesn't show up, behave, or produce in the way that she projected onto him (or as he promised to her). A man may intend to be faithful to his partner, to take care of her financially, and to be emotionally available, only to hide his feelings and focus his attention, time, and money on his hobbies or other women once the thrilling effect of the "romance hormones" are gone.

POLYAMOROUS RELATIONSHIPS

The dynamic between the triangles becomes really interesting in polyamorous relationships, where more than two partners, each of them with their own three triangles, are lovingly involved with each other…just to make your head spin a little if it isn't already.

In Summary

In this chapter we integrated the three core elements of love relationships (passion, intimacy, and dependence) into eight forms of love. We recognized that the actual partnership manifests through (1) the lower left "we" and (2) lower right "its" quadrants, plus (3) five facets of the unconscious that lead to commitment through various forms of dependence. The intensity of passion, intimacy, and dependence are experienced differently by each partner and form three pairs of metaphorical triangles whose shapes indicate each lover's experienced, projected, and intended degree of intimacy, passion, and commitment. The various shapes of the triangles point to eight general forms of love (non-love, friendship, infatuation, dependence, crazy love, romance, companionship, and Integral love) that you and your partner may experience.

Chapter 10

Differences in Male and Female Consciousness Development

Is it possible to evolve beyond the need to be in a romantic relationship?
No, that would be like playing checkers with ourselves.[385]
~ Ken Wilber ~

People sometimes wonder why partners who love each other, share many interests, and are compatible in their development still experience relationship conflicts from time to time. The reasons can be found in the fundamentally different ways in which males and females grow through the levels of consciousness and the resulting unconscious pathologies that they develop along the way.

As the physiological and biological makeup of males is geared towards production and protecting, and that of females towards reproduction and caretaking, their evolutionary role in the development of consciousness and growth through the stages are different. In short, males tend to grow in response to the demands of females by transcending and excluding, while females adapt to the male-created stages by transcending and including. In the course of transcending, errors in the process of excluding (a.k.a. differentiation) and including (a.k.a. integration) create unconscious pathologies through various forms of repression, dissociation, negation, fusion, and attachment, which later resurface as negative emotional reactions in challenging situations, especially in intimate love relationships. Let's take a separate look at each of these dynamics:

THE MALE-FEMALE CO-CREATION OF CONSCIOUSNESS

The general reasoning about why humans evolve in consciousness is their constant search for better answers to life's questions and challenges. Most immediate are those for our daily survival, such as finding food, shelter, and safety. Why we developed cultural norms and social skills such as language, art, science, religions, ethics, etc., and made technological advancements that go **way beyond** the satisfaction of our basic needs for survival can now be explained by our unique sexual selection process.[386]

In the 1980s, evolutionary psychologists and anthropologists confirmed the earlier Darwinian notion that the size and complexity of the human brain, and therefore our mental abilities and consciousness, evolved through males who not only proved their (exterior) physical abilities as protectors and providers to females, but also used their (interior) minds to compete for, dazzle, and woo the prettiest[387] (and therefore most demanding) females with ever-increasing levels of linguistic, artistic, and social skills. In return, females selected not only the tallest and strongest, but also the most intelligent, creative, entertaining, fun, inventive, and ethical males for procreation. Thus, males with the highest physical AND mental fitness indicators had much higher chances to have their genetic material handed down to future generations than their weaker and duller competitors did.[388] The sexual selection process by females ended up having a much higher impact on human evolution than natural selection through survival of the fittest did, since one needs to be conceived and born first to prove his or her ability to survive.

Because of its emotional and political charge, the vital role that the sexual selection process plays in the evolution of human consciousness and co-creation of our social, cultural, economic, and ecological reality remains largely unknown, ignored, or socially taboo.[389]

Today's displays of male physical and mental fitness, such as status symbols, academic and professional titles, sport trophies, creation of art (music, paintings, writings, sculptures, etc.), architecture, athletic prowess, and career success are the underlying and often unconscious response to the sexual selection process, which is sometimes likened to the development and display of the peacock's tail. Tail size, which actually poses a handicap for the peacock's day-to-day survival,[390] has no other function than to intimidate other males and to provide peahens with an indicator of his fitness as a mate, just as a man's ability to spend excess time and money on a woman (such as taking her to a gourmet dinner in an expensive car, spoiling her on a luxury vacation, or buying her a big diamond ring)[391] fends off competitors and indicates his fitness as a partner to her, without providing any survival benefit to him.[392]

By choosing the fittest males as mates, attractive females not only challenged our forefathers to realize ever-higher levels of consciousness, but also guided their development by recognizing and rewarding those efforts that served her and her children (and hence humanity) best.[393] It is therefore a "chicken or egg" question of what came first: the male creativity that catered to the needs and desires of females, or the female intuition to know which challenges to pose and which efforts to reward and which to punish.[394]

This dynamic between the sexes also explains why there haven't been many major female inventors,[395] explorers, artists, commanders, philosophers, chefs, founders of religions, or state leaders throughout human history. Females don't need to be creative and dominant to attract males; they simply need to be healthy-looking, vital, sexy, receptive, open, available, supportive, and appreciative. As the saying goes, "behind every successful man there is a woman," (presumably a beautiful and demanding woman) or, as Alison Armstrong puts it, "if a woman is sexy, charming, and enchanting, men will fall in love with her and willingly spend their time/money on her."[396]

To this day the dynamic of sexual reward and punishment serves its function, as modern men aspire to grow in consciousness to win the hearts and commitment of increasingly desirable and demanding women, or to deal with the emotional challenges of insecurity, shame of not being good enough, rejection, relationship conflicts, breakups, and divorce.[397]

From Archaic to Transpersonal

Below is a basic outline of the historical male-female growth dynamic that involves the process of an initial identification with a level of consciousness, differentiation from it, and integration of the next higher stage, or, as Jean Gebser put it, "the self of one stage becomes the tool of the next":[398] Please note that not all people advance into the higher stages, but that each individual has reached a particular level, and that there are also parallels to childhood development that are beyond the scope of this manual.[399]

In the archaic infrared stage, males and females were fused with their environment and driven by instinctual survival mechanisms (food, warmth, shelter, sex) that were largely unconscious. With an emerging self-awareness, females realized that they were separate from their environment and different from males, which made them feel vulnerable.

In response, some males advanced into the superstitious magenta stage with its magical belief systems and close-knit family clans to protect females from hostile male intruders, dangerous animals, forces of nature, and evil spirits. This provided women with a sense of safety until they wanted more freedom.

In response, some males advanced into the egocentric red stage in which they claimed their independent power. This won them the admiration of females who sought a protector[400] who allowed them to break free from the safety and limitations of their family-clan or tribe and venture out into the world, until they wanted to enter into a more settled lifestyle.

In response, some males advanced into the conformist amber stage in which they became stable and committed providers of food and safe homes/communities for their wife and children by consistently working hard and following rules of right and wrong conduct (such as the Ten Commandments).[401] This satisfied their spouses until they wanted to have more comfort, luxury, and leisure time.

In response, some males advanced into the rational orange stage in which they used their minds to compete for power, money, and status to provide their partners with more freedom, spending money, a bigger home, expensive diamond ring, safer car, extravagant boat, international travel, upper-class social access, etc. This satisfied women until they started to miss a deeper emotional bond, and wanted to be self-fulfilled and claim their own authority (animus stage 4). Today women in this stage often leave their partner, especially if he fails to make enough money for her to spend (loser men),[402] or is rich enough to allow her to "divorce well."[403]

In response, some males advanced into the pluralistic green stage in which they explored their sensitive self (anima), got in touch with their feelings, became emotionally available, discovered spirituality as a path to happiness, and started to care for the well-being of all humanity and our ecosystem. They were then often puzzled when women appreciated them as sensitive and conscious friends or activists, but not as potential life partners, who could lead with their masculine (protect/provide) while connecting through their feminine.[404]

In response, some males advanced into the Integral teal stage in which they realized that postmodern green women want to be met at all the previous levels of consciousness development in a healthy feminine and masculine way at the adequate time and situation. But even if women felt uniquely met by teal men who fulfilled their Primary Fantasy and who were an unconscious fit, they would still desire more—a deeper, authentic connection without any ego-driven neediness or dominance on their part.

In response, some males advanced into the transpersonal turquoise stage in which they transcended their ego and felt secure in their deepest essence, and neither needed nor rejected women. Today these men live their deepest life purpose in a loving, balanced, and harmonized way inside or outside a partnership and without competing for women with other men.

Only the future will tell how women will challenge men in this latest stage of development and how couples will co-create future stages of consciousness together.[405]

Transcend and Include/Exclude

The sexes not only play different roles in the co-creation of consciousness development, but also grow through the stages differently. Males, who tend to be single-focused (agentic) and growth-oriented (ascending), advance through them by transcending and excluding the limited views of the previous levels through negation, dissociation, and repression. Females, who tend to be relational (communal) and fulfillment-oriented (descending), tend to transcend and include previous stages through attachment, fusion, and preservation. As a consequence, males act more consistently from the highest level of consciousness that they have reached, and have a hard time tolerating the behavior, values, and worldviews of people in stages below or above them (i.e., let's force our views onto others by getting them up to our standards or rein them in to our level).[406] Females, who are conditioned by evolution to rear children (who naturally all start out at the infrared level) and to accommodate a male protector/provider, unconsciously float between the stages that they have transcended.[407] This makes their personality seemingly more complex than that of males, which is portrayed in many male-female jokes, literature, movies and the image, below.[408]

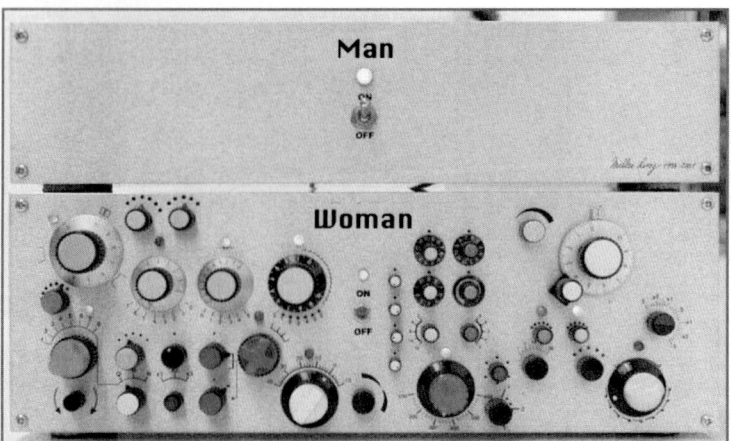

Figure 32: Joke about divergent psychological complexity of men and women

Differences in Male and Female Consciousness Development | 123

For example, a postmodern green woman may at times experience irrational existential fears (infrared), trust her horoscope to make decisions (magenta), selfishly emasculate her partner to protect her emotional wounds (red), subscribe to family- and home-oriented magazines to improve her skills as a mother and wife (amber), pursue a career in the corporate world to become financially independent (orange), and support an environmental organization to stop global warming (green). This fluidity between the stages also explains why most women in first-tier consciousness don't think hierarchically and either reject the idea of vertical stage development in adults altogether, experience growth and development as a smooth horizontal expansion rather than a clumsy vertical climb up a hierarchical ladder, or see only men as moving through individual stages of development after adolescence but not women.[409]

Because men in first-tier consciousness relate to others predominantly from their highest level of consciousness development, they resonate with their partner (or other people for that matter) only at the highest common denominator that they share.[410] For example, a postmodern green wife with a husband at the orange level may feel met by him in her rational and material needs, but disconnected when she flows to lower or higher stages. She can then either repress the feelings, views, and needs that originate from the spectrum of her consciousness outside his range, and feel unfulfilled; constantly nag him to connect with her (by being emotionally available); or meet her needs with respect to others, such as joining a conformist church (amber), a feminist group (green/red), an astrology class (magenta), and/or a pagan circle (infrared/green). In other words, a woman feels increasingly disconnected from her first-tier partner with every higher stage that she has adapted to. This is one of the reasons (the others being socioeconomic and psychological) why there are so many single women (and consequently men who can't attract a partner) in the orange and green stages.

This all changes in second-tier consciousness, where relationships are no longer driven by deficiency needs, but by Being values. Teal males begin to integrate, and turquoise males embody, the healthy feminine and masculine qualities of every previous stage, which allows them to meet their partner and others with empathy at any level (or state) of consciousness that they may experience.

Figure 33: Male-female dynamic in consciousness growth

Feminine Flow and Masculine Structure Create the River

The metaphor of the river from Chapter 2 can serve us again to visualize the co-creation of the developmental stages between males and females. The height (ascending) and width (agency) of the banks symbolize the male growth in consciousness, while the rise and fall (descending) and span (communion) of the water illustrate that of the female adaptation. Together, males and females create the river. The male buildup of the banks (consciousness) is a result of the female's desire to flow, deepen, widen, and to be contained (protected/provided for). The levels of the banks are constructed layer by layer in a predetermined order (from archaic to transpersonal) by the flow of the water.[411] No layer (level) can be skipped. The female's altitude is symbolized by the ever-fluctuating surface level of the water, while the highest level of consciousness of males is indicated by the top of the banks.

If there is more water and flow than the banks can contain, the female will overflow and feel uncontained/unsupported by the male, which creates fear in her. At the same time, the male will feel overwhelmed and inadequate, which creates shame in him. The males can then either build up higher banks (ascend to the next level of consciousness) or widen (become more agentic) to contain the females flow. Alternatively, the female can try to limit her flow (which leads to resentment and frustration), or swing to her masculine side and try to build her own banks (while feeling stressed and burned out). If there is not enough flow (female energy) to fill, deepen, and widen the riverbed, the male will feel unmotivated, unchallenged, uninspired, and unappreciated, which leads him to become more feminine (while losing direction and purpose).

For the early magenta and red stages of development, we can envision how males and females co-created meandering rivers in a natural and harmonious way through clearly separated gender roles of the male banks and female flow.

In the amber stage, patriarchal structures can be seen as a system of manmade canals and locks that forces the direction and levels that the water can flow in.

In the orange stage, females feel empowered to control the creation and direction of their own waterways by trying to alternate back and forth between flowing and containing, while males continue to be the banks only—often without the fulfillment from the feminine.

In the green stage, males swing over to their feminine side and become "flow boys"[412] while females fully embrace their masculinity and often become hardened feminists. This leads to a complete role reversal that is contrary to the way that the sexes have evolved, with women being the banks, and men the flow.

In second-tier consciousness, males and females recognize that they can't be simultaneously the banks and the flow. They return to the natural embodiment of their sexual essence, but now with a full appreciation of the opposite polarity. This allows them to co-create the river with a complementary opposite and equal partner by taking turns in flowing and containing to fully express their humanness.[413]

ERRORS ALONG THE WAY

As we established in Chapter 4 under "Spiritual Development," growth appears when the subject of one level becomes the object of the subject of the next. Along the way, errors occur when the self (subject) either continues to stay unconsciously fused with the limited views of lower stages by failing to transcend them through differentiation, or misses including healthy core functions that each level provides.

In this context, *limited views* refers to developmental lines such as morals, values, and worldviews, where healthy growth means letting go of the narrow perspectives of the lower level that prevent the cultivation of ever deeper and wider capacities for love, insight, compassion, understanding, integrity, humility, etc. For these lines, regression and attachment to lower levels is unhealthy. *Core functions* refers to intrinsic physical and cognitive skills, capacities, and structures, where healthy growth means fully developing, integrating, and retaining the qualities from lower levels that serve the individual, such as the ability to go to the bathroom, eat healthily, be sexually functional, creative, assertive, considerate, rational, sensitive, etc. For these lines, dissociation from and repression or negation of lower levels are unhealthy.

The failure to correctly transcend limited views and include core functions results in distorted perceptions and behavior that often become apparent through problems in intimate love relationships when otherwise psychologically healthy people experience emotional turmoil and act out in unexpected ways. In severe cases of fusion or dissociation, deeper forms of dysfunction (such as obsessive-compulsive disorders, phobias, anxiety, or depression) may appear in a variety of intensities (such as neurosis, borderline, or psychosis).[414]

Below is a brief outline of the process of differentiation and integration for our eight-stage model:

In the infrared stage of development, the self is completely identified with its body and undifferentiated from its environment.

In the magenta stage, the self starts to notice a healthy difference between body and matter. Failure to differentiate at this level can cause difficulties to control bodily impulses, such as eating disorders or sexual addiction; failure to integrate leads to an alienation from the body, such as repressing one's sexuality.

As the conceptual mind (ego) emerges in the red stage of development, the self learns to differentiate the body from feelings and emotions, and develops a sense of autonomy. Failure to differentiate at this level may lead to uncontrolled expressions of emotions such as anger, fear, or hatred, when the ego feels threatened; failure to integrate will lead to a lack of will, as well as emotional disconnection and unavailability. Both dysfunctions at this level are major complaints by women about men.

In the conformist amber stage, the self learns to take a second-person perspective, as in "do unto others as you would have them do unto you." Individuals in this stage learn to take on the roles and rules of others. This allows these individuals to obey mythical and government laws, to consider the needs of their fellow human beings, and to put those needs above their own.

Failure to differentiate at this level leads the self to false beliefs in concepts, stories, scripts, and myths of right/wrong that are imposed on it (e.g., you are dumb, ugly, not talented, no good, will go to hell, etc.); failure to integrate results in a lack of consideration, concern, compassion, and empathy for others.

With the emergence of the rational orange stage, the self learns to evaluate the world and itself from an objective third-person perspective, and determines independently what it believes. It develops the capacity to define its own identity, which is based on facts rather than myths, stories, roles, and rules that had been previously assigned to it by others, such as parents, peers, society, religion, etc. Failure to differentiate at this level leads to a cold, rational, materialistic, inhumane, and mechanistic view of the self, others, and the world. Failure to integrate leads to a lack of objectivity and insight about reality and the self.[415]

In the green pluralistic stage, the self becomes aware of a holistic body/mind/soul connection, that it is part of a larger ecosystem/web-of-life, and how fourth-person cultural perspectives shape the thoughts and perceptions that create subjective realities for individuals. Failure to differentiate at this level leads to a naive assumption of the goodness of all beings/nature and lack of the ability to make tough moral judgments/choices. Failure to integrate leaves the self with a nihilistic or cynical outlook on the world and others, and can cause an identity/midlife crisis.

The second-tier Integral teal stage opens the self to the views, contributions, limitations, liabilities of, and inevitable development through all the previous stages. Failure to differentiate at this level may lead to arrogant, manipulative, inauthentic, and condescending behavior towards others. Failure to integrate leaves the self with no appreciation for the different experiences of humans, their views, and contributions.

In the latest transpersonal turquoise stage (with higher stages possible), an illumination that transcends the illusion of a separate self takes place, even though there remains a healthy sense of a highly functional body/mind that relates to the manifest world of objects. Failure to differentiate at this level may lead to the inability to function in day-to-day life, a pathological idealistic worldview, or a psychotic lack of humility when the self elevates itself to a delusional God-like guru status[416] in which earlier "a-dual" stages of development are confused with non-dual awareness. Failure to integrate this level leaves the self with a sense of separation, emptiness, and fear of its mortality.[417]

To return briefly to our metaphor of the river above, errors along the way emerge during the formation of the river, when mud banks inhibit its free flow (failure to transcend limited views), or when holes in the banks allow water to leak out (failure to integrate core functions).[418]

Ladder, Climber, View

Ken Wilber often uses the metaphor of a ladder, a climber, and his or her view (altitude) to illustrate growth in consciousness and its hazards/liabilities.[419] The **ladder** represents the potential stages from archaic to transpersonal and beyond, that are always climbed in the same order from lowest to highest and that have to be taken one step at the time. The rungs of the ladder indicate the core functions that need to be included for the healthy development of the self. The **climber** represents the self where all the action is, with its quadrants, drives, lines, types, and states. The **view** signifies the particular worldviews and number of perspectives that can be taken at each level and that are transcended with each higher rung that is reached. The failure to **include** core functions leads to incomplete or broken rungs. The failure to **transcend** limited views causes parts of the self to get stuck at lower views with false/distorted beliefs.

The rungs of the ladder (stages of consciousness) were pioneered throughout human history by males in response to female rewards. Today's men are still inspired and challenged by attractive females to climb the ladder to meet their ever-increasing expectations and demands, while females (figuratively speaking) follow them along. Females in first-tier consciousness have the tendency to unconsciously move up and down the rungs of the ladder that they have climbed, while males remain more consistently at the highest rung that they have reached. In second-tier teal, females become aware of their up and down movements, while males develop the capacity to relate to and accept the limited views from each rung in others. In turquoise, a healthy unification and embodiment of the feminine and masculine qualities of all rungs and views becomes a reality for both sexes.

Psychological Healing

As we saw above, not only does the capacity to embrace and love increase with each higher level of consciousness, but also the amount of opportunities to fail at proper integration and differentiation. Since women tend to transcend and include, and are generally more sensitive and vulnerable, they often carry more emotional baggage into higher stages than men do. It is therefore no surprise that many wounded orange and green women desire to be with a man who is simultaneously a successful protector and provider AND emotionally available, compassionate, and kind. The latter capacity is often not developed yet in orange men, who tend to be emotionally unavailable, while the former is no longer a priority for sensitive green men who prefer to embrace their anima and follow a spiritual path than to work hard and aggressively compete in the academic or business world.

Instead of accepting modern and postmodern men for who they are, supporting them on their path, and healing their own psychological wounds, many women in these higher stages (who no longer feel that they need men) end and avoid partnerships instead of seeing them as an opportunity for their own healing and growth when painful emotions such as anger, fear, hurt, insecurity, boredom, guilt, jealousy, or hatred (see list of feelings when needs are not met in Chapter 3) flare up for them, and they lash out, blame their partner, emasculate him, withdraw, or sabotage the relationship with conditioned knee-jerk "fight or flight" or passive-aggressive reactions.

As a simple rule of thumb we can say that lovers who make each other happy can also make each other unhappy. All emotional reactions (positive and negative) to a partner's reality point to some unconscious pathology[420] that can only be healed by separating the behavior (observation) from the affect (emotion) that is created and by reclaiming ownership of ALL feelings, instead of projecting them onto him or her ("you did this to me," or "you make me so happy"). The difference between projecting feelings onto others and owning them is to stop re-acting and to use emotions (the word "motion" which leads to "motivation" is embedded in the word "emotion") as a call to heal and awaken towards our full capacity to love unconditionally and live our authentic purpose (self-actualization) at each level of development in a healthy partnership.

At the same time, to own one's feelings doesn't mean to become a spineless doormat and to accept all kinds of irrational behaviors that do not serve our deepest purpose. It rather means to stop making demands and/or to punish/blame our partner for their truth/reality when our needs are not met. We can then fully accept our own AND the needs and behavior of others, and act (instead of re-acting) in a loving way from choice, rather than from our emotional wounding and fears of being hurt again.

The ability to value a partnership as an opportunity for personal development requires that a couple shares a similar level of consciousness and spiritual development, and agrees to see their conflicts as an opportunity to discover their essential nature/soul through healing and growth. If they are too far apart in their development or if their pathologies vary too much in kind and degree, their relationship will either become dull or end in irresolvable conflicts.

Intimate love relationships between compatible individuals are therefore seen by many therapists and modern Western spiritual teachers[421] as the best opportunity for unearthing and healing the emotional wounds that caused unconscious attachments and dissociations in the first place, and to test the depth and embodiment of each partner's psychological health and spiritual realization. Sharing a life at all levels of their being (material, physical, intellectual, emotional, and spiritual) can support each partner in letting go of their limited views from earlier stages that were not correctly transcended (such as "the world is a dangerous place" or "I am not responsible for my actions"), and to reclaim ownership of core functions that were not properly integrated (such as "I am the master of my body, not its slave," or "I am the co-creator of my relationships, and not a victim of others or my circumstances").[422]

Depending on the developmental stage at which the pathology occurred in the first place, and its kind and degree, different forms of therapy (or even medication) and/or spiritual practices can support the healing process that brings the unconscious into conscious awareness.[423] Choosing the appropriate form of therapy and a qualified therapist is therefore essential for the success of the treatment.[424]

Many excellent relationship books with titles such as *Perfect Love, Imperfect Relationships, Love and Awakening, Undefended Love, Real Love,* or *Love Without Hurt*,[425] that have been written by therapists, address this challenging left-hand issue that is seen in many partnerships. We will therefore leave the further exploration of dysfunctional behavior, pathology, emotional healing, and spiritual growth in their expert hands (see Appendix I for book suggestions and singles2couples.org for links to recommended therapists).

In Summary

To understand the male-female dynamic on a deeper level, we established that men grow in consciousness in response to desirable females by transcending and excluding lower levels of consciousness, while women adapt to the male-created stages by transcending and including. Errors along the way lead to pathologies that cause many financially secure and emotionally independent post-conventional orange and green women to avoid intimate partnerships with men altogether. If they heal their pathologies and transcend their stage four animus complex, they may move into second-tier consciousness, where they can open up to integrally informed men to co-create a healthy partnership that serves them both as an opportunity for responsible living, further growth, and being of service to others.

Conclusion Part II

Even though it is painfully technical and unromantic to view ourselves and women as individual holons with four quadrants and drives, multiple developmental lines, hierarchical levels of development, temporary states, and given personality types, it allows us to understand the different ways in which we form social holons in love relationships, and to predict their quality and sustainability.

The Personality Matrix weaves together the eight vertical levels of consciousness development with the feminine/masculine polarities (later illustrated by the flow and banks of a river) and personality types on a vertical axis, and the five stages of the lines for spiritual, sexual, and anima/animus complex development on a horizontal axis into one chart.

The concept of holons with their four drives explains how lovers can be simultaneously a whole and a part in a partnership. The four quadrants delineate the four basic dimensions that all individual holons (such as humans) possess. When two human holons become romantically engaged, they create a social holon (love relationship) through (1) their collective interior dimension, which allows for intimacy, (2) their collective exterior dimension, which allows for passion, and (3) their five forms of the unconscious, which create various forms of dependence. These three dimensions are illustrated by a trio of metaphorical Triangles of Love that represent the reality, projected ideal, and integrity of the relationship for each partner. The lengths of each triangle's sides represent the degree of intimacy, passion, and dependence which create differently shaped triangles that are indicative of eight basic forms of love, from *non-love* to *Integral relationships*.

By expanding on the original AQAL model, we can see how the levels of consciousness were pioneered by males (who grow through them by transcending and excluding) in response to desirable females (who adapt to them by transcending and including). Pathologies along the way may occur at each level of growth through incorrect differentiation and integration (illustrated by a ladder, climber, and his/her view). The resulting psychological wounds can be addressed through self-help books (see Appendix I), therapists, workshops, and spiritual teachers—and are better left in their expert hands.

Part III—Applying the Integral Relationship Model in the Real World

Experience without theory is blind, but theory without experience is mere intellectual play.
~ Immanuel Kant ~

As we noted in the introduction to the manual, the map is not the territory. In the first two parts we explored the growth potentials of men and women as individuals and how they form romantic love relationships.

Now that you are integrally informed, you have the roadmap to enter the territory of co-creating a healthy sustainable love relationship with a compatible partner. In Part III of the manual, we will explore how you can use observations, questions, and personality tests to assess her perspectives, developmental levels, and personality types, which will provide you with what Wilber calls her Kosmic Address. These insights into her psyche, combined with your own self-assessment, will allow you to create a Compatibility Matrix that provides you with essential information about the quality and sustainability of your partnership. You can then decide if you want to overcome challenges by working on yourself and—if she is willing—with your partner inside the relationship, end it with love and integrity, or develop empathy for her and yourself if she is leaving you. If you become or are already single, you may apply the Integral dating strategies in Chapter 12 to find/attract a compatible partner.

Chapter 11

Where Am I Coming From?
Where Is She Coming From?

The important thing is not to stop questioning. Curiosity has its own reason for existing. One cannot help but be in awe when he contemplates the mysteries of eternity, of life, of the marvelous structure of reality. It is enough if one tries merely to comprehend a little of this mystery every day.
Never lose a holy curiosity.
~ Albert Einstein ~

In this chapter, **we're going to integrate our previous discussions to create a Kosmic Address for you and your partner—a summation of where you each are. Without an awareness of your own and your partner's** *Kosmic Address,* **you are** literally stumbling naked in the dark[426] when you try to relate with her.

What is a Kosmic Address?

How lovers experience each other is determined by their individual Kosmic Address, which is a combination of their personality (see Personality Matrix in Chapter 7) with one or more perspectives of the four quadrants from which an individual holon sees the world.

The Kosmic Address isn't a single score value, rather it's the collection of the characteristics that we've been discussing all along in this book—his and her Primary Fantasy, lines of development, levels of consciousness, spiritual, sexual, and anima/animus development, states, personality types, and the perspectives of the four quadrants.

In short we can say that an individual's **Kosmic Address** is defined as

$$\text{personality} + \text{perspective}^{427}$$

In common language we would say: "Where am I coming from? Where is she coming from? How does she see me? How do I see her? How do we meet each other?"

Identifying Her Perspective and Level of Consciousness

To correctly identify your own Kosmic Address requires critical self-awareness and can be difficult, as one should never underestimate the power of denial. However, if you have read this far and if the ideas in this manual resonate with you, then you have most likely reached second-tier consciousness and are able to take a four-quadrant perspective! Various online tests, feedback from others, and assistance from professionals can provide you with further information for your self-assessment if you want to get more clarity.

In order to identify her Kosmic Address, you need to carefully observe her objective UR and inter-objective LR exterior dimensions, such as her physical appearance, body language, attire, and social environment, AND engage in a dialog about her UL interior subjective and LL intersubjective reality, such as feelings, thoughts, beliefs, values, and worldviews. Especially for the exploration of the latter, you will be in her awareness (and she in yours), which will inevitably have an effect on both of your subjective perceptions.[428] This opens up another can of worms, the world of *intersubjectivity*.

Intersubjectivity

When two or more people interact on a subjective level through their lower left cultural quadrant, for example creating shared meaning, understanding, or resonance, we speak of intersubjectivity.

We generally assume that something is *objectively true* if it remains a fact everywhere and anytime, independent of human interpretations, thoughts, or feelings—whether this is possible at all remains a deeper philosophical question. Objectivity is typically the domain of science, which looks at the physical world (e.g., energy, quarks, cells, organisms, societies, ecosystems, or the universe) and human behavior from an objective upper right (UR) perspective. If the methodology that was used to form a theory is repeated by other researchers who consistently come to the same result, we speak of a theory that appears to be objectively true. Examples include: diamonds always cut glass, water molecules are always composed of one oxygen and two hydrogen atoms, or, from the social sciences, human development appears in sequential, hierarchical stages.

Objectivity is, in a sense, black and white, yes or no, true or false. Hence, UR and LR truths in a partnership refer to your and her objective characteristics, behavior, and socioeconomic reality: Are you male or female; 5'6" or 6'0"; were you there at a certain time or not; did you bring home milk or not; how much money do you have in your bank account; are you the father of her child or not; and so on and so forth.

On the other hand, *subjectivity* refers to the interior experiences of a holon, such as perceptions, thoughts, feelings, intuitions, interpretations, desires, needs, beliefs, intentions, will, motives, etc.—the world of the left-hand quadrants. These experiences are true to the individual, and if they are communicated accurately through him or her, we speak of *subjective truthfulness* or of his/her truth (versus objective truth).[429]

Most of our day-to-day interactions with the outside world are conducted in a "subject-object" or "I-it" fashion.[430] Subjects observe, think about, or interact with the world of objects in an "objective way" (or so they believe). As long as you interact with an object that has no subjective interiority, such as a car or a computer, you are in good shape. Even though you might hate your computer when it crashes, or love your car when it runs smoothly at 90 miles per hour, your subjectivity does not affect them.[431] They have no subjective interiority that you need to be concerned about. But if the object that you interact with has an interior consciousness, such as a woman, and you interact with each other (typically via linguistic exchange but also through more subtle forms of resonance such as body language, intuition, psychic, or spiritual connections),[432] then you "interactively" affect each other's subjective perceptions and inevitably enter the realm of intersubjectivity (I–You, or I-Thou).[433] This brings forth new worlds of experiences and meaning that are neither fully subjective (since subjectivity always refers to an individual's interiority) nor fully objective (since that reality only exists between the interacting subjects).

Divergences (different ways of seeing things) in intersubjective relating emerge when people are not honest or truthful about their inner world to themselves and others (which is called a pathology), or when they have conflicting definitions and interpretations of a situation or behavior.[434]

In other words, as soon as you interact with a woman (such as using observations and language to identify her Kosmic Address) both of your subjective realities are shifting, and this new reality is intersubjectively co-created between the two of you.

Different Worlds for Different People

There are three more facets to the Integral Model that will help you to understand why she may see the world differently than you. They are called (1) Flatland, (2) Co-Emergence, and (3) The Myth of the Given.

(1) **Flatland**: Even though all individual holons (such as humans) possess four quadrants, they may not all be recognized. The failure to do so is called "taking a flatland perspective," since such an outlook does not reveal all the dimensions of the holon that is looked at. It then appears to be flat (two-dimensional) instead of multidimensional.[435] For example, a therapist may reduce your relationship problems to your UL inabilities to get in touch with your feelings; a friend may reduce them to the UR fact that you gained 60 pounds; your mother may have always known that a marriage between a LL Catholic with an Italian heritage and a Protestant Scandinavian will be troublesome; and a success coach may identify your problems to be rooted in your lousy LR financial situation and sloppy lifestyle, while in reality, they are all interrelated. They don't see that you may have UL emotional problems that are caused by your strict LL religious upbringing, so your UR body became fat by overeating to comfort yourself, which prevents you from excelling in the LR profession that you feel truly called to—and all four dimensions negatively impact your partnership with your wife.

(2) **Co-Emergence**: The four quadrants, with their respective developmental lines, co-emerge. This means that growth or regression in one quadrant usually affects all other quadrants. For example, an increase in brain function and physical health in your UR body will allow you to think and feel more clearly in your UL, which will improve your ability to create LL mutual understanding with others, resulting in more LR career and social opportunities.[436]

(3) **Myth of the Given**: Our world is literally changing as our Kosmic Address is changing. There is no single given world out there (called the myth of the given)[437] that every human perceives in the same way. Instead, the Kosmic Address brings forth different world-spaces that we then inhabit. This becomes no more apparent than in intimate love relationships, where two individual subjects with separate objective bodies, divergent cultural backgrounds, and unique social environments try to align themselves in a harmonious or complementary way, only to realize that most at the time they interpret each other and the world around them in different ways. This can either produce tremendous conflicts or lead to wonderful insights, synergies and growth opportunities. As Elisabeth Lesser[438] aptly put it, "I have my reality and he has his reality, and where the two overlap is the reality of our relationship."

Observations and Q&A

By now, it may be obvious that the reality of any person is a complex tapestry of subjective perceptions, unconscious conditioning, and objective realities that are in constant flux (with the only thing constant being change). Through a combination of careful observations, asking of specific questions, active listening, qualifying answers, and personality-type quizzes (Enneagram, Myers-Briggs, Love Languages, etc.), you can get a generalizing orientation about your partner's Kosmic Address that allows you to meet her with more integrity, empathy, love, and compassion.

Perspectives

We will start our exploration of the Kosmic Address with the four perspectives that you can take on her (and that equally she can take on you):

The **UR** (it) perspective represents how she objectively looks, feels, smells, tastes, moves, sounds, behaves, etc. For example, she may be a 5'6," 40-year-old, Caucasian, brunette, freckled, smiling, high-pitched-voice female whose skin has the smell of a fragrant rose.

Your **UL** (I) subjective perspective represents what you think, believe, and feel about her, and how you interpret your perceptions of her interior and exterior dimensions. You may see her as pleasant or disturbing, intelligent or dumb, inviting or threatening, sexy or dull, thriving or striving, spiritual or material, etc. She may make you feel calm or nervous, interested or indifferent, happy or sad.

Your **LL** (we) intersubjective perspective represents how you connect with her to create mutual understanding, show compassion, kindness, devotion, and humility. You may care for her or not, talk or listen, speak her language or not, feel a resonance or feel disconnected, be empathetic or indifferent, be devoted or uncommitted.

The **LR** (its) social perspective represents how she objectively dresses, her job, what car she drives, how she lives, her hobbies, material assets, etc.—everything that you can observe about her gender identity, social environment, and personal lifestyle. She may be a single mother who wears business suits, works as a bank manager, makes $80K a year, drives a convertible, lives in the suburbs, likes to play golf, reads biographies, and likes to work in the garden.

Note how your perception of her depends on the level of consciousness that you are looking from + the perspective that you take. If you are 5'2" she may look tall with her

5'6"; if you are 70, her being 40 may look young to you; if you have a Ph.D., her bachelor's degree may not impress you much; if you strive to reverse global warming and to end poverty in the world, her materialistic family orientation may look irresponsible to you; if she is of average build with nice hair and you are stocky and bald, she may look gorgeous to you, while a taller, adolescent, less educated, egocentric body builder would see her totally differently.

LEVEL OF CONSCIOUSNESS (ALTITUDE)

To get a sense of the highest level of consciousness from which your partner experiences herself and sees the world, you need to take all four quadrants into consideration. We will start with a look at her exterior UR appearance and then proceed clockwise to the LR, LL, and UR, as this is the most common way in which people get to know and evaluate each other (unless they have a written exchange before meeting in person). The questions for each quadrant are followed by brief interpretations that provide you with pointers to a certain altitude, from magenta to second-tier, as these are the most likely levels that you will encounter in a woman.

As you make your observations and interpret her answers, note for each quadrant if she tends towards the masculine polarities of ascending/agency or the feminine polarities of descending/communion. Also notice through which of the four quadrants she is evaluating and connecting with you, as this will inevitably influence her behavior and responses to your questions.

OBSERVING ALTITUDE FROM THE UPPER RIGHT PERSPECTIVE

Her upper right-hand quadrant, which represents her physical body, can give you a vague initial pointer. How does her body look, is she in good shape, does she take care of herself, what is her body language, tone of voice, length of hair, and how does she physically express herself? To get an accurate reading, it is important to put your observations into a cultural and social context. To gain a deeper understanding about her appearance, you may ask questions such as:

What do you like/dislike about your body?
How do you stay fit and healthy?
How do you take care of yourself physically?
How healthy is your body?

Interpretations

A plain, uncultivated appearance of her body (no shaved legs, crudely cut hair, no makeup, etc.), combined with somewhat insecure behavior, points to magenta.

A "look at me" physical appearance (seductive clothing, tattoos, flashy makeup, brightly painted long nails, etc.) with a "fuck you," "I want men to look but not you," or "I will have sex with anyone but you" attitude points to red.

An "out of shape" average or overweight physique and little or no makeup, combined with a conservative appearance and behavior, indicates amber.

A physically fit and elegant appearance with stylish makeup and a self-assured attitude points to orange.

A healthy, natural "feel-good" appearance with no makeup and an emasculating, negative, or condescending behavior towards men point to green.

Women in second-tier consciousness will radiate a positive energy from their healthy bodies that expresses an authentic but humble sense of self. They appreciate men for who they are without feeling objectified by them.

OBSERVING ALTITUDE FROM THE LOWER RIGHT PERSPECTIVE

Observations about her clothes, accessories (jewelry etc.), and lifestyle, as well as asking some of the questions below, provide you with a wealth of information about her altitude based on her social "lower right" quadrant:[443]

Why/how did you choose the jewelry and/or clothes that you wear, and what do they express/mean for you?
Where do you like to shop?
Where and how do you live?
Where and how did you grow up?
What did your parents do for a living? How did that influence you?
What schools did you go to, why did you choose them, and what degrees did you earn?
What accomplishments are you most proud of in your life?
What do you do professionally and why did you choose this career?
How do you feel about financial dependence on a partner or sharing your income and financial responsibilities?
Who are your best friends, what do you like about them, and what are they interested in?
What are your hobbies and interests?
Where and how do you spend your vacations?
What and where do you like to eat and drink?
What are your political views and how were they formed?
What do you think about environmental issues such as global warming and sustainability?
What substance addictions and/or compulsive behaviors do you have?
What kind of music, books, TV shows, and movies do you like and how do they speak to you/touch you?
What do you want to accomplish in the future?
What do you see as the role of (or how do you see) men and women in our society?
How would your lifestyle be improved if you would be in a partnership with a wonderful man?
What do you see as potential downsides of a partnership?
What changes would you be willing to make in your lifestyle and what would you give up in your life to be in a healthy love relationship?
Under which socioeconomic circumstances would you leave a committed partnership?

Interpretations

If she lives in day-to-day survival mode, depends on friends, family, and/or a clan-like community/work environment for her sustenance, and has little education and low social standards, her altitude may be magenta.

If she is alienated from her family and has a rebellious, chaotic lifestyle that lies outside the social norms, combined with a dependence on males for protection, she may be in the red stage of development. Additional pointers to red may be an aversion towards a higher education, an interest in violent sports, cars, and motorcycles, substance abuse, and a desire for instant gratification of her many needs. She displays no global perspective, does not care about politics, and has no concerns for others or for the long-term consequences of her actions—which she may call "living in the now."

Women in the amber stage tend to be family-oriented, affiliated with a local community church, and live in modest homes in middle-class neighborhoods. They often pursue traditionally female educations and conventional careers that are largely reserved for women, such as being a full-time homemaker, caretaker, secretary, or teacher, or in an administrative position. Amber women are usually conservative, dress accordingly, and prefer home-cooked meals, family-oriented entertainment, local travel, and community-oriented events.

An orange woman usually wears expensive clothes, jewelry, and makeup and pursues an independent money-making high-profile corporate, academic, or entrepreneurial career that is based on an advanced college education. This allows her an upper-class lifestyle with a luxurious home and car, international travel to urban and exotic destinations, such as the Caribbean, Hawaii, Europe, Asia, etc., fine wine and dining, access to high-society cultural events, and enjoyment of costly sports like skiing, sailing, horseback riding, scuba diving, sky diving, tennis, and/or golf. She maintains a large network of friends and associates that support her in her professional career and social advancement, tends to be politically liberal, and may attend a New Age "success church" to learn how spiritual principles such as positive thinking and the law of attraction, etc., support her in getting ahead in the world.

Green women are no longer driven to work hard to earn top dollars themselves (they still want men with money, though), as they have become financially independent from passing though orange divorces and careers, and often pursue a fulfillment-oriented vocation as artists, in a non-profit organization, or as alternative healers/teachers with a global (but often naive) focus on peace, love, care, holism, and sustainability. They prefer rural living in a naturally beautiful environment with any imaginable comfort (hybrid car or SUV, hot tub, large home and garden, electricity, etc.), eat organic foods, seek avant-garde forms of entertainment, and frequently travel to indigenous and foreign cultures (Latin America, Africa, and Asia) and spiritual sites all over the world.

Women in second-tier consciousness realize the complexity and preciousness of social and ecological structures and make an active contribution to the well being of others through altruistic service and environmentally responsible life choices, inside an integrally informed partnership with a man. Such women display healthy behaviors from all previous levels.

Observing Altitude from the Lower Left Perspective

You can get answers about her altitude in the cultural lower left quadrant by observing how she relates with others and by asking questions such as:

What is your relationship with your family, children, friends, co-workers, and neighbors?
How is your relationship with your father and mother?
What is your relationship history?
What attracted you to your former partners in the first place, why/how did the relationships end, and who ended them?
What have you learned from the ending of your significant relationships and what do you plan to do differently in the future?
What is your relationship with your former partners now?
What do you see as the downsides and upsides of being in a relationship?
What makes you feel loved?
What makes you upset?
What dreams, visions, and goals do you have for your future?
What is your responsibility towards other people and how far does it extend?
In what ways do you feel inferior or superior to others?
What has your current or former partner done that created distance/intimacy for you?
Under what circumstances would a white lie and lying by omission be OK?
Under what ethical circumstances would you leave a committed partnership?
What does the word integrity mean to you?
When have you felt betrayed?
What do you think about abortion rights?
What do you think is worth fighting for?
What are your thoughts and values around gender equality and feminism?
If there is room for 10 people in a lifeboat (otherwise it would sink) and 12 people want to get in, who do you think should drown, and by whom and how would that be decided?
When do you think civil disobedience is appropriate?
Do you believe in a God, Spirit, or Higher Power, and what is your relationship with him/her/it?
How do you feel about a child dying every second from hunger or a preventable disease and what do you think humanity should do about it (if anything)?
What are the emotional rewards and challenges of being in a relationship for you?
What would it take for you to make a long-term commitment to a partner?
What thoughts do you have about your current or former partner that you have not shared with him?
Why did or didn't you have children?

Interpretations

A fear of strangers and suspicion of anything that seems to be unfamiliar, combined with a reverence for close-knit, clan-like family relationships, superstitious beliefs in spirit ghosts, and a sole reliance on lower instincts for direction, points to magenta.

If she has strained relationships with her family of origin, glorifies violent, egocentric male figures who are benevolent towards her, asks "what's in it for me now," and lacks consideration for others (especially the weak, less fortunate, and the establishment), she may be in red.

Women who express caring consideration for their family and others who subscribe to the same belief system and moral codes (our family tradition, our religion, our country, etc.) in a conservative and disciplined way, with little to no understanding, tolerance, or compassion for people with differing values and beliefs, are most likely in amber.

If she states her capacity for emotional independence, admires successful and powerful people, values rationality over mythical or magical thinking, has a global perspective, and has little use or need for intimacy with family and friends, she has advanced into orange.

A woman in green tends to see all humans as inherently equal and good. She loves her friends that pursue an alternative lifestyle, but is quick to aggressively reject those (especially men) who don't share her values of universal love, non-violence, and need for stewardship of animals and our planet. This entangles her in constant performative contradictions as she often does not live up to her own values, especially when it comes to her sexual selection process. She is quick to blame white patriarchal males as oppressors of the weak (women, children, lower social classes, and indigenous peoples, etc.) and destroyers of Gaia (earth as a single living organism) and subscribes to radical eco-feminist ideas.

Women in second-tier consciousness will express a healthy balance between their own values and the values of those in earlier stages of development, show compassion for all sentient beings (including men), and value integrally informed male-female partnerships. These women have a high level of integrity and walk their talk.

Observing Altitude from the Upper Left Perspective

Answers to the following questions about her interior upper left reality provide you with pointers to her level of consciousness and spiritual realization, if she answers them truthfully. Since we take an all-quadrant approach, you can quickly identify incongruences between her intentions and behavior in the past and present.

Who are you?
What is of ultimate concern to you?
What are your emotional needs?
What are your values? (See list in Chapter 3)
What is beauty or beautiful to you?
What do you believe to be true?
What is the purpose of life in general and your lifes purpose and mission in particular?
What is the highest aspiration you hold for yourself?
What areas of your life would you like to grow in, and what steps are you willing to take towards your goals?
What have you been passionate about throughout your life?
How do you make choices?
What does love mean to you?
What does unconditional love mean to you?
In which way do you create your own reality?
What does spirituality mean to you and do you have a spiritual practice or path (see below for more questions)?
What do you think about paranormal experiences and have you had any?
What do you think about miracles?

Interpretations

Answers that indicate a lack of independent thought, and fearful, confused, random, and irrational views, point to magenta.

If she sees herself from a first-person I (egocentric) perspective only, wants to be in control of her own destiny without consideration for others, focuses on instant gratification of her needs and impulses, divides her experiences into good and bad, and is unconcerned about her future, she is in red.

A sense of selfless devotion to her family and friends, faith in mythic beliefs, a thought system of right and wrong, and a tendency to view the feelings and well-being of others as more important than her own, points to a woman who has reached the amber stage.

A self-motivated woman who thinks positively and rationally, doesn't share vulnerable feelings, is focused on positive outcomes for her future, values her intelligence and independence, and evaluates herself by past accomplishments and the amount of success she enjoys in the present, is in the orange stage.

If she exudes an aura of independent feminine power and focuses on her emotional sensitivities and spirituality, has a desire for self-fulfillment, tries to find a deeper purpose in her life that promotes love, peace, beauty, and abundance for all in the world, she has most likely reached the green stage.

Women in second-tier consciousness will honor feminine and masculine qualities alike, value the growth potentials that healthy male-female love relationships offer, and see the contributions and liabilities of all the previous stages.

IDENTIFYING HER SPIRITUAL STATE-STAGE

As we outlined in Chapter 4 under "Spiritual Development," spiritual experiences are temporary states that can be transformed into permanently accessible stages through practices such as meditation or contemplative prayer. As with any development, spiritual advancement is a four quadrant affair.[444]

Her answers to the following questions will provide you with pointers to her current state, past spiritual experiences, and one of the five possible state-stages of spiritual development that she may have attained:

Are you religious and/or spiritual, what does it mean to you, and what role does it play in your life?

Is there a difference between religion and spirituality for you and, if so, what is it?

Did you have any peak or mystical experiences in the past, how would you describe them, what did they mean to you, and how did they shape your perceptions of life?

Who are you in your essence?

What are you aware of?

What is of ultimate concern to you?

What gives meaning to your life and what guides your choices?

What is your concept of the world, time, and space (when did time begin, what is outside the universe)?

What are your beliefs about the interaction between the manifest and un-manifest, the physical and metaphysical, or God and creation?

What are moral and ethical standards that you subscribe to?

Do you believe in God and, if yes, describe your image of him/her (if not, do you believe in any higher power, what is it, and if not, what do you believe in)?

What is your religious or spiritual practice?

Do you pray and, if yes, to whom and for what are you praying, and what are the experiences and benefits for you?

Do you meditate and, if yes, what forms of meditation do you practice and what are the experiences and benefits for you?

Where, when, with whom, how often, and how long do you practice?

What kind of spiritual growth have you experienced in the past and how would you like to advance in the future?

What are your beliefs about evil and sin, and what causes human suffering?

What does enlightenment mean to you and do you think it exists?

Are you enlightened or who is, and how do you know this?

Do you have a spiritual teacher or teachers? What is their teaching and what do you experience through them?

What religious or spiritual books do you like and what did you learn from them?

What do presence and surrender mean to you?

What are your beliefs about death and what happens afterwards?

INTERPRETATIONS

She has not developed any spiritual awareness if she views life as inherently meaningless, and the world as a mechanistic place of cause and effect that can (or will) be entirely explained by science. This also holds true if she is completely identified with her body, objects in consciousness, the material world, her possessions, and her social status.

She is at **state-stage 1** or the gross/psychic level of her spiritual development if she speaks of a higher power or order (God, Spirit, Creator, etc.) that brings everything, including her body and nature, into existence. Her spiritual practice will focus on aligning herself with this force, often through superstitious or mythic beliefs, rituals, and petitionary prayer. She will see herself and others as sinning, evil, bad, wrong, or "not spiritual" if a given situation causes her suffering, and as holy, good, aligned, or right when things go her way. Women at this stage often talk about their experiences with spirits, angels, demons, Gods, Godhead, or other higher being, and believe in the power of sacred places, objects, and artifacts. Some believe that thoughts create their physical reality and positive/negative outcomes of future events, from manifesting a parking space, influencing the course of an illness, making money, and bringing peace to the world.[445] You may also hear them mention shamanism, energy healing modalities such as Reiki, and their affinity to indigenous tribes or nature religions. Much confusion exists in New Age spiritual circles between this largely superstitious and narcissistic state-stage, and higher forms of realization (see above under pre/post fallacy).

She is at **state-stage 2** or the subtle level of her spiritual development if she talks about the illusionary nature of the mind or ego, and how unobserved thoughts, perceptions, assumptions, and interpretations create a dreamlike false sense of the self and the world. Her spiritual practice will focus on mindfulness through contemplative prayer and insight meditation. By aligning herself with a higher consciousness or spirit, a woman in this stage believes in the power of intention, intuition, creative visioning, positive thinking, synchronicities, and divine guidance, to bring more love, peace, fulfillment, abundance, harmony, freedom, and success into her life.

She is at **state-stage 3** or the causal level of her spiritual development, if she can stay fully present in the moment and in acceptance of what is, without any needs, attachments, desires, or hatreds. She may express a resonance with mystical branches of traditional religions and New Age spirituality that realize the illusionary nature of time (past and future), and speaks of full surrender or being "In The Now."[446] Her spiritual practice will focus on quieting the mind to a point that all of her actions will arise from a place of stillness and non-attachment to any particular outcome.[447] In this stage, any identification with material objects or mental concepts cease to exist.

She has entered **state-stage 4** or the witness level when she realizes that the self that has the experiences of the previous state-stages is not separate from the experience itself. She may point to the tantric union of emptiness and form, or ascending and descending, and refer to the paradox of speaking about spirituality, as it can only be pointed to, but not truly be spoken of, and may recite certain poems and sacred texts that attempt to do so.[448]

If you happen to meet a woman in the non-dual **state-stage 5**, she will most likely not talk about her spirituality or the pursuit of a spiritual path/teaching at all, as it does not exist separate from her own being or anything else. She will, however, display an incredible sense of intuitive knowing, empathy, compassion, wisdom, and integrity. Women in this state-stage are engaged but not attached, and radiate their light into the world in an authentic, uninhibited, loving, responsible, and caring way. They are at the same time incredibly strong/functional and gentle/kind, and neither resist what is, nor desire what isn't, including enlightenment. They do not confuse the non-dual stage that they have attained with an infantile stage of fusion (which would be a-dual) and are attached neither to form nor to emptiness.

IDENTIFYING HER SEXUAL STAGE

If she is open to talking about her sexuality (which is a pointer in and of itself), then you can get an idea of her sexual stage development by asking the questions below.[449] Please be sensitive, since sexuality is often a vulnerable and private issue for women, as most of them have been approached by men as sex objects, and one out of six American women has been sexually assaulted at one point in her life.[450]

How comfortable do you feel talking about your sexuality? Please let me know if I say or ask something that is too vulnerable or intimate for you to hear or respond to.
What is your sexual orientation?
What do you think about nudity in private and in public?
What role does sex play for you in a partnership?
What has been your pattern in sexual relationships?
Do you currently have a lover or sex partner and, if yes, would you like to tell me about your feelings and experiences?
What is your definition of great sex?
Are there times when you just want to cuddle or don't want to be touched at all?
What regrets do you have about sexual aspects of your life?
Who should initiate sex?
How do you ask for what you want sexually and respond if you don't get it?
How often, how long, and where do you like to have sex?
Do you prefer the lights on or off during sex?
How do you know when the time is right to become sexual with a new partner and do you expect any form of commitment?
Are you monogamous, and how would you define sexual fidelity/infidelity?
How do you like to handle birth control?
How do you feel about practicing safe sex and getting tested for STDs (Sexually Transmitted Diseases)?
When were you last tested for HIV and other STDs, what were the results, and how were you exposed since then?
In what ways do you think sexual involvement changes a relationship?
How do you equate sex with love?
Do you prefer spontaneous love-making or prearranged encounters?
How do you feel about giving and receiving pleasure without reciprocity?
Are there things that you would like to improve, learn, or experience around your sexuality?
How much and what kind of foreplay do you like to give and receive?

What do you need to get aroused?
Which sexual positions do you like and dislike?
What forms of sexual pleasuring do you desire most?
How do feel about: oral sex, masturbation, anal sex, sex toys (which?), using oil and lubricants, watching porn, bondage, spanking, talking dirty, threesomes and orgies, sex in public?
How important are kissing and oral sex to you?
What are sexual blocks that you are aware of and what sexual practices are not acceptable to you?
What are your most erogenous zones?
Do you orgasm, what makes you come, how easily do you orgasm, and how often?
What are your fears about your sexual desirability or adequacy?
Are there any sexual behaviors that you feel uncomfortable with?
How much are you willing to stretch and experiment?
Has your sexuality evolved over the years and, if yes, how so?
Under what circumstances did you withhold sex or get turned off in the past?
Were your sexual boundaries ever violated as a child or in your youth? If yes, how has that affected your sexuality?
What have sexual partners done that felt uncomfortable or turned you off?
Have you ever used any supplements or drugs to enhance your sexual experience and how was that for you?
What are sexual fantasies that you have not realized yet?
Do you prefer your partner to be sexually passive or aggressive?
How do you handle a situation where one partner wants sex and the other does not?
How do you feel about masturbating? Yourself, and if your partner does it with or without you?
What is your level of interest, understanding, and experience with sacred, tantric, or transcendental sex?
Do you have any fetishes?

INTERPRETATIONS

She may be in **stage 1** of her sexual development if she finds it distasteful to even think about sex, let alone talk about it. Note that some women just don't want to talk about sex and are still at a higher stage. Not much more to say here, since you can't interview her, so you have to find out by "doing it" once you get to that level of physical intimacy with her.

Indicators for **stage 2** of her sexual development are answers such as "I would rather do it than talk about it" or "I like to fuck." She may use words that indicate some form of aggressive power games like "doing him, being done, fucking, fuck-buddy, one night stand, having crazy sex, etc." and sees men as sexual predators who want "the one thing from every woman." Women in this stage have usually little to no concern for agreements about certain practices, birth control, or STD's.

If she is in **stage 3**, she will see sex as something that she enjoys with a partner who is agreeable about practices and boundaries that make their encounters emotionally and physically safe, and mutually enjoyable. She may say, "I like sex," "sex is great," "I had great sex," "he was a good lover" and is specific about what gives her pleasure and what she is not willing to do, or have done to her.

In **stage 4** of her sexual development, she starts to associate sex with love, a heart connection, and sometimes real commitment. She will speak of "love making," deeper heart openings of love through sharing sexuality, overcoming sexual blocks, sexuality as practice for emotional healing, and honoring each other as sexual beings.

In **stage 5**, sex becomes a spiritual energy exchange for her that leads to a mutual experience of merging into a divine union or oneness. She may talk about tantric, sacred, transcendent, or divine sex, staying present in the body, surrender, Kundalini, or a deep resonance at the level of all seven chakras between her and her partner. Any form of unrestrained authentic sexual expression that originates from a place of pure essence and transcends the lovers' sense of separation, shame, or other limitations is desirable to her.

IDENTIFYING HER ANIMUS COMPLEX

As we established in Chapter 4, she is in one of five possible stages of her animus complex development that you can identify through her behavior and answers to the following questions. Some of the previous answers and observations may have already given you pointers.

What is a man to you?
What do you expect from a man in relationship with you?
Tell me ten things that make you feel loved, honored, and respected as a woman?
What do you think about male-female equality?
What differences do you see between men and women?
Are there different roles for men and women in a relationship and our society and what are they?
What role did your father play in your life and what is your relationship with him today?
Who were the most significant males in your life, during what period, what role did they play, and how did they influence you?
What role did your mother play in your life and what is your relationship with her today?
What roles did you and your partners play in previous relationships?
What makes men attractive to you?
What kinds of men are unattractive to you?

INTERPRETATIONS

She may be in stage 1 (men as alien outsider) if she has an ambivalent relationship with her father and other significant men in her early life. Additional indicators are reports of tumultuous love/hate relationships with former partners, longer periods in her life without a male partner, sexual relationships with women, and if she goes back and forth between a desperate clingy desire for your love and then fearful rejections when you get close.

Pointers to a stage 2 animus (men as father, God, or king) are a critical or disapproving father figure whom she never felt to be good enough for. She may speak favorably of kind men who adore, support, and treat her well, and negatively of those who criticize, challenge, or dismiss her. Women in this stage may struggle with aging, can be emotionally needy, constantly ask for approval and reassurance about their lovability, and are afraid to do things wrong.

Indicators of a stage 3 animus complex (men as her hero) are answers that favor loyal, supportive, generous, and loving men with an unwavering commitment to honor and support their wife and children. She likely had a stable childhood and a good relationship with her father and mother, or at least healed most of her earlier emotional wounds. In her eyes, men should know right from wrong, be hard-working, good fathers, family-oriented, heroic, protective (if need be, aggressive towards others), and benevolent towards her.

Women in stage 4 (men as independent being) are particularly easy to identify, as they talk about the financial and emotional independence that they have attained through their own work or through successful divorces after one or more long-term marriages. They express a desire to explore who they are, independent of a committed partnership with a man, and want to live alone, often with a dog or cat that they are proud to love more than they would any man. If women in this stage consider to be in a partnership they often exclaim…"where are all the good men?"…and of course no man within their reach is ever good enough. Successful, up-beat, entertaining, self-assured, and happy men who display empathy, understanding, and support for them while pursuing their own purpose and interests without needing a female partner for sex, approval, support, or "to mother" them are valued by women in this stage, who sometimes maintain uncommitted sexual relationships with younger lovers. Most eco-, radical, and social feminists—who resent men and what they stand for—are found in this stage (or stage 1) as well.

She has arrived in stage 5 of her animus development (men as equal partner) when she realizes the benefits of being in a committed love relationship with an integrally informed man whom she values as an opposite and equal. A woman in this stage sees the benefits of a healthy, live-together committed marriage as the foundation for her ongoing personal growth, spiritual development, physicalsexual well being, and socially, economically, and ecologically responsible livelihood. Her focus is on the inner qualities of a responsible man who lives his authentic life purpose and can love unconditionally in a committed partnership, instead of his worldly possessions and social status only. A single woman in this stage is a rare find, as she is clear in what she seeks in a life-partner, and actively pursues men who are her equal. She has no problem finding a suitable partner within a few weeks of her opening to relationship if she is attractive and sex-positive,[451] as men are naturally conditioned by evolution to be chosen by a healthy woman who honors and values them.[452]

Identifying Her Type

The viable and popular typologies that we use in the Integral Relationship Model (NLP, Five Love Languages, Enneagram, and Myers-Briggs type) are best identified through tests/quizzes in books or on the Internet. Once you know your and her type, it is extremely beneficial to gain an understanding of where you harmonize, complement, and potentially conflict with each other. This exploration can be done in a very playful and relaxed way, and is especially fruitful if the two of you share the same level of consciousness. She may also bring astrology and other typologies into the discussion that can lead to deeper insights and open up an interesting dialog about your psyche. You will quickly realize if her interpretations of types are derived from a superstitious, egocentric, mythic, rational, pluralistic, Integral, or transpersonal altitude.

Refining the Kosmic Address

The Kosmic Address of humans becomes even more refined when we integrate the feminine/masculine polarities and temporary states of consciousness. By doing so, we arrive at an Integral view that combines quadrants, lines, levels, states, and types. It becomes clear—as we noted in the introduction to the book—that everybody is right from their own point of view, how these views differ, and how the different views shape every individual's perception and interpretation of the world, including our human (love) relationships. The upper left perspective of a feminine person with a green altitude in an angry state with an Enneagram type two is different from the upper right perspective of a masculine person with an orange altitude in a calm state with an Enneagram type five.

Of course, the Kosmic Address is in constant flux—maybe even more so for females with their unconscious fluidity between the levels of consciousness, their menstrual cycles (PMS), menopause, and emotional volatility, than it is for males. Nobody can actually ever occupy the exact same Kosmic Address twice. We can also never fully see the world from another person's perspective/altitude, but we can and should make an effort to do so through empathy. It is therefore important not to make assumptions or to get overly attached to things that a woman has said or done in the past, but to meet her in the present moment with openness and a Zen-like "beginner's mind."

In Summary

In this chapter we covered the topic of intersubjectivity and how you can make a generalizing orientation through observations, questions/answers, and personality tests about (1) one or more of the four perspectives from which she sees herself, you, and your partnership, (2) the highest level of consciousness (altitude) that she has reached, (3) her state-stages of horizontal spiritual, sexual, and animus development, and (4) her personality types which, taken together, comprise her Kosmic Address at that particular moment in time.

Chapter 12

Locating Your Partner and Yourself on the Compatibility Matrix

Sometimes life is too hard to be single, and sometimes life is too good not to be shared.
~ Elizabeth Gilbert ~

Out of all the elements that comprise the Kosmic Address, the level of consciousness—or altitude—is the most crucial factor to predict the quality and sustainability of your partnership. Altitude defines how individuals view and express every other aspect of their existence (Primary Fantasy, lines, levels, states, and types), and points to the number of perspectives (first, second, third, fourth, etc. person) that an individual is capable of taking. No matter how much you may be sexually attracted to a partner and share other intelligences, interests, lifestyle choices, dreams, mutually compatible unconscious pathologies, and similar levels of vertical spiritual, sexual, and anima/animus development (which are all important), the quality and outcome of your partnership will be primarily determined by your and her altitude.

If we put the eight stages of male growth in consciousness that we outlined above on a vertical axis on the left side of a matrix, and place the female expansion along the top, then we get 64 possible combinations of compatibilities and incompatibilities. To use the matrix, simply locate the highest level of consciousness that a woman has reached in the top row and that of the man in the left column. The intersecting field between will provide you with a short description of the relationship that is most likely to exist or develop between the two.

For example, an orange woman may have a teal man as a mentor, friend, and lover. An amber woman may be frustrated with her red husband and divorce him.

Male \ Female	Infrared	Magenta	Red	Amber	Orange	Green	Teal	Turquoise
Turquoise	Caretaker / Dependent	Caretaker / Dependent / Magic-Connection	No Partnership	Friendship	Mentor / Friendship / Lovers	Mentor / Friendship / Lovers	Co-Creation / Opposites	Inter-Being
Teal	Caretaker / Dependent	Caretaker / Dependent	No Partnership	Friendship	Mentor / Friendship / Lovers	Mentor / Friendship / Lovers	Co-Creation / Opposites and Equals	Co-Creation / Opposites
Green	Caretaker / Dependent	Caretaker / Dependent Pre/Trans Fallacy	Pre/Trans Fallacy	No Partnership	Confusion Frustration Divorce	Feminine / Masculine Role Reversal Divorce	Mentor / Friendship / Lovers	Mentor / Friendship / Lovers
Orange	Caretaker / Dependent	No Partnership	Trophy Wife / Boy Toy	Opposites / Not Equals Divorce	Independence Equals / Not Opposites Divorce	Confusion Frustration Divorce	Mentor / Friendship / Lovers	Mentor / Friendship / Lovers
Amber	Caretaker / Dependent	No Partnership	Frustration / Divorce	Co-Creation / Opposites Not Equals	Opposites / Not Equals Divorce	No Partnership	Friendship	Friendship
Red	No Relationship	Red Abuse of Magenta	Codependence Marry-Divorce Cycle	Frustration / Divorce	Trophy Wife / Boy Toy	Pre/trans fallacy	No Partnership	No Partnership
Magenta	Survival-Bond	Survival-Bond	Red Abuse of Magenta	No Partnership	No Partnership	Caretaker / Dependent Pre/Trans Fallacy	Caretaker / Dependent	Caretaker / Dependent / Magic-Connection
Infrared	Survival-Bond	Survival-Bond	No Relationship	Caretaker / Dependent	Caretaker / Dependent	Caretaker / Dependent	Caretaker / Dependent	Caretaker / Dependent

Figure 34: Compatibility Matrix for men and women at different levels of consciousness development

Generally speaking, we can say that individuals who are fully actualized at their level of consciousness are most compatible with partners who are at the same altitude, as indicated by the shaded fields. Individuals who are in transition from one stage into the next will be attracted to a partner at the level they are moving into. The biggest conflicts arise between first-tier partners who are one level apart and each fully actualized at their altitude (green fights orange, which most vehemently rejects amber, which is utterly frustrated by red.)[453] People with a greater discrepancy in their first-tier development don't share a resonance in their values at all, with the exception of the Pre/Trans fallacy between orange/green and red. **The conflicts between partners who have grown apart or realize that they are at different stages of development after the "love-struck phase" can't be simply solved through better communication or other means of reconciliation. Their relationships are basically doomed…sorry.**

Below are some generalizing orientations about the quality and dynamics of relationships between couples at certain stages of development.

Infrared

Modern adults who are exclusively in the infrared stage cannot maintain healthy partnerships for obvious reasons. They may have sex with others in infrared and bond with people in magenta. Red and magenta males may abuse infrared women for sex. Because of their advanced moral development, people in later stages will most likely not partner with infrared. They may, however, care for infrared in a homeless shelter, church, or mental institution.

Magenta

Two individuals in the magenta stage may partner with each other in a primal way to meet their basic needs for survival. Women in magenta may be abused by red men and forced into some form of prostitution or other dependence. Green women may romanticize magenta males as earthy or shamanic spirit guides, who, on rare occasions, may be highly spiritually and sexually developed. Sexually and spiritually developed magenta females may serve as mediums, or sexual/natural healers, and be attractive in this capacity to males in the green and transpersonal stages.

Red

Individuals in the red stage typically develop codependent relationships with one of their peers or people in green. Red women seek fearless, heroic, potent protectors, and red men seek a sexually available hot "babe" who pays them respect. Outbursts of negative emotions and physical abuse are common in these partnerships. Red couples have low moral standards and a higher rate of infidelity and break-ups, as they are quick to leave when a more exciting partner comes along. To orange and green, red can appear refreshingly sexy, seductive, uninhibited, creative, spontaneous, and alive. Green males and females are especially prone to fall into the trap of the pre/post fallacy when they confuse a pre-conventional with a post-conventional partner. Since red women initially appear as lovable, devoted (which is actually neediness), and sexy, men above red who are in a state of infatuation get easily blinded by them. The neediness of red women can be utterly seductive and easily mistaken for true love, while they end up taking whatever they can, especially from naive green rescuer types who see red as repressed victims of society. For less attractive orange men, red women are sometimes the only available sex partners, as amber women are too conservative, orange women too masculine, demanding, and busy, and green women too emasculating. They end up paying for red women in one way or another, either as prostitutes, trophy wives, in sex-related workshops, or as expensive dates. Younger red men may become "boy-toys" for older orange "cougars" who dispose of them at will and leave them stranded and heartbroken if they become emotionally and/or financially dependent. People in red who have evolved into higher stages of their spiritual and sexual development can be hard to identify and be mistaken for people who are more evolved.

Since red can only take a first-person perspective, arguments are always imbued with aggressive blaming and wronging of the other, and "won" by the physically and emotionally stronger person (usually the man).

Amber

People who are actualized in amber tend to be in relationship with mates who share their conservative mythic values and beliefs. They despise red (which they have just escaped) as undisciplined, and see most orange and green people as too liberal, opportunistic, and sinning (think abortion rights or the death penalty). Because of their family and community focus, social pressures, cultural/religious norms, and solid support systems, most people in amber stay together until one partner dies, advances into orange, or if the woman moves into her animus complex stage four. If middle-aged people in amber get divorced or become widowed, they usually seek and quickly find a new partner within their social circles.

As amber can take on a second-person perspective, differences are usually settled by compromise or female submission to the patriarchal male perspective.

Orange

In theory, people in orange have the widest choice of mates, especially if they are physically and financially attractive, and socially successful. As they have escaped the narrow moral codes of amber, they can succeed with an orange spouse, afford magenta and red people as sexual playmates, trophy wives, or "boy-toys," enjoy the support and loyalty of a partner that transitions out of amber, financially support a green mate in their desire for self-fulfillment, or find acceptance from teal, which often has no other partner choices as it struggles with green, the level it has just escaped. However, most orange women enter their animus complex stage four development level and want to pursue their own careers and independence from men, which leads to a high number of orange women filing for divorce. With their busy professional and social schedules, high incomes, fitness-oriented lifestyle, travel, care for their animals, and assortment of vibrators, they either have no time for a partnership, no longer care for a man in their life, or can't find any "good men" out there. Orange men, on the other side, often don't find androgynous, highly driven and demanding orange females to be sexually attractive, and don't know how to deal with their independent "high maintenance" attitude.[454] This makes orange, along with green, the group with the highest number of single people.

Conflicts in orange are usually settled by either agreeing to disagree, or finding a win-win solution.

Green

Green is the most puzzling stage when it comes to romantic partnerships. Men in this stage are often burned out from competing in orange to be the most successful providers for their demanding wives, and start to embrace their feminine side, sexuality, spirituality, and a socially and environmentally responsible conscious lifestyle. They become Sensitive New Age Guys (SNAGs) or "flow-boys." At the same time, green women tend to fully swing over to their masculine side and realize their vision for autonomy and self-fulfillment independent of men. While both sexes in this stage share a concern for all sentient beings, green women tend to see men and patriarchy as the prime cause of conflict, violence, injustice against women and children, and environmental problems in the world, which leads many to become men-hating social or radical eco-feminists. Because they have not transcended their Primary Fantasy yet, green women get constantly caught up in paradoxical conflicts between their sexual attraction to successful men with power, status, and wealth (who can afford them a carefree lifestyle), and their green values and fear of slipping back into some form of financial or emotional dependence that they just escaped in orange. The result can be an emasculating attitude towards men who don't know how to meet their paradoxical postmodern worldviews and complex emotions (remember that women tend to transcend and include with the resulting pathologies).[455] Green men are then often flabbergasted about why they figuratively get their balls cut off, even though they addressed women's demands to create more space in their life, got in touch with their feelings, learned to be compassionate communicators, and became emotionally available in order to act as kind and sensitive partners.

The problem is rooted in "transcend and include" versus "transcend and exclude." At different times, green women want men to be earthy (magenta), aggressive, spontaneous, uninhibited, and creative (red), loyal and devoted (amber), successful and driven (orange), **and** sensitive and caring (green), while men in this stage are overly focused on their feelings and concerns for others. To orange women, green men look like losers who have given up striving for success and amber women see green men as late hippies or in their midlife crisis that can't be trusted. The salvation for green men and women often comes in the form of red, which, on the surface, can look and act like green. Green men may still have enough financial resources to impress a sexy red woman who enjoys their care, understanding, and support, while green women often feel drawn to the raw "bad boy" masculinity of red men (which puzzles green men to no end). Both see red as victims of orange cold-heartedness and amber's oppression that exploits and marginalizes red. After green "rescued" and fell in love with red, disappointment about their emotional and financial neediness, insensitivity to their partner's values and needs, disloyalty/infidelity, and the resulting heart-break lurk right around the corner.

An interesting emergence in green is the practice of polyamory, which—you guessed it—also attracts red, but for different reasons (red takes the sex and throws the love, open communication, honesty, responsibility, care, compassion, and sharing of vulnerable feelings out the window).

Conflicts in green are resolved through sharing of feelings, exploration of underlying childhood wounds (often with the help of a therapist), expression of needs, and making requests (see Non-Violent Communication in Chapter 3 under "Feelings"). This often leads to endless processing without reaching any workable solution.

Teal

For the small group of people who have entered teal, and if you read this far, you are most likely one of them, the big "aha" about the limitations of deficiency-motivated first-tier partnerships and the resulting conflicts arises. This insight feels extremely liberating and provides men and women with the opportunity to vastly improve their relationships with all people. Unfortunately, teal can become quickly frustrated and isolated, as it no longer resonates with the singular worldviews of people in first-tier consciousness, who may perceive them as arrogant, manipulative, condescending, passive-aggressive, or cynical—and sometimes for good reasons. As there are very few people in second-tier consciousness to begin with, and even fewer women (almost all Integral pioneers[456] and their followers are men), teal men have a hard time finding an equal partner. While they can empathically relate to women below teal, they either get quickly bored with them, or get dumped because they don't exclusively subscribe to their partners' partial perspectives. On the other side, teal men may use their second-tier awareness to befriend one or several women from various first-tier stages for uncommitted relationships. Females who are entering the teal stage open up to males again and value their unique contribution to humanity, just as males in second tier honor and value females. This ends the battle of the sexes and opens the door for truly interdependent partnerships.

Conflicts in teal are resolved through an understanding of intersubjectivity, the ability to take multiple perspectives, and the finding of creative solutions that take both partners' emotional and practical needs for growth and purpose into account.

Turquoise and Above

In this and all higher stages (indigo, violet, ultraviolet, and clear light),[457] the Primary Fantasy of both sexes shifts to partners who care about their body, mind, heart, and soul in a balanced and harmonized way in order to live their true life's purpose while being economically, environmentally, and socially responsible, to love all sentient beings unconditionally, and to be of altruistic service to others. For turquoise, partnerships become an act of authentic loving between two human beings, and not a twisting of the self or others into objects to be lovable. As a result, pathological desires and fears to be alone or in a partnership vanish. Men no longer compete with their peers for financial status and social power at the expense of others and the ecosystem to earn a woman's "love," company, and sex (which is at the root of all major challenges that humanity is facing today), while women's attraction to men is no longer unconsciously dominated by their former desire for an irresponsible protector and provider, but rather for a responsible integrated partner.

As the term "transpersonal" suggests, this allows couples who have been divinely appointed to support each other in their growth and further awakening at all levels of their being—beyond their biological, cultural, and social conditioning.[458] They honor and value each other's authentic feminine and masculine expression of their sexual essence and invite the naturally arising conflicts between them as opportunities for further healing and growth, without attachment to any particular outcome. Couples at this level have entered the state of "inter-being" which allows them to fully be themselves, while staying consciously devoted to the co-creation of the larger whole (or social holon) of their partnership, which they experience as "the miracle of us" or as a "third body."[459] Once they commit to their soul mate they have no incentive to leave their partner, or to have multiple lovers, which leads to mature monogamy.

Transpersonal partnerships are still extremely rare, as there are very few people (and predominantly males) in turquoise and above.[460] Turquoise females with an animus complex stage five are usually in partnerships, while turquoise males without a partner embrace the growth opportunities of their singlehood while staying fully open to embrace their soul mate when she arrives.[461] They no longer exploit women at earlier stages of development for company and sex, but support them in their growth and, if they like, in finding a suitable partner. Once a woman in this stage chooses a man, they co-create partnerships that are neither based in fear, desire, or attachment, nor in a need for emotional/financial safety, nor conventional contracts/agreements[462] as seen in need-based relationships of first-tier developmental stages.

Conflicts in turquoise are resolved by the desire of each partner to transcend their limited views that created the differences in the first place, and by brining any unconscious aspects of their being into the conscious.

Conflict Resolution and Forgiveness

As we have seen above, each level creates its own conflicts and takes different approaches to resolving them. Several relationship experts and therapists have concluded that disagreements cannot be resolved through better communication skills,[463] while others claim to have developed effective strategies to overcome differences and to create mutual understanding/acceptance through techniques such as correct understanding of each partner's language and behavior, active listening, mirroring, sharing of vulnerable feelings, stating needs, making requests, showing empathy, and effective negotiation tactics for win-win agreements.[464]

The former group bases their opinion on couples who are at different levels of their consciousness development, while the latter proves the effectiveness of their methods with couples who are equals. To an integrally informed person it is obvious that red will not accept amber's mythic rules of right and wrong conduct and will rather violently fight things out if they can't force their partner to accept their ideas.[465] Amber will usually not submit to red violence or rational orange arguments to resolve conflicts, but rather follows established (patriarchal) mythic laws and rules of right and wrong, such as "Do unto others as you would have others do unto you," or "A husband should honor his wife, who should respect him in return." Orange will reject crude red violence and mythic amber rules, and ridicule needy green emotional sensitivities where everybody is heard (which leads to endless processing without any tangible results), and instead focus on common interests (versus individual positions) and long-term goals to negotiate effective win-win agreements that guarantee future material gains and benefits.[466] Green, will of course, loathe all of the former approaches and tries to focus on establishing emotional connections and acceptance of everybody's perspective by making requests (versus demands) that are based on objective observations and subjective need-based feelings to create mutual understanding—without attachment to a specific outcome.[467] Unlike orange and below, green would rather NOT win the argument and lose the relationship, which often leads to later resentment and bitterness when deep structural conflicts cannot be resolved by green means, e.g., fundamental differences between men and women or environmentalists and the global industry.

The big break out of gridlock comes in teal, where at least one party uses the appropriate tools to address conflicts at the level that they were created at—such as protective force to rein in red; enforcement of (hopefully democratic) laws of right and wrong to create functional societies, objective assessments, and rational forward-looking solutions for practical problems; **and** sensitivity towards the feelings and needs of others in order to maintain the healthy relationships that—as we realize more and more—are vital for our overall health and well being. Finally, turquoise adds the intuitive understanding that any form of inner conflict is ultimately an outward projection of the egoic mind, which it has transcended. It therefore welcomes any inner conflict with "what is out there" as an opportunity for further ego transcendence and awakening, instead of thinking in me-other polarities. This allows turquoise and higher to co-create peaceful relationships with its peers and to avoid conflict with others, and so contributes to the healing of the world.

Effective conflict resolution also requires forgiveness,[468] which is an often overlooked practice in relationships. As with conflict resolution, forgiveness is easier to achieve between people at the same altitude: red may forgive insults from peers who are submissive, but cannot forgive amber's humiliations; amber may forgive wrongdoing when it is confessed and forgiveness is asked for, but cannot easily forgive orange's rational questioning of their mythic worldviews; green may forgive if an emotional connection is restored, but has a hard time forgiving teal's condescending, superior, or arrogant attitude; while turquoise and above does not harbor resentment in the first place, so it has nothing to forgive later, and can also easily express their feelings in a compassionate way if they hurt others, which often removes the need to ask for forgiveness for events that occurred in the past.

TO BE OR NOT TO BE—THAT IS THE QUESTION

This most famous line from Shakespeare's *Hamlet*[469] about ending one's life or continuing to suffer can also be applied to love relationships. If you are in a troubled partnership, is it worth it to stay or better to leave? If you are happily or unhappily single, is it wise to be alone or to try to find a partner? The answer is, of course, "it depends."

IN RELATIONSHIP - HAPPY

Congratulations to you and your partner. If you read this far, you most likely know why your partnership is healthy, happy, satisfying, and rewarding. You have been (1) lucky, (2) used your insightful experience to attract a compatible mate, and/or (3) did your growth work to co-create a healthy partnership—most likely a combination of all three. By reading this manual you may have gained a clearer understanding of your individual developmental levels and the opportunities, challenges, and rewards that may lie ahead as you and your partner evolve further.[470] You will be able to identify early warning signs if you drift apart and so start an integrally informed dialog that may keep you together on your path, or allow you to separate amicably if you have taken different directions. It also allows you to welcome any potential conflict as an opportunity to support each other in your healing and growth.

IN RELATIONSHIP - UNHAPPY

If your Triangles of Love are not balanced and harmonized, then you are not having the most fulfilling relationship possible. If you lack intimacy (left side), you are most likely at different levels of your consciousness and/or spiritual development, and/or have different interests, needs, dreams, and goals. If you lack sexual passion (right side), then you may no longer meet each other's Primary Fantasy, be at different stages of your sexual development, have lost your feminine/masculine polarity, or have a different lifestyle. If you no longer experience commitment (bottom), then you have either completed the emotional healing and shadow work that attracted you emotionally in the first place, or (more likely) are dissociated from your feelings and repress negative emotions into your unconscious to avoid conflicts whose resolution could be beneficial for your healing and personal growth. If the left and right sides of your Triangles of Love are mostly balanced, and you have occasional fights (apply the 80/20 rule that 80% of the relationship should be harmonious and up to 20% can be dissonant), it will be beneficial to stay and to heal the underlying wounds.

If you are in a partnership and at different levels of consciousness and/or vertical development, then you want to assess the potential for the less evolved partner to grow. Nobody can be legitimately asked to constantly regress in order to make another person happy. If you are more than one stage apart in any of the four lines that we integrated above in the Personality Matrix (consciousness, spiritual, sexual, anima/animus development), it may be beneficial for both of you to end your partnership in a peaceful way. This is especially true if you are in amber or above and with a partner in red, which happens most often to green.

If you are one stage apart and the partner in the earlier stage is transitioning up, then it is wise for the more evolved partner to stay and to provide loving support for his or her transformation.

If you are at the same vertical and horizontal levels and have conflicts because of communication problems, gender differences, feminine/masculine polarity issues, pathologies, or shadows and complexes, then it is most certainly wise to stay and to heal—if necessary with the support of a therapist, or, in less severe cases, by participating in workshops or working together with an applicable relationship book (see Appendix I for book suggestions). Otherwise, the same problems will emerge in your next relationship or haunt you in your single life.

It is challenging, and maybe impossible, for men at any altitude to be in partnership with a woman that moved into stage four of her animus complex development. Unless she is willing to stay and he can give her all the freedom and space that she requires to transition through stage four, she will inevitably leave him or make his life miserable. In either case it is **NOT HIS FAULT**. Red men in such a situation often threaten women physically, amber men may plead and use shame/guilt tactics for years to hook their wives, orange men often try to use their financial and/or intellectual power to buy/talk her into staying or make her divorcing him as expensive and painful as possible for her, and green men tend to use manipulative emotional blackmailing to hang on to her. All these strategies will ultimately offend and alienate her. The only way for partners in their anima/animus stage four development to stay together is to be at a similar altitude and to make the transition into stage five a conscious process.

There may be other good reasons for staying in an unhappy partnership, such as caring for others (children, parents, community) and economic or political reasons, but ultimately you are doing neither yourself nor your partner a favor by prolonging a hopelessly unrewarding relationship that fulfills neither one of you.

Single - Happy

Being genuinely happy and fulfilled without a partner is unquestionably the best place from which to enter a new love relationship, because you will not come from a place of emotional, economic, sexual, or social neediness, but from a sense of contentment, fullness, satisfaction, abundance, and wholeness. People in this phase of their life have usually arrived at stage four of their anima/animus development and orange and above, which is quite an accomplishment that should be celebrated. Unfortunately, especially in New

Age circles, these stages are often hailed as the ultimate level of personal development by women who conveniently overlook that any integrated personality development appears in intimate self-other relationships and that all their living spiritual teachers of caliber live in committed partnerships.[471] It is therefore a good idea for them to look at possible pathologies that show up as fears of being in a partnership, and their unhealthy desire/attachment to being alone. Both can be expressions of denial, repression, or narcissism. Once their underlying wounds are healed and they realize that human beings are always partial and already whole, they can fully open up to invite a compatible man into their life again.

Single - Unhappy

It can be a fine line between the neediness that originates from a sense of lack and deficiency that insecure people try to fill with sex or romance, and the desire of mature singles who want to share the joy and richness of their life, body, mind, heart, and soul with another human being in an intimate love relationship. The former is indicated by compulsive serial dating and a desperate behavior towards the opposite sex that dominates the afflicted people's lives and overshadows any other activity. Their sense of urgency causes repetitive cycles of highs when falling in love, clinging while in partnership, heartbroken when abandoned by a lover (or abandoning others), and desperate searching when alone. These people are perfect candidates for "SLAA"—Sex and Love Addicts Anonymous.

The latter represents the healthy yearning of the soul to find a mate and is experienced as openness towards potential partners that are good for him or her. This yearning leads to a consciously focused approach to find/attract him or her while living one's life purpose.[472]

In Summary

Who we fall in love with is primarily determined by unconscious processes in our limbic system and reptilian brain. The hormones that are released when individuals have their Primary Fantasy met and experience chemistry cause them to temporarily regress to lower, or rise to higher states of consciousness and to ignore red flags of incompatibilities. Once the honeymoon is over, each partner inevitably returns to their original stage. If the couple was lucky—or the man was integrally informed—they will have matching levels of consciousness, which is the prerequisite for any effective conflict resolution and the co-creation of a sustainable, healthy partnership. It is therefore vital for men to be aware of their own and their partner's level of consciousness and growth potentials, to decide if a partnership can have a happy future or will end in separation.

Chapter 13

Dating Using the Integral Relationship Model

Your task is not to seek for love, but merely to seek and find all the barriers within yourself that you have built against it.
~ Rumi ~

People date for various reasons, such as finding a life-partner/spouse, having children, making new friends, going out for fun, finding a sex partner (mostly men), being wined and dined (mostly women), getting over a former partner, figuring out what they want in a mate, estimating their "market value," avoiding loneliness, or boosting their self esteem.[473]

Today, most singles try to attract people who are outside their league (meaning that they have an unrealistic Primary Fantasy). These singles are guided by their experience of chemistry only (which is triggered by a combination of sexual attraction and mutually compatible pathologies), and are otherwise unaware of additional compatibility criteria—especially their levels of consciousness—that are necessary to co-create a healthy, sustainable love relationship.

The Integral Approach

An integrally informed man who desires to be in a healthy partnership takes a four-quadrant approach to find, attract, and be chosen by a partner with a compatible (opposite and equal) Kosmic Address and similar interests, passions, dreams, and lifestyle choices to his own.

Answering the questions below before you start to date can save you from unnecessary frustrations, and support you in staying realistic and focused:

1) Why do you want to be in a partnership; how would your life be enhanced by a partnership?
2) What does a healthy partnership mean to you?
3) What qualities do you have, and want to develop further to be ready for a healthy partnership?

4) What are possible roadblocks to a healthy partnership for you?
5) What are you improving to become attractive to your perfect mate?
6) Who/what do you want to become in the future; what is your purpose; what are your goals/dreams?
7) What do you bring to the table and what do you look for in a partner?
8) What are you willing to change or to give up for a healthy partnership?
9) What do you (1) have to have, (2) would like, (3) can tolerate and (4) can't stand in a partner in the following eight areas?[474]
   A. Physical/Material
   B. Intellectual
   C. Interests
   D. Values/Lifestyle
   E. Psychological/Emotional
   F. Creativity/Passions
   G. Spirituality/Essence
   H. Sexuality
10) What qualities do you have to develop to sustain a healthy partnership?

Once you are armed with your list of answers, you can develop a dating strategy.

DATING STRATEGIES

Dating is defined as "a form of courtship, and may include any social activity undertaken by two people with the aim to assess the other's suitability as their partner in an intimate relationship or as a spouse. The word refers to the act of meeting at a certain date/time and engaging in a mutually agreed upon social activity."[475] In contrast, flirting means "to act romantically without a serious interest in forming a committed partnership" or "to gauge another person's interest in dating, or to have casual sex."[476]

As all interactions with other human beings, dating/flirting is a four-quadrant affair, with our UL inner dreams, desires, and fears, UR physical fitness and Primary Fantasy, LL cultural conditioning and skills to create mutual understanding, and LR social status and means. Men who seek a partner are usually expected to do the pursuing by approaching women and showing off their fitness and social status (and to take the risk of rejection), while women are expected to display their physical attractiveness, openness, and sexual availability to attract men (and to carry the burden of choosing the right partner by rejecting unsuitable males).

Detailed advice about the intricate dynamics of the "dating game" and strategies for men and women to find/attract/choose the most desirable member of the opposite sex are abundantly available from self-help books (see Appendix I), websites, newsgroups, and dating coaches. We will therefore only briefly touch on today's most common ways of finding/attracting a partner.

Law of Attraction

The Law of Attraction is based on the idealistic idea that thoughts create our reality. This is certainly true in the context of developing a positive attitude towards life and partnership, and to set clear intentions instead of believing that one is unlovable, ugly, undesirable, or a powerless victim.[477] As Henry Ford said, "Whether you believe you can, or you can't, you are right." On the other side, thoughts (or consciousness) do not miraculously deliver to our doorsteps what the ego wants, let alone manifest physical reality or a partner out of thin air, as it is implied in New Age books *(Love Will Find You or Ask and It Is Given)* and movies *(The Secret, or What The Bleep Do we Know?).* Simple wishful thinking (without a deep alignment with your true life-purpose/essence, followed by the appropriate actions) seldom produces the desired results.

The Law of Attraction seems to work best for sexually available and attractive women (who often need to open up, become realistic, and encourage men instead of playing hard to get, emasculating them, and pushing them away) if they have enough opportunities to meet potential mates through family and friends, recreational and social activities (sports, dances, travel, concerts, coffee shops, bars, etc.), workshops, groups, work, school, church, or the Internet. Since women typically attract, and men pursue, the best advice for single men is to engage in activities alone which they would otherwise enjoy with a partner, to stay open to the cues that interested women send their way, and to make a move if they are interested. Building a network of friends, joining a group or community, taking classes, and going out and having fun are all good strategies to meet compatible women with similar interests.

Singles Events

Using the Internet, you should be able to find local events, groups, and workshops that cater to singles. Consider speed dating, dances, seminars, church groups, and vacations for singles. Unlike Internet dating, these events provide you with a personal right-hand quadrant experience of the available women. If you are physically attractive, an entertaining extrovert, a good communicator, experienced dancer, and secure enough to approach women (doing the pick-up line thing), these events can work in your favor. The downside of singles events is the lack of upfront information about a woman's other quadrants and her intentions, which you can only assess once you engage her in a conversation. This can be challenging, especially if you are nervous, afraid to approach women and to ask questions, or if she is reluctant to talk, uncertain what she wants in a partner, or not truthful.

Internet Dating

Like it or not, Internet dating is becoming increasingly popular, is a numbers game, and is most likely here to stay. Depending on your approach, personality, integrity, skills, and style, the use of dating websites for finding/attracting a partner can be either extremely effective or utterly frustrating.

Keys to success are (1) your full availability, (2) a truthful essay of who you are and what you are looking for in a partner, (3) selecting the appropriate website(s), (4) posting attractive current pictures (a professional portrait with a smile, and shots that show you in different situations that are consistent with your profile text), (5) realistic expectations, (6) effective use of search options, (7) contacting all women that appear to be compatible, (8) receiving satisfying answers to qualifying questions before investing time, money, and hopes in an unavailable woman, (9) having at least one encouraging phone conversation before meeting in person, and (10) only going on dates with women who are interested in you and have a compatible Kosmic Address, similar interests, lifestyle choices, passions, and dreams/goals for the future.

Before Internet dating became available, most singles only had access to potential mates within their social circles at school, work, bars, or church. The perceived scarcity of potential partners led to a natural sexual selection process[478] in which each bachelor settled for the most attractive single woman who would choose him. Because most couples lived in close proximity, shared a similar cultural background, came from the same social class, knew each other for some time before becoming romantically involved, and shared similar interests, they had no need to be concerned about different levels of consciousness, values, lifestyles, worldviews, or spiritual beliefs. They were naturally aligned.

Now, for the first time in human history, with tens of millions of people dating online, the Internet provides an illusory abundance of mate choices and removes all geographic, social, and cultural barriers that had previously separated singles from each other. Unfortunately, most seekers are still exclusively focused on the fulfillment of their Primary Fantasy, experiencing chemistry, and sharing interests, only to be utterly surprised, confused, and frustrated when a date goes bad because of incompatibilities in their Kosmic Address. Some lovers get lucky (about 30% of middle-aged newlyweds met online), but most repeat the same patterns over and over until they throw in the towel in frustration. The good news is that online dating can be very effective when conducted with integrity and from an integrally informed perspective.

CREATING AN ONLINE PROFILE

The first step is to write down who you are, why you want to be in a partnership, what qualities you are looking for in a woman, and what kind of partnership you are seeking. You may write in a funny, serious, poetic, or pragmatic style. There really is no right or wrong way, as long as you find your authentic voice (as you would normally talk), avoid typos and grammatical blunders, and are positive, considerate, respectful, entertaining, real, and truthful.[479] If you fake it, she will find out sooner or later, so why lie? It can help to read the profiles of other men or to hire a dating coach to create the profile that represents you best. The goal is to attract the most compatible women, and not to get as many responses as possible (unless you want to play the field). In other words, go for quality over quantity.

Next, find a current (or take a new) photograph that shows your smile and eyes (no sunglasses!), and a few more digital photos that were taken in different situations that visualize your text. If you like to hike, play piano, travel to China, and sail, then have pictures that show you alone in these situations (avoid cropped pictures with a hand or arm of another person around your shoulder). Most women don't care about pictures of your car, motorcycle, boat, bare chest, or exposed genitals, so save those for later.

Selecting the appropriate dating website(s) from hundreds of possibilities comes next.[480] Many sites cater to specific interest groups and demographics. Prices range from free (plentyoffish.com, okcupid.com, or craigslist.org), to thousands of dollars (ge-dating.com or tableforsix.com), with most of them charging $20-$50 per month. Matchmaking sites like eharmony.com and chemistry.com don't display member profiles publicly. They provide their subscribers with pre-selected candidates based on elaborate personality and interest profiles, and only allow direct communication with access to pictures and personal information after a guided—choice exchange, which can be tiresome.

Most other dating sites are public and provide instant access to the profiles and pictures of all their members, allowing direct unmediated communication. After their merger with the number-two *yahoopersonals.com*, *match.com* has over 30 million mostly conventional amber/orange members at the time of this writing, while specialty sites such as *greensingles.com*, *spiritualsingles.com*, or *veggieconnection.com* focus on specific pre- and post-conventional demographics and interest groups, and are much less populated.

Post your profile once you have freed up enough time to communicate and to meet women who respond to you and give satisfying answers to your pre-qualifying questions. After posting for the first time you are "fresh meat" and may get some heightened attention, which will subside within a few weeks, so don't get too excited and think the sky is the limit. The most active times are usually from Thursday to Saturday when women look for weekend dates, and before holidays such as Thanksgiving and Christmas, when some singles feel especially lonely. The time to be proactive comes once the initial interest that you may receive subsides. Most women expect to be contacted by men, so you need to put in some leg (ah…finger) work.

THE SEARCH

The best approach is a twofold strategy, to be focused and to go wide. Use detailed search criteria to find the women that seem to be most compatible with what you are looking for. Include profiles that don't have pictures, as attractive women are often tired of being "hit on" for their good looks, want to hide their identity (especially if they hold public positions), are shy, don't have pictures, can't decide which shots to use, or don't know how to upload them. Most men **do not** write to women without pictures in their profiles, so considering postings without pictures increases your chance of getting a favorable response. Don't ask for a picture in your first contact but rather show an interest in her exercise routines and eating habits to get an idea about her body type and how she stays in shape, fit, and healthy. This way you may find a highly attractive woman who has transcended selling her looks only, and values her (and your) inner and outer qualities equally.

If she has posted pictures, don't go by them only (they may be old or flattering anyway) and carefully read profiles (which most men don't do) through your AQAL lens. Through their prose and pictures, most women give you pointers to the type of love relationship they envision and their level of consciousness. But don't make assumptions too quickly and always ask open-ended questions (what, why, how, when, who…) that pertain to her profile.

What kind of love is she looking for?

Use your insight from the Triangles of Love to identify the degree of passion, intimacy, and commitment that she is looking for in a partnership.

Infatuation is her priority if she only mentions the importance of chemistry, and your looks, status, and material assets. Friendship is her focus if she expresses the importance of similar interests, doing things together, good communication, feelings, going slow, getting to know each other, and sharing values. Commitment is important to her if her profile centers on patience, willingness to work through stuff, devotion, overcoming difficulties, shadow-work, and growth opportunities in a love relationship. She seeks **romance** (passion + intimacy) if she mentions that relationships should be easy and fun, and that she doesn't want to deal with your baggage, negative emotions, or dependency issues. A **companionate love relationship** (intimacy + dependence) is her desire if she asks for dedication to friendship, trust, loyalty, integrity, going through thick and thin together, being there for each other, and a long-term commitment without mentioning chemistry, falling in love, or physical intimacy/sex. **Crazy love** (passion + dependence) is on her mind if she wants to fall in love at first sight, be crazy about each other, unable to think about anything but each other, passionate sex, to leave the past behind, and to be together forever—but does not mention shared values, interests, or intimacy. A vision for an **integrally informed love relationship** (healthy forms of passion + intimacy + dependence) has emerged in her if she touches on all the healthy dimensions mentioned above, including the feminine and masculine qualities at the level of body, mind, heart, soul/spirit, and shadow.

Pointers to Her Level of Consciousness

Magenta women express naive, irrational, and superstitious beliefs about the world, themselves, and relationships, such as astrology, ghosts, past lives, voodoo, or magical powers.

Red women express many egocentric needs such as freedom, respect, and having fun without concerns for others or the future

Amber women speak of conservative family and religious values, marriage, creating a home, pride in their country, ideas of right and wrong, and being a good person. They want a man with a secure job, who is loyal and knows right from wrong.

Orange women boast about their independence, education, success, possessions, career, early retirement plans, expensive sports and hobbies, international travel, interest in exquisite wine and food, and their big social networks. They usually seek tall, good-looking, accomplished men with no or grown children, who are generous, educated, fit, and healthy, and have an independent career, high income (usually in the top 5%), and a solid retirement fund.

Green women go on and on about unconditional love, their feelings, spirituality, care for animals and nature, world peace, feminist values, compassion, nonjudgmental-ism, their self-fulfillment, and activism. They want to attract independent, educated, world-centric, strong but feminine, open, tolerant, successful, wealthy, accomplished, nonjudgmental, emotionally available men with enough free time to travel with them and enough money to support them on their path.

If you would happen to find a teal woman online, she would desire true interdependence with her partner, embrace feminine and masculine qualities, value all people (including men), seek beauty and function, thrive in the world, and have a diversity of interests without being demanding or needy. She would seek a man who has integrated his feminine and masculine polarities, has balanced and harmonized his seven chakras, and is available to co-create a purposeful partnership of opposites and equals in order to live responsibly and to make a positive difference in the world.

Turquoise women, who most likely don't date online, as they see many potential partners to choose from and are not alone for long, would mention their deep connection with all creation, an embodiment of their realization, living their lives' true purpose without regrets, surrender to what is, and the yearning of their soul to be met and seen by an equal partner. They would actively approach and choose a man who has balanced a deep spirituality with his worldliness, and is at peace with himself and all sentient beings, while living his life with intention and purpose.

Pointers to Her Animus Complex

An ambivalence towards men (can't live with or without them), or an overall insecurity about dating, points to stage 1 (men as alien outsiders). In stage 2 (men as father, God, or king) she may mention that men adore her and that she wants to be treated with kindness and respect. In stage 3 (men as hero) she is partner-oriented and wants a man who will take care of her. In stage 4 (men as independent beings) she will write about her autonomy, that she is her own "man," and doesn't want a committed relationship or marriage. She typically seeks an affluent and sophisticated man as occasional lover and generous travel/social companion who respects her need for freedom and therefore maintains his own interests, living space, and independence. In stage 5 (men as equal and opposite partners) she appreciates men as opposites and equals without needing or rejecting them, and desires to be in a co-created live-together committed partnership.

Sexual and Spiritual Development

You may also find pointers to her level of sexual and spiritual development, but they are usually too vague to make any assessment, so you need to ask questions when the time is right. It is good advice not to pose questions about her sexuality or to talk about yours too early, unless she takes the initiative. Women know (or assume) that men want sex as quickly as possible, and most of them feel offended if they are asked or approached that way during the initial contact.

Be Proactive

Most women who post profiles expect men to make the initial contact with them. Send a message to all the women that look interesting to you. Briefly introduce yourself, reflect on what resonated with you in her profile, and ask up to five specific open questions about things she mentioned that caught your eye. Depending on how available she is, how well you meet her expectations, how attractive you are, and how far outside your league you date, 5-20% of the women that you approached will respond favorably. Don't take the lack of responses personally. Most women think that not writing back is the most polite way of saying "no thanks." It actually has little to do with you. A lot of women who post profiles are not fully available for a partnership. They might just be curious, like the attention, still grieve over a breakup, want to prove that nobody is good enough for them, don't have time for dating, completely date outside their league, or just want to have fun and be wined and dined (or in the case of men, just looking for sex) instead of answering any serious questions. To get encouraging feedback on questions about her relationship history, availability, intentions, and dreams for the future is therefore paramount before you meet, unless you enjoy dating for the sake of it, to pay for the fun, and to be rejected a lot.

If you get a favorable response to your initial contact, then ask more of the qualifying questions that are listed in Chapter 10 until you have some certainty that you will be good for each other. Most women complain that men don't show enough genuine interest in them, initially talk too much, and try to sell themselves. It is not your goal to impress her by telling stories about yourself. Answer her succinctly if she has specific questions, but don't fall into the "being interviewed trap." Try to maintain an open and relaxed dialog, which means two people exchanging questions, answers, ideas, and opinions. Your goal is to identify her Kosmic Address, to verify that she seeks the same type of love relationship as you do, and to find out if you share similar interests, passions, dreams/goals, and lifestyles.

The First Phone Call

Offer to call her at a time that is convenient for her if your email exchange is positive. Most women like to be called first instead of calling you, and will offer their number on request. If the call goes well, then ask if she has any more questions before she would feel comfortable meeting you in person. Singles who are seriously looking for a partner often want to know if there is chemistry or at least some physical attraction before they spend more time exploring deeper questions of compatibility or going on a "real date."

The Meeting

Schedule a one-hour maximum "low maintenance" meeting at a coffee shop or similar place. Otherwise you may get stuck on a lengthy and expensive date with somebody that you don't share a mutual attraction with. Be early, wait around the entrance or counter, and offer to pay for what she is having. Sit face-to-face so that you can make eye contact, interpret her eye movements, and mirror her body language to create rapport (see Chapter 6 under NLP). Even if there is no mutual interest, retain your positive attitude, as any meeting is an opportunity to show kindness and humility, and to learn and practice.

Dating

Find out what she likes to do on a first date (what, where, when, how long, who pays) if there is a mutual resonance at the first meeting. Make a suggestion that feels comfortable to you and choose a setting that suits your common interests, available time, and financial budget, and allows you to get to know each other better. Most women prefer that you take the initiative and are creative (search the Internet for more novel ideas than the classic dinner, movies, walk in the park, or day at the beach). During the first date, you should be able to get a better idea about your areas of compatibility (physical, material, intellectual, interests, lifestyle, values, sexual, and spiritual), and her level of interest to become sexual with you. Women usually know that men (except for some amber) want to have sex as quickly as possible, and appreciate men who are secure in their sexuality, know what they want, are not pushy, and guide them in moving at a comfortable speed (I am ready whenever you are). Most women want some exclusivity and clarity about STDs, contraception, and sexual history before they have intercourse with a new man, so it is a good idea to initiate this conversation before things get too heated in the bedroom.

If you start to date a woman frequently, sooner or later the question of dating each other exclusively will arise. Only about 10% of committed couples experienced love at first sight, such as Ken Wilber and Treya describe in their book *Grace and Grit*. If you are unsure when to commit, you may follow the simple rule to date 12 quality women, remember the best, and then stick with the one that tops your favorite from the first dozen.[481]

Cast a wider net

Go broader in your search once you exhaust the close matches. Often, women don't know how to express themselves or find the whole online dating thing unnerving and awkward. Their profiles may start with "I am new to this...," "This is really hard/awkward ...," "I don't know how to describe myself...," or "friends tell me that I am...." Go back to step three above but send a standard message such as:

> Hello [screenname],
> My name is [name]. Thank you for posting your profile on www.xxx.com. I read it carefully and was so intrigued by it that I would like to learn more about you. I hope that you will enjoy my profile as much as I did yours. Please tell me why you are single, why you want to be in a partnership, what you look for in a man, what you are most passionate about, what ultimately concerns you, and what your dreams/goals for the future are.
> Thank you for your time to respond and I look forward to hearing back from you.
> Make it a wonderful day.
> Respectfully,
> [Your Name]

As always, find your own authentic voice for this general approach and send this message to as many women as you like, to see what happens.

Please pick one of the many excellent dating and romance self-help books (see Appendix I) that matches your Kosmic Address and intentions, and consider workshops or personal coaching if you need more guidance to find a wonderful partner.

In Summary

Most singles experience a desire to be in a partnership at some point or another and want to make a proactive effort to find/attract a suitable partner. The Integral Relationship Model provides you with the basic tools to identify the underlying motives for this desire and the type of partnership that you and women are seeking. Use your AQAL lens to look beyond your Primary Fantasy and chemistry to identify a partner within your league who has a compatible Kosmic Address and shares your lifestyle choices, interests, values, and dreams/goals for the future. Depending on your personality and goals, you may then develop a dating strategy that can include the law of attraction, singles groups, or Internet dating.

Conclusion Part III

An integrally informed man applies the AQAL map to the territory of love relationships by identifying the Kosmic Address of his partner through observations, asking questions, and personality tests. This gives him information about her perspective, altitude, feminine/masculine polarity, and levels of spiritual, sexual, and anima/animus development, as well as her personality type. This information allows him to understand how she sees him and their partnership and to meet her with the understanding, integrity, strength, kindness, and compassion that she is yearning for. He can then determine if he can satisfy her as an opposite and equal partner and grow with her in a healthy love relationship, or if it is better for both of them to end their partnership in peace and harmony if they are incompatible or have grown apart. Single men may then live purposeful lives while developing and implementing an Integral dating strategy to find and attract a new partner with whom they can further heal, grow, live responsibly, and be of service to others.

Epilogue

After reviewing over 200 relationship books, integrating their wisdom into this manual, and applying the Integral Relationship Model in my personal life, I have come to the following overall conclusions about love relationships:

Successful couples (as described in *The Exceptional Seven Percent*) have compatible Kosmic Addresses, share interests, lifestyle choices, and dreams/goals for the future, and make their partnership the highest priority in their life—above children, job, pets/animals, money, lifestyle, travel, possessions, their individual purpose, friends, religion, spirituality, and hobbies, as well as cultural, social, and family pressures. The dedication of these couples to each other and their relationship is a recurring pattern, from conformist to transpersonal levels of consciousness. Even though this commitment to a partnership/marriage may seem like a sacrifice, all the above areas and stakeholders—including children—benefit from the couple's commitment to each other in a co-created healthy partnership.

Successful couples also continuously practice to balance and harmonize agency and communion, which takes on different qualities at every level of consciousness development. This ability, as many relationship experts and spiritual teachers have confirmed, is a sign of psychological health and spiritual maturity. As a consequence, successful couples evolve together vertically in both directions—eros and agape, heaven and earth, wisdom and compassion, ascending and descending.

Last but not least, successful couples are committed to doing the individual and joined personal growth work that every lasting relationship requires, and seek professional help if they get stuck.

A second group of individuals consists of those who evolve in consciousness through several love relationships—with a new partner or several consecutive partners for each vertical level of their development. At some point these individuals may enter into second-tier consciousness, which will allow them to sustain a committed partnership.

A third group of people (mostly modern and postmodern women) with an uneven personality or spiritual development (the latter also called spiritual bypassing) have become diehard singles that settle for pathological agency, have unrealistic expectations from a partner, make themselves deliberately unattractive, display constant "seduce and withdraw" patterns, or prefer uncommitted relationships.

Men who seek a woman for a healthy, committed, long-term love relationship should be aware of women in group two and wary of (and avoid) women in group three. In the words of the eminent philosopher Smokey Robinson, "You better shop around."

Individuals who want to co-create a healthy love relationship with an existing or a new partner should therefore (1) make their relationship central to their life, (2) continuously heal and grow with a mate with whom they share a compatible Kosmic Address, lifestyle choices, passions, interests, dreams, and goals for the future, (3) balance and harmonize their healthy feminine and masculine polarities, (4) seek professional help when serious problems persist, and (5) be of altruistic service to others.

The future of love

There is overwhelming evidence that the sexual selection process that we discussed in this manual and the subsequent co-creation of male-female partnerships—instead of the often assumed male oppression of females—have defined our evolutionary past and will shape our future. Throughout the ages, human males have developed ever-higher levels of consciousness (from archaic to integral) to compete for and to be chosen by the sexiest (healthiest) females who, by and large to this day, reward the most successful/powerful providers and protectors with their love, support, companionship, and sex. Consequently, modern men still advance through the stages of consciousness to satisfy the ever-increasing demands of the women they desire.

Only in the rare transpersonal turquoise and above stages may women be attracted to and reward men who pursue a non-violent and environmentally sustainable lifestyle instead of competing with their peers for status and success in order to attract the sexiest females. At the same time, males in turquoise and above gain the choice to only enter into partnerships with environmentally and socially responsible women who have transcended their need and deficiency-driven first-tier Primary Fantasy and subscribe to Gender Mainstreaming, which honors the differences between the sexes while giving them equal social and political rights **and** responsibilities.

This potential shift in the sexual selection process—along with support for our youth to grow more responsibly through the stages of first-tier consciousness—may be the only way to address the global problems and challenges that humanity is facing in today's complex world, such as social injustice, starvation, violence, wars, modern day slavery, and the destruction of our ecosystem, to name a few.

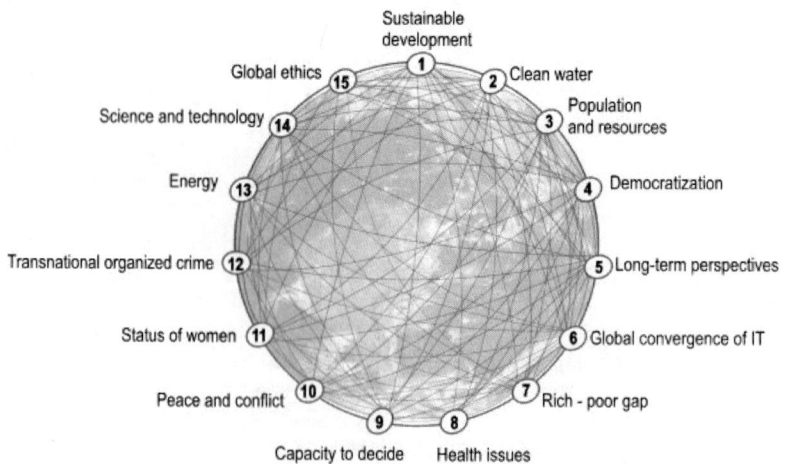

Figure 35: Global challenges facing humanity

Together, second-tier couples are poised to become the role models for the co-creation of male-female partnerships that integrate the healthy feminine **and** masculine polarities at every level of consciousness development. Their goal will not only be to support people in their transitioning into second-tier consciousness as swiftly and responsibly as possible, but also to inspire singles and couples to co-create healthy partnerships along the way that enable them to evolve together in peace and harmony with all creation.

May this manual empower you to grow in or into second-tier consciousness, to live your authentic life purpose in a joyful and responsible way, to co-create a healthy partnership with a fully available woman who has transcended her animus complex and pathological Primary Fantasy, and to show compassion and support for those women who have not been able to do so yet.

Thank you for reading and, if you feel so inclined, for sending me your feedback at martin@singles2couples.org

Appendix I: Relationship Books for All Levels/Colors

Every reader finds himself. The writer's work is merely a kind of optical instrument that makes it possible for the reader to discern what, without this book, he would perhaps never have seen in himself.
~ Marcel Proust ~

In this appendix we evaluate selected relationship books from an Integral perspective. The reviewed authors support singles and/or couples with a certain Kosmic Address (altitude + perspective) with advice for getting the love they want, either by manipulating the opposite sex, effectively dealing with gender differences, better translation (balancing and harmonizing the four polarities) at their current altitude, and/or transformation to the next higher level of consciousness.

For example, books for red take an upper right-hand perspective, objectify the opposite sex, and outline how to "exploit her psyche," "catch a millionaire," "apply manipulative rules," or see "men as scum and women as stupid."

Advice for amber singles and couples usually focuses on acceptance (versus transcendence) of gender differences in the lower right-hand quadrant, such as John Gray's *Men are from Mars, Women are from Venus* series of books or Alison Armstrong's *Making Sense of Men*, or focus on secrets and principles that make marriages last, such as Gregory K. Popcak's *The Exceptional Seven Percent: The Nine Secrets of the World's Happiest Couples* or John Gottman's *The Seven Principles for Making Marriage Work*.

Authors in orange either rationalize love with brain-activities and hormonal processes in the upper right, such as Helen Fisher's *Why We Love*, or favor psychological and behavioral measures in the two lower quadrants to overcome relationship conflicts—typically by instructing workaholic men to become more emotionally available, and women to heal their emotional scars and support their partner to give them what they want, e.g., Harville Hendrix's *Getting the Love You Want* or David Schnarch's classic *Passionate Marriage*.

Green writers tend to address the unconscious and spiritual dimensions in the upper left-hand quadrant to empower singles and couples to use their relationship conflicts for deeper psychological healing and spiritual insights that allow them to move towards unconditional love (e.g., John Welwood's *Love and Awakening*, Jett Psaris and Marlena Lyons' *Undefended Love*, or Joyce and Barry Vissell's *The Heart's Wisdom*).

Most self-help relationship books are written by therapists and coaches who view committed partnerships as essential for healthy personality development and promise that their particular approach will have a high success rate in resolving relationship problems.[482] As long as we keep in mind that everybody is right from their own view, and put the advice of each book into an Integral context, we can appreciate its content as a contribution to our deeper understanding of the entire territory of love relationships, and choose the material that best supports us in our own healing and growth work, and understanding of our partner.

Please note that the page numbers that are specified in the reviews below refer to the American paperback editions of the books, unless otherwise noted. If you have a different edition, the page numbers may slightly vary.

Books for Red Singles

The Rules: Time-tested Secrets for Capturing the Heart of Mr. Right by Ellen Fein and Sherrie Schneider, is the infamous bestseller (2,000,000 copies sold) that teaches women how to manipulate "Mr. Right" to become obsessed with her by playing hard to get (page 6). The first suggested step in the plot is for women to do everything they can to look their best, by eating right, getting into shape, wearing sexy clothes, growing long hair, undergoing plastic surgery, and being feminine (pages 15-21). What follows are 35 rules,[483] such as #4 don't meet him halfway or go Dutch on a date, #5 don't call him and rarely return his calls, #6 always end phone calls first, #7 don't accept a Saturday night date after Wednesday, #11 always end the date first, #13 don't see him more than once or twice a week, #16 don't tell him what to do, #18 don't expect a man to change or try to change him, #30 Next!—how to deal with being dumped, #31 don't discuss the rules with your therapist, #34 love only those who love you, and #35 be easy to live with. *The Rules* assumes that men want to pursue women and will become bored and eventually lose interest if she is too available or seems to pursue him. By following *The Rules*, the authors (one of them got divorced in 2001) promise marriage in the shortest time possible to a man whom they love and who loves them back even more. This right-hand approach objectifies men and manipulates them in an egocentric manner.

The Pickup Artist: The New and Improved Art of Seduction is the playbook of the infamous living-large playboy and pickup/seduction artist Mystery, who is portrait in Neil Strauss's *New York Times* bestseller *The Game* (see below). Pickup artists generally strive for better short-term sexual and romantic success with as many attractive women (who are rated by their looks from 1-10) as possible through self-improvement and exploitation of their selfish psyche. The general assumption is that women like to be approached and seduced by relaxed, carefree, confident, happy, smiling, playful, and entertaining alpha males. By making seduction of women into an art—which requires knowledge, skill, and practice—an AFC (Average Frustrated Chump) can become a successful PUA (Pick-Up Artist). The book features an extensive glossary (page 239) that explains many of the PUA's acronyms.

The basic strategy is "find, meet, attract, and close" or FMAC (page xviii). Step one is to identify places with lots of beautiful women (clubs, bars, malls, museums, concerts, etc.). Step two requires men to overcome natural nervousness and to approach as many targets as possible, from a 45-degree angle within three seconds of seeing them, and to strike up a situational conversation or use a prepared pickup line. Step three involves conveying a personality that provides added value to the target (see list on page 179) by doing 80% of the talking (page 184) and performing certain magic and ESP tricks. Since 9s and 10s—the PUA's goal—get hit on by men all the time, they are initially ignored or slightly insulted (Are these nails real or fake? Have you noticed that your nose wiggles in a funny way when you talk? Is she always that demanding? – see list on page 201), while 8s and below get positive attention (see summary pages 152-153). This supposedly motivates the "bombshell" to pursue the PUA through some reverse psychology, sometimes called "the negative close." Objects who respond negatively are abandoned as quickly as possible (even PUA's get rejected 90% of the time—so it is a numbers game), women who send positive signals (smile, touch their hair, respond to physical touch) get touched and are asked for a kiss to test their willingness. Step four involves isolating the target if she was in a group of friends, striking up a more intimate conversation with her, and asking for her number and a date.

The Game: Penetrating the Secret Society of Pickup Artists by Neil Strauss, who is a book author and contributing writer for the New York Times and Rolling Stone, describes his adventures with Mystery (see above) into the seduction community to become a pickup artist. This entertaining book covers 12 steps: Select a Target, Approach and Open, Demonstrate Value, Disarm the Obstacles, Isolate the Target, Create an Emotional Connection, Extract to a Seduction Location, Pump Buying Temperature, Make a Physical Connection, Blast Last-Minute Resistance, Manage Expectations.

The Pickup Artist and *The Game* are similar in their content and try to be entertaining in their story telling style—with *The Game* providing more self-critical insights into the psyche of PUA's and the women they attract. Despite the sad objectification of females and the hard-to-pull-off manipulative techniques to get sex, only naive and unassuming female targets would be at risk of falling for the true narcissists, while mature women would quickly see through the plot, set their own healthy boundaries, and reward more authentic and truthful men with their attention. Since many men with integrity and good intentions are often nervous and at a loss how to approach attractive women in public, the advice given (taken with the necessary grain of salt) can support them in building more self-confidence and skills around women—who generally appreciate this quality in men if it is authentic.

The Potency Principles: Transforming Sexual Energy Into Spiritual Power by Victor Gold, tells the author's story of how he learned to pleasure women through focusing on them instead of himself, especially by providing erotic vulva and G-spot massages, and delaying or avoiding ejaculation by squeezing his PC muscle. According to Gold, this leads to physical health and fulfilling relationships as well as spiritual transformation and growth in consciousness. Mr. Gold is certainly well-meaning, but grossly reduces relationships to the upper quadrants "I/it" realm by focusing on the physical body, sex, and his and her interior experience without a deeper emotional connection. Written from a first-person amber perspective, it can support red men to move from the "fucking" into the "having sex" stage. For lovers in higher stages, more in-depth books about sexuality and Tantra, such as Margo Anand's classic *The Art of Sexual Ecstasy* or John Maxwell Taylor's *Eros Ascending* are recommended.

Books for Amber Couples

The Art of Loving by Erich Fromm (which sold over 6,000,000 copies worldwide) was written in 1956 and opens with the question of whether love is an art that requires knowledge and effort, or if it is a pleasant sensation that people fall into by chance. In the following pages he advocates for the former, while thinking that most people believe in the latter—wanting to be loved, but not knowing how to love (which seems to be even truer today than it was in 1956). He outlines that any mastery of art requires theory and practice (page 5). According to Fromm, our need for love (return to oneness—versus fusion—or to find at-one-ment) is the most fundamental passion of humans (page 17) that stems from our awareness of separation, which—without reunion by love—is the source of shame, guilt, and anxiety (page 9). The following pages outline developmental stages up into orange, in which "the polarities of the sexes disappear and with them erotic love" and "men and women become the same without opposite poles" (page 15). He then goes on to touch on codependence, ascending (sadism) and descending (masochism), agency and communion, giving and receiving, care, responsibility, respect and knowledge, and the feminine and masculine (pages 18-35). Five objects of love (brotherly, motherly, erotic, self, and God) distinguish between love among equals, love for the helpless (compassion), love for one other person (fusion), self-love and selflessness (love is an active striving for the growth and happiness of the loved person, rooted in one's own capacity to love, page 55), and various forms of love for God.[484] A chapter on real love and its disintegration in contemporary Western society is followed by a guide for the practice of love, which, according to Fromm, requires qualities such as discipline, presence, patience, faith, humility, concern for others, ability to listen, sensitivity, overcoming one's narcissism, reason, courage, and fairness.

Writing mainly from a lower quadrant perspective, Fromm is critical of the rogue capitalist orange and New Age narcissistic green worldviews and decries a loss of amber values in relationships and Western societies at large. However, most of his observations in this visionary book are relevant to this day, and have provided the basis for many modern relationship books. It provides a great foundation for singles and couples who want to take an Integral perspective on love relationships and is highly recommended.

The Exceptional Seven Percent: The Nine Secrets of the World's Happiest Couples by Gregory K. Popcak, covers the two lower quadrants in an exceptional way. Based on Maslow's hierarchy of needs, he identifies five major categories of marriages (page 24) that vaguely resemble the stages of consciousness from magenta to green. He calls them (1) deadly marriages, (2) shipwrecked marriages, (3) storybook marriages, (4) partnership marriages, and (5) spiritual peer marriages. The latter display exceptional qualities in nine areas: shared vision, fidelity (not only sexual), love, service, rapport, negotiation, gratitude, joy, and sexuality. Through worksheets and quizzes, couples can create what he calls "a marital imperative" (a shared vision statement) and determine the stage of their marriage for each of the nine crucial areas (pages 7-21). What follows are chapters to sharpen the partnership skills that he identified as crucial for the sustainability of an exceptional marriage. Since Maslow's hierarchy of needs represents a horizontal translation for each stage of vertical consciousness development (you can be self-actualized at each level), Popcak's book can serve couples at almost any altitude, including second-tier partnerships. It is highly recommended.

Appendix I: Relationship Books for All Levels/Colors | 183

The Seven Principles for Making Marriage Work by John Gottman and Nan Silver, has become a classic among couples and therapists. This amber book opens with a strong argument for the benefits of traditional marriages and the liabilities that result from divorce. After closely monitoring 49 couples for a weekend each in an apartment-like setting called The Seattle Love Lab, Gottman was able to predict with 91 percent accuracy if his clients would soon divorce or stay together, after watching and listening to them for just five minutes (pages 2-3). He found that happy marriages don't depend on good communication skills, effective conflict resolution, or shared interests, but rather thrive on intimacy and friendship (shared lifestyle, personality, and values, page 23) that are based in seven principles: (1) Enhance your love maps—know about your spouse's everyday life, priorities, interests, desires, dreams, goals, etc., (2) nurture your fondness and admiration—remember and appreciate positive qualities in your spouse, (3) turn toward each other instead of away—fill the emotional bank account through active listening, empathy, affection, and validation, (4) let your partner influence you—husbands should listen to their wives, yield, and share power and the decision-making process with them, (5) solve your solvable problems—communicate, be tolerant, and compromise—and accept the irresolvable ones, (6) overcome gridlock—accept and support each spouse's individual goals and dreams, and (7) create shared meaning—through similar spiritual values and life purposes.

The overall message of this lower-quadrants focused book is that husbands can make their marriage work if they become less dominant and more understanding, supportive, emotionally available, and compromising. This is certainly good advice for most conventional couples, but will not prevent most modern and postmodern wives from leaving their relationships.

For Men Only: A Straightforward Guide to the Inner Lives of Women by Shaunti and Jeff Feldhahn (hardcover edition) is the perfect little book for conventional men who NEVER read or learned anything about gender differences between the sexes. Written from an amber Christian perspective (page 19) it suggests that "husbands need to love their wives just as Jesus does us—which means to love, serve, and be willing to sacrifice everything for her good, even above our own." In seven short and to-the-point chapters, the authors explain (1) that even after the wedding a man needs to constantly reassure his wife of his love and to continually pursue (romance) her, (2) how her painful emotions from the past and nonlinear thinking often prevent her from being rational and that it is not his fault if she suffers, (3) that 70% of [amber] women would choose emotional over financial security and prefer their husbands to work less/make less money in order to spend more time with them, (4) how her feelings about a problem are more important than the problem itself and that a man should not try to offer solutions but simply listen to her and show empathy (unless it is a technical versus an emotional problem, like a flat tire), (5) that most women want sex less often than men do, and need more warm-up time, (6) that she needs ongoing affirmation that she is the most beautiful woman to him, and (7) that [amber] women see their husbands as heroes who make them happy, even if they don't tell him that. If none of this common lower right-hand advice is news to you, or if your orange (or above) partner is more complex and demanding, then you may save your time/money for a more advanced relationship book.

For Women Only: What You Need to Know about the Inner Lives of Men by Shaunti Feldhahn (hardcover edition) is the companion to the book above, but geared towards women. The book suggests that men (1) would rather be alone and unloved than to feel disrespected and inadequate, which leads them to anger and withdrawal, (2) are imposters who hide a deep inner insecurity behind their confident mask, (3) feel obligated to be the provider even if their wives have enough income to support them both, (4) feel affirmed through sex from their wife, (5) like to look at sexy women—even if they are married, (6) want romance as much as women do but are sometimes not sure how she wants to be romanced, (7) want their partner to stay fit and healthy, and (8) want her to know how much they love her. This little book with its lower right-hand focus is great to be given to your conventional partner if you would like her to be informed about and follow its advice, and you don't know how to convey it to her otherwise.

Why Mars and Venus Collide: Improving Relationships by Understanding How Men and Women Cope Differently with Stress by John Gray (hardcover edition) is the latest contribution to his famous Mars and Venus series of books (see Bibliography below) that traditionally focus on gender differences in the lower right-hand quadrants of conventional and modern singles and couples. It is based on new upper right-hand scientific findings of hormonal and brain differences in males and females that lead to different causes and coping mechanisms for stress. As usual, the book starts out with a list of typical complaints from men and women about each other (pages 8-10) that result from evolutionary differences (men are single-focused hunters, women are multitasking gatherers/caregivers) and the shifting gender roles in the past forty years (modern working women expect men to be more like wives, while men expect women to be more like their care-giving mothers, page 13), followed by a "he says–she says" chart (page 32). According to Gray, a first step to solving these problems is for women to be more realistic, ask for what they need, and appreciate men for what they contribute—while men should be more sensitive to her needs instead of becoming green Sensitive New Age Guys (SNAGs) (page 21). Next the book addresses why many successful orange and above women leave their partners and remain single rather than be in a love relationship (page 28), before explaining different behavior (e.g., women talk more) with questionable differences in male and female brain structures (pages 37-51).

Chapters three to five dive into the nitty-gritty of hormones that cause stress (e.g., adrenalin and cortisol), and those which alleviate it (e.g., oxytocin) and how women can increase their production of the latter (see lists on pages 98-101 and 109-112). Chapters six to nine are dedicated to fights between Mars and Venus, outlining the causes of conflict, the common mistakes during arguments that women (page 140-143) and men (page 144-146) make, and how to take a time-out to cool off. As the typical advice for amber and orange goes, he suggests that men should listen to and validate her feelings, while they should process their own with someone other than their romantic partner (e.g., a therapist or coach–see page 196), as women otherwise swing over to their masculine side and feel that they have to take care of him, which is a huge "sexual" turnoff for her. In the conclusion to his book, Gray observes that successful modern women still need attention, love, romance, and sex (pages 221-222), which all produce oxytocin—the antidote to stress—and how to keep romance alive (pages 223 and 226-227).

Like most books that address amber and below from a right-hand perspective, *Why*

Mars And Venus Collide does not create deeper levels of intimacy by healing childhood wounds and transcending gender differences, but teaches couples how to cope with their conflicts and to get what they want on a surface level, which is usually sex and appreciation for men, and money, status, and support for women.

How to Improve Your Marriage Without Talking About It, by Patricia Love and Steven Stosny, makes an interesting connection between the evolutionary differences of the sexes in the upper right-hand quadrant and the resulting left-hand experiences of fear in women and shame in men. They conclude that improving communication skills does not address the underlying conflicts that many couples experience. Instead, the authors suggest to accept the different views and needs of each partner (taking a second person perspective) and to connect with him or her emotionally and sexually instead of stonewalling or trying to fix the other. Through compassion and taking action (the root of emotion is motion that motivates behavior), couples can learn to act lovingly towards each other without having to address the root of painful feelings and dysfunctional behavior. While the insights about the fear/shame dynamic seem to be helpful for couples at any altitude that are entangled in it, the suggested solutions seem to be most suitable for partners in amber and orange.

BOOKS FOR SINGLE AMBER WOMEN

Making Sense of Men: A Woman's Guide to a Lifetime of Love, Care and Attention from All Men, by Alison Armstrong is an overpriced summary of, and advertisement for her similarly overpriced (but entertaining) **Celebrating Men, Satisfying Women**® weekend workshops that teach women how to "turn frogs into princes—instead of the other way around" (page 5). She teaches that a man's romantic behavior is a direct response to a woman's skillful means (pages 7-10), that men are not hairy women—who are multitasking gatherers—but single focused hunters (pages 11-17), and that four qualities in women (shiny hair, shapely body, sensuality, and sexual energy) will attract men who will want to have sex with them (pages 18-33). Once a woman has charmed and enchanted him with her self-confidence, authenticity, passion, and receptivity (pages 35-46), he will fall in love with her and make her happy by spending time, taking care, protecting, and contributing (pages 47-61). This is the perfect right-hand quadrant book for attractive "sex-positive" amber women who have never heard of gender-specific differences and want to manipulate men to satisfy their right-hand needs.

BOOKS FOR ORANGE COUPLES

Why We Love: The Nature and Chemistry of Romantic Love, by Helen Fisher, provides an in-depth analysis of the upper right-hand chemical processes in our bodies and brains that are experienced when we feel attracted, fall in love, commit ourselves, or get left by a partner. As an anthropologist, she identifies our deep-seated desire to have our Primary Fantasy met (to experience chemistry and to fall in love) as hardwired into our brains through millions of years of evolution. Through brain scans and chemical analysis she was able to link the states of sexual lust, infatuation, romance, commitment, and heartbreak to specific hormones and brain activities. Even though (or because) it grossly reduces love to the upper right-hand quadrant, it is a perfect, fascinating, and contemporary companion to all other relationship books.

Real Love: The Truth About Finding Unconditional Love & Fulfilling Relationships, by Greg Baer, addresses orange and below that is engaging in what he calls "imitation love" of getting (demanding what makes us happy—or else) and protecting (emotional wounds) versus "real love" or "unconditional love." His rational right-hand approach suggests making our partner happy by swallowing any kind of behavior by him or her without having expectations, emotionally reacting, blaming, fixing, or criticizing—unless a promise is broken (pages 54-55). According to Baer, we will attract a partner who sees, accepts, and loves us for who we are if we are truthful about ourselves without protecting our childhood wounds. In an interesting section about choice (pages 37-40) he outlines that we can either live with our relationship and like it, live with it and hate it, or leave it (for example if our partner is physically abusive—see page 233). As the title suggests, Baer often talks about "The Truth" and therefore gets frequently stuck in "performative contradictions," as he assumes that happiness is derived from doing (behavior) instead of being, and does not recognize vertical development or the interior (unconscious, healing, and growth). However, the book is certainly useful for angry people (a major theme) who suffer and cause suffering to others by living in constant opposition to life and their partner.

Getting The Love You Want: A Guide for Couples, by Harville Hendrix, addresses unconscious childhood wounds that either lead to what he calls "unconscious marriages" that are codependent and full of power struggles or a "conscious marriage" in which the couple learns to heal and grow by (1) closing the exits (dedicating themselves to healing and growth instead of leaving), (2) creating a zone of safety, (3) engaging in pleasurable activities (creating intimacy), (4) increasing knowledge of themselves and their partner through better communication (active listening, mirroring, validation, and empathy),[485] and (5) containing rage. His amber/orange approach covers all four quadrants by drawing from a number of disciplines, including the behavioral sciences, depth psychology, cognitive therapy, and Gestalt therapy, but ignores vertical development. Out of his own experiences in a failed marriage and his work with thousands of singles and couples, he and his current wife developed *Imago Couples Therapy* which is outlined in 10 steps and 16 exercises in Part III of the book. Hendrix's classic book (not to be confused with pop psychology authors Kathlyn and Gay Hendricks's 25+ books, and academic researchers Clyde and Susan Handrick's work—see Bibliography below) is profound and practical, with many stories and examples. The advice and exercises are helpful for modern and postmodern couples who truly want to enter the challenging path of mutual healing and growth inside their partnership, instead of choosing the easy way out through divorce.

The New Rules Of Marriage: What You Need to Know to Make Love Work, by Terrence Real, is yet another book that recognizes how the liberation of modern women at the

Appendix I: Relationship Books for All Levels/Colors | 187

end of the twentieth century challenged men who want to be in a partnership not to only be successful protectors and providers, but also to be emotionally available (pages 6-9). It provides "a new set of rules that can help men become more responsible and more emotionally available while helping women become less resentful and more effective." Real defines intimacy as "a process of connection [receiving and transmitting] in the five areas of human experience: intellectual, emotional, physical [social], sexual, and spiritual" (pages 21-24) which essentially covers the four quadrants. He advises men to take an inventory in these five areas and to start practicing their intimacy skills (pages 25-32). Chapter two focuses on five *losing strategies* that prevent intimacy: (1) needing to be right, (2) controlling your partner, (3) unbridled self-expression, (4) retaliation, and (5) withdrawal. By learning to stop projecting their childhood related CNI's (Core Negative Images) onto their partner, couples can break the vicious cycle of losing strategies by addressing psychological boundary violations such as yelling and screaming, name-calling, shaming or humiliating, telling what the other should do, breaking agreements/contracts, lying, and manipulating—if need be through individual psychotherapy (page 104). Developing good boundaries (staying protected AND connected) and healthy self-esteem (your intrinsic worth and value as a human being) become the foundation for the level of intimacy that the reader hopes to generate (pages 120-157). The failure to do so is illustrated by a grid on page 147 (resembling the four unhealthy feminine/masculine polarities) with grandiosity (ascending), shame (descending), boundaryless (communion), and walled-off (agency) as their coordinates. The ability to balance and harmonize the four polarities in a healthy way leads to the five winning strategies of (1) shifting from complaint to request, (2) speaking out with love, (3) responding with generosity, (4) empowering each other, and (5) cherishing [what you have] that are outlined in detail and with practices on pages 163-279. *The New Rules Of Marriage* will work best for orange couples with a willingness to rescue and improve their partnership by learning how to (1) identify their wants and needs, (2) listen well and respond generously, (3) set limits and stand up for themselves, (4) know when to back off, (5) know when to get help, (6) know when to embrace what they have with appreciation and gratitude, (7) share themselves and receive their partner, and (8) actively cherish each other (page 18) by becoming more emotionally available.

Passionate Marriage: Keeping Love and Intimacy Alive in Committed Relationships, by David Schnarch, has become a classic of the genre, integrating for the first time sex therapy (body) and couples counseling (mind). Starting out with the question "If sex is a natural function, why are some people not responding or not willing to respond?" (page 41), he found the answer in misconceptions about sexual behavior and emotional blocks which prevent deeper intimacy between couples, to which his answer is—you guessed it—ongoing healing and personal development. According to Schnarch, this healing and development can be accomplished by focusing on the present without unearthing childhood wounds. Hence, the book is about resilience rather than damage, health rather than old wounds, and human potential rather than trauma (page 43). In a process he calls "differentiation" (pages 53-74), which balances and harmonizes individuality (agency) and togetherness (communion)—or to be simultaneously a whole and a part—he establishes the importance of self-validated (versus other-validated) emotional intimacy through sharing of feelings and thoughts independent of our partner's "validation" (pages

106-111), which leads to a more satisfying sex life and fulfilling marriage. At the end of part one of the book we learn that "the brain/heart is our largest sex organ" (page 134) that generates sexual desire, and about its role in experiencing erections, sexual joy, and orgasm.

Part two of *Passionate Marriage* focuses on practical strategies for emotional and sexual connection, with chapters on hugging till relaxed, kissing and love making with open eyes, eyes-open orgasm, the mental dimensions of sexual experience (such as staying present in your body or with your partner during sex), and finally "fucking, doing, and being done"—a chapter on uninhibited wet sex.

Part three of the book is titled "Observations on the Process," with chapters on the dilemma of choice between agency and communion,[486] holding on to yourself during conflict (self-mastery, self-control, learning about yourself, confronting yourself, self-validated intimacy, taking care of yourself—page 324), couples in the crucible of growth (balancing growth and stability—page 355), and the last chapter on sex, love, and death in which—surprise—he discovers Wilber's book *Sex, Ecology, and Spirituality*. From it he picks the four drives of a holon (and ignores everything else) which resemble his model of differentiation and "explains" why couples who continuously differentiate and integrate grow in consciousness towards more spiritual and Integral awareness and hence Integral Relationships. WOW!

In his conclusion, Schnarch outlines that partners who share underlying values (level of consciousness) can change their behavior without losing their individual identity. This allows them to want for their partner what he or she wants, instead of changing each other to get their own way. Even though this lengthy 432-page book looks at relationships from a left-hand perspective and only differentiates between pre-conventional, conventional, and post-conventional stages, it may be the most Integral relationship book and speaks to sex-positive and radical growth-oriented orange and above couples.

Hold Me Tight: Seven Conversations for a Lifetime of Love, by Sue Johnson (hardcover edition) is a new bestseller and concludes that "A sense of secure [emotional] connection between romantic partners is key in positive loving relationships and a huge source of strength for the individuals in those relationships" (page 22). Inspired by the findings of British psychiatrist John Bowlby, Johnson developed Emotional Focused Therapy (EFT), which has a simple message: "Forget about learning how to argue better, analyze your early childhood, making grand romantic gestures, or experimenting with new sexual positions. Instead, recognize and admit that you are emotionally attached to and dependent on your partner in much the same way that a child is on a parent for nurturing, soothing, and protection" (page 7). Her therapy—which claims a 70-75 % success rate (page 7) for her self-selecting clients—is based on three components that encourage emotional connection: (1) Accessibility: Can I reach you? (2) Responsiveness: Can I rely on you to respond to me emotionally? (3) Engagement: Do I know you will value me and stay close? (pages 49-50). These components are exemplified in "Seven Transformative Conversations" (pages 63-203) that are titled (1) Recognizing the Demon Dialogs, (2) Finding the Raw Spots, (3) Revisiting a Rocky Moment, (4) Hold Me Tight, (5) Forgiving Injuries, (6) Bonding Through Sex and Touch, and (7) Keeping Your Love Alive. The process is similar to non-violent communication, which teaches owning and sharing of feelings, and asking partners to meet emotional needs for connection. Unlike *Passionate*

Marriage (which suggests using relationship-conflict for healing and personal growth by balancing and harmonizing healthy agency and communion), and *How to Improve Your Marriage Without Talking About It* (which advises couples to break the fear/shame cycle by taking responsibility for their own feelings and behavior), *Hold Me Tight* advocates for undifferentiated dependence (communion) and requires reciprocity to work. Written from a feminine perspective of need for emotional safety (page 22) and fear if it is lost (page 30), *Hold Me Tight* claims that "healthy dependence is the essence of romantic love" (page 253) and that men, in addition to being providers and protectors, need to learn that to "cuddle and connect emotionally is vital for a healthy love relationship" (page 255). It is therefore best suited for orange couples who transition into green and want to rescue their marriage, and women who are in relationship with emotionally needy green men. People in second-tier will most likely find the attachment- and need-driven approach to be unbalanced and counterproductive to their healing and growth, while it is unlikely that amber and below will be able to master the required "interior" emotional work.

Books for Orange Single Women

Is He Mr. Right?: Everything You Need to Know Before You Commit by Mira Kirshenbaum (hardcover edition) is the typical book for attractive and affluent single orange women who seek the elusive good-looking, successful, and entertaining "hot guy" who also makes them feel secure by being able to control his negative emotions (anger) and commits himself exclusively to give her his time and money (see cover with the man on his knees holding a diamond ring and pages 74-95, *"Hot Guy/Safe Guy Ping Pong"*).

As we know there is a big discrepancy in our modern society between the many attractive and successful orange women who look for such men, and the few available bachelors who fit both, the "Hot" and "Safe" criteria. Since there is no shortage of so called duds (loser men—pages 95-108) who compete for attractive orange women, *Is He Mr. Right* focuses on getting rid of the ones who don't fit both criteria as quickly as possible. According to Kirshenbaum, the criterion for Mr. Right is NOT compatibility, but how he *feels* in five dimensions of what she calls chemistry (pages 11-38); (1) comfortable and close, (2) safe, (3) fun to be with, (4) sexually attractive, (5) respectable by being smart, powerful, and successful—and respectful of her ambition and accomplishments. If any of these areas do not feel 100% right, dump the dud and move on (pages 61-72 *"Can You Dump The Duds"*)—otherwise he is a keeper and everything else will work itself out (pages 132-135 *"Chemistry trumps lifestyle differences"*). If this strategy does not work for a woman, it may be that she is not ready for a partnership because of unresolved issues from past relationships (pages 139-152), lack of self love (pages 153-159), inability to deal with his emotional baggage and financial obligations (pages 160-166), her insecurity (pages 167-181), and/or negative family and peer pressures (pages 182-186).

The final part of the book focuses on "stages" (states) of relationships and what to do: (1) on a first date, interview him about how he spends his time, how he feels about women, how he likes his job, if he has roommates, how his previous relationships ended, how available he is, and any other questions that are important to her (pages 194-195),

(2) not to fall in love before it is clear that there is chemistry and that he is hot AND safe —otherwise dump the dud (page 213), (3) not to make a commitment during the love struck-phase, (4) only to have sex when it feels right for her, not to confuse "horniness" with love, and to see great sex as an important microcosm of the relationship, (5) not to try to work on the relationship if things get worse after the six-month love-struck phase and to say good-bye to the guy (page 235), (6) not to negotiate with him once she is ready to break up and move on (page 246), (7) how to get him on his knees, to offer her a ring, and to drag him to the altar (pages 247-252), and last but not least (8) how to say good bye to Mr. Maybe (page 253). This genre of books (of which there are many—e.g., Barbara DeAnglis' *Are You the One for Me*, Dr. Phil McGraw's *Love Smart: Find the One You Want—Fix the One You Got*, or Dale Koppel's book below) works well for highly attractive career women who are relationship- and sex-positive. They are also a good read for "loser men" who get constantly rejected by attractive women and don't understand why.

The Intelligent Woman's Guide to Online Dating, by Dale Koppel is an inspiring book for orange career women and men who seek an affluent "fuck buddy" or "friend with benefits" (the author's words' pages 89 and 95). It provides very useful tips for a rational and efficient right-hand approach to proactive Internet dating. Its central message is: Don't sit around and grieve after a breakup, life is too short (the author posted her profile 12 days after her husband of 25 years left her). Get into shape (she is very slender/sexy and had cosmetic surgery), make dating your second job, take great pictures, make a list of what you want, write a witty profile (consider lying about your age, marital status, drinking habits, and location—pages 24-25), cast a wide net, actively contact all men that look even remotely interesting, quickly eliminate the losers (her favorite word is "Next!"), learn from your mistakes, meet as soon as possible for a short interview, play the numbers game as efficiently as possible, and stay open to possibilities. The book is well written, contains many pragmatic tips for Internet dating, is succinct, comes to the point, and has some fun little stories. It is recommended for driven single orange women and men, and also serves all men who want to identify women like her before paying for dates, wasting their time, and being humiliated.

BOOKS FOR ORANGE SINGLE WOMEN AND MEN

Relationship Roulette: Improve Your Odds at Lasting Love by Carol Diamond (hardcover edition) traces "unhealthy" partner choices back to unconscious childhood memories that created a lack of love that later attract adults to a partner with a mutually compatible pathology (chapters 1 and 2). Once smitten, these couples struggle with creating healthy closeness (balancing agency and communion) because they either fear to become engulfed or abandoned (pages 21-23). Page 24 provides a list of early indicators for emotionally unavailable individuals that can't commit to becoming interdependent. In order to "undo the damage" (page 33), singles are asked if they are fully available to do the healing work and create the necessary space in their life to overcome their ambivalence towards being in a healthy partnership. If the answer is yes, then chapter four provides some basic dating advice, before the author touches on the definition of the word "love" in a historical context in chapter 5, covering the Greek notions of eros, agape, philia, and storge,[487] as well as the opinions of Freud, Jung, and Adler about romance. The following chapters focus on partners that are wrong for each other (page 63) with examples of various (dysfunctional) relationships and living-arrangements that they form. Chapter 9 covers communication problems between the sexes, followed by some basic advice on how to overcome them (reflective listening, validation, honesty, responding (instead of reacting), showing respect, avoiding projections (called transference and displacement), making "I" statements, negotiation and compromise, and, last but not least, non-verbal behaviors). The final chapter 11 outlines an action plan with examples to (1) recognize your relationship patterns, (2) dentify the changes you want to make, (3) set your goals, (4) develop a plan of action, and (5) implement your plan. This short and easy to read book focuses on unconscious conditioning in the interior quadrants and provides many stories of dysfunctional couples to illustrate its left-hand approach to finding lasting love.

A Book for Orange Single Men

Stumbling Naked In the Dark: Overcoming Mistakes That Men Make with Women, by Bradley Fenton, is a short book that promises men more sexual success by learning how to be more confident and how to break out of the adversarial game-like patterns that are often created when they approach women in an aggressive way that feels pushy. Instead of using the self-centered red PUA's techniques (see above) of deception and persuasion, Fenton suggests changing the old behavior patterns of men (who do anything to get sex) and women (who protect themselves from being hurt) that make dating difficult (pages 8-10) by trading the win-lose game for a more assertive, direct, and honest approach. By recognizing the evolutionary condition of women to choose successful providers as mates (pages 21-23), he teaches men to lead by following women's cues. Concept one is to develop an "I can take it or leave it" or "selectively indifferent" attitude, the middle path between being a jerk who does not give a shit about her and the desperate neediness of an insecure man (pages 24-47). Concept two covers building trust by making her feel comfortable through skillful conversation techniques that focus on her needs instead of his sexual desires, and by applying NLP techniques such as mirroring of her body language and communication style (pages 48-60). Concept three involves opening a conversation with a "No" agreement, which puts you at ease to accept her rejection and gets her to say yes more often by putting her in control of her choices (pages 61-66). Concept four teaches how to ask good questions and to listen actively (pages 67-97). Concept five advises to ask her at the end of a first date how interested she is in you on a scale from 1 (not interested) to 10 (very interested and wants to see you again). If the answer is between 7 and 9, he suggests to ask what it would take to get you to a 10, and to assume that she is ready for physical contact such as kissing—which will lead to sex if you express your desire AND that you want to respect her pace (and you are ready whenever she is). The final concept addresses the removal of roadblocks to success such as fear of approaching women and striking up a natural conversation, negative self-images, need for approval, and sexual neediness. This is a useful little guidebook for men who seek basic advice on how to be more successful with orange women by applying techniques that focus on the lower quadrants.

BOOKS FOR GREEN SINGLES AND COUPLES

The Path to Love: Spiritual Strategies for Healing, by Deepak Chopra, explores the topic of love from a left-hand, spiritual, green perspective, with its basic premise that we ARE love and that we are lovable the way we are. In essence, Chopra—like so many other spiritual teachers—makes a convincing case that our capacity for human love is a direct reflection of the depth and embodiment of our psychological health, spiritual realization, and level of ego transcendence—the three areas that support us in removing blocks to love such as anger, fear, egotism, insecurity, and mistrust (page 14). His book is a wonderful complement to this rather technical Integral relationship manual, as it addresses the idealistic and spiritual dimension with emotional insight, depth, and many heartwarming stories, for example when he states that "A man and a woman can reflect divine love in their love for each other." He offers a path that unites (or equates) spirit with romantic love by outlining the benefits of giving and receiving of affection, the psychosomatic stressors in the absence of love (pages 29-50), the four states of love (attraction, infatuation, courtship, and intimacy—page 64), positive thinking, realistic expectations, avoiding projections, equality, surrender that fosters (sexual) intimacy, non-attachment, allowing, passion (for life), and cultivating inspiration/ecstasy.

As always when ignoring certain quadrants and vertical levels, we get a limited view, and this book is no exception, as it downplays or ignores perspectives of the right-hand quadrants and worldviews of orange and below (even though he mentions lower and higher levels of the seven chakras on pages 316-321). It is however a wonderful guide for lovers in green and above who see partnership predominantly as a spiritual path.

Undefended Love, by Jett Psaris and Marlena Lyons, may be the most radical book to address the upper left-hand quadrant from a green altitude. This book for committed couples was inspired by the work of A. H. Almaas and other spiritual psychologists. The focus throughout is to uncover the essential self by transcending any emotional defenses that may prevent unconditional (or undefended) love. By claiming that our essential capacity to love lies within and does not depend on a loving, compatible, or perfect partner, the authors outline various false identities and defenses that we have developed to avoid re-experiencing the psychological wounds that were inflicted upon us during childhood. The book offers many useful practical exercises (see pages 55, 68, 76, 89, and 155) that support readers in owning their emotional reactions to their partner's reality and to effectively uncover, release, and heal old pain. This allows for ever-increasing healthy closeness (intimacy) that the book clearly differentiates from unhealthy codependency. By learning how to stop reacting to a partner's reality and moving from needs (or neediness) into "no-preference," (pages 139-150), the authors suggest that we can co-create partnerships that don't require any agreements (page 97) or certain agreeable behaviors from our partner (pages 18-20).

The premise of this book is highly challenging, especially for women, as it takes an ascending approach (being present) and requires healthy descending (surrender) in a partnership. Since it ignores all other quadrants and addresses couples instead of singles, it gets lost on many green women who avoid partnerships with men for the very reasons that are outlined in the book, such as "I love myself too much to endure any more pain in a partnership," "it is on men to become more conscious," "a man needs to have status and money to be worthy of me," etc. *Undefended Love* is the perfect guide to support couples in second-tier to heal their remaining UL psychological wounds.

How to Be an Adult in Relationship: The Five Keys to Mindful Loving, by David Richo, starts with the premise that "all the love in the world will not bring us happiness or make a relationship work. That requires skill [and practice], and this skill is quite attainable" (page 1). According to him, most people feel loved when they receive the five A's: (1) attention, (2) acceptance, (3) appreciation, (4) affection, and (5) are allowed the freedom to live in accord with their deepest needs and wishes. The ability to bestow these five elements unconditionally onto a partner—and ultimately the world—requires working through childhood and personal conundrums, and the practice of compassionate mindfulness and ego transcendence, which transforms relationships into a path of psychological healing and spiritual growth. The book discusses each of the five A's and how they apply to childhood wounds, relationships, and spiritual maturity—with the goal that the reader becomes a more loving person, with the world as his or her beneficiary. After the obligatory chapters on healing psychological wounds in part one of the book, part two provides advice on (1) choosing a partner who meets a list of criteria (page 85),[488] (2) providing "full disclosure" of positive and negative character traits, (3) rising in love (instead of falling into addictive behaviors) during the romance phase, with a helpful list to identify the difference between the two on pages 118-119, (4) dealing with conflicts (if need be with the help of a therapist), (5) introverted and extroverted types, (6) healthy conflict versus stressful drama, (7) neediness versus needs, (8) fear of abandonment and engulfment (see list on pages 165-166), (9) jealousy, (10) infidelity, (11) letting go of ego, and (12) ending a relationship—with a list on pages 203-204 that can help to make this often difficult choice. Part three of the book is dedicated to the spiritual potentials of committed partnerships between soul mates who support each other in their healing and growth.

As many other authors who address singles and couples at the green level, Richo calls them to balance and harmonize the four drives in the interior quadrants through psychosocial healing and a spiritual practice that will allow them to move into second-tier consciousness, where healthy committed partnerships between opposites and equals can become a reality. Unlike others, he has a talent to interweave spiritual and therapeutic aspects with pragmatic advice on how to choose a partner and make a relationship work.

Love and Awakening: Discovering the Sacred Path of Intimate Relationship, by John Welwood, presents a "psychospiritual" approach to relationships that focuses largely on the upper left-hand quadrant. He believes that we can know another, and be known, only as deeply as we know ourselves. To create a sacred relationship that reaches beyond amber duty and orange pleasure requires coming into a deeper connection with our true essential nature—both psychological and spiritual. Seen in this light, love becomes a path of awakening—rousing us from a sleep of old, unconscious patterns into the freshness and immediacy of living more fully in the present, in accord with who we really are (introduction, page XIII). Defining love as "be-ing fully present" in the moment (page 3) without having or doing, he notes that most couples are not really there with each other. What separates them are outer pressures of life and inner obstacles such as old beliefs, emotional reactions, fears, and patterns of denial and avoidance (page 6). By confronting these obstacles, they can regain their capacity for compassion, which is the antidote to human suffering (page 13). According to Welwood, there is no time to lose, because only between one person and another can the renewal of our world begin (introduction, page XVI). The chapters that follow outline how humans develop a false self and unconscious identity (ego) during childhood that becomes defensive when a romantic partner brings them up against the prison walls of their personality structure—which needs to be pushed against before it can be broken through (Sartre—hell is other people—page 32). In Chapter four, Welwood distinguishes between a universal kind of love that we can feel towards many human beings and the unique connection that soul mates (which he calls worthy opponents—page 54) experience as "the opening of a further dimension—seeing and loving each other for who they could become under each other's influence" (page 50). Overcoming the inner enemy that is all too often projected outwardly onto our partner is the topic of chapter five, which opens with a Hermann Hesse quote: "Whenever we hate someone, we are hating some part of ourselves that we see in that person. We don't get worked up about anything that is not in ourselves." As soul mates bring out the best and worst in each other (see chapter six, co-emergence, pages 95-99) they can use their partnership for transformation once they realize that their conflicts are rooted in a "fourfold truth" (page 103)—each partner's objective behavior and distorted emotional reaction. Working with the chaos of conflict by bringing the shadow into the open (page 126) through truth–telling (pages 131-138), exposing the raw edges (pages 138-139), and no-fault listening (pages 139-142) will lead to a new birth of consciousness, which is the topic of chapters seven, eight, and nine. Chapter ten outlines the inner marriage of the feminine yin and masculine yang—the balancing and harmonizing of agency, communion, ascending, and descending.[489] The next chapter is dedicated to men in relationship because "despite all their expertise in worldly affairs, they are still primitives in their relationships with women—because fully engaging with a woman means probing the uncharted depths of their own inner life. "This is the new frontier for men today" (pages 181-182). In "the dialectic of male (animus) development," Welwood calls for "a different brand of heroism" that overcomes men's fear of women and to meet them "with an open heart and mind, to be receptive to what they have to teach or to hold their own ground in the face of their emotional intensity or earthy strength" (page 184). Seeing the feminine as activator (the anima that *animates*), balancing his strength and softness, and channeling his forcefulness (anger and potency) in a conscious and mindful way, can be used in the service of his sacred vision and purpose (page 199). In the final two short chapters, "Suchness and magic" and "The broken-hearted warrior and the renewal of the world" Welwood reminds us that the deeper meaning of love is not to get our needs met by an object of our desire, but a longing for the sacred presence that lies at the heart of our being and at the heart of the world. Intimate relationship is therefore the outer reflection of this sacred love affair (page 231), and "broken hearts" are actually "hearts that are broken open" to this deeper reality (page 236). Like most other green books, *Love and Awakening* ignores aspects of the right-hand quadrants, but is a wonderful book for green and second-tier couples who want to explore and deepen the sacred dimension of their partnership.

The Heart's Wisdom: A Practical Guide to Growing through Love, by Joyce and Barry Vissell, is the latest book by this couple that has walked their talk since they met in 1964, married in 1968, and started to teach relationship seminars in 1972. Interlacing many personal stories from their own journey, workshop participants, and clients, the Vissells introduce their readers to the importance of a committed love relationship as a soul mirror that allows the couple to see parts of themselves that would otherwise remain invisible (page 3). At the heart of their book are three upper-left red/green beliefs: (1) that love continuously brings us back to ourselves, (2) that each of us is ultimately in relationship with ourselves, and (3) that this inner relationship is the spiritual path that most of us in Western culture are following (page 20). Hence their teaching embraces the idea that we cannot open to the fullness of love until we stop pointing the finger at our partner and see ourselves as the source of all our feelings, including our reactions, independent of what he or she did to cause them (page 24). They follow the masculine logic that a deeper view of ourselves provides a deeper view of everyone else (page 22) and that who we are attracted to or repelled by represents aspects of our psyche that we need to cultivate or deal with in a better way (page 23) in ourselves. While they acknowledge that a deep connection with another soul is one of life's most precious treasures (page 26), they frequently return to the importance of agency and the connection to the self, which can be contradictory and confusing at times, as they don't seem to make the leap to see the relationship as a new whole. The book, which is not very linear in its approach and sometimes mixes pre-conventional believes with post-conventional experiences, has 23 chapters that cover topics such as gratitude and appreciation, constructive criticism, unspiritual and spiritual partners, overcoming fears and doubts, codependence and interdependence, learning from the mirror, anger management, saying "no," passion and compassion, dealing with jealousy and disappointment, relationship transitions, being of service, and making love last. Each chapter closes with questions and suggestions for practices that allow motivated couples to deepen their heart connection by strengthening their ego (sense of self, self-esteem, self-love, boundaries etc.) instead of transcending it, while making their partnership central to their life. This book seems most suitable for green and above couples with her on an ascending ego-strengthening, and him on a descending ego-transcending path.

BOOKS FOR GREEN SINGLES

If the Buddha Dated: A Handbook for Finding Love On a Spiritual Path, by Charlotte Kasl, provides a short and easy read for singles who seek a vibrant human relationship based on authenticity, equality, spirituality, and joy (page xiv). Drawing from Buddhism, Sufism, and Christianity, part one focuses on grounding through spiritual wisdom, such as awareness, compassion, and loving kindness, that leads to transcendence of needy desires or fears to be in a relationship, which she describes as manifestations of the egoic mind. Chapters six and fourteen cover the dance of oneness (communion) and separateness (agency), followed by her insight on page 44 that dating and relationship advice for red and amber singles focuses on understanding and accepting the differences between men and women, that orange experts encourage the sexes to express themselves authentically, and that green teachers do not differentiate between the two. Part two of the book is dedicated to attracting a partner who is an equal on the level of: physical/material, intellect, interests, values/lifestyle, psychological/emotional, creativity/passion, spiritual, essence, and sexuality (pages 62-68 and 120-127),, with chapters containing practical examples to formulate what we want and have to give in these areas (pages 75-81), when to trust our attraction to another person (pages 81-84), how to free the heart from unfinished business of the past (pages 85-93), and how to open up wholeheartedly to a love relationship without reservations (pages 94-96.) Part three covers the actual dating process with chapters on staying conscious and going slow, how to overcome fears, first dates, children and dating, sexuality, and giving and receiving. Part four dives into the process of choosing a mate who will join us on a spiritual path, covering how to deal with fear and ambivalence, tonglin (often spelled tonglen) meditation for healing and compassion, four lists to set a bottom line (1) unacceptable behavior of others, (2) unacceptable behavior of our own, (3) rationalizations and stories we use to disregard our bottom line, and (4) consequences of disregarding our bottom line or not taking care of ourselves), handling obsessions, astrology, and graphology. The penultimate chapter instructs the reader how to go deeper with a partner to create a "durable fire" and how to deal with the bittersweet moments of love, before the final chapter reminds us of the universe's gift of a lover, with a 14-point list to rate the doubts, fears, and joys that partners may experience in their love relationship. Written from a feminine left-hand perspective, the book also addresses practical lower right-hand strategies and how to balance agency and communion. It is highly recommended for green singles of both sexes who want to attract/find a partner to join them on a spiritual Buddhist path.

Calling In "The One": 7 Weeks to Attract the Love of Your Life, by Katherine Woodward Thomas, starts with her confession that—despite her longings to be in partnership—she was "unconsciously" unavailable to good available men until a friend asked her what she was avoiding by choosing to be alone in life (page xvi). In her early forties, childless and never married, she started to take responsibility for her attitude and hidden agendas that made her avoid love, material abundance, and commitment. A few weeks after this decision she reconnected with an old lover that she had turned down twice before, soon after got married to him, had a child, and has been doing the "happily ever after thing" for several years now.

From her own experience and work as a psychotherapist, she realized that there is a huge chasm between wanting to find an ideal partner and being truly available for that partner when he appears (page xxi). Based on this insight she developed a seven-week course with 7 x 7 = 49 lessons that instruct women to take the less-traveled intimidating and frightening path that leads to freedom from the past and love in the future, instead of repeating the same old safe patterns that ultimately lead to more of the same disappointments.

Week one, "Preparing For Love," is dedicated to honoring the human need for others and making the space for love.

Week two, "Completions," contains lessons on how to let go of the past and relinquish unconscious patterns.

Week three, "Healing Core Wounds," provides suggestions for healing old childhood wounds, releasing old beliefs, and reclaiming the disowned self.

Week four, "Setting Your Course," outlines how to set clear intentions, clarify the soul's purpose, receive inner guidance, and make wise choices.

Week five "First Things First," focuses on making commitments, body acceptance, a woman's sense of self-esteem, sexual healing, and cultivating solitude.

Week six "A Life Worth Living," makes suggestions on being happy, listening with an open heart, and speaking up.

Week seven "Living Love Fulfilled," teaches how to move from "me" to "we," and to live a loving enchanted life.

The book provides an upper left-hand spiritual, idealistic, "law of attraction" path to love that will speak to attractive new-age red and green women, as well as Sensitive New Age Guys (SNAGs).

A Book for Green Men

The Way of the Superior Man: A Spiritual Guide to Mastering the Challenges of Women, Work, and Sexual Desire, by David Deida, is one of several books by this author that focus on the spiritual and sexual dimensions of the feminine and masculine polarity between men and women (for his other books see the Bibliography below). It challenges men to grow beyond the macho-jerk, "all spine but no heart," and the sensitive New-Age wimp "all heart but no spine" ideals by mastering the second-tier challenges of living an authentic masculine life while embracing the feminine in themselves and in women. Although written for heterosexual men with a masculine essence (page 10), this controversial book is mostly read by women who are either outraged by Deida's suggestions that women want to be sexually taken, fucked, and ravished by a man with an unabashed masculinity, or yearn to be with a partner as described by him. In the introduction, Deida outlines how society has moved from clearly divided feminine/masculine gender roles that are found up to amber, into a 50/50 sameness—with a disappearance of sexual attraction/polarity—in orange, and a complete role reversal in green. The 52 short chapters that follow are divided into 8 parts that cover (1) A Man's Way—how to live fearlessly on the edge of your authentic purpose NOW, (2) Dealing with Women—that her words usually express momentary "nonlinear" feelings/emotions instead of logical finite positions, and how to stay present and love her in the NOW, (3) Working with Polarity and Energy—outlining the masculine desire for pleasurable oneness with the feminine, (4) What Women Really Want—the committed, unwavering man of her choosing with a directed divine masculine presence and integrity that she can trust, (5) Your Dark Side—a man's drive towards freedom and to "fuck it or kill it" that attracts the feminine, (6) Feminine Attractiveness—the masculine desire for the union of its consciousness with the fullness of life in general, and a woman's body in particular, (7) Body Practices—how to control and "redirect" ejaculation up the spine through conscious breathing, and (8) Men's and Women's Yoga of Intimacy—how to balance the masculine life mission/purpose with the feminine need for connection/flow that fosters love between couples and their capacity to be of service to others.

The Way of the Superior Man will elude or annoy most men in orange and below, and provoke, frustrate, or disturb men in green, as it challenges them to evolve into second-tier consciousness. If your partner reads or suggests this book to you, it is a clear sign that she yearns for you to lead with your masculine while deeply connecting with her through your feminine.

Conclusion to Appendix I

In their essence, all relationship self-help books give advice to singles and/or couples on how to effectively balance and harmonize agency and communion at a particular Kosmic Address. Picking the book that best addresses the quadrant and level of consciousness/pathology at which the relationship problem occurs is therefore crucial for its effectiveness.

Visit www.singles2couples.org/literature.asp for additional book reviews.

Appendix II: Links and References

The links and references given throughout the book, especially in the endnotes, were correct at time of printing. For clickable links, updates, corrections, errata, additional resources, etc. please visit:

www.singles2couples.org/ir.asp

Bibliography

Alice, Kathryn. 2007. *Love Will Find You: 9 Magnets to Bring You and Your Soulmate Together.* Marlow & Company.

Almaas, A.H. 1987. *Diamond Heart Series Book One: Elements of the Real in Man.* Diamond Books.

Almaas, A.H. 1998. *Facets of Unity: The Enneagram of Holy Ideas.* Diamond Books.

Amodeo, John. 2001. *The Authentic Heart: An Eightfold Path to Midlife Love.* Wiley.

Anand, Margo. 1989. *The Art of Sexual Ecstasy: The Path of Sacred Sexuality for Western Lovers.* Tarcher Putnam.

Andreas Connirae and Steve. 1989. *Heart of the Mind: Engaging Your Inner Power to Change with Neuro-Linguistic Programming.* Real People Press.

Armstrong, Alison. 2003. *Keys to the Kingdom.* Pax Programs.

* Armstrong, Alison. 2007. *Making Sense of Men: A Woman's Guide to a Lifetime of Love, Care and Attention from All Men.* Pax Programs.

Bader, Michael J. 2002. *Arousal: The Secret Logic of Sexual Fantasy.* Thomas Dunne Books.

* Baer, Greg. 2003. *Real Love: The Truth About Finding Unconditional Love & Fulfilling Relationships.* Gotham Books.

Baren, Renee and Wagele, Elizabeth. 1994. *The Enneagram Made Easy: Discover the 9 Types of People.* Harper.

Barnet, Rosalind and Rivers, Caryl. 2004. *Same Difference: How Gender Myths Are Hurting Our Relationships, Our Children, and Our Jobs.* Basic Books.

Brandenburger, Adam M. and Nalebuff, Barry J. 1996. *Co-Opetition: A Revolutionary Mindset That Combines Competition and Cooperation.* Doubleday.

Baucum, Don. 1996. *Barron's EZ 101 Study Keys: Psychology.* Barron's Educational Series.

Beck, Aaron. 1988. *Love Is Never Enough: How Couples Can Overcome Misunderstandings, Resolve Conflicts, and Solve Relationship Problems through Cognitive Therapy.* Harper and Row.

Behrendt, Greg and Tuccillo, Liz. 2004. *He's Just Not That Into You. The No-Excuses Truth to Understanding Guys.* Simon Spotlight.

Claremont de Castillo, Irene. 1973. *Knowing Women: A Feminine Psychology*. Harper & Row Publishers.

Beck, Don Edward and Cowan, Christopher. 2006. *Spiral Dynamics: Mastering Values, Leadership and Change*. Blackwell.

Block, Joel D. and Neuman, Kimberly Dawn. 2009. *The Real Reason Men Commit: Why He Will – or Won't – Love, Honor, and Marry You*. Adams Media.

Bloom, Charlie and Linda. 2010. *Secrets of Great Marriages: Real Truth from Real Couples about Lasting Love*. New World Library.

Brings, Felicia and Winter, Susan. 2000. *Older Women, Younger Men: New Options for Love and Romance*. New Horizon Press.

Brizendine, Louann. 2006. *The Female Brain*. Morgan Road Books.

Brown, Byron. 1999. *Soul without Shame: A Guide to Liberating Yourself from the Judge Within*. Shambala.

Buss, David M. 2003. *The Evolution of Desire: Strategies of Human Mating*. Basic Books.

Campbell, Susan. 2004. *Truth in Dating: Finding Love by Getting Real*. New World Library.

Campbell, Susan. 2005. *Saying What's Real: 7 Keys to Authentic Communication and Relationship Success*. New World Library.

Chadha, Yogesh. 1997. *Gandhi*. John Wiley & Sons.

Chafetz Saltzman, Janet. 2006. *Handbook of the Sociology of Gender*. Springer.

Chapman, Gary. 1992. *The Five Love Languages: How to Express Heartfelt Commitment to Your Mate*. Northfield Publishing.

Chapman, Gary. 2004. *The Five Love Languages for Singles*. Northfield Publishing.

Chödrön, Pema. 2002. *Comfortable With Uncertainty: 108 Teachings on Cultivating Fearlessness and Compassion*. Shambhala.

Chögyam, Trungpa. 1973. *Cutting through Spiritual Materialism*. Shambhala.

*Chopra, Deepak: 1997. *The Path to Love: Spiritual Strategies for Healing*. Three Rivers Press.

Claremont de Castillejo, Irene. 1973. *Knowing Women: A Feminine Psychology*. Harper.

Cloke, Bill. 2008. *Love-Making from the Inside Out: A New Approach to Creating and Maintaining a Loving Relationship: How to Transform Conflict, Complaint, and Criticism*. Self.

Cloud, Henry and Townsend, John. 1999. *Boundaries in Marriage: Understanding the Choices That Make or Break Loving Relationships*. Zondervan.

Coleman, Emily and Edwards, Betty. 1980. *Brief Encounters: How to Make the Most of Relationships That May Not Last Forever*. Anchor Press.

Collins, Bryn C. 1997. *Emotional Unavailability: Recognizing It, Understanding It, and Avoiding Its Traps.* Contemporary Books.

Combs, Allan. 2009. *Consciousness Explained Better: Towards an Integral Understanding of the Multifaceted Nature of Consciousness.* Paragon House.

Covey, Stephen R. 1990. *The 7 Habits of Highly Effective People: Powerful Lessons in Personal Change.* Fireside.

DeAngelis, Barbara. 1992. *Are You the One for Me: Knowing Who's Right & Avoiding Who's Wrong.* Dell.

de Quincey, Christian. 2005. *Radical Knowing: Understanding Consciousness through Relationship.* Park Street Press.

de Quincey, Christian. 2008. *Consciousness from Zombies to Angels: The Shadow and the Light of Knowing Who You Are.* Park Street Press.

Crenshaw, Theresa L. 1996. *The Alchemy of Love and Lust: How our Sex Hormones Influence our Relationships.* Pocket Books.

Deida, David. 1995. *Intimate Communion: Awakening Your Sexual Essence.* Health Communications, Inc.

* Deida, David. 1997. *The Way of the Superior Man: A Spiritual Guide to Mastering the Challenges of Women, Work, and Sexual Desire.* Sounds True.

Deida, David. 1997. *It's a Guy Thing: An Owner's Manual for Women.* Health Communications.

Deida, David. 2005. *Blue Truth: A Spiritual Guide to Life & Death and Love & Sex.* Sounds True.

Dyer, Wayne. 2004. *The Power of Intention: Learning to Co-Create Your World Your Way.* Hay House.

* Diamond, Carol. 2010. *Relationship Roulette: Improve Your Odds at Lasting Love.* Praeger.

Dowling, Colette. 1981. *The Cinderella Complex: Women's Hidden Fear of Independence.* Pocket Books.

Ellis, Thomas. 2005. *The Rantings of a Single Male: Losing Patience with Feminism, Political Correctness,… and Basically Everything.* Rannenberg Publishing.

Esbjorn-Hargens, Sean and Zimmerman, Michael E. 2009. *Integral Ecology: Uniting Multiple Perspectives On the Natural World.* Integral Books.

Eschner Hogan, Eve with Hogan, Steve. 2000. *Intellectual Foreplay: Questions for Lovers and Lovers-to-Be.* Hunter House.

Etcoff, Nancy. 2000. *Survival of the Prettiest: The Science of Beauty.* Anchor Books.

Faludi, Susan. 1991. *Backlash: The Undeclared War Against American Woman.* Anchor Books.

Faludi, Susan. 1999. *Stiffed: The Betrayal of the American Man*. Perennial.

Farrell, Bill and Pam. 2001. *Man Are Like Waffles, Women Are Like Spaghetti: Understanding and Delighting in Your Differences*. Harvest House Publishers.

Farrell, Warren. 1986. *Why Men Are the Way They Are: The Male-Female Dynamic*. Berkley Books.

Farrell, Warren. 1993. *The Myth of Male Power: Why Men Are the Disposable Sex*. Berkley Books.

Farrell, Warren. 2001. *Women Can't Hear What Men Don't Say: Destroying Myths, Creating Love*. Finch.

Farrell, Warren. 2001. *Father and Child Reunion: How to Bring the Dads We Need to the Children We Love*. Tarcher Putnam.

Farrell, Warren. 2005. *Why Men Earn More: The Startling Truth Behind the Pay Gap— and What Women Can Do About It*. Amacom.

Farrell, Warren and Sterba, James P. 2008. *Does Feminism Discriminate Against Men: A Debate*. Oxford University Press.

* Fein, Ellen and Schneider, Sherrie. 1995. *The Rules: Time- tested Secrets for Capturing the Heart of Mr. Right*. Warner Books.

* Feldhahn, Shaunti. 2004. *For Women Only: What you need to know about the inner lives of men*. Multnoma.

* Feldhahn, Shaunti and Jeff. 2006. *For Men Only: A straightforward guide to the inner lives of women*. Multnoma.

* Fenton, Bradley. 2008. *Stumbling Naked In the Dark: Overcoming Mistakes that Men Make with Women*. Simon & Brown.

Ferrini, Paul. 1998. *Creating a Spiritual Relationship: A Guide to Growth and Happiness for Couples on the Path*. Heartways Press.

* Fisher, Helen. 2004. *Why We Love: The Nature and Chemistry of Romantic Love*. Henry Holt and Company.

Fisher, Helen. 2009. *Why Him? Why Her? Finding Real Love by Understanding Your Personality Type*. Henry Holt and Company.

Frankl, Victor. 1997. *Man's Search for Meaning*. Pocket.

* Fromm, Erich. 1956. *The Art of Loving*. Harper Perennial.

Gendreau, Geralyn (Editor). 2006. *The Marriage of Sex & Spirit*. Elite Books.

Gerson, Mark. 1992. *Coming Into Our Own: Understanding the Adult Metamorphosis*. Delacorte Press.

Gibson, Valerie. 2001. *Cougar: A Guide for Older Women Dating Younger Men*. Key Porter Books.

Gilbert, Elizabeth. 2006. *Eat, Pray, Love: One Woman's Search for Everything Across Italy, India and Indonesia.* Penguin.

Gilbert, Elizabeth. 2010. *Committed: A Skeptic Makes Peace with Marriage.* Viking.

Gilligan, Carol. 1982. 1993. *In a Different Voice.* Harvard University Press.

Gilligan, Carol. 1992. *Meeting At the Crossroads: The Landmark Book about the Turning Points in Girls' and Women's Lives.* Ballantine.

Gilligan, Carol. 2002. *The Birth of Pleasure.* Knopf.

Gladwell, Malcom. 2007. *Blink: The Power of Thinking without Thinking.* Back Bay Books.

* Gold, Victor. 2008. *The Potency Principles: Transforming Sexual Energy into Spiritual Power.* iUniverse.

Goleman, Daniel. 1995. *Emotional Intelligence.* Bantam.

Goleman, Daniel. 2006. *Social Intelligence: The Revolutionary New Science of Human Relationships.* Bantam.

Gosse, Richard. 1997. *You Can't Hurry Love: An Action Guide for Singles Tired of Waiting.* Marin Publications.

* Gottman, John and Silver, Nan. 1999. *The Seven Principals for Making Marriage Work.* Orion.

Gray, John. 1992. *Men Are from Mars, Women Are from Venus: The Classic Guide to Understanding the Opposite Sex.* Harper Collins.

Gray, John. 1993. *Men, Women and Relationships: Making Peace with the Opposite Sex.* Quil.

Gray, John. 1994. *Mars and Venus Together Forever: Relationship Skills for Lasting Love.* Harper Perennial.

Gray, John. 1997. *Mars and Venus On a Date: A Guide for Navigating the 5 Stages of Dating to Create a Loving and Lasting Relationship.* Harper Perennial.

* Gray, John. 2008. *Why Mars and Venus Collide: Improving Relationships by Understanding How Men and Women Cope Differently with Stress.* Harper.

Greenwald, Rachel. 2003. *Find a Husband after 35: Using What I Learned at Harvard Business School.* Ballantine Books.

Greenwald, Rachel. 2009. *Why He Didn't Call You Back: 1000 Guys Reveal What They Really Thought about You after Your Date.* Crown.

Hanauer, Cathi. 2003. *The Bitch In the House. 26 Women Tell the Truth about Sex, Solitude, Work, Motherhood, and Marriage.* Perennial.

Harding, Esther M. 1970. *The Way of All Women.* Shambala.

Hawkins, David R. 1995. *Power Versus Force: The Hidden Determinants of Human Behavior*. Hay House.

Hellinger, Bernd; Weber, Gunthard; and Beamount, Hunter. 1998. *Love's Hidden Symmetry: What Makes Love Work in Relationships*. Zeig, Tucker & Co.

Hendrick, Clyde and Susan S. 2000. *Close Relationships: A Sourcebook*. Sage.

Hendricks, Gay and Kathlyn. 1990. *Conscious Loving: The Journey to Co-Commitment: A Way to Be Fully Together without Giving Up Yourself*. Bantam.

Hendricks, Gay and Kathlyn. 2004. *Lasting Love: The Five Secrets of Growing a Vital, Conscious Relationship*. Rodale.

Hendricks, Gay and Kathlyn. 2004. *Attracting Genuine Love: A step-by-step program to bring a loving and desirable partner into your life*. Sounds True.

* Hendrix, Harville. 1988. *Getting the Love You Want: A Guide for Couples*. Owl Books.

Hendrix, Harville and LaKelly-Hunt, Helen. 2003. *Getting the Love You Want Workbook*. Atria Books.

Hoffman, Edward. 1988. *The Right to Be Human: A Biography of Abraham Maslow*. McGraw Hill.

Hoffman, Glynda-Lee. 2003. *The Secret Dowry of Eve: Woman's Role in the Development of Consciousness*. Parker Street Press.

Holstein, Lana L. 2001. *How to Have Magnificent Sex: The Seven Dimensions of a Vital Sexual Connection*. Harmony Books.

Hooks, Bell. 2001. *All About Love: New Visions*. Harper Perennial.

Hooks, Bell. 2002. *Communion: The Female Search for Love*. Harper Perennial.

Hill, Gareth S. 1992. *Masculine and Feminine: The Natural Flow of Opposites and the Psyche*. Shambala.

Howard, Lew. 2005. *Introducing Ken Wilber: Concepts for an Evolving World*. Author House.

* Johnson, Sue. 2008. *Hold Me Tight: Seven Conversations for a Lifetime of Love*. Little, Brown.

Joudry, Patricia and Pressman, Maurie. 1993. *Twin Souls: A Guide to Finding Your True Spiritual Partner*. Carol Souther Books.

Jung, Emma. 1957. *Animus and Anima: Two Essays*. Spring Publications.

* Kasl, Charlotte. 1999. *If the Buddha Dated: A Handbook for Finding Love On a Spiritual Path*. Arkana.

Katie, Byron. 2002. *Loving What Is: The Four Questions That Can Change Your Life*. Three Rivers Press.

Katie, Byron. 2005. *I Need Your Love – Is That True: How to Stop Seeking Love, Approval, and Appreciation and Start Finding Them Instead*. Harmony Books.

Keagan, Robert. 1994. *In Over Our Heads: The Mental Demands of Modern Life*. Harvard University Press.

Keen, Sam. 1991. *Fire In the Belly: On Being A Man*. Bantam.

Kempton, Jared. 2008. *Men are Scum, Women are Stupid*. Partigen Publishing.

Kennedy, Barbara. 2009. *Baby Boomer Men: Looking for Love*. Madison Avenue Publishers.

Kingma, Daphne Rose. 1998. *The Future of Love: The Power of the Soul in Intimate Relationships*. Broadway.

Kingma, Daphne Rose. 2000. *Coming Apart: Why Relationships End & How to Live Through the Ending of Yours*. Conari Press.

Knight, Sue. 1995. *NLP At Work: Neuro-Linguistic Programming: The Difference that Makes Difference in Business*. Nicholas Brealey Publishing.

Koppel, Dale. 2008. *The Intelligent Woman's Guide to Online Dating*. Peterman Samuelson.

* Kirshenbaum, Mira. 2006. *Is He Mr. Right?: Everything You Need to Know Before You Commit*. Harmony Books.

Leeds, Lilo and Gerard with Real, Terrence. 2008. *Wonderful Marriage: A Guide to Building a Great Relationship That Will Last a Lifetime*. Benbella.

Lewis, Thomas; Amini, Fari; and Lannon, Richard. 2000. *A General Theory of Love*. Vintage.

Louis, Ron and Copeland, David. 1998. *How to Succeed with Women*. Reward Books.

* Love, Patricia and Stosny, Steven. 2007. *How to Improve Your Marriage without Talking about It*. Broadway.

Luskin, Frederic. 2009. *Forgive for Love: The Missing Ingredient for a Healthy and Lasting Relationship*. Harper One.

Malach Pines, Ayala. 2005. *Falling in Love: Why We Choose the Lovers We Choose*. Routledge.

Maslow, Abraham H. 1971. *The Farther Reaches of Human Nature*. Penguin.

Masters, Robert Augustus. 2007. *Transformation through Intimacy: The Journey toward Mature Monogamy*. Tehmenos Press.

McGraw, Phillip C. 2000. *Relationship Rescue: A Seven-Step Strategy for Reconnecting with Your Partner*. Hyperion.

McGraw, Phil. 2005. *Love Smart: Find the One You Want—Fix the One You Got*. Free Press.

McIntosh, Steve. 2007. *Integral Consciousness and the Future of Evolution: How the Integral Model is Transforming Politics, Culture and Spirituality*. Paragon House.

Merzel, Dennis Genpo. 2007. *Big Mind, Big Heart: Finding Your Way*. Big Mind Publishing.

Miller, Geoffrey. 2001. *The Mating Mind: How Sexual Choice Shaped the Evolution of Human Nature*. Anchor.

Mitchell, Stephen. 1988. *Tao Te Ching*. Harper Perennial.

Moore, Thomas. 1994. *Soul Mates: Honoring the Mysteries of Love and Relationship*. Harper.

* Mystery – a.k.a. Markovik von, Erik. 2010. *The Pickup Artist: The New and Improved Art of Seduction*. Villard.

Nelson, Noelle. 1997. *Dangerous Relationships: How to Identify and Respond to the Seven Warning Signs of a Troubled Relationship*. DaCapo.

Norwood, Robin. 1985. *Women Who Love Too Much: When You Keep Wishing and Hoping He'll Change*. Pocket Books.

Page, Susan. 1998. *If I'm So Wonderful, Why Am I Still Single?* Three Rivers Press.

Paget, Lou. 2000. *How to Give Her Absolute Pleasure: Totally Explicit Techniques Every Woman Wants Her Man to Know*. Broadway.

Paul, Pamela. 2002. *The Starter Marriage and the Future of Matrimony*. Random House.

Peck, Scott M. 1997. *The Road Less Traveled and Beyond: Spiritual Growth in an Age of Anxiety*. Simon & Schuster.

Pickens, W. James. 1989. *The Art of Closing Any Deal: How to Be a Master Closer in Everything You Do*. Warner Business Books.

* Popcak, Gregory K. 2000. *The Exceptional Seven Percent: The Nine Secrets of the World's Happiest Couples*. Citadel Press.

* Psaris, Jett and Lyons, S. Marlena. 2000. *Undefended Love: The way you felt about yourself when you first fell in love is the way you can feel all the time*. New Harbinger Publications.

Real, Terrence. 1997. *I Don't Want to Talk About It: Overcoming the Secret of Male Depression*. Scribner.

Real, Terrence. 2002. *How Can I Get Through to You: Closing the Intimacy Gap between Men and Women*. Fireside.

* Real, Terrence. 2007. *The New Rules of Marriage: What You Need to Know to Make Love Work*. Ballantine.

René, Lucia. 2009. *Unplugging the Patriarchy—A Mystical Journey into the Heart of a New Age*. Crown Chakra.

Rengel, Peter. 1995. *Living Life in Love: Integrating Western Psychology with Eastern Spirituality*. Imagine Publications.

Reynolds, Brad. 2006. *Where's Wilber AT?: Ken Wilbers Integral Vision in the New Millenium*. Paragon House.

* Richo, David. 2002. *How to Be an Adult in Relationship: The Five Keys to Mindful Loving*. Shambhala.

Riso, Don Richard, and Hudaon, Russ. 1999. *The Wisdom of the Enneagram: The Complete Guide to Psychological and Spiritual Growth for the Nine Personality Types*. Bantam.

Rosenberg, Marshall. 2003. *Nonviolent Communication: Create Your Life, Your Relationships, and Your World in Harmony with Your Values*. Puddle Dancer.

Rudman, Laurie A. and Glick, Peter. 2008. *The Social Psychology of Gender: How Power and Intimacy Shape Gender Relations*. Guilford Press.

Ruiz, Don Miguel. 1997. *The Four Agreements*. Amber-Allen.

Ruiz, Don Miguel. 1999. *The Mastery of Love*. Amber-Allen.

Salmon, Caterine and Symons, Donald. 2001. *Warrior Lovers: Erotic Fiction, Evolution and Female Sexuality*. Yale University Press.

Scantling, Sandra R. 1998. *Extraordinary Sex Now: A Couples Guide to Intimacy*. Doubleday.

* Schnarch, David. 1997. *Passionate Marriage: Keeping Love and Intimacy Alive in Committed Relationships*. Owl Books.

Schucman, Helen and Thetford, William. 1975. *A Course in Miracles*. Viking.

Sheehan, Donna and Reffell, Paul. 2009. *Redefining Seduction: Women Initiating Courtship, Partnership and Peace*. Redefining Seduction.

Sheehy, Gail. 1998. *Understanding Men's Passages: Discovering the New Map of Men's Lives*. Ballantine Books.

Sheehy, Gail. 2006. *Sex and the Seasoned Woman: Pursuing the Passionate Life*. Ballantine Books.

Sherven, Judith and Sniechowski, James. 2001. *Be Loved for Who You Really Are: How the Differences between Men and Women Can Be Turned into a Source of the Very Best Romance You'll Ever Know*. St. Martin's Griffin.

Silverstein, Judith and Lasky, Michael. 2004. *Online Dating for Dummies: The Fun and Easy Way to Find That Special Someone On the Web*. Wiley Publishing.

Singer, Irving. 2009. *Philosophy of Love: A Partial Summing-Up*. MIT Press.

Smith, Huston. 1991. *The World's Religions: Our Great Wisdom Traditions*. Harper San Francisco.

Smith, Huston. 2001. *Why Religion Matters: The Fate of the Human Spirit in an Age of Disbelief.* Harper.

Sobel, Alan. 1989. *Eros, Agape, and Philia: Readings in the Philosophy of Love.* Paragon House.

Stanger, Patti. 2009. *Become Your Own Matchmaker: 8 Easy Steps for Attracting Your Perfect Mate.* Atria Books.

Stills, Judith. 1993. *Excess Baggage: Getting Out of Your Way.* Penguin Books.

Stills, Judith. 1996. *Loving Men More, Needing Men Less.* Penguin Books.

Sternberg, Robert J. and Weis, Karin. 2006. *The New Psychology of Love.* Yale University Press.

Stoeker, Fred and Stoeker, Jason. 2009. Hero: *Becoming the Man She Desires.* Water Brook.

Stosny, Steven. 2006. *Love without Hurt: Turn Your Resentful, Angry or Emotionally Abusive Relationship into a Compassionate, Loving One.* Da Capo Press.

* Strauss, Neil. 2005. *The Game: Penetrating the Secret Society of Pickup Artists.* William Morrow.

Symons, Donald. 1997. *The Evolution of Sexual Desire.* Oxford University Press.

Tannen, Deborah. 1990. *You Just Don't Understand: Women and Men in Conversation.* Ballantine Books.

Tate, Brett. 2007. *The Professional Bachelor: How to Exploit Her Inner Psycho.* TPB Publishing.

Tavris, Carol. 1992. *The Mismeasure of Women: Why Women Are Not the Better Sex, the Inferior Sex, or the Opposite Sex.* Simon & Schuster.

Taylor, John Maxwell. 2009. *Eros Ascending: The Life-Transforming Power of Sacred Sexuality.* Frog Books.

Taylor, Maurice and McGee, Seana. 2000. *The New Couple: Why the Old Rules Don't Work and What Does.* Harper.

Temple-Thurston, Leslie. 2000. *The Marriage of Spirit: Enlightened Living in Today's World.* Core Light Publications.

* Thomas, Katherine Woodward. 2004. *Calling in "The One": 7 Weeks to Attract the Love of Your Life.* Three Rivers Press.

Time. 2009, October 26. "The State of the American Woman: Why they are more powerful – but less happy." Time, Inc.

Tolle, Eckhart. 1999. *The Power of Now: A Guide to Spiritual Enlightenment.* New World Library.

Tolle, Eckhart. 2003. *Stillness Speaks.* New World Library.

Tolle, Eckhart. 2005. *A New Earth: Awakening to Your Life's Purpose.* Penguin.

Ulanov, Ann and Barry. 1994. *Transforming Sexuality: The Archetypal World of Anima and Animus.* Shambala.

Vissell, Barry and Joyce. 1984. *Shared Heart: Relationship Initiations and Celebrations.* Ramira Publishing.

* Vissell, Joyce and Barry. 1999. *The Heart's Wisdom: A Practical Guide to Growing through Love.* Conari Press.

Weinberg, George. 2002. *Why Men Won't Commit: Getting What You Both Want without Playing Games.* Atria Books.

Wade, Jenny. 1996. *Changes of Mind: A Holonomic Theory of the Evolution of Consciousness.* State of New York University Press.

Wade, Jenny. 2004. *Transcendent Sex: When Lovemaking Opens the Veil.* Paraview Pocket Books.

Wallerstein, Judith S.; Lewis Julia M.; and Blakeslee, Sandra. 2000. *The Unexpected Legacy of Divorce: A 25 Year Landmark Study.* Hyperion.

Walsh, Roger and Vaughan, Frances. 1993. *Paths Beyond Ego: The Transpersonal Vision.* Tarcher Putnam.

Warren, Neil Clark. 1992. *Finding the Love of Your Life: Ten Principals for Choosing the Right Mate.* Pocket Books.

Webb, Michael. 2000. *The Romantic's Guide: Hundreds of Creative Tips for a Lifetime of Love.* Hyperion.

Welwood, John. 1985. *Challenge of the Heart: Love, Sex, and Intimacy in Changing Times.* Shambala.

Welwood, John. 1990. *Journey of the Heart: The Path of Conscious Love.* Harper Perennial.

* Welwood, John. 1996. *Love and Awakening: Discovering the Sacred Path of Intimate Relationship.* Harper Perennial.

Welwood, John. 2000. *Toward a Psychology of Awakening: Buddhism, Psychotherapy, and the Path of Personal and Spiritual Transformation.* Shambala.

Welwood, John. 2006. *Perfect Love, Imperfect Relationships: Healing the Wound of the Heart.* Trumpeter.

Wilber, Ken. 1980. *The Atman Project: A Transpersonal View of Human Development.* Quest Books.

Wilber, Ken. 2000. *Integral Psychology: Consciousness, Spirit, Psychology, Therapy.* Shambhala.

Wilber, Ken. 1991, 2000. *Grace and Grit: Spirituality and Healing in the Life and Death of Treya Killam Wilber.* Shambhala.

Wilber, Ken. 2001. *Sex, Ecology, Spirituality: The Spirit of Evolution, Second Edition.* Shambhala.

Wilber, Ken. 2001. *A Brief History of Everything.* Shambhala.

Wilber, Ken. 2007. *Integral Spirituality: A Startling New Role for Religion in the Modern and Postmodern World.* Shambhala.

Wilber, Ken. 2007. *The Integral Vision: A Very Short Introduction to the Revolutionary Integral Approach to Life, God, the Universe, and Everything.* Shambhala.

Wray, Robert A. 1999. *The Guide: A Man's Field Guide to Dating.* netImage.

Young, Ben, and Adams, Samuel. 1990. *The 10 Commandments of Dating: Time-Tested Laws for Building Successful Relationships.* Nelson.

Young-Eisendrath, Polly and Wiedeman, Florence. 1987. *Female Authority: Empowering Women through Psychotherapy.* Guilford.

Young-Eisendrath, Polly. 1993. *You're Not What I Expected: Love After the Romance Has Ended.* Fromm International.

Zinczenko, David. 2006. *Men, Love & Sex: The Complete User's Guide for Women.* Rodale.

Zukav, Gary. 2010. *Spiritual Partnership: The Journey to Authentic Power.* Harper One.

* Reviewed in Appendix I of the manual.

Endnotes

Preface

1   See Institute of American Values (www.americanvalues.org/) *Why Marriage Matters, Second Edition: Twenty-Six Conclusions from the Social Sciences,* and Patricia Love and Steven Stosny *How To Improve Your Marriage Without Talking About It* introduction page 3: "Research and clinical experience also tell us that marriage and committed love relationships are more important to the health and well-being of men than women. Divorced men do not work as well or live as long or "survive" with anything like the quality of life enjoyed by married men. They are at considerably higher risk of alcoholism, suicide, physical and mental illness, unemployment, car crashes, and other accidents. They lose contact with friends, stop going to church or social groups, and eventually isolate themselves completely, except for whatever company they can find in a bar. In short, they lose meaning and purpose. *Without a partner, men just go through the motions of living.*"

2   See John Gray, *Why Mars and Venus Collide* page 230: "Divorced woman are often happier, because they have finally taken responsibility for their own happiness." Also note the declining number of women in marriages in recent decades:

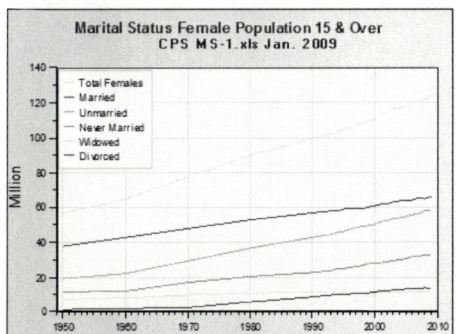

From www.biblenews1.com/marriage/marriags.htm#Total%20Marriages

3   John Gray in an interview with Ken Wilber: "My first book, *Men and Women in Relationship* that was first published in 1993, was a much more intelligent work than my later *Mars* and *Venus* books. But it was too dense for the mass population, as there are only a few people who have the patience and lifestyle to read a densely written intelligent book. So I wrote a watered down version which was more fun and easy to digest, had fewer points, and was something that people could apply right away in their relationships. These simpler books, beginning with *Men are from Mars Women are from Venus* became a pop phenomena with over 40 Million copies sold." See www.integrallife.com/editorial/resurrecting-postmodern-sex-life

4   See www.factfinder.census.gov/servlet/ADPTable?_bm=y&-geo_id=01000US&-ds_name=ACS_2008_3YR_G00_&-_lang=en&-_caller=geoselect&-format= and Helen Fisher, *Why We Love* page 217.

5   See Helen Fisher, *Why We Love* page 217 and www.datingsitesreviews.com/staticpages/index.php?page=Online-Dating-Industry-Facts-Statistics

6   See www.center.americanvalues.org/?p=5

7   See www.divorcerate.org/ for details about age distribution of divorced men and women as well as statistics for first, second and third marriages. Also see www.divorcereform.org/nyt05.html for an explanation of the variations in such statistics.

8   See Gregory K. Popcak *The Exceptional Seven Percent* page 4 and 5 where he cites the findings of several researchers such as Dr. Judith Wallerstein (author of *The Good Marriage*) who found that 15% of all marriages and 7% of first time marriages are exceptional; Lilo and Gerald Leeds *Wonderful Marriage* page 2: "Some research indicates that only 7% of all marriages can be considered to be great marriages"; www.divorcemag.com/statistics/statsUS.shtml for marriage and divorce statistics, and the research of Steven L. Nock and W. Bradford Wilcox, University of Virginia: *What's love got to do with it? Equality, equity, commitment, and women's marital quality*.

9   See John Tierney *The Big City; A New Look At Realities Of Divorce* published July 11, 2000 in the NY Times: "Researchers who have interviewed divorcing couples have repeatedly found that, in cases where the divorce is not mutually desired, women are more than twice as likely to be the ones who want out. After the split, women are typically happier than their exes." Also Margaret Brinig, Notre Dame Law School and Douglas Allen, Simon Fraser University *These Boots Are Made for Walking: Why Most Divorce Filers Are Women*, and Patricia Love, Steven Stosny *How to Improve your Marriage Without Talking About It* page 162, and AARP *The Divorce Experience: A Study of Divorce At Midlife and Beyond* http://assets.aarp.org/rgcenter/general/divorce_1.pdf

10 See Patricia Love, Steven Stosny *How to Improve your Marriage Without Talking About It* page 46: "The devastating effects of divorce on men present a strong argument for the fact that his partner provides the meaning of his life." Also Laurie A. Rudman and Peter Glick *The Social Psychology of Gender* pages 223-225: "Thoughts of ending the relationship are especially physically taxing and aversive for men."

11 See www.fathersforlife.org/suicides/US_suicide_deaths.htm and Warren Farrell *Does Feminism Discriminate Against Men* page 8.

12 See www.archives.cnn.com/2000/HEALTH/03/15/divorce.suicide.wmd/ and www.afsp.org/ "in 2004 overall US male suicides 25,907 of 145,973,538 = 17.8 for every 100,000, overall US female suicides 6,730 of 150,533,523 = 4.5 for every 100,000.

13 See Warren Farrell *Why Men Are the Way They Are* page 105—based on studies by Donald Symons, author of *The Evolution of Human Sexuality*.

14 See books in Appendix I of this manual with books such as such as *Is He Mr. Right* with a chapter on "How to dump the duds" or *An Intelligent Woman's Guide to Online Dating* in which the author describes how she rejected (and sometimes broke the hearts) of over 100 men until she found "Mr. Right." Her favorite word is "Next!"

15 Age Distribution by Sex, 2000

	Male		Female	
	Number	Percent	Number	Percent
Total Population	138,053,563	49.06%	143,368,343	50.94%
0-4	9,810,733	3.49%	9,365,065	3.33%
5-9	10,523,277	3.74%	10,026,228	3.56%
10-14	10,520,197	3.74%	10,007,875	3.56%
15-19	10,391,004	3.69%	9,828,886	3.49%
20-24	9,687,814	3.44%	9,276,187	3.30%
25-29	9,798,760	3.48%	9,582,576	3.41%
30-34	10,321,769	3.67%	10,188,619	3.62%
35-39	11,318,696	4.02%	11,387,968	4.05%
40-44	11,129,102	3.95%	11,312,761	4.02%
45-49	9,889,506	3.51%	10,202,898	3.63%
50-54	8,607,724	3.06%	8,977,824	3.19%

	Male		Female	
	Number	Percent	Number	Percent
55-59	6,508,729	2.31%	6,960,508	2.47%
60-64	5,136,627	1.83%	5,668,820	2.01%
65-69	4,400,362	1.56%	5,133,183	1.82%
70-74	3,902,912	1.39%	4,954,529	1.76%
75-79	3,044,456	1.08%	4,371,357	1.55%
80-84	1,834,897	0.65%	3,110,470	1.11%
85+	1,226,998	0.44%	3,012,589	1.07%

16 See Patricia Love and Steven Stosny *How to Improve your Marriage Without Talking About It* page 49: "Most relationship books and marriage–enrichment programs are designed to appeal to the women who buy or attend more than 90 percent of them."

17 See www.hai.org for powerful *Love, Intimacy, and Sexuality* workshops. Also numerous other providers of *Tantric Sex Workshops* that typically have waiting lists for men who are often asked to pay women to gender balance the group.

18 As one die-hard single female *Science Of Mind* Minister who facilitates *Undefended Love* groups put it: "Men who come to these groups are not really interested in the work, they just want to pick up women." Women may also feel manipulated, controlled, taken advantage of, or disconnected when a man mentions that he reads relationship books and applies their wisdom. Lastly they may feel uncomfortable about losing their "competitive edge" or "authority" as the relationship expert in a partnership if a man is equally or better informed and has better relationship skills than she has.

19 The French *Encyclopédie* was the first attempt at a systematic analysis of the "order and interrelations of human knowledge" in the late 18th century. Diderot called it the attempt to collect all the knowledge that now lies scattered over the face of the earth, to make known its general structure to the men among we live, and to transmit it to those who will come after us. To make men not only wiser, but also "more virtuous and more happy." Wilber has taken it a significant step further, by not only collecting much of the essential knowledge and wisdom available today from the East and West, but also by putting it into a cohesive map, framework or model.

20 Bill Clinton called Ken Wilber brilliant and mentions him in speeches (see www.youtube.com/watch?v=GEjKr2gA8Wk). Wilber has also consulted with advisors to Al Gore, Tony Blair, and George W. Bush.

21 See for example Sean Esbjorn-Hargens's, and Michael Zimmerman's landmark book *Integral Ecology*.

22 See for example Alex Grey's integral art and Wilber essay at www.alexgrey.com/essay/kenwilber.html in which he says "I first encountered Ken Wilber's phenomenal philosophical genius some seventeen years ago."

23 If this manual inspires you to learn more about the AQAL model you may want to read some of Ken Wilber's books. For a short, simple and up-to-date overview: *The Integral Vision: A Very Short Introduction to the Revolutionary Integral Approach to Life, God, the Universe, and Everything*. For more detail: *A Brief History of Everything*. For Wilber's latest thoughts: *Integral Spirituality* (which can be challenging at times). Also highly recommended are Allan Combs's current and excellent book *Consciousness Explained Better* and Lew Howard's 2005 book *Introducing Ken Wilber* (which does not cover the important Wilber-Combs Lattice and the eight Zones, which were introduced later in *Integral Spirituality*, but is otherwise quite complete and easy to read.) For a collection of critical articles about Wilber's model visit www.integralworld.net

24 To have integrity means to live according to your values and beliefs in the face of adversity and opposition, or to say what you do and to do what you say.

25 Abraham Maslow saw and formulated a hierarchy of human needs. Simply put it states that we all have a need to live (survive), love (feel well in our relationships), learn (grow), and leave a legacy (make a difference in the world that we will be remembered for) and that these needs unfold in that

216 | Integral Relationships: A Manual for Men

hierarchical order. He called this process self-actualization. Eckhart Tolle subtitled his book *A New Earth* with *Awakening to your Life's Purpose*. David Deida's *The Way Of The Superior Man* empowers men to discover and live their true purpose in a spiritual context.

26 See Irvin Singer *Philosophy of Love* page xvii: "I realized that understanding love or its related conditions required an investigation into problems about meaningfulness in life as a whole and the human creation of values in general."

Chapter 1: Understanding the Dimensions of Love

27 See for example Jenny Wade *Transcendental Sex* page 181: "Lovers tell of losing all touch with everyday reality to become One with an unfathomable, ineffable mystery so great and so free of content that it can only be realized once the person returns [to duality]."

28 Lao Tzu, the first Taoist philosopher writes in the first line of the Tao Te Ching (translated by Stephen Mitchell): "The Tao that can be told is not the eternal Tao." He says "Those who know do not speak, those who speak do not know." Also see Rumi and Hafiz for wonderful poetry about the longings of the heart and soul to return to this oneness and Eckhart Tolle's little book *Stillness Speaks*.

29 Famous statement by Stephen Hawking, professor of mathematics at the University of Cambridge for thirty years and author of popular books on science such as *A Brief History of Time*.

30 Our deep yearning for Love as a return to oneness or non–separation may also be explained by longing for a return to the fusion that we experienced with our mother before birth.

31 See Hillary Mayell, National Geographic News, February 16, 2005.

32 See www.en.wikipedia.org/wiki/Punctuated_equilibrium for a comparison between Darwinian evolution theory and cladogenesis. Also see Rupert Sheldrake *Morphic Resonance* page 131-143 for his model of Formative Causation.

33 Sexual Selection (also called *Survival of the Prettiest*) occurs through mate choices in which males and females with the strongest fitness indicators (e.g., the tail of a peacock) mate with each other to produce offspring with the highest chance of survival. Natural selection occurs through survival of the fittest after birth. There is mounting evidence (see Geoffrey Miller *The Mating Mind*) that sexual selection plays a much larger role in the evolution of species than natural selection does.

34 See www.archaeologyinfo.com/species.htm for an in-depth review of human evolution.

35 Katharine Milton, a physical anthropologist at the University of California, Berkeley, and authority on primate diet states that our human ancestors who roamed the dry and open savannas of Africa about 2 million years ago routinely began to include meat in their diets to compensate for a serious decline in the quality of plant foods. It was this new meat diet, full of densely-packed nutrients that provided the catalyst for human evolution, particularly the growth of the brain.

Without meat, said Milton, it's unlikely that they could have secured enough energy and nutrition from the plants available in their African environment at that time to evolve into the active, sociable, intelligent creatures they became. Receding forests would have deprived them of the more nutritious leaves and fruits that forest-dwelling primates survive on, said Milton.

Her thesis complements the discovery by UC Berkeley professor Tim White and others that early human species were butchering and eating animal meat as long ago as 2.5 million years. Milton's article integrates dietary strategy with the evolution of human physiology to argue that meat eating was routine. It was published in the journal *Evolutionary Anthropology* (Vol.8, #1).

Milton said that her theories do not reflect on today's vegetarian diets, which can be completely adequate, given modern knowledge of nutrition. www.berkeley.edu/news/media/releases/99legacy/6-14-1999a.html

36 Most anthropologists believe that the strategy of monogamy was chosen by pre-modern human females. It ensured the loyalty of one male protector and provider, instead of trying to leave several males wondering who had fathered her children, without having any of them committed to her. It is also quite possible that strong males had small harems and that attractive females engaged in serial

monogamy or polyandry (having more than one husband) as long as they were fertile. The idea that humans are not naturally programmed to be monogamous does not make sense from an evolutionary perspective, as humans have relatively long periods of gestation and their offspring take the longest to raise to adulthood. See for example Geoffrey Miller *The Mating Mind* pages 194-198 and articles on the Internet.

37   Nuclear family means a woman and man with child (or children), versus single parents, childless family or single adults living alone, with their parents, or any other family construct.

38   See Helen Fisher *Why We Love* page 132, Daniel Goleman *Social Intelligence* page 198-210, Harville Hendrix *Getting The Love You Want* page 6, Erich Fromm *The Art of Loving* page 1-2, John Gottman *The Seven Principles For Making Marriage Work* page 37 -38 … (to name a few).

39   See Catherine Salmon and Donald Symons *Warrior Lovers* which outlines how the stark contrasts between romance novels and pornography underscore different female and male erotic fantasies. These differences reflect human evolutionary history and the disparate selection pressures that women and men experienced. The authors review the fundamental importance of evolutionary history to human psychology, discuss how male and female sexual psychologies differ, and then demonstrate how sex differences in erotica illustrate this. This difference is further evidenced by homosexual men who have between 100 and several 1000 sexual partners over a lifetime, while lesbian women rarely have more than 100. Also see Nancy Etcoff *Survival of the Prettiest* page 58, Donald Symons, *The Evolution of Human Sexuality*, David M. Buss, *The Evolution of Desire*, and Robert J. Sternberg and Karin Weis (editors) *The New Psychology of Love* pages 65-86.

40   See Geoffrey Miller *The Mating Mind* page 258 -291, Helen Fisher *Why We Love* pages 143-145, and www.news.bbc.co.uk/2/hi/science/nature/733747.stm

41   With the rise of agriculture, for the first time in human development food production became the main domain of men, since pregnant and nursing women could not handle a heavy plow. Enough food could be produced this way so that women could focus more on caring for home and children.

42   Patriarchy literally means "hierarchy of priests" (who were called fathers) or simply "Father ruled." It is the structuring of families, communities, and societies where fathers (men) assume the primary responsibility for the welfare (protection and providing) of these units. The word patriarchy is now often misused to indicate abusive male control and domination over women and children (and other males), while in actuality it was a co-created mutually beneficial system for the survival of men, women, and their offspring. The opposite of patriarchy is a matriarchy. Theoretically, matriarchies develop when humans live in peaceful environments with abundant food supply. It is now believed that matriarchies never existed. Some feminists romanticize matriarchies as the better alternative to patriarchy. Matriarchy is also sometimes confused with matrifocal societies. See Laurie A. Rudman and Peter Glick *The Social Psychology of Gender* page 32 and 33, and www.en.wikipedia.org/wiki/Matriarchy

43   See Ken Wilber *A Brief History of Everything* page 47.

44   Philosophy is the love of knowledge. Its disciplines are concerned with questions of how one should live (morals/ethics), what sorts of things exist (ontology), and the nature/limits of knowledge (epistemology).

45   The Greek philosophers Socrates, Plato, and Aristotle have provided much of the foundation of Western thought, including morals, religions, and the resulting civilizations. The influence of Plato has been persistent and unbroken. His Academy at Athens, which opened in about 387 BC, was the forerunner of today's colleges and universities. It was a school devoted to philosophy, law, and scientific research—primarily mathematics—and it endured as an institution until 529 AD when it and other non-Christian schools were closed by the emperor Justinian. Alfred North Whitehead wrote in *Process and Reality* page 39: "The safest general characterization of the European philosophical tradition is that it consists of a series of footnotes to Plato."

46   See www.en.wikipedia.org/wiki/List_of_inventors Note that practically all of them are males. This also holds true for art, philosophy, science, agriculture, and religions etc.

47 See Ken Wilber *A Brief History of Everything* pages 40-51 for a more detailed description of human evolution.

48 In 1792 Mary Wollstonecraft published *A Vindication of the Rights of Woman*, which was a call for equality between the sexes in particular areas of life, such as education and morality. However she did not explicitly state that men and women are equal.

49 The different waves and forms of feminism are: **First wave feminism** promoted women's equal right to contract, property, and suffrage, and opposed the ownership of married women by their husbands.

Second wave feminism concerned itself with ending any type of discrimination against women, with a tendency to dictate to women what is good and bad for them, often implying that men are bad.

Third wave feminism coexists with second wave feminism and started a debate between women about whether women are different from men or not. It raised question of class- and race-related subjectivities.

Post feminism assumes that equal rights and opportunities are being achieved and that any kind of view that separates the sexes rather than uniting them is not feminist but sexist.

Liberal feminism asserts the equality of men and women through political and legal reform. It focuses on women's ability to show and maintain their equality through their own actions and choices.

Radical feminism claims that a male-based authority and power structure is responsible for the oppression of women and their inequality, and that as long as this system and its values are in place, society will not be able to be reformed in any significant way. Radical feminism is anti-patriarchy.

Socialist feminism connects the oppression of women to Marxist ideas about exploitation, capitalism, and labor. Socialist feminists see women being held down as a result of their unequal standing in both the workplace and the domestic sphere.

Eco-feminism believes that the oppression of women comes from the same ideologies that bring about the destruction of the natural environment. Eco-feminists argue that men in power control the land, are able to exploit it for their own profit and success, and exploit women for their pleasure. Like radical feminists, eco-feminists also tend to hate men and are therefore often called radical eco-feminists.

50 In the US as a whole in 1920. → TOO GENERALIZED

51 Women obtained 19 percent of all undergraduate college degrees around the beginning of the 20th century. By 1984 the figure had increased to 49 percent. Women also increased their numbers in graduate study. By the mid-1980s women were earning 49 percent of all master's degrees and about 33 percent of all doctoral degrees. In 1985 about 53 percent of all college students were women, with more than one quarter above age 29. See www.wic.org/misc/history.htm

52 The myth that women get paid less for equal work was debunked by Warren Farrell in his book *Why Men Earn More: The Startling Truth Behind the Pay Gap—and What Women Can Do About It*. He asked the question why companies would not put their competitors out of business by hiring women if they would do the same work for much less. He found out that women on average work fewer hours and don't take jobs that are highly stressful, competitive, strenuous, or dangerous. Instead they are more fulfillment-oriented. In the end it turned out to be a question of supply and demand. It is also a certain paradox that women generally expect their husbands to earn significantly more money than they do themselves, but on a large scale demand equal pay. Finally, today, single childless women earn on average 20% more than their male peers.

53 The Pill, as it became known, was invented by Dr. Gregory Pincus and approved by the US Food & Drug Administration in 1960. Pregnancy was no longer inevitable for married, and later single women (the pill was initially illegal in some states and only prescribed to married women in others) but became a choice in which may now men have no or little say.

54 Signed into law in 1969 by then-Governor of California Ronald Reagan, soon to be adopted in other US States.

55 See *These boots are made for walking: Why most divorce filers are women* a study by Margaret Brinig and Douglas Allen (American Law and Economics Review, Vol. 2, pp. 126-169, 2000) which states: "Because of the financial and social hardship faced after divorce, most people assume that generally husbands have instigated divorce since the introduction of no-fault divorce. Yet *women* file for divorce and are often the instigators of separation, despite a deep attachment to their children and the evidence that many divorces harm children. Furthermore, divorced women in large numbers reveal that they are happier than they were while married. They report relief and certainty that they were right in leaving their marriages. This fundamental puzzle suggests that the incentives to divorce require a reexamination, and that the forces affecting the net benefits from marriage may be quite complicated, and perhaps asymmetric between men and women. This paper considers women's filing as rational behavior, based on spouses' relative power in the marriage, their opportunities following divorce, and their anticipation of custody." Also see www.divorcereform.org/rates.html

56 Feminism fought for and, by and large achieved, equal rights and opportunities for modern and postmodern women in comparison to men, but did not advocate for the same rights of men compared with women. It also did not demand the same responsibilities for women. Feminists continue to expect men to be success-oriented providers, risk their lives in the workplace and in wars as protectors, take the risk of rejection, court women, open doors, and buy the diamond ring, while women retain their rights to be fulfillment-oriented and to use their interior emotional strength and exterior sexual power to take advantage of men.

57 See any book by Warren Farrell for details, especially *The Myth of Male Power* and *Does Feminism Discriminate Against Men* where he redefined power as "control over one's life," saying that "men learn to define power as feeling obligated to earn money that women spend while they die sooner." Farrell argues that "men's weakness is their facade of strength while women's strength is their facade of weakness." He concludes that we had much less need for a women's movement or a men's movement, but needed instead a gender transition movement that frees both men and women form the rigid gender roles of the past. Also see Gail Sheehy *Understanding Men's Passages* page 18: "Being a good provider is still the primary way men define themselves. What has drastically changed is that fewer men and more and more women can fill that role" and Terrence Real *The New Rules Of Marriage*, page 6: "The reason things have been so difficult between men and women in the last several decades can be pared down to this: In the *last generation women have radically changed and men, by and large, have not.* This is not a criticism of men. It is a simple fact."

58 See Laurie A. Rudman and Peter Glick *The Social Psychology of Gender* pages 25-28.

59 According to www.bls.gov/news.release/cfoi.t04.htm in 2007, 5071 men and 417 women died in the workplace in the US. Also see Patricia Love and Steven Stosny *How to Improve your Marriage Without Talking About It* page 65.

60 American Male/Female Casualties of Wars:

World War I: 116,516 men died. At least 359 servicewomen died, mostly from influenza and vehicle and aircraft accidents.

World War II: 405,399 men died. 543 women died, mostly from vehicle and aircraft accidents. Sixteen Army nurses died from enemy fire.

Korean War: 36,574 men died. 17 women died, mostly from vehicle or aircraft accidents.

Vietnam War: 58,190 males died. 8 females died, one from hostile fire, one suicide, and the rest from vehicle and aircraft accidents.

Gulf War: (Operations Desert Shield and Desert Storm): 367 men died. 16 women died, mostly from vehicle and aircraft accidents and hostile fire.

Iraq War: As of May 3rd 2008: 3,965 men died: 94 women died from hostile fire, and 378 have been wounded in action.

5,396 men died at work in the U.S. in 2006, compared to 444 women.

SOURCES: Women in Military Service for America Memorial Foundation; Defense Department. www.fas.org/sgp/crs/natsec/RL32492.pdf

www.purplemotes.net/tag/life-expectancy/

61 See Brett Tate *The Professional Bachelor* pages 216-226 for a men's perspective on women divorcing well. According to him, each year about $45 billion of wealth are transferred from men to women through divorce.

62   The Assistant Secretary-General and Special Adviser to the Secretary-General on Gender Issues and the Advancement of women has been charged with supporting and overseeing the implementation of Gender Mainstreaming, a globally accepted strategy for promoting gender equality. Equality between women and men refers to the equal rights, responsibilities, and opportunities of women and men and girls and boys. Equality does not mean that women and men will become the same, but that women's and men's rights, responsibilities and opportunities will not depend on whether they are born male or female. Gender equality implies that the interests, needs and priorities of both women and men are taken into consideration—recognizing the diversity of different groups of women and men. Gender equality is not a women's issue but should concern and fully engage men as well as women. Equality between women and men is seen both as a human rights issue and as a precondition for, and indicator of, sustainable people-centered development. See www.un.org/womenwatch/osagi/gendermainstreaming.htm

63   See www.time.com/time/specials/packages/article/0,28804,1930277_1930145_1930309-2,00.html

64   See Jean Houston in an interview at www.womenontheedgeofevolution.com where she said: "It is important that women rise to full partnership with men in the whole domain of human affairs. This is happening whether men like it or not. As women rise, men are regaining some of their deepest capacities, instead of being so patterned by their traditional roles, which don't work so well anymore as the economy and the ecology are collapsing. This is the time for women to get together WITH men and make them see what women can offer, such as the sensibility for process, patterns of connection, and—above all—creative wonderful strategies for issues in local communities; not as power, but with love. This is giving us a very great and different perspective on the relationship; men and women are *deeply, deeply, deeply* needful of each other."

CHAPTER 2: UNDERSTANDING THE DIFFERENCES BETWEEN THE SEXES

65   A waist to hip ratio (WHR) of 0.7 for women and 0.9 for men has been shown to correlate strongly with general health and fertility. Women within the 0.7 range have optimal levels of estrogen and are less susceptible to major diseases such as diabetes, cardiovascular disorders, and ovarian cancers. Men with WHR's around 0.9 have been shown to be more healthy and fertile with less prostate cancer and testicular cancer. See Helen Fisher *Why We Love* page 107, and Nancy Etcoff "Survival of the Prettiest" pages 140-143.

66   See for example Helen Fisher, *Why We Love* page 108-113, David Deida Intimate Communion page 45, Alison A. Armstrong *Making Sense of Men* pages 18-33, Ayala Malach *Pines Falling in Love* pages 83-104, Harville Hendrix page 5.

67   See Nancy Etcoff *Survival of the Prettiest* pages 172-176, and Malcom Gladwell *Blink: The Power of Thinking Without Thinking*: "There's plenty of evidence to suggest that height—particularly in men—does trigger a certain set of very positive, unconscious associations." Gladwell polled about half of the Fortune 500 companies and found that the majority of their CEOs were tall, white men:
- The average CEO was just under 6 feet (the average American man is 5'9")
- Among the CEOs, 58 percent were 6 feet or over
- In the United States, 14.5 percent of men are 6 feet or over
- Some 30 percent of the CEOs were 6'2" or taller
- Only 3.9 percent of U.S. men are 6'2" or taller"

"Height matters for career success," said Timothy Judge, a University of Florida management professor who co-conducted a study on the topic.

68   Helen Fisher *Why We Love* page 114-116 and David Deida *Intimate Communion* page 44.

69   It is difficult to estimate the porn industries' overall revenue. Numbers range between $5 and $10 billion for the US and approx. $40 billion worldwide. Through affordable video technology and the Internet, a lot of free "fan websites" have been established that compete with magazines and DVD sales. X-rated movies are still the top sellers in hotel room entertainment.

70   Reports say that romance fiction generated $1.37 billion in sales in 2008 and remained the largest share of the consumer book market at 13.5 percent. What makes romance so popular? The diversity of

the genre, titles aimed mostly at women, who read 90.5 percent of all romance novels, and the low price point helped make romance the number one category on best-seller lists in 2008 see www.rwanational.org/cs/the_romance_genre/romance_literature_statistics/industry_statistics

71   Mahatma Gandhi struggled throughout his adult life to transcend his Primary Fantasy and shared his bed with much younger and attractive female devotees to overcome his sexual desires in his later years. See page 423 in *Gandhi, A Life* by Yogesh Chadha "… Gandhi publicly stated that in his quest to master his sexual drive, he had been experimenting by sharing his bed with women disciples. He was 77 years old."

72   "Time, money, and sex" (TMS – sometimes also called "the big three" – not to be confused with "the Good, the True and the Beautiful") have been identified as the main reasons for couples to get together AND the main cause for later conflict and breakups.

73   See Theresa L. Crenshaw *The Alchemy of Love and Lust* for an in-depth analysis of all the hormones that affect male/female sexuality and relationships, and Harville Hendrix *Getting The Love You Want* page 47. In *Is He Mr. Right* Mira Kirshenbaum defines Chemistry as (1) comfortable and close, (2) safe, (3) fun to be with, (4) sexually attractive, (5) respectable by being smart, powerful, and successful – and respectful of her ambition and accomplishments.

74   See Helen Fisher, *Why We Love* in its entirety and specifically page 78 and 195-196.

75   See Helen Fisher, *Why We Love* pages 153-180.

76   See Ayala Malach Pines *Falling in Love* page 79, Nancy Etcoff *Survival of the Prettiest*, and many movies where he initially goes crazy over her (and wants to have sex) while she is not so sure and wants to get to know him better.

77   In 2008 the American cosmetics and beauty aid industry generated over $20 billion in sales, predominantly by hair and skin care products that are heavily advertised in print media and on television. Fashion industry sales were approx. $200 billion.

78   Research has shown that men who are sexually aroused are willing to take higher financial and physical risks. www.huffingtonpost.com/2008/04/04/sex-drives-men-to-take-ri_n_95169.html and www.usatoday.com/tech/science/2008-04-07-sex-financial-risk_N.htm

79   See Geoffrey Miller *The Mating Mind* page 206: "If a woman is interested in assessing a man's personality, intelligence, and experiences, it may take weeks of conversations before she has (unconsciously) gathered all information she needs to fall in love …. while men's sexual decision-making may appear faster, because physical appearance can be judged much faster than character," and Donald Symons *The Evolution of Sexual Desire* page 166: "Since human female parental investment may typically exceed male investment, females might be expected to be choosier than males."

80   See Helen Fisher, *Why We Love* pages 116-118 and Geoffrey Miller *The Mating Mind* pages 85-87 where he writes: "Robert Trivers realized that females make fewer eggs (one per month) than males make sperm (300-500 million per ejaculate). Thus it makes sense that males should compete more intensely to fertilize eggs than females do to acquire sperm, and that females should be choosier than males. Males compete for quantity of females, while females compete for quality in males."

81   Warren Farrell in his books *Father and Child Reunion* and *Does Feminism Discriminate Against Men* makes a case for a similar investment of fathers, as they may have to diminish their life quality and longevity by working harder to pay for a child that they may not have wanted, and that is turned against them if the mother hates him. While that may be true, it seems to be a rather rational argument and does not hold up well from an evolutionary perspective.

82   See Ayala Malach *Pines Falling in Love* page 89.

83   See Patricia Love/Steven Stosny page 66 in *How to Improve your Marriage Without Talking About It*: "Many women have no clue how critical and demeaning they are to men" and Harville Hendrix *Getting The Love You Want pages 76-81*: "In despair, people begin to use negative tactics to force their partners to become more loving. They withhold their affection and become emotionally distant."

84 To deprive of strength; vigor or weaken. Allison Armstrong of www.understandmen.com calls it "ripping his balls off and not giving them back to him." Also see Patricia Love/Steven Stosny *How to Improve your Marriage Without Talking About It* pages 65-71.

85 See Terrence Real *I don't want to talk about it* about male depression.

86 The PAX program created by Alison Armstrong teaches women how to appreciate men in order to get celebrated by them (see www.understandmen.com). Also see John Gray *Why Mars And Venus Collide* for tips on how to understand and resolve this conflict.

87 This dynamic was aptly captured in the movie *Love Actually* when Karen exclaims: "Would you wait around to find out if it's just a necklace, or if it's sex and a necklace, or if, **worst of all**, it's a necklace AND love?" Note how she feels that the necklace is OK (no emotional connection) and even sex would be OK, as long as she is clear about what is behind it, but the necklace (support) AND love (emotional infidelity) are unacceptable.

88 Patricia Love and Steven Stosny wrote an excellent book about the fear/shame dynamic between men and women called *How To Improve Your Marriage Without Talking About It*.

89 Irvin Singer (Professor of Philosophy at M.I.T) writes in his book *Philosophy of Love* page xvi: "I began my labors in the philosophy of love at a time when hardly any reputable philosopher in the Anglo Saxon world considered that subject professional or even respectable." And on page 109: "I was cautioned to avoid it because – I was told – I would ruin my career, I would suicidally destroy my professional standing, I would be ostracized by the American Philosophical Association." Geoffrey Miller states in *The Mating Mind*: "Prudery has also marginalized the public discussion of sexual selection – which is, after all, about sex. Many people, especially scientists, are ambivalent about sex: fascinated but embarrassed, obsessed yet guilty, alternately ribald and puritanical. Scientists still feel awkward teaching sexual selection to students, talking about it with journalists, and writing about it for the public."

90 See Millionaire Matchmaker Patti Stanger in *Become your own matchmaker* pages 50-72. Under "mirror mirror" **she** writes: ".... you know I can be harsh. I tell girls [who want to catch a millionaire] that they are too fat or too thin, their hair is too frizzy/curly or the wrong color. This may sound crude, but men are measuring your 'fuckability factor.'"

91 See endnote #49 in Chapter 1 for the various forms of feminism.

92 A rather crass example can be seen in the docudrama *Downfall* that chronicles the last two weeks of Hitler's life. In it, women who enjoy the safety and relative luxury of living with him beg him not to surrender, while thousands others die outside.

93 See specifically Helen Fisher, *Why We Love* page 103, 114, and the top of page 202, Daniel Goleman *Social Intelligence* page 199, Laurie A. Rudman and Peter Glick *The Social Psychology of Gender* page 211-222, and Ayala Malach Pines *Falling in Love* pages 83-104, to name a few.

94 For a sobering account of an intelligent woman who literally rejected one hundred men after dating them see Dale Koppel *The Intelligent Woman's Guide to Online Dating*.

95 See Ayala Malach Pines *Falling in Love* pages 100-103.

96 See David M. Buss, *The Evolution of Desire* in which he found that "in the pursuit of a mate, women prefer men who possess money, resources, power, and high social status, while men tend to seek attractive, youthful women who will remain sexually faithful." These findings emerged from a global survey by Buss and his colleagues of 10,047 adults in 37 cultures, from Australia to Zambia. Also see Donald Symons *The Evolution of Human Sexuality* page 191: "The human female tendency to detect and to be attracted to high status males may constitute one such innate rule."

97 See Laurie A. Rudman and Peter Glick *The Social Psychology of Gender* pages 6-24.

98 See Warren Farrell et al. *Does Feminism Discriminate Against Men* pages 60-68 for separate lists for men and women of typically assigned work around the house, debunking the myth that women work "two shifts" while men do little to no work at home (according to Farrell, American men work an average of 59.5 hours per week on their job and at home combined, while women work an average of 56.4 hours combined).

99 See Laurie A. Rudman and Peter Glick *The Social Psychology of Gender* page 89.

100 See most famously John Gray *Why Mars And Venus Collide* and earlier titles such as *Mars and Venus Together Forever, Men are from Mars, Women are for Venus, Mars and Venus on a Date, Mars and Venus in the Bedroom*, workshops at www.understandmen.com/ and fun videos and advice at www.laughyourway.com/

101 See John Gray *Why Mars And Venus Collide* pages 38-41.

102 See Ken Wilber *Integral Spirituality* page 11-15. Note that the Integral Relationship Model does not see the feminine and masculine polarities as types that remain consistent throughout vertical human development in consciousness (as defined in the AQAL model), but as potentials that can be actualized and embodied by both sexes as they age and evolve to various degrees, as Wilber states himself on page 26 in the same book: "The masculine principle identifies more with agency, and the feminine identifies more with communion, but the point is that every person has both of these components." Also see Erich Fromm *The Art of Loving* page 34: "There is masculinity and femininity in character as well as in sexual function … and it must always be kept in mind that in each individual both characteristics are blended."

103 Ascending qualities are wisdom, emptiness, and stillness. Practices include mediation, contemplation and solitude. The archetype is the wise father. Ascenders seem to be otherworldly and think in absolutes. They ascend from matter to spirit. It is the love that reaches up (Eros), towards God in the heavens, ever striving to find greater wholeness and wider union, to break the limits and to reach for the sky, to rise to the unending revelations of a greater good and glory, always rejecting the shallower, in search of the deeper, rejecting the lower in search for the higher.

The God of the ascenders is otherworldly to the core, his kingdom is not of this world. Ascending is puritanical, monastic, and ascetic, and sees the body, the flesh, and especially sex as archetypal sin. Ascenders are pessimistic about finding happiness in this world and shun time in favor of eternity.

Descending is seen as evil and sin. This world is seen as illusory, shadowy, and corrupted.

Healthy ascending is the desire to improve and to become better, to go beyond and to grow into a more illumining nature by gaining a wider perspective of the true self and the nature of things. Self transcendence is a personal journey of self discovery. It requires personal effort and the willingness to change by letting go of old paradigms. Spiritual seekers experience self transcendence as emptiness, infinite consciousness of inner peace, freedom, and joy by going beyond the limitations of the ego and becoming aware of a higher source.

Unhealthy ascending (also called phobos) represses and dissociates from the lower instead of embracing it, e.g., by denying feelings, the body, sexuality, and gaia (as seen in many ascending religions such as Christianity, Buddhism and Islam.) The unhealthy ascender is afraid of being dragged down and contaminated by the lower. Phobos is the ultimate source of all repression, denial, fear, and sometimes even hatred of anything this-worldly like vital life, sexuality, sensuality, often neglecting body and nature.

104 See Ken Wilber *A Brief History of Everything* pages 227-235.

105 Descending is expressed in Goddess- and earth-based religions such as paganism. Descending is the path of compassion. It sees that the One actually manifests as the many and so all forms are to be treated equally with kindness, compassion and mercy in a this-worldly descend from spirit to matter. The One empties itself into all creation, is in all forms and celebrates the visible and sensible. Presence, surrender, aliveness, feelings and emotions are expressions of descending. It is the love that reaches down, expressed as embodiment, bodily incarnation, relationship, relational and manifest embrace, touching each and every being in perfect and equal grace, rejecting nothing, embracing the many with goodness and immanent care. The descender is in love with the visible, sensible God, celebrates the senses, the body, sexuality and earth, and embraces a creation-centered spirituality.

Spiritual seekers experience self immanence as total surrender to what is—a total connectedness with earth and all manifestation, fullness, form and flow.

106 See Ken Wilber Sex, Ecology, Spirituality Page 340.

107 From "agent" which means "an entity that is capable of action."

108 Masculine means "having qualities appropriate to or usually associated with a man or being mannish." Feminine means "characteristic of or appropriate or unique to women or being womanish."

109 See David Deida *Intimate Communion* pages 19-36.

110 David Gordon White offers the following definition: Tantra is that Asian body of beliefs and practices which, working from the principle that the universe we experience is nothing other than the concrete manifestation of the divine energy of the Godhead that creates and maintains that universe, seeks to ritually appropriate and channel that energy, within the human microcosm, in creative and emancipatory ways. www.en.wikipedia.org/wiki/Tantra

111 See John Maxwell Taylor *Eros Ascending* pages 18-19: "The sexual aspect was one small part of a larger whole and required, of a true follower, years of dedication to prepare for an enlightened ultimate evening of love with a Tantra goddess or "Sacred Temple Prostitute.""

CHAPTER 3: LINES OF DEVELOPMENT FOR HUMAN INTELLIGENCES

112 In his book *Frames of Mind* (1983) Howard Gardner suggested that there is not just one intelligence that can be reduced to a single number as IQ. He listed 7 basic intelligences (and later added an eighth) that can all develop independently:
   1. Linguistic Intelligence: The capacity to use words effectively, whether orally (e.g., as a storyteller, orator, or politician) or in writing (e.g., as a poet, playwright, editor, or journalist).
   2. Logical-Mathematical Intelligence: The capacity to use numbers effectively (e.g., as a mathematician, tax accountant, or statistician) and to reason well (e.g., as a scientist, computer programmer, or logician).
   3. Spatial Intelligence: The ability to perceive the visual-spatial world accurately (e.g., as a hunter, scout, or guide) and to perform transformations upon those perceptions (e.g., as an interior decorator, architect, artist, or inventor).
   4. Bodily-Kinesthetic Intelligence: Expertise in using one's whole body to express ideas and feelings (e.g., as an actor, a mime, an athlete, or a dancer) and facility in using one's hands to produce or transform things (e.g., as a craftsperson, sculptor, mechanic, or surgeon).
   5. Musical Intelligence: The capacity to perceive (e.g., as a music aficionado), discriminate (e.g., as a music critic), transform (e.g., as a composer), and express (e.g., as a performer) musical forms.
   6. Interpersonal Intelligence: The ability to perceive and make distinctions in the moods, intentions, motivations, and feelings of other people.
   7. Intrapersonal Intelligence: Self-knowledge and the ability to act adaptively on the basis of that knowledge.
   8. Naturalistic Intelligence: The ability to easily recognize and classify plants, animals, and other things in nature.

113 See www.wilderdom.com/personality/L4-1IntelligenceNatureVsNurture.html to read more about nature versus nurture.

114 Lew Howard lists 27 lines of development/intelligences in his book *Introducing Ken Wilber* page 23, and Allan Combs provides a similar list of 10 lines in *Consciousness Explained Better* on pages 47-48.

115 David M. Buss, *The Evolution of Desire* page 36, Helen Fisher, *Why We Love* page 103, Ayala Malach Pines *Falling in Love* pages 48-60, and Nancy Etcoff *Survival of the Prettiest* pages 147-149.

116 Unconditional Love means to fully accept, feeling one with, and wanting the best for him/her beyond egoic needs, judgment, or selfish motives.

117 See John Welwood *Towards a Psychology of Awakening* pages 236-237: "Becoming fully human involves working with the totality of what we are – both our conditioned nature (earth) and our unconditioned nature (heaven). On the one hand, we developed a number of habitual personality patterns [interests, lifestyle, passions, dreams etc.] …. , on the other hand, the human heart is an unconditioned awake presence, a caring, inquisitive intelligence, and openness to reality. Each of us has these two forces at work in us."

118 Gregory K. Popcak lists 28 values and ideals page 62 in his book *The Exceptional 7 Percent* and Abraham Maslow enumerated 14 universal being values.

119 See Erich Fromm *The Art of Loving* page 20-21.

120 In Intellectual Foreplay, Eve Eschner-Hogan and Steven Hogan identify 29 categories of values, needs, qualities, interests, and passions, and provide many questions for each topic that you can answer by yourself or with a partner.

In *If The Buddha Dated* Charlotte Kasl lists 9 categories to consider for partner selection page 62 –68.

121 From *Nonviolent Communication* by Marshall Rosenberg page 54-55 and Abraham Maslow's hierarchy of needs.

122 Manfred Max Neef, a Chilean economist and environmentalist defined nine fundamental human needs that are distinct from economic "wants" that are infinite and insatiable. According to him, these needs are consistent throughout all human cultures and across historical time periods. There is no hierarchy of these needs, apart from the basic need for subsistence or survival. These needs are "subsistence, protection, affection, understanding, participation, recreation (in the sense of leisure time to reflect, or idleness), creation, identity, and freedom." These needs are defined according to the existential categories of "being," "having," "doing" and "interacting," and from these dimensions, a 36 cell matrix can be developed.

123 See *Undefended Love* by Marlena Lyons and Jett Psaris pages 139-150.

A "need" is something that you need right now for your survival or well-being. If the need is not met, you will most likely make it your highest priority to get it met as soon as possible. Meeting needs usually require something external, such as air, food, water, or a certain behavior or contribution from others.

A "want" is something you want to have eventually such as I want to be loved, I want to travel.

A "desire" is something that you have a longing for but that you can live without. You are open to receive it but don't feel that you have to actively pursue it or demand it from others, e.g., I have a desire to be in a healthy partnership.

A "preference" is a leaning or tendency in a certain direction, but the alternative is just as fine, such as I have a preference for rice over noodles or warm weather over cold.

"No preference" is a spiritual state of acceptance and non-choosing, which requires a high level of presence and surrender to what is.

It is questionable if anyone can be completely without needs, wants, desires, or preferences if he or she fully engages in life without repression or dissociation.

124 David Richo in *How to be an Adult in Relationship* defines the five A's of a healthy relationship as:
1. **Attention** to the present moment; observing, listening, and noticing all the feelings at play in our relationships.
2. **Acceptance** of ourselves and others just as we are.
3. **Appreciation** of all our gifts, our limits, our longings, and our poignant human predicament.
4. **Affection** shown through holding and touching in respectful ways.
5. **Allowing** life and love to be just as they are, with all their ecstasy and ache, without trying to take control.

125 Examples for unclear communication between couples may be the desire to have children without discussing the when, how (e.g., adoption versus the wife's pregnancy), and how many, e.g., the reason Elizabeth Gilbert gives in *Committed* for divorcing her husband, or financial issues – whether it's OK to have credit card debt (and whether the individuals have it), how to allocate funds when one partner earns more (divide it equally or the higher income one gets to call the shots more), let's save up for a house, versus let's borrow from parents, or if it's OK to accept money, cars, houses from wealthy relatives.

126 The concept of emotional intelligence dates back to Charles Darwin and Howard Gardner identified it as an interpersonal intelligence. The term Emotional Intelligence was first used in Wayne Payne's doctoral thesis, *"A study of emotion: Developing emotional intelligence"* in 1985 and was later widely popularized in Daniel Goleman's book *Emotional Intelligence*.

226 | INTEGRAL RELATIONSHIPS: A MANUAL FOR MEN

127 Salovey and Mayer (1990) defined Emotional Intelligence as: "The ability to monitor one's own and others' feelings and emotions, to discriminate among them and to use this information to guide one's thinking and actions." Also see Daniel Goleman's bestsellers *Emotional Intelligence* and *Social Intelligence*.

128 See Tony Robbins in a dialog with Ken Wilber on www.integralnaked.org and the website www.eqi.org/fw.htm which lists over 3,000 words for feelings.

129 See the book *Power vs. Force* by David R. Hawkins pages 67-94 and 145 – 149 or www.stevepavlina.com/blog/2005/04/levels-of-consciousness/

130 See Louann Brizendine *The Female Brain* pages 18-19, 117-134, and Patricia Love/Steven Stosny *How to Improve your Marriage Without Talking About It* page 59-60.

131 See for example Terrence Real *The New Rules Of Marriage* on page 7: "Most of all, [women want] an emotional partner who shows interest in and appreciation for her feelings."

132 One of the major themes of John Gray's *Mars and Venus* books.

133 See Patricia Love and Steven Stosny *How to Improve your Marriage Without Talking About It* pages 60-61 under "Not Those Feelings," Warren Farrell *Women Can't Hear What Men Don't Say* page 74: "Being in touch with feelings is very different from expressing feelings. Being in touch with feelings gives a man the option of expressing them when appropriate. It is the choice that empowers him – if he makes the right choices" and a cartoon on page 73 where a woman complains to a fortune teller: "He never talks about his feelings" to which she replies "Next year at 2:00 PM, men will start talking about their feelings; and at 2:05 women all over America will be sorry," and John Gray *Why Mars And Venus Collide* page 196.

134 To express emotions, especially in an excessive or theatrical manner.

135 Vulnerability means taking the risk of sharing information, thoughts, and feelings that will most likely provoke a negative reaction or criticism in others. [handwritten note: WRONG – NOT THE DEFINITION]

136 See David Deida *The Way of the Superior Man*, page 116 and 117 under "Her Complaint Is Content-Free": "You must listen to your woman more as an oracle than as an advisor. She usually is speaking in a very tangential, but revelatory, style. She is revealing your unconscious habits that prevent your fullest awakening in consciousness. Your unconsciousness causes her pain. If she can't trust you with living your life from your deepest wisdom and fullest capacity, she can't trust you with her life. She can't trust your masculine impeccability, so she naturally will compensate by overdeveloping her own. And this results in stress [for her]."

137 See Eckhart Tolle *A New Earth* pages 129-184, and *The Power Of Now* pages 33-45 (paperback) or 27-37 (hardcover) for the latter. His suggestion that therapy is not necessary if you just learn to witness your negative feelings and emotions is questionable, as it may lead to spiritual bypassing. See Ken Wilber *Integral Spirituality* pages 126-141.

138 From *Nonviolent Communication* by Marshall Rosenberg page 43.

139 See *Nonviolent Communication* by Marshall Rosenberg.

140 The core principles of NVC are:
Avoid:
    Criticism and "should"ing
    Denial of responsibility
    Demands with threat of blame or punishment
    Declarations of who deserves reward or punishment
Do not confuse an observation with an evaluation:
    When I see you do X (when you say X) I think/feel you are (a) Y (jerk, idiot, insensitive, liar, etc.)
Make doable requests in less then 15 words:
    When I observe X, I feel Y because I have a need for Z. Would you be willing to …
Listen and paraphrase but do not:
    Advise, compare, educate, re-assure, story-tell, tell not to feel, sympathize, or gather data.
Focus on how people are and what they request:

What observed?
Feeling created?
Unfulfilled need?
What can I do?

Behind every message is a person with unmet needs (typically to be loved, understood, accepted, heard, etc.)

Focus on all feelings, wait until all is expressed.

When you can't give empathy you need empathy.

Empathy guess:

When you hear/experience X are you feeling Y because you need Z? Would you like me to …?

141 An alternative and compatible strategy is outlined in the book *Getting To Yes Without Giving In* by Roger Fisher and William Ury.

142 In the movie *The Fog of War* Robert McNamara shares his 11 tenets, among them "empathize with your enemy," "rationality will not save us," "there is something beyond one's self," "believing and seeing are often both wrong" and "be prepared to re-examine your reasoning."

Chapter 4: Levels of Growth

143 There is a lot of carefully conducted research that supports the idea that humans develop in sequential stages in ALL the developmental lines, e.g., you need to learn algebra first before you can move on to calculus, or in stages of moral development from selfish to care to universal care.

Men need to be sensitive towards women who have been (or feel like) victims of patriarchal dominator hierarchies. Therefore natural hierarchies need to be distinguished from dominator hierarchies, which occur when a higher level in the hierarchy assumes unjustified control over the lower levels, for example a dominant man over a woman.

144 For a comprehensive (mind dazzling) overview of developmental systems and their sources see *Integral Psychology* by Ken Wilber pages 197-217.

145 For a broader overview of developmental lines and stages, see Ken Wilber *Integral Spirituality* pages 4-11 and 50-70, *Integral Psychology* pages 38-53, and *A Brief History of Everything* 125-142, *Spiral Dynamics* by Don Edward Beck and Christopher Cowan (based on initial research by Prof. Claire Graves), the CD-Set Spiral Dynamics by Don Beck, *Changes of Mind* by Jenny Wade, *Integral Consciousness* by Steve McIntosh pages 29-96, development of worldviews by Jean Gebser, self-identity/ego development by Jane Loevinger and Susanne Cook-Greuter, moral developmental stages by Lawrence Kohlberg and in the book *In A Different Voice* by Carol Gilligan, and consciousness development in *In Over Our Heads* by Robert Kegan.

146 See Ken Wilber *Integral Spirituality* page 202-205, and Ken Wilber, Terry Patten, Adam Leonard, and Marco Morelli in *Integral Life Practice—A 21st Century Blueprint for Physical Health, Emotional Balance, Mental Clarity, and Spiritual Awakening*.

147 Consciousness in medicine simply means wakefulness and is assessed by observing a patient's alertness and responsiveness. In psychology it usually refers to human awareness and experiences, while in philosophy it covers a wide range—from subjectivity to choice, interiority, volition, intention, or prehension. "Volition" means "the act of making a choice or decision; or the power of choosing or determining." "Prehension" means "the act of taking hold, seizing, or grasping; or mental understanding."

148 See Christian de Quincey *Radical Knowing* page 78-90 for a brief introduction to consciousness with the differences between psychological, philosophical, and spiritual consciousness. Also Allan Combs *The Radiance Of Being* pages 7-27.

149 See Christian de Quincey *Radical Knowing* page 78.

150 See Allan Combs *Consciousness Explained Better*.

151 Ego is Latin for "I." Sigmund Freud used the German word "ich" in his writings, which were later translated into "Ego" (instead of the correct "I") to sound more scientific. Psychology speaks of ego as the self-organizing principle and acknowledges that it is important to have a healthy sense of self or to strengthen the ego. Spiritual teacher and psychologist Jack Engler said "you have to be somebody before you can be nobody." Women often use the word "ego" in a negative way to describe men who are full of themselves, too much in their head, egocentric, narcissistic, or don't adopt women's feminist way of seeing the world—not realizing that they actually commit the same fallacy, defending their own limited worldview. In spirituality, the term "ego" is often used to describe a false or illusionary sense of self that defends its separate identity, is completely indentified with objects in consciousness, and its own narrow way of seeing the world—and therefore separates itself from others and sees everything as objects that it can use for its own gain. Eckhart Tolle said "The ego cannot Love, it always wants something." Spiritual books such as Eckhart Tolle's *A New Earth and The Power Of Now* which are popular among women, A.H. Almaas's *Diamond Heart* series of books, and basically all Eastern traditions try to point to an authentic and functional self that lies beyond the ego. At www.livereal.com/psychology_arena/what_is_ego.htm you can find a few dozen definitions for ego.

152 It is called the "hard problem," because it has not been explained yet how the immaterial or transpersonal is related to matter and vice versa. From Christian de Quincey *Radical Knowing* page 22 -24:

There are 4 general suggested answers to the hard problem:
1. The materialists claim that there is only matter and that everything else will be ultimately explained by mechanistic science, we just need to stay with it long enough. They can't however explain experiences such as meaning, love, purpose, consciousness or spirit, at least not yet.
2. The idealists claim that everything material is ultimately an illusion of the mind, or is created from spirit through the mind and therefore not real, or only real to the extent that we believe in it or create it. Movies such as The Secret and What the bleep do we know claim that we create our own physical reality. They can't however explain how the connection really works.
3. The dualists acknowledge that there is emptiness and form and say neither can be reduced to the other. They can't however explain how they are connected or interacting and say they might just be the same thing, just seen from different perspectives, or that everything that is not material is supernatural.
4. Panpsychism claims that both matter and mind are equally real, that neither is above the other, that everything is sentient (has prehension) and that there are either many separate minds, or one single mind that unites everything that is.

Also see Rupert Sheldrake *Morphic Resonance* pages 15-17.

Just think a few generations back. There was no "you," just your ancestors. Then your father and mother were born, met, and had sex, with you as a result. Out of emptiness arose (your) form. And you can now think about yourself and, sorry to say, in less than 100 years you (the egoic self) will go back to .... ??? .... you get the idea why it is called the hard problem.

The idea that the connecting force is "Love" in the deepest sense is probably as good as any other, and has been experienced by anybody who ever loved deeply (see Ken Wilber *Grace and Grit*), because it brings the subjective (emptiness) and objective (manifest) world into direct contact.

153 The word "creates" in this context does not imply that our mind or consciousness creates physical objects or the world around us (a.k.a. collapsing the Schroedinger wave equation) as suggested in New Age movies such as *What the bleep do we know* or *The Secret*. Instead, the word "creates" suggests that each individual interprets and therefore sees the world in a unique way and co-creates parts of their external reality through intentions. These intentions may create physical objects (artifacts) through human actions (such as a house or painting), put us into certain places such as a supermarket, or make us prone to certain outcomes, such as attracting somebody to get married to. People sometimes confuse their own role and responsibilities with the role of given factors in this intricate process of co-creation. The challenge is to distinguish between what is given (called critical realism), and what is created through our human interpretation (the myth of the given) and to distinguish our circle of influence from our circle of concern. See Ken Wilber *Integral Spirituality* pages 175-178.

154 See the pioneering work of Jean Gebser regarding the evolution of human consciousness, and Jean Piaget or Erik Erikson for stages in child development, (nicely summarized by Allan Combs in *Consciousness Explained Better* page 21–34 and 49-76.) See also Susanne Cook-Greuter, *Ego*

Development: Nine Levels of Increasing Embrace which can be downloaded for free from www.cook-greuter.com/

155 See the work of Abraham Maslow, Jenny Wade, Robert Kegan, Lawrence Kohlberg, Jane Loevinger, Carol Gilligan, and Susanne Cook-Greuter, to name a few men AND women who conducted developmental research and designed developmental models.

156 Two examples of natural hierarchies are: letters form words, words form sentences, sentences form paragraphs; atoms form molecules, molecules form cells, cells form organisms and so on.
Nobody would see letters or atoms as repressed or dominated, because they are "lower" or of "less depth/complexity" than the words and molecules that they form.
Most people also see the value of hierarchies pertaining to academic, musical, or athletic skills that can be objectively evaluated and measured, or for the functioning of institutions such as hospitals, corporations, the military, or churches. Because we, and especially females, are all too familiar with dominator hierarchies, fascism, and misguided Darwinian thinking (survival of the fittest), some people throw the baby out with the bathwater. In dominator hierarchies, people at higher levels with more power force their values (violently) onto others, and dominate them instead of taking care of them. Growth in consciousness causes individuals to show increased levels of care, love, compassion, and responsibility towards others and is therefore the antidote to dominator hierarchies.

157 Roger Walsh suggested that integrally informed people show:
Care and compassion for those at earlier stages, because these are the people we may be privileged to help and serve.
Love for those at the same stage, because these are our peers, our community, and our sangha.
Gratitude to those at later stages, because these are our teachers, role models, and way-finders. See www.integrallife.com/node/54698

158 In the Integral Model, these stages are often called "memes" (rhymes with creams). While a "gene" contains the inheritable traits of an organism, a "meme" (rhymes with theme) contains cultural information, such as practices, ideas or values, that get transmitted verbally or by repeated action from one person to another.
Memes or levels of development are often color coded to deflect from ranking/labeling and to avoid confusion between systems that have a different number of levels and/or names.
The color system and developmental stages can also be related to the Seven Chakras, which are subtle energy centers in our body that can be active at different levels.
Spiral Dynamics (SD), Ken Wilber (KW) and the Seven Chakra System (CS) are using a slightly different color coding:
Stage 1 - (SD) Beige = Survival, (KW) Infrared = Archaic, (CS) Red = Root or Base Chakra
Stage 2 - (SD) Purple = Kin-Spirits, (KW) Magenta = Magic , (CS) Orange = Sacral Sex Chakra
Stage 3 - (SD) Red = Power-Gods, (KW) Red = Egocentric, (CS) Yellow Solar = Plexus Emotion Chakra
Stage 4 - (SD) Blue = Truth-Force, (KW) Amber = Conformist/Mythic, (CS) Green = Heart Feeling Chakra
Stage 5 - (SD) Orange = Strive-Drive, (KW) Orange = Rational, (CS) Blue = Self Expression Chakra
Stage 6 - (SD) Green = Human Bond, (KW) Green = Pluralistic, (CS) Indigo = Intuition Chakra
Stage 7 - (SD) Yellow = Flex-Flow, (KW) Teal = Integral, (CS) Violet = Pure Consciousness Chakra
Stage 8 - (SD) Turquoise = Global View, (KW) Turquoise = Higher Mind (CS) N/A

159 The lower stages are often perceived as non-dual enlightened, but are in actuality a-dual and pre-conventional, which may look like non-dual post-post-conventional, since they are both unconventional (also see pre/trans fallacy and non-dual awareness under "spiritual development" in this chapter.)

160 Ken Wilber coined the term "pre/trans fallacy" to describe the confusion between pre-rational and trans-rational stages of development, because they are both non-rational. Any confusion between the pre- and trans-stages such as pre-formal and post-formal, pre-conventional and post-conventional, pre-personal and transpersonal, etc. fall under the pre/trans fallacy. See Ken Wilber *Integral Psychology* endnotes page 244/245, *Integral Spirituality* page 51-53, and *Eye to Eye* pages 332-373 (in Collected Works).

161 Red constantly underestimates that men are more frequently engaged in adjusting their ideas to circumstances, and much less successful at adjusting circumstances to their ideas.

162 See Roger Fisher and William Ury *Getting To Yes Without Giving In*.

163 In the movie *The Fog of War* Robert McNamara says "in order to do good, you may have to engage in evil," "maximize efficiency," "get the data," "never say never."

164 A line from the Oscar-winning musical *Swing Time* (1936), used by President Obama during his inauguration speech on 1/20/09.

165 A "performative contradiction" is a lack of fit between the content and the performance of a speech act. The *truth* of statements is a central element of communicational ethics. Statements which contradict the performance of the statement are considered a performative contradiction. The example "all statements must be false" is a performative contradiction because the speaker performs the action of stating something that contradicts the truthfulness of the speech act. We could also imagine speech acts whose content contradict the very act itself. For example, someone saying "I am mute" or "I don't speak English" would commit a performative contradiction. To elevate lateral above hierarchical thinking is another example, as it creates its own hierarchy.

166 With the exception of NOW, which was founded by Betty Friedan, all these organizations have been founded by men!

167 The evolutionary stages of the sexes from archaic to transpersonal that we just reviewed are all embedded in the layers of our brains. See for example Helen Fisher, *Why We Love* page 70, and Jenny Wade *Changes of Mind* page 68-75. Each stage lives as a potential to emerge inside every human being, waiting to be awoken as we mature. In an integrally informed relationship, we resonate at all these levels with our partner.

Indian mystics recognized these evolutionary developmental stages over 3,000 years ago in the seven chakra system.

7	Crown of Head	Totality of Beingness. Spiritual Perfection.	Violet
6	Forehead (3rd Eye)	Visualization. Psychic Sight.	Indigo
5	Pit of Throat	Communication. Creative Expression.	Blue
4	Heart	Universal Love. Compassion. Empathy.	Green
3	Solar Plexus	Creation of Self. Perception and Projection of Self.	Yellow
2	Sacral (Pubic)	Desire, Including Sexual Energy.	Orange
1	Base of Spine	Physical Vitality. Survival.	Red

168 Sri Aurobindo, an Indian nationalist and freedom fighter, poet, philosopher, and yogi developed his vision and philosophy of human progress and a spiritual path, which he called "Integral Yoga". He wrote: "Man is a transitional being. He is not final. The step from man to superman is the next approaching achievement in the earth's evolution. It is inevitable because it is at once the intention of the inner spirit and the logic of Nature's process." Jean Gebser used the term to describe the emergence of a new structure of consciousness in the West which he termed "Integral." Wilber adopted the term "Integral" for his theory that is based on Aurobindo and Gebser (among many others) in the late 1990s.

169 Clare Graves, Lawrence Kohlberg, Jane Loevinger, Susanne Cook-Greuter, and Robert Kegan, to name a few.

170 A term first used by Kurt Goldstein and popularized by Abraham Maslow that generally means "the full realization of one's potential [at each level of consciousness development]."

171 Translation means the healthy balancing and harmonizing of agency and communion at each stage of development. See www.enlightennext.org/magazine/j41/guru-pandit.asp?page=2 "The main point is that you want all four of those fundamental drives to be healthy."

172 For a long time the Integral stage was seen by researchers as the highest level of human consciousness that integrated all lower levels. Later, higher stages where discovered, e.g., by Susanne Cook-Greuter, which now sometimes creates confusion as "Integral" no longer stands for highest or most integrated. In a dialog with Allan Combs, Ken Wilber gave four definitions for Integral: (1) the highest level of development possible, (2) the integration of all lower levels, (3) a horizontal integration of the four quadrants (discussed in Part II of the manual) at a particular level, and (4) to be integrally informed.

173 Transpersonal stages are sometimes called holistic, transcendent, post-Integral, unity stage, implicate order, illumined mind, para mind, higher mind, super mind, meta mind, trans-global mind, or intuitive mind, depending on the particular line or developmental model.

174 See A.H. Almaas *Diamond Heart: Book One*: "'Being in the world but not of it' means that you continue doing what you do, you continue to pursue your career as a physicist, a gardener, a mother and so on, but all the time you remember and realize that it is only a reflection of something else, that what you wish most deeply is to actualize a part of yourself."

175 See Susanne Cook-Greuter's dissertation *Postautonomous Ego Development: Ego Development: Nine Levels of Increasing Embrace* (free download from www.cook-greuter.com/), and Jenny Wade *Changes of Mind*, which are some of the first systematic approaches to map out stages of higher consciousness development as outlined by Ken Wilber in *Integral Psychology*.

176 See Ken Wilber *Integral Spirituality* pages 51-53 and 104.

177 This makes it difficult to even talk about spirituality without making it into a mental concept. A wonderful book that addresses this very issue is *Cutting through Spiritual Materialism* by Chogyam Trungpa.

178 See Robert Kegan's book *In Over Our Heads*, an interview with him in *What Is Enlightenment* Magazine Fall–Winter 2002, online at www.wie.org/j22/kegan.asp?page=1 , Douglas E. Harding's classic *On Having No Head: Zen and the Rediscovery of the Obvious*, and Eckhart Tolle *A New Earth* pages 129-137 (Hardcover).

179 See Ken Wilber *Integral Spirituality* pages 71-83, *A Brief History of Everything* pages 179-217, and Lew Howard *Introducing Ken Wilber* pages 196-279 for more details.

180 Emotions are feelings that are physically expressed through the body, for example screaming, crying, laughing, cheering, sweating, recoiling, getting a red face, shaking, or a knot in the stomach. They are different from higher felt experiences such as intuition, wholeness, presence, meaning, purpose, empathy, compassion, faith, humility, devotion, love, or surrender.

181 Many New Age or New-Thought ideas arose from this state-stage such as *Science of Mind* churches (based on the work of Ernest Holmes) and movies/books like *The Secret, Ask and It is Given* (Abraham Hicks), and *What the bleep do we know* who all promote positive thinking with the idealistic idea that thoughts not only create our *interpretations* of reality and our intentions (which then may or may not create certain realities later), but physical reality itself (such as illnesses, social situations, financial wealth, or a partner that we *manifest* etc.) While it is an important first step towards awakening, and can empower people to take more responsibility for their lives instead of feeling victimized, it can become a highly problematic and morally questionable notion, as it makes people fully responsible for their own fate, independent of their race, cultural background, and capacities. If claimed as universal truth, it fails to pass the so called *Auschwitz Test*, as it suggests that the six million Jews who were killed by the Nazis (or the 10 million or more Native Americans who were killed by white settlers through war, starvation, and their diseases) are responsible for their own fate, because they did not "think the right way and attracted their fate." These notions not only indicate a profoundly distorted moral compass, but have also been long abandoned by serious scientists, for example Dr. David Albert on Disc One, Side Two of *Down The Rabbit Hole*, which is the in-depth version/sequel to *What the Bleep do we Know*, or Einstein's famous remark "I like to think that the moon is there even if I am not looking at it."

182 Breathing, which is usually involuntary, can serve as a bridge between the manifest and unmanifest world when we bring consciousness into it.

183 Addictions are recurring compulsions with negative consequences for our body and social life that have power over us, and that we can't control. See Eckhart Tolle *The Power Of Now* page 127 (152 paper-back): "Every addiction arises from an unconscious refusal to face and move through your own pain. Every addiction starts with pain and ends with pain. Whatever the substance you are addicted to—alcohol, food [sex, gambling, work, dating], legal or illegal drugs, or a person—you are using something or somebody to cover up your pain."

184 "Psychic" refers to the ability to perceive things that are hidden from the normal senses, associated with the body (i.e., things that you see, hear, touch, smell, taste).

185 A term that Carl Jung created for the experience of two or more unlikely events that occur together as a meaningful coincidence, such as bumping into a friend in a foreign country who was searching for a place that you had just came from, or you talking about a person and she calls you and asks a question that relates to what you just said. See Christian de Quincey *Radical Knowing* pages 91-122.

186 Ralph Waldo Emerson (1803 – 1882) was the most influential American writer about this stage and is quoted extensively by Wilber in *Sex, Ecology, Spirituality* pages 288-301.

187 See Terrence Real *I Don't Want to Talk About It* about male depression.

188 Many books have been written to describe this state-stage, such as *A Course In Miracles* channeled by Helen Schucman, *Be Here Now* by Ram Dass, or more recently, Eckhart Tolle's bestsellers *The Power Of Now*, and *A New Earth* that inspired millions.

189 Lucid dreaming means that you can watch your dream like a movie. In a less enlightened form, you may manipulate the dream, in a more advanced form you just witness it with no attachment to its context. See Roger Walsh *Paths Beyond Ego* pages 71-86.

190 Simply notice that you could not experience time if there wasn't stillness inside of you. It is also helpful to distinguish between relative "clock-time," which we use to keep appointments, to plan for the future, or remember events that happened in the past, and "psychological time" which creates a false sense of self that results from things that happened to us in the past and fear of the future such as death, illness, or losing all possessions.

191 There should be a conference for enlightened beings, and everyone who attends is automatically disqualified.

192 It is written in the *Upanishads*, the ancient Hindu scriptures, that Brahman (the Supreme Being) is that which speech does not illumine, but which illumines speech; that which cannot be thought by mind, but by which mind is able to think; that which is not seen by the eye, but by which the eye is able to see; that which cannot be heard by the ear, but by which the ear is able to hear, and that which none breathes with the breath, but by which breath is in-breathed.

193 Psychosis (an abnormal condition of the mind) is a generic psychiatric term for a mental state often described as involving a "loss of contact with reality." People suffering from psychosis are said to be psychotic.

194 See Eckhart Tolle, *The Power Of Now* page 125 (page 150 paperback): "On the physical level, you are obviously not whole, nor will you ever be: You are either a man or a woman, which is to say, one half of the whole. On this level, the longing for wholeness—the return to oneness—manifests as male-female attraction, man's need for a woman, woman's need for a man. The root for this physical urge is a spiritual one: the longing for an end to duality, a return to the state of wholeness. Sexual union is the closest you can get to this state on the physical level."

195 See diagram in Huston Smith's *Why Religion Matters* page 224 and Chapter 15 "Spiritual Personality Types" pages 234-254 where he defines four different spirituality types that pervade all major religions; (1) atheists who only believe in matter and the subjective experiences of biological organisms, (2) polytheists who find ghosts and spirits in many objects and phenomena, (3) monotheists who believe in a supreme being or creator of all that is, and (4) mystics who experience that there is only God. Also see Ken Wilber *Integral Spirituality* page 215, and Eckhart Tolle *A New Earth* page 16.

196 See Roger Walsh *Paths beyond Ego* pages 38-55 for a dozen of horizontal variables for each spiritual state-stage.

197 See Gregory K. Popcak *The Exceptional Seven Percent* pages 183-204, and David Schnarch *Passionate Marriage*.

198 See David Deida *Intimate Communion* page 59.

Endnotes | 233

199 See www.webmd.com/sex-relationships/features/10-surprising-health-benefits-of-sex Researchers found that sex: (1) Relieves Stress, (2) boosts the immune system, (3) burns calories (85 or more in 30 Minutes), (4) improves cardiovascular health, (5) boosts self esteem, (6) improves intimacy, (7) reduces pain (through release of oxytocin), (8) reduces risk of prostate cancer, (9) strengthens pelvic floor muscles, and (10) helps you to sleep better. Also see Patricia Love and Steven Stosny in *How to Improve your Marriage Without Talking About It* pages 148-150.

200 See David Deida *Intimate Communion* pages 59-60.

201 See David Schnarch *Passionate Marriage: Keeping Love and Intimacy Alive in Committed Relationships*.

202 "Kundalini" literally means coiling, like a spring or snake, at the base of the spine. It conveys the sense of an untapped energy potential or great reservoir of creativity that can be moved up the spine, often during sexual activity. When kundalini energy moves through the body, consciousness necessarily changes with it. From a psychological perspective, it can be thought of as a rich source of psychic or libidinous energy in our unconscious.

203 See poets such as Rumi, Hafiz, Rainer Maria Rilke, or Emily Dickinson, and David Deida *Dear Lover*, a book with 29 wonderful love letters that introduce each of the short chapters.

204 See David Deida *Intimate Communion* pages 60-61.

205 See Margo Anand *The Art of Sexual Ecstasy* pages 387-421 for this and other tantric positions.

206 See Victor Gold's simple and somewhat repetitive book *The Potency Principles* and www.sexualhealingnow.com/ For a more comprehensive introduction to Tantra see Margot Anand *The Art of Sexual Ecstasy* and *The Sexual Ecstasy Workbook*.

207 The PC or pubococcygeus muscle is found in males and females. It stretches from the pubic bone to the tail bone, forming the floor of the pelvic cavity. It is the same muscle that you use to stop the flow of urine. It can be strengthened by squeezing and holding it for a few seconds 30-50 times in a row three times a day.

208 See Dennis Genpo Merzel *Big Mind – Big Heart*, for a method that brings the many, often unconscious voices that compete for attention in our mind such as "the protector, the skeptic, the controller, the fearful self, the angry self, the fixer, the damaged self, the vulnerable child, the seeker, the enlightened self, etc." into conscious awareness, and leaves the practitioner with a "Satori" experience (Zen Buddhist term for understanding or enlightenment) of their authentic self.

209 See Leslie Temple Thurston *The Marriage of Spirit* page 52: "This androgynous soul form includes both the masculine and feminine frequencies, both negative and positive, and both conscious and unconscious. The second schism is the splitting away of the soul. It institutes the division between conscious-unconscious, negative-positive, and masculine-feminine. The individual is split into the masculine frequencies if in a male body or the feminine frequencies if in a female body."

210 See Ayala Malach Pines *Falling in Love* pages 109-120: "'Attachment theory' describes how children learn to feel close (attached) to their primary caregiver (usually the mother) while also feeling safe to explore their individuality. If the primary caregiver is consistent, stable, trustworthy and responsive, the toddler develops a sense of security in love and as an adult will be comfortable and satisfied in love relationships. If not, an adult will display a pattern of anxiety and ambivalence or may even avoid intimate love relationships altogether."

211 See Ayala Malach Pines *Falling in Love* pages 98-100 for a theory about how males have to suppress their emotional, but not their physical (or sexual) attachment to their mother in order to identify with their father. This attachment is then transferred to women in later life. Females have to become sexually detached from their mother but not emotionally in order to identify with father. This attachment is then transferred to men in later life. Also see John Welwood, *Love and Awakening* pages 182-184, and on page 199.

212 Carl Gustav Jung, (1875-1961) was a Swiss psychiatrist, influential thinker, and founder of analytical psychology.

213 The Anima and Animus are, in Carl Jung's school of analytical psychology, the totality of the unconscious feminine psychological qualities that a male possesses (anima) and the masculine ones possessed by the female (animus). Jung was not clear if the anima/animus archetype was totally unconscious, calling it "a little bit conscious and unconscious." Jung gave as an example a man who falls head over heels in love, then later in life regrets his blind choice as he finds that he has married his own anima–the unconscious idea of the feminine in his mind, rather than the woman herself. The anima is usually an aggregate of a man's mother but may also incorporate aspects of sisters, aunts, and teachers. The anima and animus are one of the most significant autonomous complexes of all. They manifest by appearing as figures in dreams as well as by influences in the interactions between the sexes. Jung said that confronting one's shadow self is an "apprentice-piece," while confronting one's anima and animus is the "masterpiece." See www.en.wikipedia.org/wiki/Anima_and_animus

214 In psychology, a *complex* refers to unconscious associations or strong unconscious impulses that underlie an individual's behavior. Complexes explain why some people get angry or sad about a situation while others don't, or why one person is emotionally attracted to or repulsed by a certain person's aura and behavior while others are not.

215 See Harville Hendrix *Getting The Love You Want* pages 35-36: "It was as if you had merged with the other person and became more whole" as well as pages 48-60.

216 See Harville Hendrix *Getting The Love You Want* pages 63-76.

217 See David Richo *How to be an Adult in Relationship* pages 156-158, Helen Fisher, *Why We Love* page 21-22, 97, 152, 173-175, 218, and Peter Rengel *Living Live in Love* page 46 about jealousy, which is a destructive and painful mix of anger, fear, and hurt.

218 See Patricia Love/Steven Stosny *How to Improve your Marriage Without Talking About It* about the male shame and female fear dynamic.

219 Almost all couples and many therapists/teachers confuse a negative emotional reaction to another person's reality with setting healthy boundaries. An emotional reaction such as anger or fear is **always** caused by our own pain. It is an attempt by our psyche to protect ourselves from re-experiencing the emotional hurt that was inflicted on us in our past, most likely during childhood. Instead of projecting the emotional reaction on the other person (usually through blame and "should"ing, and fight or flight reactions), we can learn to own our feelings and make "I" statements. **This does not mean** that we have to like or agree with the behavior of the other person at all, because that would make us into a doormat. It simply means that we separate the behavior of the other person from our emotional reaction to their reality. We can also learn to show empathy and/or compassion and take the others person's view. Then, without projecting, we may state our needs and desires and either accept, change or leave the situation.

220 Deepak Chopra's book *The Path of Love* beautifully covers the aspects of love, ego transcendence, spirit, and soul. A great article about intimacy and the ego can be found at www.livereal.com/relationship_arena/intimacy.htm

221 Scott Peck defined love in his book *The Road Less Traveled* as "The will to extend one's self for the purpose of nurturing one's own or another's spiritual growth." John Welwood in *Love and Awakening* pages 49-59 calls soul mates "worthy opponents." The book *Undefended Love* by Marlena Lyons and Jett Psaris (based on A.H. Almaas's (Hameed Ali) Diamond Heart Work) is an excellent tool for using relationship to awaken to your soul's essence.

222 The following article was authored by Scott Andrews, Founder of AspireNow, (AspireNow.com) and can be found at www.aspirenow.com/smooth_sailing_how_to_recognize_your_soul_mate.htm It aptly describes how to recognize a soul mate:

"You can almost always spot soul mates, because they make each other more powerful as a team than they were apart! This is the **first** way to spot your soul mate.

If you are in a relationship, and you're having to rationalize how much this other person helps you (or hinders you) then they are **not** your soul mate. Take the word soul, add the definition with the definition for mate, and you've got a strong definition of a soul mate: "the core spiritual nature, immortal, inseparable even from death, mated to be together."

Considering this definition, let us also consider the **second** way to spot your soul mate:

They are both aware of their spiritual nature. In most cases, these two will have their eyes first upon this higher calling or power (God/Spirit), second upon each other, third upon their purpose together. Their family, career, and other things will always follow in some priority after these three.

The **third** was to spot a soul mate is to recognize how the journeys of the two interrelate. All soul mates are on a spiritual life journey. These journeys, when the souls coincide for maximum impact, almost always run parallel or coincide in such a way that it creates a relationship that is more about the union, or the team, than the individual. They put the team/partnership journey above their individual journey and desires. The reason for this is that the individual's dream is complementary to the union in a soul mate relationship. At the same time, the relationship works in a way that each person's individual journey is fully supported. With soul mates, there is trust and respect. With trust and respect comes the ability to realize aspirations—both as a couple and as individuals.

The **fourth** way to spot your soul mate is to recognize how each partner brings real love into the other's life. If a person does not bring real love to you, but instead causes significant conflict, grief, angst, lack, and failure, then it is highly unlikely that this person is your soul mate. A soul mate helps to awaken your soul and makes it easier for you to learn the lessons you are meant to learn. A key difference is that the soul mate is not the lesson, they help you learn your lessons and support that growing process.

The **fifth** way to spot a soul mate is that they possess harmonious and complementary natures. Sometimes, when people are coming from ego, rather than spirit, the relationship becomes about what they have (possessions) rather than who they are (experiences). Soul-mates are about experiences far more than possessions, because they realize that they cannot take their possessions with them. Your soul does not own your possessions, but it owns your experiences." (Reprinted with permission from the author.)

223 See Erich Fromm *The Art of Loving* pages 88-89.

224 See Robert Bly *Iron John*, Sam Keen *Fire in the Belly*, and David Deida who writes in *The Way of the Superior Man* page 51: "A woman often seems to test her man's capacity to remain unperturbed in his truth and purpose. She tests him to feel his freedom and depth of love, to know that he is trustable. Her tests may come in the form of complaining, challenging him, changing her mind, doubting him, distracting him, or even undermining his purpose in a subtle or not so subtle way. A man should never think his woman's testing is going to end and his life will be easier. Rather, he should appreciate that she does these things to feel his strength, integrity, and openness. Her desire is for his deepest truth and love. As he grows, so will her testing."

225 See Mark Gerzon *Coming Into Our Own*, and the movie American Beauty.

226 Polyamory means to have more than one loving, intimate relationship at a time with the full knowledge and consent of everyone involved. Polyamorous people often have one primary partnership as an economic and family base and additional lovers. It is seen as an alternative to cheating and divorce if a person in a committed relationship falls in love with somebody else. Another motive is to keep a primary relationship fresh and alive by bringing the excitement of the new love into the existing relationship. "Poly" relationships can be very challenging, time-consuming, disruptive, and potentially damaging, and only very few couples have been successful and happy with such an arrangement over a longer period of time. Polyamorous relationships are often confused with open relationships, swinging, or simple cheating. The poly scene was created by well-meaning and mature green individuals and later infiltrated by red, which created many problems that persist to this day.

227 See David Deida's provocative book *The Way of the Superior Man* for insights into an authentic and sensitive masculine sexual essence that is attractive to many women.

228 Authority is defined as the power to validate or command one's own thought, opinion, or behavior as good and true.

229 See Robert Augustus Masters *Transformation through Intimacy—The Journey Towards Mature Monogamy*. In a mature monogamous relationship, opposite and equal partners are faithful to each other out of choice and not out of fear.

230 See David Richo *How to be an Adult in Relationship* pages 113 and 153-155.

231 Codependence develops when a person (the codependent) exhibits a controlling behavior towards an emotionally, physically, or economically depended person (the dependent), to perpetuate the dependent person's condition, because of their own desire to be needed and their fear of doing anything that would change the relationship.

232 See Polly Young Eisendrath and Florence Wiedemann *Female Authority* pages 69-74.

233 See Polly Young Eisendrath and Florence Wiedemann *Female Authority* pages 80-111.

234 See Polly Young Eisendrath and Florence Wiedemann *Female Authority* page 8: "The ability of a woman to validate her own convictions as of Truth, Beauty and Goodness (which Ken Wilber, in accordance with the perennial philosophies calls "The Big Three"—not to be confused with the three big reasons why partners get together and break up "Time, Money and Sex") in regard to her self-concept and self-interest is what we call 'female authority.'"

235 See Polly Young Eisendrath and Florence Wiedemann *Female Authority* pages 112-120.

236 See Elisabeth Kubler-Ross *On Death and Dying*, which outlines five states of grief, (denial, anger, bargaining, depression, and acceptance) that we may also experience after being left by a partner that we were in love with. Also see David Richo *How to be an Adult in Relationship* pages 199-213, Helen Fisher, *Why We Love* pages 153-180, Kathryn Alice *Love Will Find You* pages 69-100, or find more specific books on dealing with breakups with advice on how to deal with "lost love".

237 Vivid and popular examples of women in their animus stage four development are portrayed in Elizabeth Gilbert's best-selling book *Eat, Pray, Love,* and Cathi Hanauer's collection of stories about unhappy wives in *The Bitch in the House.*

238 See Polly Young Eisendrath and Florence Wiedemann *Female Authority* pages 139-143.

239 See Dale Koppel *The Intelligent Woman's Guide to Online Dating* which provides a vivid insight into the psyche of a woman in this stage and AARP *The Divorce Experience: A Study of Divorce At Midlife and Beyond* http://assets.aarp.org/rgcenter/general/divorce_1.pdf

240 See Polly Young Eisendrath and Florence Wiedemann *Female Authority* page 204.

241 See Polly Young Eisendrath and Florence Wiedemann *Female Authority* pages 222-223. Also Christian de Quincey *Radical Knowing* pages 176-180: "I as subject am never reflected in things (objects) only in other 'I's' such as you," and Gail Sheehy *Sex and the Seasoned Woman* page 159: "Dr. Judith Wallerstein scoffed at the comment from unmarried women that "they don't need a man to define them" and argues that sexual attractiveness is central to a woman's self-image, and no one develops a self-image alone."

242 Interdependence creates synergy in which the whole is greater than the sum of its parts. In other words, women and men in this stage are usually both financially and emotionally secure and independent. They can then co-create a wider economic base by living together, sharing resources, supporting each other in their growth and having lots of fun while doing it.

243 See Polly Young Eisendrath and Florence Wiedemann *Female Authority* page 225.

244 See Ayala Malach Pines *Falling in Love* pages 116-121. The five stages of anima/animus development that are described in this manual resemble Otto Kernberg's five-point scale of people's ability to love, even though he does not differentiate between males and females and focuses on the relationship with mother only (a major criticism) with the consequence that his scale seems to reflect more of a male development:
  1. Total inability to love.
  2. Sexual promiscuity.
  3. Primitive idealization of the beloved and childish dependence.
  4. Ability to create stable relationships, without the ability to enjoy full sexual satisfaction.
  5. Deep intimate relations with a healthy combination of sexuality and sensitivity to the other.

245 See Ayala Malach Pines *Falling in Love* pages 137-159 for three different theories about this attraction, (1) objects relation theory, (2) Anima/Animus and (3) evolutionary theory. The major difference to our Integral Relationship Model is that she seems to miss stage four of animus development in females.

246 See Eckhart Tolle *The Power Of Now* page 127 (page 153 in the paperback edition): "Avoidance of relationships in an attempt to avoid pain is not the answer either. The pain is there anyway. Three failed relationships in as many years are more likely to force you into awakening then three years on a desert island shut away in your room."

247 www.eve3.wordpress.com/2007/11/01/the-anima/

Chapter 5: States of Falling in Love

248 See Allan Combs *Consciousness Explained Better* page 49-61 for a more comprehensive exploration of states of consciousness and how they are different from structure stages.

249 For a comprehensive explanation of how hormones influence our romantic experiences see Helen Fisher, *Why We Love*, Theresa L. Crenshaw *The Alchemy of Love and Lust*, and John Gray *Why Mars And Venus Collide* pages 53-75. In the movie *What the bleep do we know* during the wedding scene you can see an entertaining animated segment that illustrates the function of hormones in our addiction to love.

250 From an evolutionary perspective it did not make sense for couples to stay together if pregnancy was not the result of their efforts after 6 to 24 months.

251 See Helen Fisher *Why We Love*, pages 170-173, where she suggests that depression emerged millions of years ago to protect abandoned infants and to cause compassionate reactions from others when adults were suffering from loss or abandonment.

252 See www.genepartner.com/index.php/science "With genetically highly compatible people we feel that rare sensation of perfect chemistry. This is the body's receptive and welcoming response when immune systems harmonize and fit together. Genetic compatibility results in an increased likelihood of forming an enduring and successful relationship. Research has also shown that the sex lives of genetically compatible partners are more satisfying than average. Additionally, fertility rates are higher in genetically compatible couples and they have healthier children."

253 See Erich Fromm *The Art of Loving* page 4: "[These lovers] take the intensity of the infatuation, this being crazy about each other, for proof of the intensity of their love, while it may only prove the degree of their preceding loneliness."

254 See Ayala Malach Pines *Falling in Love* page 215, as well as the account of Ken Wilber and Terry (Treya) Killam when they first met—told in Wilber's book *Grace and Grit* pages 8-12.

255 People are far more susceptible to falling in love when they go through major transitions in their lives that make them feel unsettled and unbalanced, such as losing a job or a loved one, moving to a new place, a major illness, or traveling. Even getting aroused by watching a suspenseful or emotionally moving movie, rides at an amusement park, or other adventures can do the trick. Seduction artists know this and arrange exciting activities with their dates.

256 See Helen Fisher, *Why We Love* pages 99-125, and *Why Him Why Her?* pages 144-145 about proximity; Geoffrey Miller *The Mating Mind* page 206: "If a woman is interested in assessing a man's personality, intelligence, and experiences, it may take weeks of conversation before she has (unconsciously) gathered all the information she needs to fall in love," and Ayala Malach *Pines Falling in Love* pages 3-71. Her research suggests that individuals who live in close proximity are more likely to mate. Frequent short contacts (at the mailbox, at a coffee shop, at work, a weekly class, a workshop or group, meeting with friends etc.) or being together over longer periods of time (on a cruise, a weeklong seminar, working together on a project etc.) and the state of arousal such as a dramatic shift in one's life circumstances, a roller coaster ride, or watching a thrilling movie, increases the chances of the release of the love hormones if the first impression was neutral or positive. However, if the first impression was negative, then ongoing contact usually deepens the negative reaction, so it is better to let go and move on.

257 Deepak Chopra lists four states in his book *A Path To Love* pages 62-131: Attraction, infatuation, courtship, and intimacy.
John Gray lists five states in his book *Mars and Venus* on a Date pages 34-109: Attraction, uncertainty, exclusivity, intimacy, and engagement.

Geoffrey Miller lists several states in *The Mating Mind* page 179: Infatuation, falling in love, ecstasy, jealousy or heartbrokenness, boredom, and forming attachment.

David Richo lists three phases in his book *How to be an Adult in Relationship*: Romance pages 106-118, conflict pages 126-141, and commitment pages 217-231.

An unknown source listed six states: (1) two separate selves, (2) symbiosis—exclusive bonding (romantic state), (3) differentiation—disillusionment, regret, doubt, fear, (4) moving from "we" back to "I," (5) rapprochement: Back and forth to Intimacy, and (6) independence and interdependence in the context of a larger "we."

258 See Louann Brizendine, *The Female Brain* page 91.

259 See Theresa L. Crenshaw *The Alchemy of Love and Lust* pages 164-174 and 190.

260 See Theresa L. Crenshaw The Alchemy of Love and Lust pages 213-217: "If you are with a woman in or past menopause, it is important to be sensitive to her changed emotional and physical needs, and to apply skill, care, and (if necessary) plenty of good lubricant to make sex pleasurable, safe, and rewarding for both of you."

261 See Nancy W. Collins and Mason Grigsby *Love At Second Sight* pages 208-209. Their research showed that in first-time marriages, men were looking for sexual attractiveness (40%) while women focused on good providers (30%). Single men over 50 look for common interests (34%) in a mate and only 13% look for sex, while sex tops the list of female requirements at 36%. The recent "cougar" movement is another indicator for this role reversal in which older women seek younger men for sex.

Testosterone patches and vaginal estrogen creams may help to restore the sex drive in males and receptivity and vaginal health in women.

262 See Helen Fisher, *Why We Love*, pages 80-83.

263 See Helen Fisher, *Why We Love*, pages 52-53. Also, researchers at Florida State University examined the nature of love by studying the brains and behavior of male prairie voles, picked for their habit of lifelong monogamy and aggression towards other females once they have found a mate. The scientists found that males became devoted to females only after they had mated. The bond coincided with a huge release of the feel-good chemical dopamine inside their brains. Brandon Aragona, who led the study, demonstrated that dopamine was the voles' love drug by injecting the chemical into the brains of males who had not yet had sex with female companions. Immediately, they lost interest in other females and spent all of their time with their chosen one. Further experiments showed that dopamine restructured a part of the vole's brain called the nucleus accumbens, a region that many animals have, including humans. The change was so drastic that when paired-up males were introduced to new females, although their brains still produced dopamine on sight, the chemical was channeled into a different neural circuit that made them go cold towards the new female.

264 See Helen Fisher, *Why We Love*, pages 53-54.

265 See Theresa L. Crenshaw *The Alchemy of Love and Lust* pages 131-132, and Helen Fisher, *Why We Love* pages 54-55.

266 See Helen Fisher, *Why We Love*, pages 188-190.

267 See David Richo *How to be in Adult in Relationship* pages 126-152 and the many other relationship books (see Appendix I) that deal with conflict resolution.

268 See John Gray, *Why Mars And Venus Collide* page 221. "Women today long for romance, because romance is the most powerful oxytocin producer. It is a powerful antidote to the stress of working in a testosterone-oriented work world." Also see www.womentowomen.com/sexualityandfertility/healthbenefitsofsex.aspx

269 See Theresa L. Crenshaw *The Alchemy of Love and Lust* pages 102-105 and Helen Fisher *Why We Love* pages 89-91.

Males rely on a second bonding hormone in addition to oxytocin, a chemical called vasopressin. It has been demonstrated that dopamine, oxytocin, and vasopressin play an important role in human society, for instance, in love, social attachment, and reward. There are great similarities between voles and humans. Vasopressin is associated with male voles' territoriality and aggression towards others after they bonded and had sex with a female. See www.nationalzoo.si.edu/Publications/ZooGoer/2004/3/monogamy.cfm

270 See John Gray, *Why Mars And Venus Collide* with many tips on how to reduce stress that kills romance, Helen Fisher *Why We Love* pages 181-208 with tips how to make romance last, *Passionate Marriage* by David Schnarch how to remove emotional blocks that prevent a satisfying sex life, and *The Exceptional 7 Percent* by Gregory K. Popcak about the nine secrets of the worlds happiest couples.

271 See Helen Fisher, *Why We Love*, page 195-196: "No wonder women are less depressed when they make love and receive this fluid [ejaculate]; perhaps they may even become more receptive to romance."

272 See Helen Fisher, *Why We Love*, pages 86-93, and Theresa L. Crenshaw *The Alchemy of Love and Lust* pages 90-97 about bonding after sex.

273 From www.slaafws.org/ "We in S.L.A.A. believe that sex and love addiction is a progressive illness which cannot be cured but which, like many illnesses, can be arrested. It may take several forms—including, but not limited to a compulsive need for sex, extreme dependency on one or many people, or a chronic preoccupation with romance, intrigue, or fantasy. An obsessive compulsive pattern, either sexual or emotional, or both, exists in which relationships or sexual activities have become increasingly destructive to career, family and sense of self-respect. Sex addiction and love addiction, if left unchecked, always gets worse. However, if we follow a simple program which has proven successful for scores of other men and women with the same illness, we can recover."

274 Open relationships give each partner the freedom to be sexual with others, usually as long as there is no love or emotional intimacy involved that could threaten the primary relationship. Sometimes there is an agreement of "don't ask don't tell".

275 See Dr. Judith Orloff *Emotional Freedom: Liberate Yourself from Negative Emotions and Transform Your Life*. Her approach to transforming fear has two stages. First, take stock of what makes you afraid and distinguish irrational fears from legitimate intuitions. Second, take appropriate steps to heed protective fears and transform the others with courage. At times you may foresee real danger, but more frequently unproductive fears clobber you. Therefore as a general rule, train yourself to question fears tied to low self-esteem; we're all worthy of what's extraordinary. For example, it is right to question the fear that you're too emotionally damaged to love; even the severely wounded can have their hearts opened again. True intuitions will never put you down or support destructive attitudes or behavior. Her guidelines to distinguishing legitimate fears from irrational ones are:
Signs of a Reliable Intuition
- Conveys information neutrally, unemotionally
- Feels right in your gut
- Has a compassionate, affirming tone
- Gives crisp, clear impressions that are "seen" first, then felt
- Conveys a detached sensation, like you're in a theater watching a movie

Signs of an Irrational Fear
- Is highly emotionally charged
- Has cruel, demeaning, or delusional content
- Conveys no gut-centered confirmation or on-target feeling
- Reflects past psychological wounds
- Diminishes centeredness and perspective

See www.drjudithorloff.com/Free-Articles/Fear-Intuition.htm

Chapter 6: Evaluating Personality Types

276 See NLP books such as Sue Knight *NLP at Work* and Andreas and Steve Connirae *Heart of the Mind*.

277 Books by Pickup Artists such as Neil Strauss's *The Game* and Mystery's *The Pickup Artist* apply NLP techniques to pick up and seduce women.

278 See the eye pattern chart below. Looking at the other person you can follow their eye movement and get clues to if they feel or think, and if they are living in the past or future.

You can test if a person displays these movements (they need to be right handed, otherwise reverse the left and right) by asking questions that indicate:

Visual Remembered (VR)
What is the color of the shirt you wore yesterday?
Which of your friends has the shortest hair?

Visual Constructed (VC)
What would your room look like if it were painted yellow with big purple circles?
Can you imagine the top half of a tiger on the bottom half of an elephant?

Auditory Remembered (AR)
What does your best friend's voice sound like?
Which is louder, your door bell or your telephone?

Auditory Constructed (AC)
What will your voice sound like in 10 years?
What would it sound like if you played your two favourite pieces of music at the same time?

Auditory Digital (AD)
What is something you continually tell yourself?
What are your thoughts about this article?

Kinesthetic (K)
What does it feel like to walk barefoot on a cool sandy beach?
What does it feel like when you rub your fingers on sandpaper?

For more see Sue Knight *NLP at Work* pages 61-90.

279 See Bradley Fenton "Stumbling Naked in the Dark" pages 52-60, and Sue Knight *NLP at Work* pages 288-307.

280 See *The Five Love Languages* by Gary Chapman. Chapman illustrates each love language with real-life examples from his counseling practice and the book has a self-test in the back.

281 www.greaterquest.com/LoveLanguages.asp

282 See A.H. Almaas *Facets of Unity: The Enneagram of Holy Ideas*.

283 Under stress and disintegration, a type 1 acts like an unhealthy 4, a 4 like a 2, a 2 like an 8, an 8 like a 5, a 5 like a 7, and a 7 like a 1. Likewise, the sequence 9->6->3->9 applies. For integration and growth, the direction is opposite, from 1->7->5->8->2->4->1 and 9->3->6->9. So for example a 7 (Enthusiast) tends towards unhealthy type 1 (Reformer) attitudes under stress, and towards 5 (Investigator) for healthy integration and growth. For more information see www.enneagraminstitute.com/intro.asp

284 Don Richard Riso and Russ Hudson integrate the horizontal types (e.g., Enneagram), vertical growth (levels/stages) and "states" in their book *The Wisdom of the Enneagram* (see pages 75-87). This book also has a simple test in the front that you can take with your partner. A simple, playful and fun book for couples and the whole family is *The Enneagram Made Easy* by Renee Baron and Elizabeth Wagele.

285 Two tests that seem to be especially useful are at www.enneagraminstitute.com/ and www.9types.com/

At www.enneagraminstitute.com/matrix.asp you can enter your and your partners Enneagram type and get an overview of the "assets and liabilities" that your pairing holds.

286 In psychology, the term "extravert" is preferred over the more commonly used term "extrovert."

287 The terminology may be misleading for some—the term "judging" does not imply "judgmental," and "perceiving" does not imply "perceptive."

288 To take a test, go to www.humanmetrics.com/cgi-win/JTypes1.htm or www.typelogic.com or google any other of the many online tests that are available.
At www.typelogic.com/products.html you can download software to compare the 256 possible combinations. It may help you to identify your general life style and your style in certain fields of activity.

289 See www.harrisinteractive.com/harris_poll/index.asp?PID=359

ELEVEN BELIEFS—BY SEX AND AGE

	All Adults	Sex		Age					
		Male	Female	18 – 24	25 – 29	30 – 29	40 – 49	50 – 64	65+
	%	%	%	%	%	%	%	%	%
God	90	86	93	84	82	91	90	91	95
Survival of the soul after death	84	78	89	85	88	81	86	82	84
Miracles	84	77	90	86	85	82	85	83	82
Heaven	82	75	89	83	71	83	84	80	85
The resurrection of Christ	80	73	86	76	68	81	82	81	84
The Virgin birth (Jesus born of Mary)	77	70	83	76	60	79	80	78	80
Hell	69	65	73	74	63	69	72	66	68
The devil	68	64	73	68	62	72	72	68	62
Ghosts	51	45	58	58	65	55	57	48	27
Astrology	31	25	36	37	43	37	23	32	17
Reincarnation	27	23	30	30	40	30	25	26	14

290 Ken Wilber finds astrology only remotely viable as a typology and certainly not as a predictor for future outcomes or specific qualities and behavior patterns in individuals. The experience of many women is different, so we need to honor that. A pro and con dialogue about astrology between Roger Walsh and Will Keepin can be found at www.noetic.org/publications/review/issue43/r43_Walsh.html

291 See www.humandesignhawaii.com/humandesignbasics/fourauratypes.html and www.humandesign4life.com/

292 See Bert Hellinger *Love's Hidden Symmetry*.

293 See Helen Fisher (now a director for chemistry.com) in her book *Why Him, Why Her?* where she outlines four personality types—the Explorer, Builder, Director and Negotiator, and how they are compatible with each other.

CHAPTER 7: PRIMARY FANTASY AND PERSONALITY

294 The value of cosmetic procedures for men and women in 2008 was $11.8 billion, according to a member survey released 3/17/09 by the American Society of Aesthetic Plastic Surgery. The number of breast augmentation procedures for women were about 356,000, fat removal was 341,000. See www.business.smh.com.au/business/world-business/cosmetic-surgery-sags-20090317-9084.html

295 There have been slight variations throughout the ages and between cultures of what is considered to be healthy/sexy; for example today we consider a tanned body to be sexy as it indicates that the woman has exercised in the sun and fresh air, while a few hundred years ago, this indicated that the woman was of a lower class who had to work outside. The same goes for weight/height proportions. During a time of scarce food resources, a well nourished heavier woman is considered to be healthy and sexy, while a skinny woman may have been considered to be starved or malnourished.

296 From the www.en.wikipedia.org/wiki/US_income statistic below you can see that only 7% of all individuals (so less than 3.5% of single males, as single childless women usually have higher incomes than men) make more than $100,000 per year, while most attractive single women (50+% of adult single female population) seek men who make significantly more than $100K a year and are willing to spend it on their partner . You can also see that the income of couples is higher above the $50K level than that of individuals, which indicates that low income males can't find partners and that it is hard for women to find single males with desirable incomes.

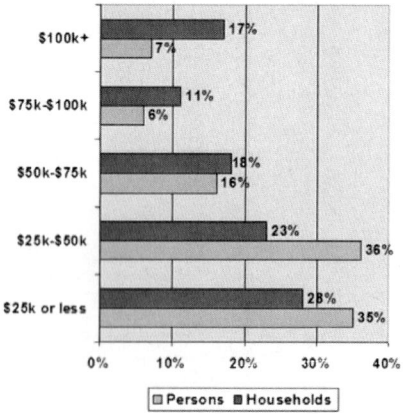

297 In this stage, women are often willing to financially support a male if it feels like a sound investment in their future, e.g., if he studies for a higher degree or starts a promising business or career. When confronted with the Primary Fantasy, they often argue that they financially supported their current partner or men in previous relationships, confusing "support" with "investment." Modern divorce laws protect the financial and time investments of wives into their husbands—often with a very good return on investment—while, of course, there isn't (and can't be) any protection for a men's investment into a woman (that she will take care of herself physically, will be sexually available, support him in his mission, and stay with him if he makes too much or too little money.)

298 True altruism is defined as giving to people that we don't know, the receivers not knowing who they received from, and supporting the receiver in their independence instead of making them more dependent.

299 See Nancy Etcoff *"Survival of the Prettiest"* pages 65-67 and 79 -80: "Men are evaluated by their income and professional statuses as harshly as woman are evaluated by their looks."

300 Millionaire matchmaker Patti Stanger in her book *Become Your Own Matchmaker* on page 50 doesn't pull any punches when she advises women to: "Take a good long look into the mirror" to evaluate their "fuckability factor" and to "get into their ideal dating condition" to catch a millionaire. In the following pages, she advises her readers about the effects that a sexy body (shiny hair, white teeth, makeup, skin care ... the works) has on men.
Alison Armstrong in her little book *Making Sense of Men: A Woman's Guide to a Lifetime of Love, Care and Attention from All Men* could not agree more when she explains what causes sexual attraction in men: "Shiny hair, shapely body, sensuality, and sexual energy."

301 See Valerie Gibson a Toronto journalist and author of *Cougar: A Guide for Older Women Dating Younger Men*. Note that this book is not about creating healthy long-term relationships, but focuses on dating and sex while *Older Women, Younger Men: New Options for Love and Romance* by Felicia Brings and Susan Winter focuses on committed monogamous partnerships between men with women ten years or more their senior. Also see www.richgosse.blogspot.com/2009/08/cougar-conventionother-singles-parties.html

> Aug 27-29, 2009: Incredible turnout for our National Single Cougars Convention, at Dinah's Garden Hotel in Palo Alto! Unfortunately we had to turn away hundreds of disappointed cougars and cubs, who were eager to attend the hottest ticket in town.

302 See Ayala Malach Pines Falling in Love page 87: "Women prefer not only to look up to their husbands, but also tend to marry up; men tend to marry down. This leaves many unmarried women at the top of the world of politics, science, and business, and many unmarried men in prison, at the bottom of the social ladder."

303 This mockup personal ad illustrates the point:

> Okay, I'm tired of beating around the bush. I'm a beautiful (spectacularly beautiful) 25 year old girl. I'm articulate and classy. I'm not from New York. I'm looking to get married to a guy who makes at least half a million a year. I know how that sounds, but keep in mind that a million a year is middle class in New York City, so I don't think I'm overreaching at all.
>
> Are there any guys who make 500K or more on this board? Any wives? Could you send me some tips? I dated a business man who makes average around 200-250. But that's where I seem to hit a roadblock. 250,000 won't get me to central park west. I know a woman in my yoga class who was married to an investment banker and lives in Tribeca, and she's not as pretty as I am, nor is she a great genius. So what is she doing right? How do I get to her level?
>
> Here are my questions specifically:
> - Where do you single rich men hang out? Give me specifics—bars, restaurants, gyms.
> - What are you looking for in a mate? Be honest guys, you won't hurt my feelings.
> - Is there an age range I should be targeting (I'm 25)?
> - Why are some of the women living lavish lifestyles on the upper east side so plain? I've seen really 'plain Jane' boring types who have nothing to offer, married to incredibly wealthy guys. I've seen drop dead gorgeous girls in singles bars in the east village. What's the story there?
> - Jobs I should look out for? Everyone knows—lawyer, investment banker, doctor. How much do those guys really make? And where do they hang out? Where do the hedge fund guys hang out?
> - How you decide marriage vs. just a girlfriend? I am looking for MARRIAGE ONLY.
>
> Please hold your insults—I'm putting myself out there in an honest way. Most beautiful women are superficial; at least I'm being up front about it. I wouldn't be searching for these kind of guys if I wasn't able to match them—in looks, culture, sophistication, and keeping a nice home and hearth.
>
> **The reply from a suitor:**
>
> Dear Pers-431649184:
>
> I read your posting with great interest and have thought meaningfully about your dilemma. I offer the following analysis of your predicament. Firstly, I'm not wasting your time, I qualify as a guy who fits your bill; that is, I make more than $500K per year. That said here's how I see it.
>
> Your offer, from the prospective of a guy like me, is plain and simple a crappy business deal. Here's why. Cutting through all the B.S., what you suggest is a simple trade: you bring your looks to the party and I bring my money. Fine, simple. But here's the rub, your looks will fade and my money will likely continue into perpetuity…in fact, it is very likely that my income increases but it is an absolute certainty that you won't be getting any more beautiful!
>
> So, in economic terms you are a depreciating asset and I am an earning asset. Not only are you a depreciating asset, your depreciation accelerates! Let me explain, you're 25 now and will likely stay pretty hot for the next 5 years, but less so each year. Then the fade begins in earnest. By 35 stick a fork in you!
>
> So in Wall Street terms, we would call you a trading position, not a buy and hold…hence the rub… marriage. It doesn't make good business sense to "buy you" (which is what you're asking) so I'd rather lease. In case you think I'm being cruel, I would say the following. If my money were to go away, so would you, so when your beauty fades I need an out. It's as simple as that. So a deal that makes sense is dating, not marriage.

Separately, I was taught early in my career about efficient markets. So, I wonder why a girl as "articulate, classy and spectacularly beautiful" as you has been unable to find your sugar daddy. I find it hard to believe that if you are as gorgeous as you say you are, that the $500K hasn't found you, if not only for a tryout.

By the way, you could always find a way to make your own money and then we wouldn't need to have this difficult conversation.

With all that said, I must say you're going about it the right way. Classic "pump and dump."

I hope this is helpful, and if you want to enter into some sort of lease, let me know.

304 Viewed by many as a gold-digger, Paul McCartney's ex-wife and former model Heather Mills has been embroiled in a lengthy battle with the ex-Beatle over his vast fortune. In March 2008 a judge ruled that she is entitled to $48.6 million (she had sued for $251 million). Considering they were only married for about four years (they wed in 2002 and McCartney filed for divorce in 2006), that comes out to just over $12 million per year, or a little over one million dollars a month see www.cnn.com/2008/SHOWBIZ/03/17/mccartney.mills/index.html Also see Barbara Kennedy *Baby Boomer Men*, a book that encourages successful middle aged men to "do their last dance," Elisabeth Gilbert's bestseller *Committed* for a successful females view on the perils of marriage, and George Weinberg, *Why Men Won't Commit: Getting What You Both Want Without Playing Games*.

305 Flatland is a term that Wilber uses to describe a view of reality (or relationship) that ignores the left-hand interior quadrants with its developmental stages of consciousness and only takes a right-hand materialistic/scientific perspective. Wilber adopted the term from the book *Flatland: A Romance of Many Dimensions* written in 1884 by Edwin Abbott. Also see the movie *Down the Rabbit Hole* DVD#1 Track 31 for a nice animation that illustrates "flatland".

306 See www.en.wikipedia.org/wiki/Personal_income_in_the_United_States

307 See www.cdc.gov/healthyweight/index.html for healthy Body Mass Index (BMI).

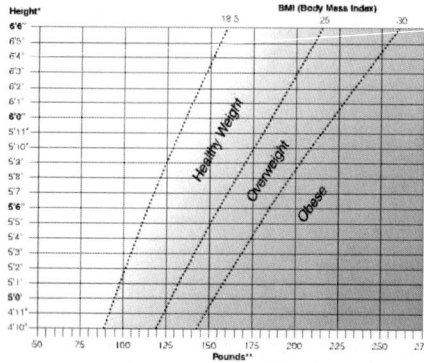

These guidelines are not generated by sexist men who want women to be "thin" and objectify them as sex objects, but because it is known to be healthier not to be overweight or obese (and of course not to be underweight and bulimic). Also see Nancy Etcoff "Survival of the Prettiest" pages 195-204 and the new initiative of First Lady Michelle Obama against child obesity www.letsmove.gov/

308 See www.msnbc.msn.com/id/3076615/

309 See Rabbi Michal Lerner's related blog at www.tikkun.org/index.php

310 For example, the 2005 per capita greenhouse gas (CO_2) emissions were 23.5 tons in the US, 11.9 tons in Germany, and 1.9 tons in India. www.en.wikipedia. org/wiki/List_of_countries_by_greenhouse_gas_emissions_per_capita [American] women reward men who drive big cars, buy big homes, allow them to spend big bucks for consumer goods, and travel frequently with them, and are therefore at least equally if not more responsible for the exploitations of the poor and global warming with its negative effects for all humanity, our ecosystem and future of our children.

Endnotes | 245

311 Inspired by the "Wilber-Combs Grid/Matrix/Lattice" as seen in Ken Wilber's *Integral Spirituality* page 88-93, *The Integral Vision* page 143, and Allan Combs's Consciousness Explained Better pages 90-102.

312 See John Gottman and Nan Silver *The Seven Principals That Make Marriage Work* page 8.

313 Similar to the Enneagram or Myers-Briggs types, Ken Wilber sees the feminine and masculine as fixed personality types (listen to disc 5 of 10 of the Kosmic Consciousness series, and *Integral Spirituality* pages 11-15) that are consistent throughout a person's life, while we see them as a fluid polarity that have the potential to shift as males and females grow in consciousness, and that can be fully embodied by both sexes in higher stages of development. This does not mean that individuals may not have a sexual essence that they feel most comfortable in or at home with at each stage of development.

314 Androgyny is a term derived from the Greek words anér, meaning man and gyné, meaning woman. It either refers to the mixing of masculine and feminine characteristics or the balancing of "anima and animus." It does not mean a healthy integration of the two, but more of a neutralizing.

315 See David Deida *Intimate Communion* pages 47-55 and *The Way of the Superior Man*, pages 86-91 and 117.

316 See Gail Sheehy *Sex and the Seasoned Woman* page 230 where she shows this very dynamic in a "sexual diamond" that is derived from her insight that "around the mid-fifties, females and males become more like each other, with a tendency for males to take on female [feminine] attributes ..... and females to take on male [masculine] attributes."

317 In the movie *The Shift* Wayne Dyer mentions a study that indicates the shift of priorities when men and women move from a modern to a post-modern worldview:

	Priorities for Women		Priorities for Men	
	Modern	Postmodern	Modern	Postmodern
1	Family	Own Personal Strength	Money	Spirituality
2	Independence	Self-Esteem	Adventure	Peace
3	Career	Spirituality	Achievement	Family
4	Fitting in	Happiness	Pleasure	God's Will/Purpose
5	Attractiveness	Forgiveness	Respect	Honesty/Integrity

Note how women shift from communion towards agency, and males from agency towards communion.

318 The vast majority of spiritual traditions and altruistic organizations such as Greenpeace, Doctors Without Borders, Amnesty International, WWF, and the Sierra Club, to mention a few, have been founded by men.

319 This dynamic is nicely portrayed in the movie *American Beauty*, where the orange wife feels forced to succeed in her career and falls in love with another orange man, while her husband enters green and falls in love with the red girlfriend of his daughter while clashing with his amber neighbor whose teal son tries to get along with everybody, and the movie *Same Time Next Year*, where she becomes a feminist and then a successful business woman, while he loses his drive to succeed, gets in touch with his feelings and becomes a bar pianist.

320 See endnote #49 in Chapter 1 about different forms of feminism. Feminism fought for—and achieved—equal rights and opportunities for modern and postmodern women in comparison with men, but did not advocate for the same rights of men compared with women. It also did not demand the same responsibilities for women. On a personal level, most feminists continue to be attracted to men who are success-oriented providers, risk their lives in the workplace and in fights/wars as protectors, take the risk of rejection, court women, open doors, and buy the diamond ring, while they retain their rights to be fulfillment oriented, and to use their interior emotional strength (covered by a façade of weakness or victimhood) and exterior sexual power to be celebrated and taken care of by men.

321 See for example www.newfemininepower.org and Glynda-Lee Hoffmann *The Secret Dowry of Eve*.

322 The Wilber-Combs Lattice outlines that all spiritual state-stages are interpreted from the individual's level of consciousness. A superstitious person may attribute it to a spirit or ghost that connected with him or her; an egocentric person may claim to be chosen to transmit some magical powers; a conformist religious person may claim a special encounter with their savior or God; a rational person may interpret it as a unique brain state (see *Zen And The Brain*); a pluralistic person may recognize it as the unity with all creation; and a person in 2nd tier as an energetic illumination (Kundalini experience) of all the seven chakras. See Ken Wilber, *Integral Spirituality* pages 88-93, *The Integral Vision* page 143, and Allan Combs *Consciousness Explained Better* pages 90-102.

323 The inspiration for arranging the state-stages of spiritual, sexual, and anima/animus complex development in the form of a lattice is derived from the Wilber-Combs Lattice.

324 See Jenny Wade *Transcendent Sex* in which she describes how "ordinary people with no special training can find themselves in different spiritual realms when making love—an experience so profound that nothing will ever be the same. Atheists have become believers; long standing psychological wounds have been healed; and the sexually abused have become whole" (from the back cover of the book).

Chapter 8: Our Drive to Connect

325 Wilber identified these four dimensions during a three year retreat from 1991-1994, when he realized that all developmental hierarchies fall into four broad categories. As he writes in *Theory of Everything* page 38, "At one point I had over two hundred hierarchies written out on legal pads lying all over the floor, trying to figure out how to fit them together." Also see *One Taste* June 12th entry. The resulting four quadrants were first outlined in his 800 page book *Sex, Ecology, Spirituality* (SES), published in 1995 and in all subsequent books.

326 The term holon was coined by Arthur Koestler in his book *The Ghost in the Machine* p. 48. Also see Ken Wilber *Sex, Ecology, Spirituality* page 48-54 and *A Brief History of Everything* page 19 -24 for a more complete exploration of holons.

327 See endnote #156 about natural growth versus dominator hierarchies in Chapter 4.

328 As Aristotle noted in his writings (later termed *Metaphysics*): "The whole is more than the sum of its parts."

329 The four types of holons are: (1) individual holons, (2) social holons, (3) artifacts and (4) heaps.
  1. Individual holons have constituent parts that they are composed of, and a single dominant subjective interior that allows some level of conscious choice. Humans fall into this category;
  2. Social holons are formed when individual holons group together. These holons also have a defining pattern, but there isn't a single subjective consciousness that makes choices; instead, social holons have certain characteristics that they have distributed or intersubjective consciousness.
  3. Artifacts are holons that are produced by individual or social holons, such as a bird's nest or a car. Artifacts have no interior or conscious choice of their own but represent the level of consciousness of their creator(s). If artifacts are removed from their environment, their creators can still find ways to survive.
  4. A heap is a random pile of holons that was not created by an individual or social holon. A heap has no defining pattern or interior consciousness, like a pile of dead leaves, a water puddle or a sand dune.

330 Only individual holons possess four quadrants. All other holons (social, artifacts, and heaps) can be looked at from the perspective of each quadrant. See Ken Wilber *Integral Spirituality* footnote page 146 and Appendix II pages 255-266 for an in-depth exploration.

331 The philosophical reasoning behind the four quadrants states that every occasion has an inside and outside, and every singular needs a plural for its existence. This idea goes all the way down to the smallest events in the universe such as quantum events and strings, and up to the whole universe. It is related to the panpsychist ideas of Alfred North Whitehead and more recently Christian de Quincey and others.

332 In humans, three of these four dimensions are so essential that they are expressed in the pronouns of every major language—the subjective 1st person "I" (the person that is speaking), the intersubjective 2nd person "you/we" (the person that is spoken to), and the objective 3rd person "he/she/them/it" (the person or thing that is spoken off). Ancient philosophers also spotted these three fundamental dimensions of human existence and called them "the Good (LL), the True (UR), and the Beautiful (UL)"; represented through (1) morals (how to act in a "good way"), (2) science (how to know what is objectively true), and (3) art (how to create and perceive beauty.) Buddhists identified these three dimensions as well and called them the Buddha (UL–being), Dharma (UR–truth), and Sangha (LL–community). The fourth dimension was added to cover the more recent discovery that reality is linked in complex systems (covered by systems theory, web of life, deep ecology, sociology, quantum physics, etc.), and is called the inter-objective "its" dimension.

333 The common interpretation "into-me-you-see" for intimacy can be misleading as it does not really require a partner to validate or "see" us in order for us to be intimate. See David Schnarch *Passionate Marriage* page 112 "Intimacy is like an orgasm during intercourse—it takes two people to create it, but only one may have it."

334 To differentiate your individual **UL** from the collective **LL** interior, imagine for a moment that you would have been locked away in a cell after your birth and never seen a human soul, as it apparently happened to Kaspar Hauser in the early 19th century Germany (now disputed but still an interesting story.) You would have neither learned a language nor have become culturally conditioned in any way (religion, acceptable behavior, gender identity, beliefs etc.) Without this cultural dimension, you would still experience your interior but have no conditioned self awareness, language, thoughts, values or beliefs etc. which are all formed through shared experiences with others (culture). This cultural conditioning (LL) would, among many other things, determine how you approach a woman. The movie *The Enigma of Kaspar Hauser* by Werner Herzog illustrates this vividly. The movie is based on a real-life event that was well documented at the time. It depicts the (questionable) story of a boy who grew up in a 3' x 6' cell without any human contact until age 16 and who was then set free and later learned to speak to tell his story.

335 See Ken Wilber *A Brief History of Everything* pages 63-122 for a more complete exploration of various developmental lines in the four quadrants, and *Sex, Ecology, Spirituality* in its entirety. For individual holons in general, Wilber uses the outline for the co-arising of developmental lines below:

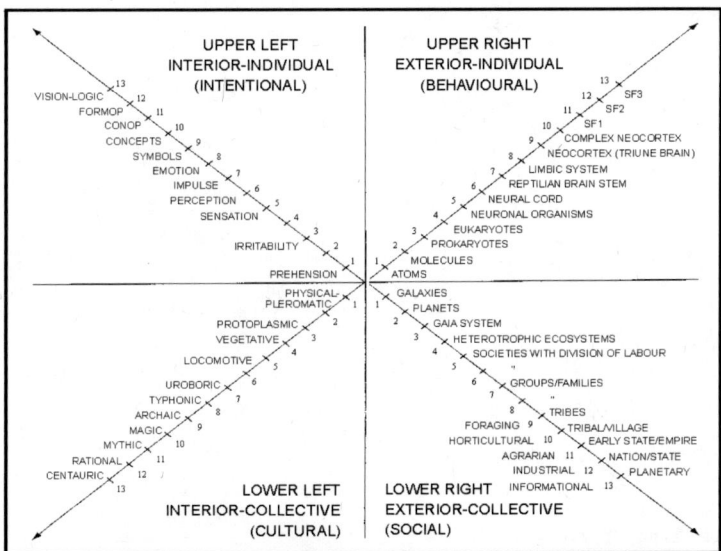

336 For more characteristics of holons according to Wilber, see his twenty tenets in *Sex, Ecology, Spirituality* pages 40-85, and a critique of the tenets at www.integralworld.net/meyerhoff-ba-toc.html

337 See Ken Wilber *Integral Spirituality* Chapter 7 "A Miracle Called We," pages 142-162.

338 Hitler's Nazi Germany or "Thousand Year Reich" lasted twelve years. For a vivid example of the madness that the imbalance created (and how males and females reacted to it) see the movie "Downfall—Hitler and the End of the Third Reich," and for an example of (mostly) successful healthy integration of the four drives the movie "Gandhi" and related literature.

339 You may take this idea even further by integrating the four polarities (a = agency, c = communion, t = self transcendence, i = self immanence) into **ALL** four quadrants, which gives you 16 possibilities:

Upper Left:
ULA = independence, introverted, introspection, keeps thoughts and feelings hidden from others, uncompromising.
ULC = emotional closeness, share ideas, open communication, teamwork, compromising, care, and responsibility.
ULT = striving for wisdom, presence, and emptiness.
ULI = striving for compassion, fullness, and surrender.
An easy way to relate to the four polarities in the UL is to think about communication. ULA you don't want to talk, ULC you want to talk, ULT you want to be heard and understood, ULI you want to hear and understand.

Lower Left:
LLA = individualism, survival of the fittest, there is only one right way to see the world.
LLC = cultural diversity, all living things have a right to be, there are many ways to see the world.
LLT = the most qualified with the widest perspective should lead and make decisions.
LLI = the most caring with the deepest connection should lead and make decisions.
An easy way to relate to the four polarities in the LL is to think about your neighborhood. LLA you don't care about your neighbors and prefer them to look and think like you, LLC know and connect with your neighbors and appreciate cultural diversity, LLT you want to grow and lead your community, LLI you want to fit into your community.

Upper Right:
URA = you don't like to be physically close, touched or intimate.
URC = you love physical closeness, touch and intimacy.
URT = you see your body as servant that needs to be controlled and disciplined around its desires for food, comfort, relaxation, and sex.
URI = you see your body as a temple and guide that is full of wisdom that points to its own needs that you surrender to.
An easy way to relate to the four polarities in the UR is to think of sex. URA you don't want to have sex, URC you want to have sex, URT you want to be on top and empty yourself, URI you want to be at the bottom and be filled up.

Lower Right:
LRA = prefer to be single, live and work alone, avoid family events and social gatherings, people should be responsible for themselves and their fate.
LRC = enjoy social gatherings, team worker, social systems should support the poor and underprivileged, we are all in this together
LRT = aspires to climb the social and corporate ladder. Cares about social status, influence, and wants to be a leader.
LRI = cares about the well-being of all people in family, community and society.
An easy way to relate to the four polarities in the LR is to think of your workplace. LRA you prefer to work alone and take full responsibility for producing results, LRC you would rather work in a team and share goals and responsibilities with others, LRT you enjoy a hierarchical structure with a clear chain of command and responsibilities, LRI you enjoy flat or no hierarchies and would rather be part than the leader of a team.

Since every quadrant can be looked at from the inside and the outside (see Ken Wilber *Integral Spirituality* pages 33-49) you may even be able to take this further, but this would be beyond the scope of this manual, so we leave it at eight/sixteen combinations for now.

340 For an in-depth discussion about the difference between individual and social holons see *Integral*

Spirituality by Ken Wilber page 142 to 162.

341 An interesting book that makes multiple references to the fact that humans cannot survive over time without a social structure is *Into The Wild* by Jon Krakauer.

342 Ken Wilber is adamant that it is incorrect to construct holarchies that stack social holons on top of individual holons and so continue from individual humans to partnerships, families, communities, societies, nations, etc. He makes a strong case that individual and social holons co-emerge. Social holons also don't form natural hierarchies (holarchies) since members can join and leave at their own will (of course we see many dominator hierarchies in social holons that may make them look like individual holons.) See *Integral Spirituality* pages 142-162 for an in-depth explanation and devastating critique of systems that commit this fallacy. His view makes sense if we take a momentary snapshot of evolution as there could be communities of humans without family structures, and holarchies—by definition—always collapse if you remove a lower part. However, if seen dynamically as a process over time, communities or societies cannot survive without partners who procreate and raise children in some family structure. So from that view it seems legitimate to construct a holarchy that extends from humans to societies. In other words, it is viable—and even vital—to have a model that stacks social holons on top of individual holons, because—over time—there will be no more individuals without couples who form families and have children. And without families we won't have communities and so on and so forth.

From everything we know today about human history and nature, we can say that men and women who raise children in stable, healthy relationships (nuclear families), that are embedded in functional communities, which form caring societies, and peaceful nations seem to best support the happiness and health of individuals, and to maintain a sustainable ecosystem to live in. So there is no reason not to acknowledge and support the healthy development of holarchies that continue from individual to social holons. We don't need to throw out the baby with the bathwater over philosophical technicalities and can still understand the differences between individual and social holons.

343 See David Schnarch *Passionate Marriage* pages 53-74 for an excellent outline of how to balance and harmonize agency and communion, which he calls "differentiation."

344 See Gregory K. Popcak *The Exceptional 7 Percent* pages 49-80 how to design a "marital imperative" which he defines as "a deeply held, mutually shared set of spiritual values, moral ideals, and emotional goals."

345 The concept of the conventional "opposites but not equals," the post-conventional "not opposites and equals," and the Integral/post-post-conventional "opposites AND equals" was developed by Chris Anderson, founder of www.manandwomanbalance.com/

346 See Erich Fromm, *The Art of Loving* page 15: "The polarity of the sexes is disappearing, and with it erotic love, which is based on this polarity. Men and women become the same, not equals, as opposite poles."

347 Inspired by Leslie Temple Thurston *The Marriage of Spirit* pages 189-196

348 An interesting and entertaining book about the conflicts in answering these questions is Elisabeth Gilbert's book *Committed*, the personal story of a woman in the rational stage with an animus complex in stage four who struggles with amber, and possibly regressing to stage three of her animus development after she falls in love with a man that she married so that he could obtain a US residency permit, or green card.

CHAPTER 9: PASSION/INTIMACY/DEPENDENCE

349 See Ken Wilber, *The Atman Project* Chapter 11 under "Types of Unconscious."

350 The term subconscious is used in many different contexts and has no single or precise definition. This greatly limits its significance as a meaning-bearing concept, and in consequence, the word tends to be avoided in academic and scientific settings. As the saying goes, you can't be a little pregnant, just as you can't be a little conscious. See www.en.wikipedia.org/wiki/Subconscious

351 See Deepak Chopra *The Path of Love* page 177, Marlena Lyons and Jett Psaris *Undefended Love*

(a book that focuses on the submerged unconscious in relationships and how to uncover our true essence, especially page 57-59), John Welwood Love and Awakening pages 31-48 and page 196 (in opening to our anger, we also find other feelings underneath it—sorrow, fear, or hurt—that are calling for attention and concern), and Harville Hendrix Getting The Love You Want page 36-39.

352 The 3-2-1 Process that is part of the five DVD/two CD Integral Life Practice (ILP) Starter Kit (available from http://myilp.com/ or www.amazon.com) is one way to learn to own your shadow.

353 See Dennis Genpo Merzel Big Mind—Big Heart for an exploration of many (unconscious) inner voices and how to make them conscious, based on the original voice dialog work of Hal and Sidra Stone.

354 The following poem describes our desire to be seen beyond our mask or false self:

The Mask I Wear:
Don't be fooled by me.
Don't be fooled by the face I wear
For I wear a mask. I wear a thousand masks-
masks that I'm afraid to take off
and none of them are me.
Pretending is an art that's second nature with me
But don't be fooled, for God's sake, don't be fooled.
I give you the impression that I'm secure
That all is sunny and unruffled with me
within as well as without,
that confidence is my name
and coolness my game,
that the water's calm
and I'm in command,
and that I need no one.
But don't believe me. Please!

My surface may be smooth but my surface is my mask,
My ever-varying and ever-concealing mask.
Beneath lies no smugness, no complacence.
Beneath dwells the real me in confusion, in fear, in aloneness.
But I hide this.
I don't want anybody to know it.
I panic at the thought of my weaknesses
and fear exposing them.
That's why I frantically create my masks to hide behind.

But I don't tell you this.
I don't dare.
I'm afraid to.
I'm afraid you'll think less of me, that you'll laugh
and your laugh would kill me.
I'm afraid that deep-down I'm nothing, that I'm just no good
and you will see this
and reject me.

I idly chatter to you in suave tones of surface talk.
I tell you everything that's nothing
and nothing of what's everything, of what's crying within me.
So when I'm going through my routine
do not be fooled by what I'm saying
Please listen carefully and try to hear
what I'm not saying
Hear what I'd like to say

but what I cannot say.
It will not be easy for you,
long felt inadequacies make my defenses strong.
The nearer you approach me
the blinder I may strike back.
Despite what books say of men, I am irrational;
I fight against the very thing that I cry out for.
you wonder who I am
you shouldn't
for I am everyman
and everywoman
who wears a mask.
Don't be fooled by me.
At least not by the face I wear.–Author unknown.
Variations can be found in several publications and on the Internet.

355 MRI scans revealed that the main activity in the brain of a person who is in love is not occurring in the cortex, the seat of conscious awareness and logical thinking, but in the reptile and limbic brain system (the Caudate Nucleus and the Ventral Tegmental Area), which are the seat of powerful emotions and long-term memories. They may direct us to choose a person who can help us to master unresolved childhood issues. Also see Ayala Malach Pines *Falling in Love* page 178, and Helen Fisher, *Why We Love* page 69-72. Additional evidence that lovers resonate with each other in mysterious ways is provided by experiments that see correlations in brain and heart activity between physically isolated pairs (see Ph.D. dissertation *Correlated Heart-Rate Measures in the Study of Nonlocal Human Connectedness* at www.dorothymandel.com) Even though not directly focused on lovers, Rupert Sheldrake's research into Morphic Resonance (the hypothesis that living organisms draw upon and contribute to a collective memory of their species) may also hold answers why humans sometimes feel magically "in-tune" with, or powerfully drawn to, a specific lover, which cannot be explained by their reproductive, cultural, social, and psychological compatibility.

356 See Ayala Malach Pines Falling in Love pages 105-159 and 181-204, John Welwood *Love and Awakening* pages 49-61 and 126-130, Thomas Moore *Soul Mates*, and endnote #222 in Chapter 4 about soul mates.

357 Source: www.bbc.co.uk/relationships/couples/love_why.shtml

358 See David Richo *How to be an Adult in Relationship* page 121.

359 Couples therapist, professor, and head of the Department of Business Administration at the School of Management at the Ben-Gurion University in Israel, and author of ten books.

360 The Rumi Poem below beautifully depicts the unconscious fit and the potential for awakening in a long-term partnership:
"It's the old rule that drunks have to argue and get into fights.
The lover is just as bad. He falls into a hole.
But down in that hole he finds something shining,
worth more than any amount of money or power.
Last night the moon came dropping its clothes in the street.
I took it as a sign to start singing,
falling up into the bowl of sky.
The bowl breaks. Everywhere is falling everywhere.
Nothing else to do.
Here's the new rule: break the wineglass,
and fall toward the glassblower's breath."

361 See an abridged excerpt of Ken Wilber's discussion with Roger Walsh about his presentation at the Integral Conference in 2008 below (http://integrallife.com/node/54698 The State of the Integral): "Relationships dedicated to growth can constitute one of the best bulwarks against stagnation. Growth-

oriented relationships provide us with honest feedback to compensate for our blind spots. After all it is far easier to see other people's limitations than our own. Two thousand years ago, Jesus famously asked: "Why do you see the speck in your neighbor's eye, but do not notice the log in your own?" Therefore, relationships aimed at recognizing and releasing psychological, spiritual and developmental limitations are invaluable. There is no substitute for dialog and feedback. There are many forms of relationships, however, perhaps the supreme method for obtaining second person feedback are intimate relationships and marriage. One of the best tests of enlightenment may be that of psychiatrist Arthur Deikman who suggests: "Ask the spouse." One of the most effective ways to transform a relationship into a powerful facilitator of growth is to make an explicit agreement to use the relationship for mutual learning and awakening. Once the agreement is made, you have given each other permission to tell your truth, give feedback, and do whatever best serves mutual learning, healing, growth, and awakening. This can be a real gift to any relationship, but it requires a lot of people, such as really wanting to learn, grow, awaken, and make a contribution. There is something about this [level of truthfulness], because we often don't have permission in our culture to tell our truth. Most relationships are based at least in part on a shared covert agreement that "I won't call you on your act if you don't call me on mine," and so relationships unconsciously protect one's fears, defenses, and neurosis. So if you want to turn a relationship from a mutual admiration agreement into something that serves your own growth and transformation, give each other the permission to tell your truth and then "fasten your seatbelts." It won't be necessarily easy, but it will by valuable. Ideally, the relationship will then serve a purpose larger than either individual, larger than the self, and is offered in service to do service as well as awakening. www.in.integralinstitute. org/holons/Walsh_State_of_the_Integral_Enterprise_Part_I.pdf

362 See *The New Psychology of Love* edited by Robert J. Sternberg and Karin Weis pages 149-170, *Styles of Romantic Love* by Clyde and Susan S. Hendrick, and Helen Fisher, *Why We Love* page 94 where they list the styles as follows:
1. Eros — a passionate physical and emotional love based on aesthetic enjoyment; stereotype of romantic love
2. Ludus — a love that is played as a game or sport; conquest
3. Storge — an affectionate love that slowly develops from friendship, based on similarity
4. Pragma — love that is driven by the head, not the heart; undemonstrative
5. Mania — highly volatile love; obsession; fueled by low self-esteem
6. Agape — selfless altruistic love; spiritual; motherly love

Also see pages 184-199 "A Duplex Theory of Love" by Robert J. Sternberg who lists them as
1. Non Love
2. Friendship
3. Infatuated Love
4. Empty Love
5. Romantic Love
6. Companionate Love
7. Fatuous Love (silly, stupid, ridiculous, meaningless, or foolish)
8. Consummate Love (complete, perfect and highest).

363 See Ayala Malach Pines *Falling in Love*, pages 3-11: "Repeated exposure is yet another requirement for a romantic spark to turn into the steady flame of a love relationship. If the first impression is negative, it is best to cut contact," Helen Fisher, *Why Him Why Her*? page 144-146, and the service *Over 40 Dating* (www.dateoverforty.com) where singles meet over several consecutive weekends for social activities to get to know each other in a "natural" setting.

364 Truthfulness refers to the subjective truth about the interior of a person, while "truth" refers to the objective "factual" truth in the exterior. The answer to the question of whether you had intercourse with a woman during a business trip would be an objective, factual truth. If you are in love with her or not would be subjective truthfulness. People can only be truthful to their level of consciousness (and—by definition—not about their unconscious). Children and adults are deeply conditioned to lie, because telling the truth has often negative consequences. This is often a big challenge in relationships, where telling the truth or being truthful would hurt the other partner and may get him or her to leave.

365 See Susan Campbell *Truth in Dating: Finding Love by Getting Real*, and *Saying What's Real: 7 Keys*

to Authentic Communication and Relationship Success.

366 Lovers who regress to a state devoid of any useful discrimination, or of being completely carried away by unreasoned passion or "love" that leads to addictive love.

367 Many mystics, poets, philosophers, theologians, and even scientists have pointed to this mystery; as the mathematician Blaise Pascal (1623-1662) mused "the heart has reasons that reason cannot know."

368 The three primary causes for psychosis are *functional* (mental illnesses such as schizophrenia and bipolar disorder), *organic* (stemming from medical, non-psychological conditions, such as brain tumors or sleep deprivation), and *psychoactive drugs* (e.g., barbiturates, amphetamines, and hallucinogens).

369 Below is an alphabetical list of psychotherapies. The list contains some approaches that may not call themselves psychotherapy but have a similar aim to improve mental health and well-being through talk and other means of communication. Choosing the best therapy and practitioner is essential to the success of the treatment. See Ken Wilber *Integral Psychology* pages 98-100 for more information.

- Adlerian therapy
- Analytical psychology
- Art Therapy
- Autogenic psychotherapy
- Behavior therapy
- Biodynamic psychotherapy
- Bioenergetic analysis
- Biosynthesis
- Brief therapy
- Classical Adlerian Psychotherapy
- Co-Counseling
- Cognitive analytic psychotherapy
- Cognitive behavioral psychotherapy
- Concentrative movement therapy
- Contemplative Psychotherapy
- Core process psychotherapy
- Daseins analytic psychotherapy
- Depth Psychology
- Dialectical behavior therapy
- Emotional Freedom Techniques (EFT)
- Encounter groups
- Eye Movement Desensitization and Reprocessing (EMDR)
- Existential analysis
- Family systems therapy
- Feminist therapy
- Focusing
- Freudian psychotherapy
- Gestalt therapy
- Gestalt Theoretical Psychotherapy
- Group therapy
- Holotropic Breath work
- Humanistic psychology
- Hypnotherapy
- Integrative Psychotherapy
- Internal Family Systems Model
- Jungian psychotherapy
- Logo therapy
- Multimodal Therapy
- Narrative Therapy
- Neuro-linguistic programming (NLP)
- Object relations theory
- Personal construct psychology (PCP)
- Positive psychotherapy
- Postural Integration
- Primal integration
- Process Oriented Psychology
- Primal therapy
- Provocative therapy
- Psychedelic psychotherapy
- Psychoanalysis
- Psychodrama
- Psychodynamic psychotherapy
- Psycho-Organic analysis
- Psychosynthesis
- Pulsing (bodywork)
- Rational emotive behavior psychotherapy
- Re-evaluation Counseling
- Reality therapy
- Reichian psychotherapy
- Rogersian (or Rogerian) psychotherapy
- Rolfing
- Sophia analysis
- Self Relationship (or Sponsorship)
- Systemic therapy
- SHEN Therapy
- T Groups
- Transactional analysis (TA)
- Transpersonal psychology

370 Such as obsessive-compulsive disorders, chronic anxiety, or phobias.

371 See Polly Young Eisendrath and Florence Wiedemann *Female Authority* pages 222-223: "Thus we claim that personality is always a tandem development of self-other conceptions and never a discovery of an independent self. The fallacy of individualism, a misleading notion that we are separate units contained in private bodies like machines in little houses, leads to endless confusion about human relationship and a general repression of dependence and vulnerability. We have encountered many people—especially women—who literally believe that living alone is a condition of psychological independence. In other words, they have confused personal agency (choice, etc.) with the social condition of living alone. The idea of "living alone" is, itself, a distortion based on misconceptions about privacy because people never live alone. As organisms, we have a variety of both biological and psychological needs that prevent us from being able to survive in isolation."

372 See Christian de Quincey *Radical Knowing* pages 176-180: "I as subject am never reflected in things (objects) only in other "I's" such as you." Famous feminist activist Gloria Steinem who had quoted Irina Dunn saying "A woman needs a man like a fish needs a bicycle" married David Bale in 2000 at age 66.

373 See www.integrallife.com/awaken/shadow/practice-3-2-1-shadow-process

374 See Robert Kegan in *In Over Our Heads* page 313: "Couples in 4th order consciousness begin with the premise of their own completeness and see conflict as an inevitable by-product of interaction of two psychologically whole selves, while couples in 5th [Integral] order of consciousness begin with their "own tendency" to pretend to completeness (while actually being incomplete) and see conflict as the inevitable, but convertible by-product of the pretension to completeness."

375 Adyashanti, a married Zen teacher in an interview with Bert Parlee stated: "The proof of the depth and embodiment of your realization is seen in your love relationship. That's where the proof is in the pudding. If it all collapses in your relationship, you have some work to do. And people do have a lot of difficulties in their relationships."

Eckhart Tolle, (in relationship with Kim Eng) writes in *The Power Of Now* page 127 (page 153 in the paperback edition) "Three failed relationships in as many years are more likely to force you into awakening than three years on a desert island shut away in your room" and on page 132 (page 159 paperback edition): "Humanity is under great pressure to evolve because it is our only chance of survival as a race. This will affect every aspect of your life and close relationships in particular. Never before have relationships been as problematic and conflict ridden as they are now. As you may have noticed, they are not here to make you happy or fulfilled. If you continue to pursue the goal of salvation through a relationship, you will be disillusioned again and again. But if you accept that the relationship is here to make you conscious instead of happy, then the relationship will offer you salvation, and you will be aligning yourself with the higher consciousness that wants to be born into this world. For those who hold on to the old patterns, there will be increasing pain, violence, confusion, and madness."

376 See Robert Augustus Masters *Transformation through Intimacy—The Journey Towards Mature Monogamy* on the page before the Introduction: "The passage from immature to mature monogamy is not just a journey of ripening intimacy with a beloved other, but also a journey into and through zones of ourselves that may be quite difficult to navigate, let alone get intimate with and integrate with the rest of our being. But however much this passage might ask of us, it gives back even more, transforming us until we are established in the unshakable love, profound passion, and radically intimate mutuality that epitomize mature monogamy. And even if we don't end up in such a relationship, our having taken the journey toward it will immeasurably benefit us in whatever we do."

377 See David Deida *Intimate Communion* pages 263-267.

378 When women who seek this form of love speak of healing, learning, growth, and awakening in a partnership, they often mean that *men* need to do so in order to adapt to the female perspective and so no longer challenge them emotionally. These women say: "I am done growing, very evolved and happy. I love myself way too much to have a partner to make my life miserable again." They may be right in some cases if they date men who are less conscious or balanced/integrated in their development, but all too often it is just an avoidance to take responsibility for their own uneven development. And to assume that women are more evolved than men is a ridiculous fallacy.

379 See Helen Fisher, *Why We Love* pages 52-56.

380 Women initiate domestic violence about as often as Men do when either of them feels powerless to resolve their conflicts through non-violent means (such as talking things through.) The myth that males are more abusive than women stems from the fact that women report physical abuse more often to the authorities than their partners, while males feel shame to do so and are often laughed at if they

report physical abuse to the police. See Warren Farrell *Does Feminism Discriminate Against Men* pages 33-39 and *Women Can't Hear What Men Don't Say* pages 123-162.

381 David Schnarch's *Passionate Marriage* is a classic.

382 Any kind of couples Tantra workshops or the excellent HAI workshops about love intimacy and sexuality (www.hai.org) are recommended.

383 See *The New Psychology of Love* edited by Robert J. Sternberg and Karin Weis page 185 under intimacy about the qualities of integrally informed relationships which they describe as:
1. Desire to promote the welfare of the loved one.
2. Experienced happiness with the loved one.
3. High regard for the loved one.
4. Being able to count on the loved one in times of need.
5. Mutual understanding with the loved one.
6. Sharing of one's self and ones possessions with the loved one.
7. Receipt of emotional support from the loved one.
8. Giving of emotional support to the loved one.
9. Intimate communication with the loved one.
10. Valuing of the loved one.

384 See Shunryu Suzuki *Zen Mind, Beginner's Mind*, which suggests to approach life, and hence our relationships, without the thought of gaining anything special. Or, as Eckhart Tolle mentioned: "The ego cannot love, it always wants something."

CHAPTER 10: DIFFERENCES IN MALE AND FEMALE CONSCIOUSNESS DEVELOPMENT

385 Ken Wilber responded to this question by saying that on the "manifest side of the street" things tend to manifest in polarities all the way up in the gross, subtle and causal body, and that the boy/girl duality is pretty fundamental to our existence. Even though you want to embody both qualities as well as you can, you can't be feminine and masculine simultaneously. In order to engage in the dance between the two polarities requires a man and a woman—all the way up. And where the two—the ultimate masculine pushing, clarity and drive, and the ultimate feminine compassion and embrace—come together in "one taste" is on the other side of manifestation. See http://www.in.integralinstitute.org/live/view_ken.aspx#Too_Evolved_for_Relationships

386 See Geoffrey Miller *The Mating Mind* for a deeper exploration of sexual versus natural selection.

387 See Nancy Etcoff *"Survival of the Prettiest."*

388 In today's world, these male and female ideals can represent by models, porn stars, actors, characters in novels or video games. In our culture, and increasingly throughout the world via the Internet and satellite TV, both sexes are constantly bombarded with ideal images of the opposite sex that hardly anybody can live up to. For women this means, if I look a certain way, I can have the dream man who takes care of me and supports me in my desire for self-fulfillment. For men this means, if I succeed in a certain way, I can attract my dream woman who looks good on my arm, meets my sexual desires, satisfies my need for company and supports me in my purpose/mission. Also see Geoffrey Miller *The Mating Mind* page 8-12.

389 To discuss the Primary Fantasy, mutually compatible pathology, and male/female co-creation of developmental stages of consciousness in a group-setting or in public upsets most people. Especially women get defensive when confronted with the fact that they fell in love with a man who met their Primary Fantasy and complements their unconscious pathology. It is not only embarrassing to admit, it also makes them co-responsible for the atrocities that women so often criticize as being committed by males, such as violence against others (especially women and children), wars, and the increasing destruction of our environment. The Primary Fantasy of males (i.e., I fell in love with her because she is beautiful and I wanted to have sex with her) is usually easy to see and admitted by them, at least if there are no other women (including their spouses) around. And no man wants to believe that she only fell for him because he met her Primary Fantasy and matched her pathological shadow. Couples don't want to (or can't) talk about their mutually compatible pathology and the resulting conflicts that are either repressed or fought out behind closed doors. As a result, the only politically correct way to rationalize why a couple fell in love and stayed together is for their friendship, the children, religious, cultural, and maybe spiritual connection. Single men and women may get defensive around the topic because they have been deeply wounded by being rejected as inadequate success or sex objects, could not deal with their pathology or are otherwise not emotionally healthy and spiritually mature enough to be in a relationship. To mention that almost all advancements in consciousness along with art, science, and religion came from men, driven by their desire to have sex with attractive women, is largely taboo in today's egalitarian society, including scientists who are at best ambivalent to talk/write publically about sex and the sexual selection process (see Geoffrey Miller *The Mating Mind* page 15 and 16), endnote #89 in Chapter 2, and Nancy Etcoff in *"Survival of the Prettiest"* pages 79-80 where she states: "Simply put, there are forces that make both sexes uncomfortable in such situations. Men are evaluated by their income and professional status as harshly as women are evaluated by their looks."

390 See Nancy Etcoff *"Survival of the Prettiest"* pages 169-170.

391 The US jewelry retail industry generates annual revenues of $30 billon. See www.hoovers.com/jewelry-retail/--ID__66--/free-ind-fr-profile-basic.xhtml

392 See Geoffrey Miller *The Mating Mind* page 3-4, and 63-65.

393 In an interview with www.womenontheedgeofevolution.com/access/index.php (password "women") Barbara Marx Hubbard replied to the question about the role of females in the evolution of men: "Men do what women want [reward]. Women attract the male shifting from the patriarchy into their own inner essence. Women are the leaders of the liberation of men. We don't reject or see men as inferior or oppressive. Men can be liberated and guided through women. I love men and I have always been inspired by men, fulfilling a lot of the impulses from men by being a woman as I saw their genius. I have been "inseminated" logically by the ideas of great men. I have always been inspired by the great men who were evolutionaries. They were all men! I was attracted to their ideas and their seed, and it awakened in me the feminine co-creator. And then I became a guide to the men who were not yet evolutionaries but who were brilliant.

394 The insight about the interior and sexual power of females is not new. In 411 BC, a play by Aristophanes shows Lysistrata convincing the women of Greece to withhold sexual privileges from their husbands as a means of forcing them to negotiate peace in the Peloponnesian war. www.en.wikipedia.org/wiki/Lysistrata

395 See www.en.wikipedia.org/wiki/List_of_inventors for a list of inventors. This also holds true for art, philosophy, science, agriculture, religions, etc. Also see David Deida *The Way of the Superior Man* page 61: "The masculine grows by challenge."

396 Alison Armstrong *Making Sense of Men* page 56.

397 An example of this is seen in *Groundhog Day*, a lovely movie in which actor Bill Murray plays a character who evolves from "egocentric" to "care" to "universal care" (or ability to take a first, second, and finally third person perspective) to win the heart of a woman, played by actress Andy MacDowell.

398 The process of growth or transcendence typically involves three phases; (1) identification, (2) differentiation, and (3) integration.
In the *first* phase of *identification*, the self (the subject) is "at one" or fully identified with its level of consciousness (or the way of seeing itself and the world), such as a magenta fortune teller, a red self centered rock star or athlete, an amber religious follower, an orange success-driven Wall Street broker, a green philanthropist or activist, a teal corporate trainer, or a turquoise spiritual teacher.
The *second* phase of differentiation is triggered when the present level of consciousness no longer provides satisfying answers to the questions and challenges at hand, for example, a man trying to attract and satisfy a desirable woman that he is in love with and who rejects him. To get out of his confusion, suffering, and frustration, his "self" will start to seek different solutions by looking at "itself" which triggers the process of separating (differentiating) the "I" (self/ego/subject) from the "it" (object).
In the *third* phase the self integrates, and so *identifies* with the more complex and advanced perspectives,

values, and worldviews of the next higher stage of development, until they no longer provide the answers to life's questions and challenges at hand, and the process starts anew.

Even though we may feel at times that we have reached the ultimate stage of development, or that we can grow without suffering, the cycle of growth through identification, differentiation (triggered through some form of suffering or challenge), and integration never seems to end.

399 See Allan Combs *Consciousness Explained Better* pages 25-34 about childhood development.

400 See Laurie A. Rudman and Peter Glick *The Social Psychology of Gender* page 48: "The more men threaten women, the more women seek out men for protection (ironically) from other men."

401 Note how eight of the ten Judeo/Christian commandments deal with creating stability in family and community:

1. Remember the Sabbath and keep it holy
2. Honor your father and mother
3. You shall not murder
4. You shall not commit adultery
5. You shall not steal
6. You shall not bear false witness against your neighbor
7. You shall not covet your neighbor's wife
8. You shall not covet anything that belongs to your neighbor

402 See Nancy Etcoff *"Survival of the Prettiest"* page 76.

403 See (as one of many examples) the movie *Intolerable Cruelty* when gold digger Marylin Rexroth exults after her rich husband is caught on video tape cheating on her: "Whilst I don't find this terribly amusing, I am delighted that you found this material. This is going to be my passport to wealth, independence... and freedom."

404 See David Deida—whom Ken Wilber calls the savior of green men—especially *The Way of the Superior Man*.

405 For more details about the process of growth see Jenny Wade *Changes of Mind* page 262-270, Beck/Cowan *Spiral Dynamics* pages 71-103, Ken Wilber *A Brief History of Everything* page 131 and Robert Kegan *In Over Our Heads* page 32 with his insight that the "subject of the previous stage becomes the object of the subject of the next stage."

406 See Jenny Wade *Changes of Mind* page 268: "[for people in first-tier consciousness] differences in values threaten the ego to some extent, so they are unable to be tolerant or accepting of people at a different level of awareness." *Spiral Dynamics* maintains that humans operate 50% of the time from their central stage of development (center of gravity), 25% from the stage below, and 25% from the stage above.

407 See Carol Gilligan *In A Different Voice* introduction page xx where she outlines that: "men think by knowing themselves they will understand women, while women think by knowing others they will come to know themselves," and page 16 where she quotes Virginia Woolf as saying: "it is obvious that the values of women differ very often from the values which have been made by the other sex. Naturally this is so. Yet, it is the masculine values that prevail" and adds; "as a result, women come to question the normality of their feelings and alter their judgments in deference to the opinion of others."

408 There are many jokes and books who point to this fact, for example *Men are like Waffles, Women are like Spaghetti* by Bill and Pam Farrell.

409 Ken Wilber does not get tired of interpreting Carol Gilligan's work (see her book *In a Different Voice*) that women don't think hierarchically, but develop hierarchically. Alison Armstrong of PAX (www.understandmen.com) and her facilitators maintain that men go through four developmental stages (1) page, (2) knight, (3) prince, and (4) king (which is more likely a vertical translation than a vertical transformation) while she identifies no developmental stages in women. Also see Alison Armstrong's book *The Amazing Development of Men: Everyman's Journey from Knight to Prince to King*.

410 As Abraham Maslow famously noted: "If the only tool you have is a hammer, you tend to see every problem as a nail." (He was not the first to express this sentiment, but he is widely credited for it.)

411 With the exception of falling in love, or in times of crisis such as a breakup/divorce, when, as you certainly experienced, temporary peak experiences of higher stages or regression to lower stages of consciousness (called "states" since they are not permanent) may occur.

412 See David Deida *Blue Truth* pages 100-102 where he describes feminine men who go with the flow instead of being directed by their purpose as "flow boys".

413 The river metaphor also works well if we envision our life's purpose as a return to the Ocean (ever present origin) in a co-creation with our life-partner and soul mate.

414 Neurosis is a class of functional mental disorders involving distress (but neither delusions nor hallucinations), where behavior is not outside socially acceptable norms. Psychosis means "abnormal condition of the mind," and is a generic psychiatric term for a mental state often described as involving a "loss of contact with reality." Borderline personality disorder (BPD) falls between the two and describes a prolonged disturbance of personality function, characterized by depth and variability of moods. BPD typically involves unusual levels of instability in mood, "black and white" thinking or splitting, chaotic and unstable interpersonal relationships, self-image, identity, and behavior, as well as a disturbance in the individual's sense of self. These disturbances can have a pervasive negative impact on many or all of the psychosocial facets of life. This includes difficulties maintaining relationships in work, home, and social settings. Attempted suicide and completed suicide are possible outcomes, especially without proper care and effective therapy.

415 Jenny Wade points out that there might be one exception for the growth from stage 4 (amber) to 6 (green). Both males and females may skip stage 5 (orange) if they have the economic base to so. This may create some form of pathology through insecurity later with the realization that they never had to—and most likely can't—provide for themselves. In this case, they may regress to orange or even to red during a crisis situation.

416 A classic example is Adi Da who was recognized by many as a highly realized human being, but in later life drifted into some kind of delusion, claiming a form of his own divinity that no other human had ever attained before him, or could ever attain after him, other than through him. He died on November 27, 2008 at age 69.

417 Wilber calls the major milestones (or stages of psychological development) "fulcrums" and goes into some detail about this process in *A Brief History of Everything* pages 131-135 and Integral Psychology pages 102-108.

418 The river metaphor also works well if we envision our life's purpose as a return to the Ocean (ever present origin) in a co-creation with our life-partner and soul-mate.

419 For a more in depth explanation of ladder, climber, and view, see Ken Wilber *A Brief History of Everything* pages 125-136. Note that Wilber does not differentiate between feminine and masculine growth other than repeatedly referencing Carol Gilligan's work from her book *In A Different Voice* which, according to Wilber, outlines that women grow with an emphasis on care, relationships, and responsibility, while males grow with an emphasis on justice, agency and rights. Our metaphor of the river is compatible with ladder, climber, and view, and expands on it by differentiating between the static masculine and the fluid feminine.

420 The Greek root of the word pathology is "pathos," which means "suffering." Any kind of attachment dependence, desire, or expectation for another person to make us happy (or hating them if they don't), or their power to make us unhappy, will eventually lead to suffering. It can be transcended if happiness (or joy/peace) originates from within us, as the Buddha already noticed some 2500 years ago.

421 Eckhart Tolle, Gangaji, Michael Beckwith, Byron Katie, Steven Harrison, Deepak Chopra, Tony Robbins, Adyashanti, Leonard Jacobson, Bernie Prior, Saniel Bonder, Jack Kornfield, Roger Walsh, Stephen Covey ... the list goes on and on.

422 An amazing book about the creation of meaning is Victor Frankl's account of his experiences in the concentration camps of Nazi Germany in *Man's Search For Meaning*, which later lead him to the development of Logo Therapy.

423 See Ken Wilber *Integral Spirituality* pages 126-129 and the list of various forms of therapies in endnote #369 in Chapter 9 of this manual.

424 See *Integral Psychology* by Ken Wilber pages 91-114 for a full account of the self and its pathologies, sub-personalities, and suggested forms of therapy.

425 See John Welwood *Perfect Love Imperfect Relationships* and *Love and Awakening*, Greg Baer *Real Love*, Marlena Lyons and Jett Psaris *Undefended Love*, or Steven Stosny *Love Without Hurt*.

CHAPTER 11- WHERE AM I COMING FROM? WHERE IS SHE COMING FROM?

426 Title of an orange relationship book by Bradley Fenton (see Appendix I).

427 See Ken Wilber *Integral Spirituality* pages 69 and 249-266 where he initially defines the Kosmic Address as altitude (level of consciousness) + perspective and later adds other dimensions of our personality such as states and types.

428 As we now know from quantum physics, we cannot even observe/measure particles without affecting them in some mysterious way, and always need to take the observer or the observing apparatus into account. This does not mean that the observer or human consciousness is necessary or responsible for bringing things into existence (aka collapsing the Schroedinger Wave Equation), as stated in New Age books and movies such as *What the bleep do we know*, but that it is part of the larger quantum field. See www.en.wikipedia.org/wiki/Observer_effect_(physics).

429 See Ken Wilber *Integral Spirituality* pages 267-269.

430 See Daniel Goleman *Social Intelligence* pages 105-116.

431 Some people (often women) believe that their thoughts or consciousness actually influence or create physical objects/reality. There is indeed some evidence of this on a very small scale. For example the Institute of Noetic Sciences (www.ions.org) performs experiments to that end with random number generators, but the effect is extremely small (1 in 50,000). See for example www.noosphere.princeton. edu/ and the movie *Down The Rabbit Hole* DVD#3, Side 2, Chapter 2 interview with Dean Radin, chief scientist at the Institute of Noetic Sciences. As of this writing, none of the scientists who study these phenomena know what this really means and what causes this effect.

432 At www.wilber.shambhala.com/html/watch/042301_i.cfm/ Sean Esbjorn-Hargens outlines that Ken Wilber uses the term intersubjectivity to refer to at least five different dimensions of intersubjectivity. He briefly introduces them with terms that he generated:
  1. *Intersubjectivity-as-spirit*: the transcendental quality of all relationships that allows for any dimension of intersubjectivity to manifest. The only reason that two subjectivities can touch simultaneously (co-presence) is that they are ultimately only one Subject.
  2. *Intersubjectivity-as-context*: the context created by multiple intersubjective structures (i.e., meshworks) which are constitutive of the subject and create the space in which both subjects and objects arise (e.g., physical laws, morphic fields, linguistic, moral, cultural, biological, and aesthetic structures). These cultural contexts, backgrounds, and practices are non-discursive and inaccessible via direct experience.
  3. *Intersubjectivity-as-resonance*: the occurrence of "mutual recognition" and "mutual understanding" between two holons of similar depth. Within this dimension there are Worldspaces and Worldviews.
     a. *Worldspaces*: ontological resonance between two subjects who share emergent domains (e.g., physical, emotional, mental, and spiritual). Here, mutual recognition is simple co-presence prior to reflection (precognitive).
     b. *Worldviews*: epistemological resonance between two subjects who share a level of psychological development (e.g., archaic, magic, mythic, rational, and centauric). Here mutual understanding is co-presence via cognition, which increases in complexity with development. This is the cognitive component of a shared worldspace.
  4. *Intersubjectivity-as-relationship*: the way we identify with and have relationships with other subjects and objects. Within this dimension there are at least three types of relationships.
     a. *It-It relationships*: an objective subject in relation with an objective object.
     b. *I-It relationships*: a subject in relationship with an object (or a subject seen as an object).

c. *I-I relationships*: a subject in relationship with a subject. This last subdivision has two general forms, either solidarity or difference.
      1) *Relationship-as-solidarity*: relating to another subject because they mirror your values, ethnicity, gender, or nationality etc.
      2) *Relationship-as-difference*: relating to another subject as a subject despite the fact that they are different from you in important ways.

   It is also helpful to keep in mind a related quality to intersubjectivity, namely:
   5. *Intersubjectivity-as-phenomenology*: the felt-experience of different dimensions of intersubjectivity, including: spirit, resonance, and relationships. Note that intersubjectivity-as-context is not available as "felt-experience" by its very nature of constituting the subject prior to experience.

433 The famous Austrian/Jewish philosopher and mystic Martin Buber made the statement "Ich und Du" which means "I and you" or more often translated as "I and Thou" to express the very personal, even intimate German "Du," which has no direct equivalent in English. Buber's somewhat outdated philosophy was that two subjects can meet one another in their authentic existence, without any qualification or objectification of one another. He also spoke of the "Ich und es," translated to "I and it," the subject-object relationship.

434 See Ken Wilber *Integral Spirituality* pages 157-162.

435 In *Integral Spirituality* page 33-49, Ken Wilber expands on this concept by giving each of the four quadrants an inside and an outside perspective; for example the singular interior "I" dimension can be looked at from the perspective of the individual OR from the perspective of a researcher who studies consciousness development (or a woman who intuitively senses what is going on inside of you).

436 See Stephen Covey *The Seven Habits of Highly Effective People* page 288: "Habit #7: Sharpening the Saw." He suggests that you develop habits for the renewal of your UR physical body (exercise, nutrition, stress management), UL mind (reading, visualizing, planning, writing), LR social/emotional relations (service, empathy, synergy, intrinsic security), and LL spiritual dimension (value clarification & commitment, study, and meditation). Also see Ken Wilber *Integral Spirituality* page 23.

437 See Ken Wilber *Integral Spirituality* pages 175-178, 234, and 283, where he describes the myth of the given as "the (false) believe that reality is simply given; that the consciousness of an individual will deliver truth; that the truth that a subject delivers is independent from intersubjective cultural networks and that the mirror of nature is an adequate methodology." This is of course not advocating for an idealistic worldview, but for what Wilber calls "critical realism."

438 Elisabeth Lesser, co-founder of Omega Institute and author of several books (e.g., *Broken Open— How Difficult Times Can Help Us Grow*) in an interview with Ken Wilber.

439 Active listening is a way of listening and responding to others that focuses attention on the speaker without distraction through the environment, thinking about other things, or preparing a response. The listener then often paraphrases the speaker's words, including underlying feelings and perceptions, and/or asking deeper questions until a mutual understanding is reached. Mutual understanding does not mean consent.

443 See Eve Eschner-Hogan and Steven Hogan *Intellectual Foreplay* for a wealth of questions to ask.

444 See Ken Wilber *Integral Spirituality* pages 71-102.

445 At the time of this writing, there is evidence for a body-mind connection, but it is often totally blown out of proportion by individuals in spiritual development stage one. Noetic sciences use scientific methods to explore the "inner cosmos" of the mind (consciousness, soul, spirit) and how it relates to the "outer cosmos" of the physical world. In other words, they study how people come to know things or affect things through experiences or capacities (intuitions, synchronicities, psi, "after-death" communication, energy healing, etc.) that have no apparent rational explanation, and what this says about the nature of human consciousness (from www.noetic.org)

446 The major theme of books such as *The Power Of Now* by Eckhart Tolle, *Be Here Now* by Ram Dass, or *Facets of Unity* by A.H. Almaas, and many other spiritual teachers who have access to this level of spiritual awareness.

447 This stage is beautifully expressed in the following (abridged) Zen Poem by Seng Ts`an:

The perfect way knows no difficulties
Except that it refuses to make preferences;
Only when freed from hate and love
Does it reveals itself fully and without disguise;

A tenth of an inch's difference,
And heaven and earth are set apart.
If you wish to see it before your own eyes
Have no fixed thoughts either for or against it.

To set up what you like against what you dislike -
That is the disease of the mind.

The Way is perfect like unto vast space,
With nothing wanting, nothing superfluous.

It is due to making choices
That its suchness is lost sight of.

The One is none other than the All, the All non other than the One.

Take your stand on this, and the rest will follow on its own accord;
I have spoken, but in vain, for what can words tell
Of things that have no yesterday, tomorrow or today.

From Huston Smith *The World's Religions* page 138 (paperback).

448 See for example Eckhart Tolle *Stillness Speaks*, Coleman Barks *The Illuminated Rumi*, or Stephen Mitchell's translation of the *Tao Te Ching*.

449 See Eve Eschner Hogan and Steven Hogan *Intellectual Foreplay* pages 246-256, and Susan Campbell *The Truth In Dating Card Game* for fun and inspiring questions.

450 See www.rainn.org/statistics

451 See for example Katherine Woodward Thomas *Calling In The One: 7 Weeks to Attract The Love Of Your Life*, or Kathryn Alice *Love Will Find You: 9 Magnets To Bring You And Your Soulmate Together*.

452 See Donna Sheehan *Redefining Seduction*. This book teaches post-feminist women about men, seduction and Darwin's theory of sexual selection. Based on Geoffrey Millers book *The Mating Mind* and Donna's personal love story, it explains how "women who take the lead in courtship and in choosing and guiding their mates, fulfill their biological role as the drivers of civilization. *Redefining Seduction* gives women the skills and confidence to allow themselves to meet, choose and seduce the men they know are right for them. Combining science, intuition and a personal love story, Redefining Seduction begins the shift to a partnership society in which women and men complement each other's biological strengths in harmony.

CHAPTER 12: LOCATING YOUR PARTNER AND YOURSELF ON THE COMPATIBILITY MATRIX

439 David Deida *The Way of the Superior Man* page 58: "In the feminine reality, words and facts take a second place to emotions and the shifting moods of relationship. When she says "I hate you," or "I'll never move to Texas," or "I don't want to go to the movies," it is often more a reflection of a transient feeling-wave than a well considered stance with respect to events and experiences. On the other hand, the masculine means what it says. A man's word is his honor. The feminine says what it feels. A woman's word is her true expression in the moment."

440 See Marshall Rosenberg *Non Violent Communication* pages 91-111 about empathy guesses.

441 A very basic but still profound spiritual book is *The Four Agreements* by Don Miguel Ruiz who outlines four qualities that help us in our relating with others:

1. Be impeccable with your word
2. Don't take anything personally
3. Don't make assumptions
4. Always do your best

442 Active listening is a way of listening and responding to others that focuses attention on the speaker without distraction through the environment, thinking about other things, or preparing a response. The listener then often paraphrases the speaker's words, including underlying feelings and perceptions, and/or asking deeper questions until a mutual understanding is reached. Mutual understanding does not mean consent.

453 Think of someone who just quit smoking. He or she is usually most intolerant of people who still smoke. The same is true for stage development. Since it takes a tremendous effort to transcend a lower stage, it makes total sense to reject the values of the lower stage a person just left behind. Ken Wilber states in an interview with Roger Walsh that individuals in first-tier consciousness take up particular interpretations (from archaic to pluralistic) of the world. And because these people don't know that their limited views are merely interpretations of the world, they think that they are seeing reality itself. And so they think that people who are at different levels of development are categorically, absolutely wrong.

454 The *Celebrating Men, Satisfying Women®* PAX workshops (*www.understandmen.com/*) by Alison Armstrong try to address these problems by teaching orange women who want to be in a relationship to be more understanding and accommodating towards men, but can't address the problem that successful orange men want (and can have) younger women, and orange women want way above-average successful same-aged or younger men, which are hard for them to attract.

455 Ken Wilber wrote a whole "tongue-in-cheek" novel called *Boomeritis* in which he ridicules extreme postmodernism.

456 Sri Aurobindo, Jean Gebser, Ken Wilber, Sean Esbjorn-Hargens, Allan Combs, Terry Patten, Craig Hamilton, Steve McIntosh, Erwin Laszlo, Don Beck, and Christian de Quincey, to name a few (see www.en.wikipedia.org/wiki/Integral_theory_(philosophy))

457 See Ken Wilber *Integral Spirituality* Page 69 with a chart of 3rd tier consciousness. These stages refer mainly to transcendental stages of the mind and higher mind.

458 Bernie Prior writes on www.bernieprior.org/man-and-woman.php "To put it very simply, man has to return to pure presence, his true timeless state, (his golden essence) which is the faint echo he hears within himself, calling him home to once again truly honor the feminine (woman and the whole of creation) and unconditionally adore her with no egoist projection; to truly serve her in truth and bring her home into the deep. She, woman, has to be the love she is, in order to return to her radiant essence. She knows of the intimacy I am speaking of in the deep of herself, within the attraction to man. She has the knowledge that she is not being met in the deepest place by man and hears and feels a deep longing calling her home in this, to be true to the love that she is, and not compromise. And yet she does, just like her mother's mother's mother, wrapped up and consumed in the many layers of masculine projection (including her own). Man, consciously or unconsciously using her feminine essence to manifest his world of distance from the source, his expectations and his goal orientated existence. The many promises of tomorrow, the better future, away from home in the present, from the presence of true loving, true meeting.

As a stream turns into a river to enable it to meet the ocean, man and woman's distraction must die in order to dissolve into the 'already great' ocean of love."

459 The following poems by Robert Bly and Rumi point to this third body:

> A man and a woman sit near each other, and they do not long
> at this moment to be older, or younger, nor born
> in any other nation, or time, or place.
> They are content to be where they are, talking or not talking.
> Their breaths together feed someone whom we do not know.
> The man sees the way his fingers move;
> he sees her hands close around a book she hands to him.

> They obey a third body they have in common.
> They have made a promise to love that body.
> Age may come, parting may come, death will come.
> A man and woman sit near each other;
> as they breathe they feed someone we do not know,
> someone we know of, whom we have never seen.
> –Robert Bly

> Out beyond ideas of wrongdoing and rightdoing,
> there is a field. I'll meet you there.
> When the soul lies down in that grass,
> the world is too full to talk about.
> Ideas, language, even the phrase each other
> doesn't make any sense.
> –Rumi

460 See dissertation of Jenny Stitz *Intimacy and Differentiation in Couples at Post-Conventional Levels of Ego Development*, Institute of Transpersonal Psychology, Palo Alto, CA 9/13/2004 UMI Microform 3153925.

461 A poem by the Sufi Poet Hafiz illustrates the journey of turquoise males who can't find a partner and utilize their singlehood for their ever deeper awakening.

> Don't surrender your loneliness so quickly
> Let it cut more deep
> Let it ferment and season you
> As few human
> Or even divine ingredients can
> Something missing in my heart tonight
> Has made my eyes so soft
> My voice so tender
> My need of God
> Absolutely clear

462 See Marlena Lyons and Jett Psaris *Undefended Love* pages 97-101 about the limitations of agreements.

463 See John Gottman and Nan Silver in *The Seven Principals That Make Marriage Work* page 8: "Perhaps the biggest myth of all is that communication—and more specifically, learning to resolve your conflicts—is the royal road to romance and an enduring, happy marriage." Patricia Love/Steven Stosny *How to Improve your Marriage Without Talking About It* page 1: "Research and our combined fifty-plus years of clinical experience show repeatedly that, despite your best intentions, talking about your relationship has more of a chance of making things worse than making it better. And it has nothing to do with your partner's lack of interest or poor communication skills." David Schnarch *Passionate Marriage* page 50: "We like to believe that "communication problems" underlie most relationship difficulties ... but this is not what happens."

464 Marshall Rosenberg, Susan Campbell, John Gray, Warren Farrell, Steven Covey, Roger Fisher and William Ury, etc. ... the list goes on and on.

465 See James W. Pickens *The Art Of Closing Any Deal* about manipulative sales techniques.

466 See Roger Fisher and William Ury *Getting To Yes Without Giving In*.

467 See Marshall Rosenberg *Non Violent Communication*.

468 See Frederic Luskin *Forgive for Love: The Missing Ingredient for a Healthy and Lasting Relationship*.

469 To be, or not to be: that is the question:
   Whether 'tis nobler in the mind to suffer,
   The slings and arrows of outrageous fortune,
   Or to take arms against a sea of troubles,
   And by opposing end them?

To die: to sleep;
No more; and by a sleep to say we end,
The heart-ache and the thousand natural shocks
That flesh is heir to, 'tis a consummation.

470 The wonderful movie *Same Time Next Year* follows the developmental stages from red to teal of a men and woman—both married to different partners, that meet each other once a year to share some extramarital romance and their life story.

471 Many modern spiritual teachers and coaches are in partnerships (Eckhart Tolle, Gangaji, Michael Beckwith, Byron Katie, Steven Harrison, Deepak Chopra, Tony Robbins, Adyashanti, Leonard Jacobson, Bernie Prior, Saniel Bonder, Jack Kornfield, Roger Walsh, Stephen Covey ... the list goes on and on), and make references to the fact that relationships are the best or even the only path to full realization. This makes sense, as you can't avoid parts of the human experience (having a partner, co-habitation, sex, and children) and claim full enlightenment. This raises the question if monks and saints such as the Dalai Lama, Ramana Maharshi, the Buddha, or Jesus can be fully realized. One answer to this is that while they may have pioneered new depths of certain aspects of our human existence, we would not want their (assumed) way of being replicated in a majority of humanity, which is the ideal of a modern integral spiritual teacher/teaching.

472 A sentimental poem that depicts this notion in a nice way is:
People come into your life for a reason, a season, or a lifetime. When you figure out which it is, you know exactly what to do.
When someone is in your life for a *reason*, it is usually to meet a need you have expressed outwardly or inwardly. They have come to assist you through a difficulty, to provide you with guidance and support, to aid you physically, emotionally, or spiritually. They may seem like a godsend, and they are. They are there for the reason you need them to be. Then, without any wrongdoing on your part or at an inconvenient time, this person will say or do something to bring the relationship to an end. Sometimes they die. Sometimes they walk away. Sometimes they act up or out and force you to take a stand. What we must realize is that our need has been met, our desire fulfilled; their work is done. The prayer you sent up has been answered and it is now time to move on.
When people come into your life for a *season*, it is because your turn has come to share, grow, or learn. They may bring you an experience of peace or make you laugh. They may teach you something you have never done. They usually give you an unbelievable amount of joy. Believe it! It is real! But only for a *season*.
Lifetime relationships teach you lifetime lessons; those things you must build upon in order to have a solid emotional foundation. Your job is to accept the lesson, love the person/people anyway; and put what you have learned to use in all other relationships and areas of your life. It is said that love is blind but friendship is clairvoyant.

Chapter 13: Dating Using the Integral Relationship Model

473 See AARP *The Divorce Experience: A Study of Divorce At Midlife and Beyond* http://assets.aarp.org/rgcenter/general/divorce_1.pdf pages 40-41.

474 See Charlotte Kasl *If The Buddha Dated* page 62 –68.

475 See www.en.wikipedia.org/wiki/Dating_(activity)

476 See www.merriam-webster.com/dictionary/flirt and www.en.wikipedia.org/wiki/Flirting

477 See Kathryn *Alice Love Will Find You*, Wayne Dyer, *The Power Of Intention*, Kathlyn and Gay Hendricks *Attracting Genuine Love*, *The Secret*, *What the bleep do we know* (book and movie), *Science of Mind* and other "Success Churches," and Abraham Hicks's *Ask and it is Given* (www.abraham-hicks.com). There are groups and coaches for *The Law of Attraction* that you can find through the Internet.

478 See Geoffrey Miller *The Mating Mind* pages 195-208.

479 See Susan Campbell *Truth in Dating*.

480 Visit the links page at www.singles2couples.org or do a Google search for a list and reviews of dating websites.

481 See Geoffrey Miller *The Mating Mind* pages 206-207, and John Gray *Mars and Venus on a Date* in

the chapter on exclusivity page 65-90.

APPENDIX I- RELATIONSHIP BOOKS FOR ALL LEVELS/COLORS

482 Since therapists work primarily with clients who met each other's Primary Fantasy and partnered based on their shared interests and values (level of consciousness), and also agreed to participate in therapy/workshops, they can often reduce conflict resolution to communication and behavioral issues in the lower quadrants. With almost 50% of the adult US population being single, and most couples not even engaging in therapy, therapists address less than 10% of the population, yet make their advice sound like as it applies to all others who struggle in or outside a relationship. Because of the self-selecting process of their clients some therapists claim success rates of 75% and higher—much higher than the average 25% success rate of general couples therapy (which is a little bit like saying "90% of our patients died, but 75% of the remaining 10% are doing fine.")

483 *The Rules* for red women:
1. Be a "Creature Unlike Any Other."
2. Don't talk to a man first (and don't ask him to dance).
3. Don't stare at men or talk too much.
4. Don't meet him halfway or go "dutch" on a date.
5. Don't call him and rarely return his calls.
6. Always end phone calls first.
7. Don't accept a Saturday night date after Wednesday.
8. Fill up your time before the date.
9. How to act on dates 1, 2, and 3.
10. How to act on dates 4 through Commitment Time.
11. Always end the date first.
12. Stop dating him if he doesn't buy you a romantic gift for your birthday or Valentine's day.
13. don't see him more than once or twice a week.
14. No more than casual kissing on the first date.
15. Don't rush into sex and other rules for intimacy.
16. Don't tell him what to do.
17. Let him take the lead.
18. Don't expect a man to change or try to change him.
19. Don't open up too fast.
20. Be honest, but mysterious.
21. Accentuate the positive and other rules for personal ads.
22. Don't live with a man (or leave your things in his apartment).
23. Don't date a married man.
24. Slowly involve him in your family and other rules for women with children.
25. Practice, practice, practice! (or, getting good at the rules).
26. Even if you're engaged or married, you still need the rules.
27. Do the rules, even when your friends and parents think it's nuts.
28. Be smart and other rules for dating in high school.
29. Take care of yourself and other rules for dating in college.
30. Next! and other rules for dealing with rejection.
31. Don't discuss the rules with your therapist.
32. Don't break the rules.
33. Do the rules and you'll live happily ever after!
34. Love only those who love you.
35. Be easy to live with.

484 These ideas on self-love and love of God are well summarized by Meister Eckhart who wrote: "If you love yourself, you love everybody else as you do yourself. As long as you love another person less than you love yourself, you will not really succeed in loving yourself, but if you love all alike, including yourself, you will love them as one person and that person is both God and man. Thus he is a great and righteous person who, loving himself, loves all others equally."

485 David Schnarch writes in *Passionate Marriage* on page 107 that he never saw this approach to work.

486 On page 298 Schnarch states: "We can agree to disagree as long as we are focused on feelings and perceptions. When the issue is *behavior*, however, flexibility is reduced significantly. You can't agree to disagree about sex [or any other vital right-hand aspect of a partnership such as time and money]. When your spouse says he or she is never doing a particular sexual behavior—or never having sex again—you don't feel like saying, "Thanks for sharing!""

487 See endnote #362 in Chapter 9 for classic forms of love.

488 The list includes: proximity, full availability, free of addictions, agreement on children, sexual and financial compatibility, friendship, shared interests and intellect, realistic expectations, emotional health, similar values and wishes, commitment, and the approval of head, heart and gut.

489 On page 170, Welwood regards compassion as masculine and wisdom as feminine, which is opposite from the Integral Relationship Model.

INDEX

Abbott, Edwin 244
abraham-hicks.com 264
Absolute 9
active listening 262
Adyashanti xvii, 254, 258, 264
Agape 9, 24, 175, 252
agency. *See* polarities
Albert, David 231
alexgrey.com 215
Alice, Kathryn 236, 261, 264
Allen, Douglas 214, 218
All Quadrants, All Levels. *See* AQAL, Integral Model
Almaas, A. H. 192
Almaas, A.H. 228, 231, 234, 240, 260
altitude 139, 179
   critical factor in predicting quality of partnership 153
amber 46-47, 48, 49, 84, 89, 90, 103, 110, 115, 121, 123, 124, 125, 139, 141, 143, 144, 154, 155, 156, 157, 159, 160, 161, 167, 171, 181, 182, 183, 184, 185, 186, 189, 193, 196, 197, 245, 249, 256, 258. *See* also consciousness development
   patriarchal 46
   percentage of population 47
   religious and political values 46
   self-help books 179, 182
American Society of Aesthetic Plastic Surgery 241
americanvalues.org 213, 214
Amnesty International 49, 245
Anand, Margo 233
Anderson, Chris 249
Andrews, Scott 234
anima/animus 153, 233
   and dating 169
   bridge to soul 58
   compatible 59
   development 58-66
   development in men 60-61
   development in women 62-65
   five stages 60

   growth 65
   identifying in women 149
   integrating in Personality Matrix 90
   men as alien outsiders 62
   men as equal partners 64
   men as father, God or king 62
   men as hero 63
   men as independent beings 63
   unconscious 109
   women as equal partner 61
   women as guide to creativity and awakening 61
   women as mother 60
   women as sex object 60
   women as wife 60
AQAL 17, 29, 81, 93, 95, 100, 131, 167, 172, 173, 215, 223. *See* also Integral Model
Aragona, Brandon 238
archaeologyinfo.com 216
archaic level of consciousness 44. *See* infrared
archaic unconscious 109
architecture 12
Aristophanes 256
Aristotle 12, 217, 246
Armstrong, Alison 120, 179, 185, 220, 222, 242, 256, 257, 262
art 12
ascending 223. *See* polarities
aspirenow.com 234
astrology 78
atheist 55
Athens 12, 217
attachment 119
Aurobindo, Sri 230
Auschwitz Test 231
Baer, Greg 186, 259
Bale, David 254
Barks, Coleman 261
Baron, Renee 240
bbc.co.uk 251
Beck, Don 227, 262

Beckwith, Michael 258, 264
beer 12, 19
Beginners Mind 54, 117
Big Bang 10
biological differences between men and
    women 15-20
Blair, Tony 215
bls.gov 219
Bly, Robert 235, 262
body mass index (BMI) 86
Body Mass Index (BMI) 244
body ornaments 11
Bonder, Saniel 258, 264
Bond, James 11
borderline personality disorder (BPD) 258
boy-toy 19, 90, 156
Brings, Felicia 243
Brinig, Margaret 214, 218
Brizendine, Louann 226, 238
Buber, Martin 260
Buddha 264
Buddhism 195, 247
Bush, George W. 215
business.smh.com.au 241
Buss, David M. 217, 222, 224
Campbell, Susan 252, 261, 263, 264
Caudate Nucleus 251
cave paintings 11
cdc.gov 244
Celexa 69
Chapman, Gary 74, 240
chick flicks 18
China 12
Chopra, Deepak 192, 234, 237, 249, 258,
    264
Christianity 195
Clinton, Bill 215
Cloud of Unknowing 54
cnn.com 214
codependent 70, 113, 236
Co-Emergence (of quadrants) 137
cohabitatation 1
Collin, Rodney 81
Collins, Nancy W. 238
colors. *See* consciousness development
Columbus, Christopher 12
Combs, Allan 215, 224, 227, 228, 237, 245,
    246, 257, 262
    Wilber-Combs Lattice 215, 245

commitment 113
communication 38
communion. *See* polarities
companionate love 115
Compassionate Communication. *See* Non-
    Violent Communication (NVC)
Compatibility Matrix 133, 153
    conflict resolution 159
    constructing 153
Connirae, Andreas 239
Connirae, Steve 239
conscious development
    alternate color systems 229
consciousness
    definition 42
consciousness development 42-51. *See*
    also infrared, magenta, red, amber,
    orange, green, teal, turquoise
    advantages of higher levels 43
    altitude 139
    and dating 168
    and opposite polarities 103
    and quadrants 98
    and sexual selection process 120
    and unconscious 110
    and women's demands of men 84
    changes in how women are attracted
        to men 83
    characteristics of levels 44
    Compatibility Matrix 154
    differences in male/female 119-127
    eight stages (colors) 43
    first-tier 43
    growth in adults 43
    levels and underlying values/
        worldviews 44
    male-female growth dynamic 121
    second-tier 43
    seven chakra system 230
    sexes grow through them differently 122
    shifting polarities 89
    ways it appears 43
consciousness, states of 67
Constitution of the United States 47
contemplative prayer 51. *See also* prayer
contraception 19, 171
conventional 46. *See* amber, orange
Cook-Greuter, Susanne 227, 228, 229,
    230, 231

Copernicus 12
cougar 242
Covey, Stephen 258, 260, 263, 264
Cowan, Christopher 227
craigslist.org 167
Crenshaw, Theresa L. 221, 237, 238, 239
Da, Adi 258
Dalai Lama 264
dances 11
Darwin, Charles 225, 261
dateoverforty.com 252
dating
   compatible Kosmic Address 166
   Internet 165
   online profile 166
   singles events 165
   strategies 164
DeAnglis, Barbara 190
Deida, David 197, 216, 220, 224, 226, 232, 233, 235, 245, 254, 256, 257, 258, 261
Deikman, Arthur 252
descending 223. *See* polarities
Desert Shield 219
Desert Storm 219
desire 11, 18, 19, 60, 64, 68, 113, 188, 191, 194, 225, 256, 258, 264
Diamond, Carol 190
Dickinson, Emily 67, 233
Diderot 215
dissociation 119
divorce 67
   initiated by women 2, 13
   no-fault 13
   rates doubled after no-fault laws 13
   statistics 2
   suice rate of divorced fathers 2
divorcemag.com 214
divorcerate.org 214
divorcereform.org 214, 219
Doctors Without Borders 49, 245
domestic violence 254
dominator hierarchies 43
Don Juan 60
dopamine 18, 68, 69, 70, 115, 238
Dostoevsky, Fyodor 41
drjudithorloff.com 239
drug induced states 10
drumming 11

duality 10
Dunn, Irina 254
Dyer, Wayne 245, 264
Eckhart, Meister 265
Eckhart Tolle 216, 226, 228, 231, 232, 237, 254, 255, 258, 260, 261, 264
ecosystem 13, 14
egocentric level of consciousness 45. *See* red
eharmony.com 167
eight forms of love 112
Einstein, Albert 2, 24, 47, 51, 83, 93, 135
Eisendrath, Polly Young 236, 253
embedded unconscious 109
emergent unconscious 110
Emerson, Ralph Waldo 232
emotional infidelity 20
emotional intelligence 35
emotionally available 35
emotional pain 36
emotions
   definition 231
empathy guess 39
Eng, Kim 254
Engler, Jack 228
enlightenment 10
Enlightenment, The 12, 47
Enneagram 73, 75-76, 91, 150, 240, 245
   compatibility between different types 76
   personality types 75
enneagraminstitute.com 240
environment
   destruction as byproduct of pursuit of money and power 86
eqi.org 226
Eros 9, 24, 175, 252
Esbjorn-Hargens, Sean 215, 259, 262
Eschner-Hogan, Eve 225
estrogen 18, 68, 70, 96, 220, 238
Etcoff, Nancy 217, 220, 221, 224, 242, 244, 255, 256, 257
ethics
   pursuit of money and power 86
European states 12
eve3.wordpress.com 237
Ever Present Origin 9
extraverts. *See* extroverts
extroverts 73, 77

Eye Accessing Cue technique 74
Farrell, Bill and Pam 257
Farrell, Warren 214, 218, 219, 221, 222, 226, 255, 263
fas.org 219
fathersforlife.org 214
fear of abandonment 64
fear-shame dynamic 19
feelings 35, 231. *See* also emotions
 communicating 38
 interpretations 37
 when needs are satisfied 36
 when needs not satisfied 37
Fein, Ellen 180
Feldhahn, Jeff 183
Feldhahn, Shaunti 183, 184
female liberation. *See* feminist movement
females
 infatuation 113
 monogamy in exchange for protection 11
 shadow 36
 spirituality 89
 terminology 17
feminine 28
 polarities 27
 terminology 17
feminism 13. *See* feminist movement
 eco 218
 first wave 218
 liberal 218
 post-feminism 218
 radical 218
 radical eco 218
 second wave 218
 socialist 218
 third wave 13, 218
feminist movement 13, 14, 89
Fenton, Bradley 191, 240, 259
fight or flight 36
first-tier consciousness development 43, 123. *See* consciousness development
Fisher, Helen 179, 185, 213, 217, 220, 221, 222, 224, 230, 234, 236, 237, 238, 239, 241, 251, 252, 254
Fisher, Roger 227, 230, 263
Five Love Languages 73, 91, 150
flatland 244
flirting 164

Ford, Henry 165
Formative Causation 216
Frankl, Victor 258
Freud, Sigmund 109, 227
Friedan, Betty 230
friendship 112
Fromm, Erich 182, 217, 223, 225, 235, 237, 249
fuckability 84, 222, 242
fusion 119
Galileo 12
Gandhi 51, 248
Gangaji 264
Gardner, Howard 224, 225
Gates, Bill 47
Gebser, Jean 227, 228, 230, 262
ge-dating.com 167
gender, 22
 definition, 22
 expressions, 22
 hard to break out of gender roles, 22
 nature vs nature, 22
 stereotypes, 22
Gender Mainstreaming 13, 14, 79, 176, 220
gender roles. *See* also sex (evolution of)
 evolution 14-17
genepartner.com 237
genetic success 11
Gerzon, Mark 235
Gibson, Valerie 242
Gilbert, Elizabeth 113, 153, 225, 236, 244, 249
Gilligan, Carol 227, 229, 257, 258
Glick, Peter 214, 217, 219, 222, 257
God 9
 male 12
Godhead 26, 54
Goldstein, Kurt 230
Gold, Victor 181
Goleman, Daniel 217, 222, 225, 226, 259
Gore, Al 215
Gottman, John 179, 183, 217, 245, 263
Graves, Claire 227
Gray, John 179, 184, 213, 222, 223, 226, 237, 238, 239, 263, 264
greaterquest.com 240
Greece 12
green 48-49, 50, 84, 87, 89, 103, 121, 123,

124, 126, 127, 129, 140, 141, 143, 144, 154, 155, 156, 157, 159, 160, 161, 182, 184, 189, 192, 193, 195, 196, 197, 198, 235, 245, 249, 256, 257, 258. *See* also consciousness development
   percentage of population 49
   self-help books 179, 192
Greenpeace 49, 245
greensingles.com 167
Grey, Alex 215
Grigsby, Mason 238
Ground of all Being 9
ground unconscious 108
Gulf War 219
Hafiz 216, 233, 263
hai.org 215, 255
Hamilton, Craig 262
Hamlet 160
Hanauer, Cathi 236
Harding, Douglas E. 231
harrisinteractive.com 241
Harrison, Steven 258, 264
Hauser, Kaspar 247
Hawking, Stephen 216
Hawkins, David R. 226
Hellinger, Bert 241
Hendricks, Kathlyn and Gay 264
Hendrix, Harville 179, 186, 217, 220, 221, 234, 250
Herzog, Werner 247
Hicks, Abraham 231, 264
hierarchical structures in social holons 101
history of male/female evolution 10-14
Hitler, Adolf 99, 222, 248
Hoffmann, Glynda-Lee 245
Hogan, Eve Eschner 261
Hogan, Steven 225, 261
holarchies 93
Holmes, Ernest 231
holonic structures
   definition 93
holons
   and quadrants 246, 247
   artifacts 246
   characteristics 94
   conflicts between drives of individual holons 100
   constructing holarchies 249

   definition 93
   differentiating drives of individual holons 99
   dominant monad 95
   drives of individual holons 98
   heaps 246
   individual 94-97, 246
      governing force 95
      independent will 95
   quarants of 97
   social 101-103, 246, 249
      balancing drives 102
      hierarchies 101
      power structure 101
   types 246
homemaking 12
hoovers.com 256
hormones 18, 19, 67, 69, 70, 71, 87, 96, 97, 113, 115, 117, 162, 184, 186, 221, 237
horoscopes 78
Houston, Jean 220
Howard, Lew 215, 224, 231
Hubbard, Barbara Marx 256
Hudson, Russ 240
humandesignhawaii.com 241
humanmetrics.com 241
ideals 33
Industrial Revolution 13
infatuation 113
Infinite/Eternal 9
infrared 44, 45, 50, 83, 121, 122, 123, 125, 154. *See* also consciousness development
   instinctive behaviors 45
   percentage of population 45
Institute of Noetic Sciences 259
Institute of Transpersonal Psychology 263
Integral 2
   approach to dating 163
integralinstitute.org 255
integral level of consciousness 49-50. *See* teal
integrallife.com 213, 251, 254
Integral Life Practice (ILP) 42, 56, 227
integral love 115
Integral Model xv, xvii, xviii, 3, 15, 29, 41, 73, 91, 93, 95, 137, 229

and levels to be fully realized 41
four types of holons 246
fulcrums 258
lines of development 29-40
quadrant diagram 247
Integral Relationship Model xviii, 3, 7,
    15, 17, 40, 43, 79, 133, 150, 172, 223,
    236, 266
    dating 163
    levels 41-50
    overview 3
integrity 215
intelligences
    types 224
intersubjectivity 136, 259
intimacy 8, 18, 25, 35, 36, 40, 57, 61, 78,
    96, 103, 107, 110, 112, 113, 114, 115,
    118, 131, 142, 143, 148, 160, 168, 183,
    185, 186, 187, 188, 192, 233, 234, 237,
    239, 247, 248, 254, 255, 262, 265
introverts 73, 77
ions.org 259
Iraq War 219
Islam 46
Jacobson, Leonard 258, 264
Jesus Christ 252, 264
Johnson, Sue 188
Jordan, Michael 51
Jung, Carl 29, 232, 233
    anima/animus 58-66, 233. See also
        anima/animus
Justinian 217
Kant, Immanuel 133
Kasl, Charlotte 195, 225, 264
Katie, Byron 258, 264
Keen, Sam 235
Keepin, Will 241
Kegan, Robert 227, 229, 230, 231, 254, 257
Kennedy, Barbara 244
Kepler, Johannes 12
Kernberg, Otto 236
Killam, Terry (Treya) 237
Kirshenbaum, Mira 189
Knight, Sue 239, 240
Koestler, Arthur 246
Kohlberg, Lawrence 227, 229, 230
Koppel, Dale 190, 222, 236
Korean War 219

Kornfield, Jack 258, 264
Kosmic Address 133, 135-151, 166, 175
    and dating 163
    definition 135
    identifying 136-151
    intersubjectivity 136
Krakauer, Jon 249
Krishnamurti, Jiddu 1
Kubler-Ross, Elisabeth 236
kundalini 58, 233, 246
language development in human evolution 11
Lao Tzu 54, 73, 216
Laszlo, Erwin 262
Leeds, Lilo and Gerald 214
Leonard, Adam 227
Lerner, Rabbi Michael 86
Lesser, Elisabeth 138, 260
letsmove.gov 244
levels 41-66, 153
    depend on many factors 41
    number depends on line 41
    plotting on a psychograph 41
Lexapro 69
lines of development 29-40, 153
    and compatibility with women 29
    and levels 41
    and levels to be fully realized 41
    and quadrants 98
    hardwired from birth 29
    interdependent 41
    spiritual 51-56
LL 95
Loevinger, Jane 227, 229, 230
Logo Therapy 258
love
    addiction to hormones 70
    art of 9
    biological/physical dimension 9
    biological/psychological dimension 10
    commitment 69, 113
    companionate love 115
    crazy love 115
    dimensions of 9-10
    eight forms 112
    eight forms (diagram) 112
    falling in 67-71
    friendship 112

Index | 273

future of 176
infatuation 113
integral love 115
lust 68
nonlove 112
psychological/unconscious dimension 9
reason plus chemistry 70
romance 68
romantic 114
selfless 9
temporary states (versus permanent stages) 67
types 252
unconditional Love 10
Love Languages 73, 74
Love, Patricia 185, 213, 214, 215, 219, 221, 222, 226, 233, 234, 263
LR 95
Ludus 252
Luskin, Frederic 263
lust 18, 57, 60, 67, 68, 71, 186
Luvox 69
Lyons, Marlena 179, 192, 225, 234, 249, 259, 263
Lysistrata 256
MacDowell, Andy 256
Madonna 60
magenta 45, 48, 49, 83, 90, 103, 121, 123, 124, 125, 139, 141, 143, 144, 154, 155, 156, 157, 182, 256. *See also* consciousness development
  evolution of 45
  percentage of population 45
  superstitions 45
magic level of consciousness 45-46. *See* magenta
male production and female reproduction 12
males
  fitness to win females 14
  infatuation 113
  protecting genetic legacy 11
  terminology 17
manandwomanbalance.com 249
Mania 252
marriages
  happy 2
Marxism 46

masculine 28
  polarities 27
  terminology 17
Maslow, Abraham 215, 225, 229, 230, 257
Masters, Robert Augustus 235, 254
match.com 167
mating behaviors for heterosexual men and women 18
Mayell, Hillary 216
McCartney, Paul 244
McGraw, Dr. Phil 190
McIntosh, Steve 227, 262
McLaughlin, Mignon 107
McNamara, Robert 227, 230
meditation 51, 58
meditation practice, starting 36
Mediterranean 12
memes
  definition 229
men. *See also* relationships, singles
  advances in the 18th century 12
  anima development and separation from parents 60
  attraction to Playboy models 11
  attraction to women 2
  average and disadvantaged men finding partners 14
  balancing partnership with individuality 93
  becoming more successful to attract women 13
  benefit more from committed relationships 1, 2, 213
  benefits of Primary Fantasy 86
  biological makeup 15, 18-21
  casualties in war 219
  characteristics of women that attract 18
  competitive sports 12
  cycle of amassing wealth destroying ecosystem 13
  development of specialized warfare 12
  disposable sex (in wars) 13
  doing stressful/dangerous work 12, 13, 19
  dominating public spheres (government, education, religion and politics) 12
  drawn to spend money on women 19
  effort to gain love of women 12
  emotionally available 35

evolution of protectiveness for
    females 11
evolution of skills 11
fighting wars 12
freeing men to realize potential 13
inventors 12
monotheistic religions 12
need to be success-oriented 13
physical attraction to biological features
    of women 18
power/status/wealth to attract
    women 13
Primary Fantasy 18
    based on appearance 19
scientific discoveries 12
secondary fantasies 18
separation from parents (animus development) 59-60
shame dynamic re biological differences
    between the sexes 19
shifts in polarity with growth in consciousness 89
suffering after divorce 2
suicide rate after divorce 2
terminology 17
menopause 68, 238
merriam-webster.com 264
Merzel, Dennis Genpo 233, 250
Michelangelo 51
Miller, Geoffrey 216, 217, 221, 222, 237,
    238, 255, 256, 261, 264
Mills, Heather 244
Milton, Katharine 216
Mitchell, Stephen 216, 261
monogamy
   development of 11
monotheist 55
monotheistic religions 12
Monroe, Marilyn 60
Moore, Thomas 251
Morelli, Marco 227
Morphic Resonance 251
Moses 46
Mozart, Wolfgang Amadeus 51
MRI scans and love 251
Mr. Right 85, 180, 189, 204, 207, 214, 221
msnbc.msn.com 244
Murray, Bill 256
Myers-Briggs personality types 73, 77,
    150, 245
   combinations 77
   introvert / extrovert 77
   judging / perceiving 77
   sensing / intuition 77
   thinking / feeling 77
mystical 55
mythic level of consciousness 46. See
    amber
Myth of the Given 138
National Organization of Women
    (NOW) 49
National Single Cougars Convention 243
nationalzoo.si.edu 239
near death experience 10
needs 34-35, 225
   communicating 38
   feelings when not satisfied 37
   feelings when satisfied 36
   vs wants 34
negation 119
Neuro-Linguistic Programming (NLP)
    73-74, 150
   eye movements 239
   personality types 73-74
   techniques 74
neurosis
   definition 258
New Age 46, 55, 61, 89, 146, 165
newfemininepower.org 245
Newton, Sir Isaac 12
Nile River 12
Nock, Steven L. 214
no-fault divorce 13
non-dual awareness 50
nonlove 112
non-violence 14
Non-Violent Communication (NVC)
    39, 226
norepinephrine 18, 68, 69, 70, 115
nuclear families 11
Obama, Barack 47, 230
Obama, Michelle 244
Observation-Feeling-Need Request
    (OFNR) 38
   examples 38
Obsessive Compulsive Disorder(OCD) 69
okcupid.com 167
Omega Institute 260

one-night-stand 19
orange 46, 47, 48, 49, 84, 87, 89, 90, 103,
    110, 115, 121, 123, 124, 126, 127, 129,
    139, 141, 143, 144, 154, 155, 156, 157,
    159, 160, 161, 167, 182, 183, 184, 185,
    186, 187, 188, 189, 190, 192, 193, 196,
    197, 198, 245, 256, 258, 259, 262. *See
    also* consciousness development
  materiality 47
  percentage of population 48
  pursuing goals 47
  self-help books 179, 185
Orloff, Judith 239
out of body experiences 78
oxytocin 19, 69, 70, 184, 233, 238
Parlee, Bert 254
partnerships. *See* relationships
Pascal, Blaise 253
past life experiences 78
patriarchy 217
Patten, Terry 227, 262
Paxil 69
Payne, Wayne 225
Peck, Scott 234
Personality Matrix 87-91
  and personality types 91
  and shifts in polarity 89
  diagram 87
  merging consciousness, polarities,
    anima/animus, sexual, spiritual,
    types 87
personality type
  identifying in women 150
personality types 73-74, 153
  Enneagram 73, 75
  extroverts 73
  Five Love Languages 73
  introverts 73
  love languages 74
  Myers-Briggs 73, 77
    combinations 77
    introvert / extrovert 77
    judging / perceiving 77
    sensing / intuition 77
    thinking / feeling 77
  NLP 73-74
    auditory 73
    kinesthetic 73
    techniques 74
    visual 73
  Type-A 73
  Type-B 73
  Zodiac 73
perspective 135, 138, 153, 179
Phobos 24
Pickens, James W. 263
Pill, The 13, 218
Pincus, Dr. Gregory 218
Pines, Ayala Malach 111, 220, 221, 222,
    224, 233, 236, 237, 243, 251, 252
Plato 12, 217
  Academy at Athens 217
Playboy 11, 60
plentyoffish.com 167
pluralistic level of consciousness 48-49.
    See green
polarities 23-28
  agency 25
  and altitude 139
  and drives of holons 98
  ascending 24
  balancing 27
  balancing drives in social holons 102
  communion 25
  creating sexual attraction 30
  descending 24
  diagram 25
  division of labor in pre-conventional 85
  drives toward 26
  feminine not necessarily associated with
    women 27
  integrating with quadrants 248
  masculine not necessarily associated
    with men 27
  mutually exclusive 26
  opposites attract 103
  river metaphor 28
  shifting with consciousness
    development 89-90
  shifting with growth 89
polyamorous 70, 235
  relationships 117
polytheist 55
Popcak, Gregory K. 179, 182, 214, 225,
    232, 239, 249
porn 11, 18

post-conventional 48, 50. *See* green
personal freedom 50
post-post-conventional 49. *See* teal, turquoise
poverty 13
Pragma 252
prayer 51
pre-conventional 44, 50. *See* infrared, magenta, red
pregnancy 19, 57, 67, 69, 225, 237
pre/post fallacy 50
pre/trans fallacy 50, 229
Primary Fantasy 15, 18-21, 19, 30, 67, 70, 83, 84, 86, 87, 89, 113, 121, 153, 156, 158, 160, 163, 164, 166, 172, 176, 177, 186, 221, 242, 255. *See* also secondary fantasies
  and compatibility 83-86
  creating sexual attraction 30
  cultural consistency 18
  positive in men, liability in womern 86
Prior, Bernie 258, 262, 264
Proust, Marcel 179
Prozac 69
Psaris, Jett 179, 192, 225, 234, 249, 259, 263
psychic
  definition 232
psychograph 41
psychological healing 127
psychosis
  causes 253
psychotherapies 253
Pure Awareness 9
purplemotes.net 219
quadrants 17, 93
  and altitude 139
  and holons 95, 97
  and Kosmic Address 135
  development inside 98
  full diagram 247
  NOT part of social holons 101
Quincey, Christian de 227, 228, 232, 236, 246, 254, 262
Radical Emptiness 54
Radin, Dean 259
raising children 12
Ramana Maharshi 264

Ram Dass 232, 260
rational level of consciousness 47-48. *See* orange
Reagan, Ronald 218
Real, Terrence 186, 219, 222, 226, 232
recorded history 12
red 45, 46, 47, 48, 49, 50, 84, 89, 103, 121, 123, 124, 125, 139, 141, 143, 144, 154, 155, 156, 157, 159, 162, 181, 191, 195, 196, 197, 231, 235, 245, 256, 258, 264, 265. *See* also consciousness development
  in street gangs 46
  percentage of population 46
  self-help books 179, 180
  selfish behaviors 45
Reiki 78
relationships
  as social holons 94
  capacities 33
  chemistry xviii, 8, 18, 20, 67, 70, 71, 97, 107, 115, 163, 166, 167, 168, 170, 172, 186, 189, 190, 237, 241
  compatibility 160
  compatible anima/animus complex 59
  compatible emotional development 36
  compatible Kosmic Addresses 175
  compatible passions and interests 30
  compatible personalities 88
  compatibley psychological makeup 83
  define past, present, future 7
  emotional infidelity 20
  empathy guess 39
  Enneagram compatibility 76
  feelings 35
  gay 7
  gender equality 14
  ideals 33
  improving through balancing polarities 27
  integral approach 2
  limitations of statistics about 7
  monogamy 11
  needs 34-35
  new possibilities 14
  Non-Violent Communication (NVC) 39
  nuclear families 11
  OFNR 38

partnerships between integrally in-
    formed men and post-feminist
    women 14
Personality Matrix 87
polyamorous 117
sexual infidelity 20
statistics 1-2
terminology 8, 17
unconscious 111
unconscious fit 110
values 33
religion
    summary of world religions 56
Rengel, Peter 234
repressed sexuality 56
repression 119
Republican Party 47
Rexroth, Marylin 257
richgosse.blogspot.com 243
Richo, David 193, 225, 234, 235, 236,
    238, 251
Rilke, Rainer Maria 233
Riso, Don Richard 240
Robbins, Tony 258, 264
Robinson, Smokey 175
romance 68
romance novels 18
Roman empire 12
romantic love 114
Rosenberg, Marshall 226, 261, 263
Rudman, Laurie A. 214, 217, 219, 222, 257
Ruiz, Don Miguel 261
Rumi 51, 163, 216, 233, 251, 262
Sagan, Carl 9
Salmon, Catherine 217
satori 233
Schnarch, David 179, 187, 232, 233, 239,
    247, 249, 255, 263, 266
Schneider, Sherrie 180
Schroedinger Wave Equation 259
Schucman, Helen 232
Science Of Mind 215
secondary fantasies 18, 30. See also Pri-
    mary Fantasy
second-tier consciousness 49, 123
second-tier consciousness development 43.
    See consciousness development
Selective Serotonin Reuptake Inhibitors
    (SSRIs) 69

self-actualization 42
self-help books 1, 2, 179-198
    amber 179, 182
    green 179, 192
    orange 179, 185
    red 179, 180
self-identification as boys or girls 58
self-immanence 24
semen 19
seminal fluid 70
Seng Ts'an 261
sense of self 51, 58
Sensitive New Age Guys (SNAGs) 89,
    156, 197
serotonin 18, 69, 115
Seven Chakra System (CS) 229
sex
    evolution of 10-14, 119
        advanced farming producing sur-
            plus food 12
        African jungles 10
        development of male
            protectiveness 11
        foundations of Western thought 12
        gene mutation 10
        herding animals 11
        hunting 12
        hunting in bands 11
        Industrial Revolution 13
        invention of the plow 12
        language development 11
        large domesticated animals
            (oxen) 12
        mammals 10
        meat protein and brain growth 11
        men freed for creative
            endeavors 12
        men stuck in traditional roles 13
        monogamy 11
        monotheistic religions 12
        nomadic horticulture 11
        nomadic hunters and gatherers 11
        nutrition improvements 11
        patriarchal social structures 12
        predecessors to our human ances-
            tors 10
        rising population leads to
            conflict 12
        scientific discoveries 12

specialization into hunting and
    gathering 11
  survival of the fittest 10
  unaffected by social change 18
  women as gatherers 11
  women's right to vote 13
  written documents 12
 summary of male-female differences 28
 tantric xvii, 10
Sex and Love Addicts Anonymous (SLAA)
    70
sexual development
  and dating 169
sexual infidelity 20
sexuality
  development 56-58
  fucking 56
  having sex 57
  lovemaking 57
  repressed 56
  transcendent sex 58
sexually transmitted diseases (STDs) 56
sexual revolution 13
sexual stage
  identifying 147
Shakespeare, William 160
Shakti 28
shamanic voyages 78
Sheehan, Donna 261
Sheehy, Gail 219, 236, 245
Sheldrake, Rupert 216, 228, 251
Shiva 28
Sierra Club 49, 245
Silver, Nan 183, 245, 263
Singer, Irvin 216, 222
singles. *See* also relationships, men,
    women
  balance of men and women 2
  statistics 1
singles2couples.org xvii, 177, 198,
    199, 264
slaafws.org 239
Smith, Huston 232, 261
Socrates 12, 217
soul-mate
  how to find 234
Spiral Dynamics (SD) 229, 257
Spirit 9

spiritual
  categories 51
  definition 51
  state-stages 51-56. *See* also state-stages
spiritual but not religious 55
spiritual development 51-56
spiritual realization
  practices 51
spiritualsingles.com 167
Sri Aurobindo 262
Stanger, Patti 222, 242
starvation 13
state-stages (spiritual) 51-56
  causal/deep sleep 53
  definition 51
  development 52
  feminine/masculine 52, 53, 54, 55
  gross/waking 52
  matching with a partner 56
  non-duality 52, 54
  subtle/dreaming 53
  witness 52
  witnessing 54
steam engines 13
Steinem, Gloria 254
Sternberg, Robert J. 217, 252, 255
stevepavlina.com 226
Stitz, Jenny 263
Stone Age 11
Storge 252
Stosny, Steven 185, 213, 214, 215, 219,
    221, 222, 226, 233, 234, 259, 263
Strauss, Neil 180, 239
submerged unconscious 36, 109, 113
suffrage 13
Sufism 195, 263
sugar daddy 244
super-ego 109
Suzuki, Shunryu 255
Symons, Donald 214, 217, 221, 222
tableforsix.com 167
tantric sex xvii, 10, 28, 51, 58, 69, 84, 90,
    115, 215, 224, 233, 255
Taoism 216
tarot card readings 78
Tate, Brett 219
Taylor, John Maxwell 224
teal 49, 50, 84, 89, 121, 126, 127, 156, 157,

158, 159, 160, 168, 245, 256, 264. *See also* consciousness development
encompasses other stages 49
Ten Commandments, the 46, 257
testosterone 18, 19, 68, 69, 70, 87, 89, 96, 115, 238
tetra arise 98
Thanatos 24
Thomas, Katherine Woodward 196, 261
Thurston, Leslie Temple 233, 249
Tierney, John 214
time.com 220
Time Magazine 13
Toltecs 261
transcendence
  process 256
transpersonal level of consciousness 50. *See* turquoise
triangle of love 107-118
  aligning 116, 117
  intentions 117
Trivers, Robert 221
Trungpa, Chogyam 231
Turner, Ted 47
turquoise 49, 50, 84, 90, 122, 123, 126, 127, 158, 159, 160, 176, 256, 263. *See also* consciousness development
Type-A 73
Type-B 73
typelogic.com 241
types. *See* personality types
UL 95
unconscious
  anima/animus 109
  archaic unconscious 109
  embedded unconscious 109
  emergent unconscious 110
  fit with others 110
  ground unconscious 108
  patterns of fit 110
  role in love 108
  submerged unconscious 109
understandmen.com 222, 262
Unified Field 9
United Nations 13
un.org 220
Upanishads 232
UR 95

Ury, William 227, 230, 263
values 33
vasopressin 19, 69, 70, 238
veggieconnection.com 167
Ventral Tegmental Area 251
Vertical Drop, the 54
Vietnam War 219
Vipassana 53
Vissell, Joyce and Barry 179, 195
voles and monogamy 69
Wade, Jenny 216, 227, 229, 230, 231, 246, 257, 258
Wagele, Elizabeth 240
Wallerstein, Judith 214, 236
Wall Street 48, 256
Walsh, Roger 229, 232, 241, 251, 258, 264
weapons 13
webmd.com 233
Weinberg, George 244
Weis, Karin 217, 252, 255
Welwood, John 179, 193, 224, 233, 234, 250, 251, 259, 266
White, David Gordon 224
Whitehead, Alfred North 217, 246
White, Tim 216
Wiedemann, Florence 236, 253
wie.org 231
wikipedia.org 217, 224, 234, 242, 244, 249, 256, 259, 262, 264
Wilber-Combs Lattice 245, 246
Wilber, Ken xv, xvii, xviii, 2, 3, 15, 17, 29, 81, 93, 95, 98, 119, 126, 133, 171, 188, 215, 217, 218, 223, 224, 226, 227, 228, 229, 230, 231, 232, 236, 237, 241, 244, 245, 246, 247, 248, 249, 251, 253, 255, 257, 258, 259, 260, 262. *See also* Integral Model
  all quadrants diagram 247
  flatland 137, 244
  ladder metaphor 126
  quadrants 15, 17
wilber.shambhala.com 259
Wilcox, W. Bradford 214
Williamson, Marianne 15
Winter, Susan 243
witness 52, 54
Wollstonecraft, Mary 218
women. *See also* relationships, singles,

feminist movement, females, feminine
   animus development 62
   attracted to James Bond 11
   attraction to men 2, 83
   balancing partnership with
      individuality 93
   biological makeup 15, 18-21
   bombarding men with seductive
      images 19
   casualties in war 219
   characteristics of men that attract 18
   control over their reproductive
      capacity 13
   cougars 85
   declining number in marriages 213
   dominating private sphere of family,
      hearth, home 12
   emotional independence 14
   equal pay for equal work 13
   equal rights and responsibilities 14
   evolutionary reasons for selecting
      successful partner 19
   evolution of senses for gathering food 11
   exercise 86
   fear dyname re biological differences
      between the sexes 19
   fulfilment-oriented 13
   identifying animus complex 149
   identifying Kosmic Address 136
   identifying personality type 150
   identifying sexual stage 147
   initiating divorces 2, 13
   inventors 120
   liability of Primary Fantasy 86
   liberation 14
   liberation from traditional gender roles
      and economic dependence on
      men 13
   marrying up 84
   modern and postmodern 13
   modern and postmodern rights and op-
      portunities 14
   nagging out of fear 20
   perceived as inferior by monotheistic
      religions 12
   prefer to remain single 1, 2, 84
   Primary Fantasy 18
      attraction to successful men 19
      turned off by low socioeconomic
         status 19
   raising children 12
   relationship resources 2
   rewarding men 14
   right to equal education 13
   right to vote 13
   secondary fantasies 18
   self-help books 2, 265
   separation from parents (anima
      development) 59-60
   sex-positive 85, 150, 185, 188, 190
   sexual fantasies 18
   shifts in polarity with growth in con-
      sciousness 89
   sufficient to be healthy and beautiful to
      attract men 13
   tapping financial resources from men 13
   terminology 17
   want men who are emotionally
      available 35
womenontheedgeofevolution.com 220, 256
womentowomen.com 238
world religions 56
World War I 219
World War II 219
World Wildlife Federation (WWF) 245
www.integralworld.net 215, 247
yahoopersonals.com 167
yoga 51, 58
Zen 54, 117
Zimmerman, Michael 215
Zodiac 73
Zoloft 69